Human Rights Diplomacy: Contemporary Perspectives

Nottingham Studies on Human Rights

Published under the auspices of the Human Rights Law Centre of the University of Nottingham

Edited by

Michael O'Flaherty
David Harris

VOLUME 1

The titles published in this series are listed at brill.nl/nshr

Human Rights Diplomacy: Contemporary Perspectives

Edited by
Michael O'Flaherty
Zdzisław Kędzia
Amrei Müller
George Ulrich

MARTINUS
NIJHOFF
PUBLISHERS

LEIDEN • BOSTON
2011

This book is printed on acid-free paper.

Library of Congress Cataloging-in-Publication Data

Human rights diplomacy : contemporary perspectives / edited by Michael O'Flaherty ... [et al.].
p. cm. -- (Nottingham Studies on Human Rights ; v. 1)
Based on presentations from the High-Level Workshop on Human Rights Diplomacy at the European Inter-University Centre for Human Rights and Democratisation (EIUC) in Venice, 30-31 January 2009.--Forword.
Includes bibliographical references and index.
ISBN 978-90-04-19516-5 (hardback : alk. paper) 1. Human rights--Congresses.
I. O'Flaherty, Michael, solicitor.
K3239.8.H864 2011
341.4'8--dc23

2011034628

ISSN 2211-7342
ISBN 978 90 04 19516 5

CONTENTS

Foreword vii
Kyung-wha Kang
List of Contributors xi
Acknowledgements xvii

1. Introduction. Human Rights Diplomacy—Contemporary Perspectives 1
Michael O'Flaherty, Zdzisław Kędzia, Amrei Müller and George Ulrich

2. Framework for the Analysis of Human Rights Diplomacy 19
George Ulrich

3. A Short Reflection on Human Rights Diplomacy 43
Robert Archer

4. The Role of Human Rights Ambassadors in Human Rights Diplomacy—Perspectives from Spain 59
Silvia Escobar

5. Human Rights Diplomacy of Small States 69
Éamonn Mac Aodha

6. The European Union as a Human Rights Actor 77
Toby King

7. Human Rights Diplomacy and the Council of Europe Commissioner for Human Rights 101
Thomas Hammarberg and Isil Gachet

8. Human Rights Diplomacy from a UN Perspective: A Complement to Advocacy 129
Ibrahim Salama

9. The United Nations Human Rights Treaty Bodies as Diplomatic Actors ... 155
Michael O'Flaherty

10. The Human Rights Diplomacy of the UN Secretary-General ... 173
Bertrand G. Ramcharan

11. Human Rights Diplomacy of the United Nations Security Council ... 191
Joanna Weschler

12. Conference Diplomacy and Human Rights ... 201
Zdzisław Kędzia

13. Human Rights Diplomacy: The NGO Role ... 217
Peggy Hicks

14. National Human Rights Institutions as Diplomacy Actors ... 223
Kirsten Roberts

15. The Relevance of the Multi-Stakeholder Approach and Multi-Track Diplomacy for Human Rights Diplomacy ... 251
Wolfgang Benedek

Annex: Report on the High-Level Workshop on Human Rights Diplomacy, Venice, 30–31 January 2009 ... 263

Select Bibliography ... 289
Index ... 293

FOREWORD

In the three decades since the 39th President of the United States, Jimmy Carter, made human rights a cornerstone of his administration's policy overseas, human rights has come to occupy a central place in the foreign policies of many countries. Governments are investing a great deal of diplomatic capital in defending their records on human rights at home and promoting their positions on global human rights issues with interlocutors at the bilateral level and in multilateral fora. Indeed, human rights diplomacy is a growing field of work. But the literature on the topic remains scant, and the vacuum prompts a basic question: Is it diplomacy in the service of human rights, or is it human rights as a tool of diplomacy in pursuit of foreign policy goals? The answer is not so obvious when observing the actions of key players on the global stage, and in many cases the two may overlap. But clearly, the organisers of the 2009 High-Level Workshop on Human Rights Diplomacy at the European Inter-University Centre for Human Rights and Democratisation (EIUC) in Venice had the former in mind. The presentations at the workshop, now collected in this volume together with additional articles, are about making advances for universal human rights around the world through principled and skilful diplomacy. The publication could not be more timely.

Many human rights professionals are reluctant to call their work diplomacy, and find 'human rights diplomacy' an uncomfortable oxymoron that links two fundamentally different areas of human endeavour. The roots of the discomfort run deep. Diplomacy is traditionally understood as the cool-headed pursuit of national interests, where principles and morality can, and in some cases should, be left aside or compromised, a dispassionate exercise of *realpolitik* at the international level. Meanwhile, human rights work has always been about ideals and values, driven by passion and indignation over injustice. In recent decades, however, there has been a convergence of the two disparate areas of work. Governments increasingly desire to be and to be seen as respectful if not in active pursuit of human rights in their domestic and foreign policies. Thus expanded, the opportunities for dialogue with governments call for more active and thoughtful engagement by human rights professionals.

The drive behind the convergence may be enlightened leadership in some countries. But in most, it has been the demands of the people and civil society to whom the policies of democratic governments must be accountable. More than six decades after the proclamation of the Universal Declaration of Human Rights, everyday individuals around the world are keenly aware of and ready to claim their rights, though perhaps not necessarily in the terms of international human rights norms. The citizens of the 21st century global community demand that their rights and those of others be upheld by their own governments and their bilateral, regional and international partners. When the demands for the full range of human rights are not met, the discontent is expressed through the ballot box, advocacy groups, petitions to regional or international human rights mechanisms or peaceful protests. When the calls are ignored or suppressed for a long time, when human beings can no longer bear the assault to their inherent dignity, the anger over the injustice explodes onto the streets, becoming an unstoppable force for political upheaval and national transformation.

In the early months of 2011, we are witnessing one such powerful moment in history, the aftermath of which will have long-lasting, wide-spread repercussions for human rights and political orders far beyond the national boundaries within which the protests have unfolded. Indeed, the longing for human rights is at the heart of the popular uprising that has swept across many countries of North Africa and the Middle East in the 'Arab spring' of 2011. From country to country, people have taken to the streets to voice their ardent aspiration for a clean break with the past in which their fundamental rights and freedoms were denied and abused by autocratic governments. They have said 'enough' to self-serving rulers who sheltered behind thick layers of state machinery that kept them disconnected from the aspirations of their people, and relied on the complacency of friendly governments to turn a blind eye to their socio-economic plight and political oppression in the pursuit of short-sighted security or economic interests.

The disconnect and the complacency have now been exposed and rejected in these countries, with countless human lives lost in the process. They remain yet to be fully revealed in many others. While, the primary responsibility of breaking the chains of the past and moving toward a future of democratic rule with respect for human rights rests with the governments of the peoples who have risen or hope to rise, the international community also has a role to play. Governments of countries that share a genuine commitment to human rights, non-governmental human rights organisations on the ground and in the global arena, regional and international human rights entities, and researchers in academic institutions all have a contribution to make in nurturing dialogue and action on human rights toward tolerant and open societies. These are demanding and exciting times for human rights diplomacy.

One should not preach what one does not practice, it is said. For human rights diplomacy, this is more than a simple dictum. It is at the core of the credibility of any effort to advance human rights. Thus, human rights diplomacy is as much a process of self-reflection and self-correction, as it is about encouraging and urging others for improvements. Connecting the two, using the platform of universal human rights norms, is a challenge for all countries.

The authors of each of the articles in this collection are highly accomplished thinkers and practitioners of human rights. They offer valuable and much-needed insight, analysis and lessons learned at a pivotal time for both human rights and diplomacy.

Kyung-wha Kang
Deputy UN High Commissioner for Human Rights

LIST OF CONTRIBUTORS

ROBERT ARCHER co-directs Plain Sense, an editing, writing and design service based in Geneva. Until 2010 he was Executive Director of the International Council on Human Rights Policy, an independent think tank. Until 1997 he ran the Policy Programme of Christian Aid (London), where he worked on aid policy, and governance and development issues in Sub-Saharan Africa. Between 1981 and 1991 he established a policy and advocacy programme on East and South East Asia for the Catholic Institute for International Relations (now Progressio), where he worked on political reform, human rights and labour issues in the region. He spent two years in the publishing and bookshop industry in Paris and has written books on Madagascar (l'Harmattan, 1975) and South African sport (Zed Books with Antoine Bouillon, 1982) as well as many shorter articles and reports. He taught for two years at the University of Antananarivo and wrote the screen play of Taba Taba (Madagascar, 1985). He has degrees in philosophy and English literature from Cambridge University and in African Studies from the School of Oriental and African Studies, London.

WOLFGANG BENEDEK is professor and director of the Institute of International Law and International Relations of the University of Graz and of the European Training and Research Centre for Human Rights and Democracy of the University of Graz (UNI-ETC); Chairman of the Austrian Committee of World University Service (WUS) Austria; Lecturer at the Vienna Diplomatic Academy and the European Master Program on Human Rights and Democratisation in Venice and the European Regional Master Program on Democratisation and Human Rights in Sarajevo. Benedek has published in the fields of human rights and human security, internet governance and the role of human rights in the information society, the European Union and human rights and international economic law.

SILVIA ESCOBAR is a linguist, pianist and human rights expert. She holds degrees from the University of Paris, the Royal Conservatory of Music, Madrid, and the Centre for Political Studies in London. Currently, she is Special Mission Ambassador for Human Rights at the

Spanish Ministry of Foreign Affairs and Cooperation. She is a founding member of the Spanish section of Amnesty International whose president she was between 1976 and 1982. Other former positions include those of Director of the Social Services of the Spanish Red Cross, Director of the Human Rights Unit at the Spanish Ministry of Foreign Affairs, and Secretary-General of the Centre for International Humanitarian Law of the Spanish Red Cross. Escobar was a member of several diplomatic missions to the United Nations, the Council of Europe and the (former) Conference on Security and Cooperation in Europe (CECE). She was elected Councillor of Madrid 1999–2003. She also was Secretary-General and later Vice President of the CEAR Foundation (Comisión Española de Ayuda al Refugiado).

Isil Gachet is the Director of the Office of the Council of Europe Commissioner for Human Rights. She was appointed to this position in January 2009. She began her professional life with eight years as a social worker, mainly dealing with projects devoted to literacy among immigrants, immigrant women, and the integration of unemployed youths. She joined the Council of Europe in 1984, and since then has been an international civil servant of this Organisation, where she worked first in the Youth sector, and from 1989 onwards, in human rights. She spent five years working as an administrator in the Media Division in the Directorate of Human Rights, where she was responsible for questions dealing with freedom of expression. In 1994, she was asked to provide the secretarial services necessary for the setting up of the European Commission against Racism and Intolerance (ECRI). In 1997 she was appointed Executive Secretary to ECRI in the General Directorate of Human Rights.

Thomas Hammarberg is Commissioner for Human Rights of the Council of Europe. He began his six-year term of office in April 2006. Formerly, he was Secretary General of the Olof Palme International Center, Sweden. His other positions have included those of Regional Advisor for Europe, Central Asia and the Caucasus at the Office of the UN High Commissioner for Human Rights and Swedish Representative for the multilateral Middle East peace process. He was also the Personal Representative of the Swedish Prime Minister to the Special Session on Children of the UN General Assembly and Chairman of the International Council on Human Rights Policy. Previously, he was Special Representative of the UN Secretary-General for Human Rights in Cambodia, Secretary-General of Amnesty International, and Secretary General of Swedish Save the Children. He has also worked as the foreign editor of the daily newspaper Expressen, diplomatic correspondent for the Swedish Radio and as a teacher.

Peggy Hicks is global advocacy director at Human Rights Watch, where she is responsible for coordinating Human Rights Watch's advocacy team and providing direction to its advocacy worldwide. Hicks previously served as director of the Office of Returns and Communities in the UN mission in Kosovo and as Deputy High Representative for Human Rights in Bosnia and Herzegovina. She has also worked as the Director of Programs for the International Human Rights Law Group (now Global Rights), clinical professor of human rights and refugee law at the University of Minnesota Law School, and as an expert consultant for the UN High Commissioner for Human Rights. Hicks is a graduate of Columbia Law School and the University of Michigan.

Zdzisław Kędzia holds the Chair of Constitutional Law, Faculty of Law and Administration, Adam Mickiewicz University of Poznań, Poland. He is currently the Vice-Chairperson of the UN Committee on Economic, Social and Cultural Rights. He previously worked for the Office of the UN High Commissioner for Human Rights (1994–2005), most recently as the Chief of the Research and Right to Development Branch. Between 1990 and 1994 Kędzia worked for the Polish diplomatic service. His posts included that of the Minister-Counsellor at the Permanent Mission of the Republic of Poland to the United Nations Office at Geneva. In 1993 Kędzia served as the General Rapporteur of the Second World Conference on Human Rights in Vienna. Kędzia has Masters and Doctorate degrees in Law from the Adam Mickiewicz University, Poznań, Poland.

Toby King BA, LLM, MPhil, is an administrator in the Human Rights Unit of the European External Action Service (formerly DG External Relations of the European Commission) and formerly worked in the External Relations Unit of DG Justice, Freedom and Security. Before joining the Commission, he was a research fellow at the Institute of Advanced Studies, United Nations University, Tokyo and is currently a visiting lecturer at the Centre for Advanced Legal Studies, University of Leuven.

Éamonn Mac Aodha, BCL, BL, Dip CDRS is Chief Executive of the Irish Human Rights Commission, Ireland's statutory national human rights institution. Between 1990 and 2007 he served with the Irish Department of Foreign Affairs including as human rights desk officer at the Permanent Mission of Ireland to the United Nations in Geneva (2000–2002) and as the Department's Director of Human Rights (2004–2007). He also served at the Irish Embassies to the Holy See, South Africa and Israel. He is currently Adjunct Professor at the Irish Human Rights Centre at the National University of Ireland, Galway and is a member of the Press Council of Ireland.

Amrei Müller has recently obtained a PhD from the University of Nottingham, exploring the relationship of legal obligations under the International Covenant on Economic, Social and Cultural Rights and international humanitarian law. She is currently a research assistant at the University of Zurich, School of Law. She was project officer for the project on Human Rights Diplomacy at the University of Nottingham Human Rights Law Centre. She has previously worked with the German Institute for Human Rights (DIMR) on the role of national human rights institutions in the UN treaty body process, and with UNDP Regional Centre for Europe and the Commonwealth of Independent States on human rights and security issues. She holds an LLM degree from the University of Nottingham and a BA degree in International Relations from the Technical University Dresden, Germany.

Michael O'Flaherty is Chief Commissioner of the Northern Ireland Human Rights Commission and holds the Chair in Applied Human Rights at the University of Nottingham. He is Co-Director of the University of Nottingham Human Rights Law Centre. He is currently Vice-Chairperson of the United Nations Human Rights Committee and is also a member of the UN Expert Group on Human Rights Indicators. Until December 2003, Michael O'Flaherty served in a number of senior positions with the United Nations. He established the UN human rights field missions in Bosnia and Herzegovina (1994) and Sierra Leone (1998) and subsequently guided UN headquarters support to its human rights programmes across the Asia-Pacific region. O'Flaherty has led a number of applied research projects and written extensively on human rights and related issues. His most recent publication include *Human Rights Field Operations, Law, Theory and Practice* (ed., Ashgate, 2007), and *The Professional Identity of the Human Rights*

Field Officer (ed. with G. Ulrich, Ashgate, 2010). A Fellow of the Royal Society of Arts, O'Flaherty read law at University College Dublin (BCL), theology and philosophy at the Gregorian University, Rome (BPh, STB), international relations at the University of Amsterdam (MA, MPhil) and is a Solicitor of the Irish Courts.

Bertrand G. Ramcharan is a fellow at the University of Nottingham Human Rights Law Centre. He performed the functions of UN High Commissioner for Human Rights in 2003-2004 and has been professor at the Geneva Graduate Institute of International and Development Studies and Chancellor of the University of Guyana. He has previously been Director of Studies at the Research Centre of the Hague Academy of International Law and served as Director of the International Conference on the Former Yugoslavia between 1992 and 1996. Earlier, he was the Head of the UN Secretary-General's speechwriting team and a Director in the Department of Political Affairs from 1996-1998, dealing with African issues. Ramcharan is a Barrister-at-Law of Lincoln's Inn and has Masters and Doctorate degrees in Law from the London School of Economics and Political Science. He is the author of several books, including *Preventive Diplomacy at the UN* (Indiana University Press, 2008).

Kirsten Roberts BCL, M.Litt., is Director of Research, Policy and Promotion in the Irish Human Rights Commission (IHRC), Ireland's national human rights institution (NHRI). From 2008 2011 she was Coordinator of the European Group of NHRIs. Prior to joining the IHRC, Roberts worked as a legal officer in the United Nations International Criminal Tribunal for the former Yugoslavia. Her previous experience includes the Permanent Representation of Ireland to the Council of Europe, European Court of Human Rights, European Court of Justice, and Amnesty International. Roberts has spoken widely on NHRIs, and has acted as an independent expert on national institutions for the EU Commission Technical Assistance and Information Exchange (TAIEX) platform.

Ibrahim Salama studied law at the University of Cairo, obtained a diploma in International Relations from the International Institute of Public Administration in Paris, a post-graduate degree in Specialised Studies in International Organisations and a PhD in Public Law from the University Paris XI. In 1981, he joined the Egyptian Foreign

Service. After postings in Paris, New Delhi and Geneva, he became Ambassador of the Arab Republic of Egypt in Lisbon in 2003. In August 2007 he joined the United Nations Office of the High Commissioner for Human Rights in Geneva where he is currently Director of the Human Rights Treaties Division. Salama is the author of many publications and papers on various human rights topics.

George Ulrich is since August 2009 Rector of the Riga Graduate School of Law. Prior to this, he served as Secretary General of the European Inter-University Centre for Human Rights and Democratisation (EIUC, based in Venice, Italy) from 2003-2009, and as Academic Coordinator and Programme Director of the European Master's Degree in Human Rights and Democratisation (E.MA) from 2001-2004. From 1999-2001 he was employed as Senior Researcher at the Danish Centre for Human Rights, and from 1996-1998 as research fellow at the Institute of Anthropology, University of Copenhagen, and visiting researcher at Makerere University, Kampala, Uganda. He obtained his PhD as well as an MA in Philosophy from the University of Toronto, Canada, and holds the degree of Cand. Mag. in Social Anthropology and History of Ideas from Aarhus University, Denmark. Among his current research interests are issues related to: the philosophy of human rights, health and human rights, international medical ethics, professional ethics, and ethics for human rights professionals.

Joanna Weschler is Deputy Executive Director and Director of Research of the Security Council Report, and a research fellow at the Columbia University's School of International and Public Affairs. She was a reporter for the Solidarity Union press agency in Poland, in charge of covering most meetings between Union President Lech Walesa and the communist government, and meetings of the executive leadership of the Union. Between 1994 and 2005 Weschler worked as Human Rights Watch's representative at the United Nations. As the first person appointed to this position, Weschler developed and articulated HRW's strategy toward the UN. Previously, she was the researcher on Poland for Helsinki Watch; researcher on Brazil for Americas Watch; and Director of HRW's Prison Project. She has conducted human rights investigations in countries on five continents and written numerous reports and articles on human rights. She has a Masters degree in Spanish and Latin American Studies from the University of Warsaw and a Masters degree in journalism from Columbia University.

ACKNOWLEDGEMENTS

At the outset we should thank the participants at the High-Level Workshop on Human Rights Diplomacy in Venice, January 2009. It was that event that provided the context and impetus for this volume. We thank all of our authors who worked diligently in writing and revising their chapters, notwithstanding their many other commitments.

We are very grateful to the University of Nottingham Human Rights Law Centre, the European University Centre for Human Rights and Democratisation, Venice, and the Adam Mickiewicz University of Poznań for their generous financial support for the Workshop and the preparation of this volume.

Michael O'Flaherty, Zdzisław Kędzia,
Amrei Müller and George Ulrich
Nottingham, Poznań, Riga
April 2011

CHAPTER 1

INTRODUCTION

HUMAN RIGHTS DIPLOMACY—CONTEMPORARY PERSPECTIVES

Michael O'Flaherty, Zdzisław Kędzia, Amrei Müller and George Ulrich

The implementation of international human rights standards can be pursued by a range of means. These include legal redress, technical assistance, political pressure and non-governmental advocacy. Another such means which has not received much attention is the undertaking of human rights diplomacy. This volume seeks to explore the notion, dimensions and means of human rights diplomacy.

While traditional diplomacy is associated with the pursuit of national interests by states in their foreign policy, human rights diplomacy is the utilisation of diplomatic negotiation and persuasion for the specific purpose of promoting and protecting human rights. It involves a strategy of engagement with a range of actors whose goals and interests concerning human rights may be different. Accordingly, human rights diplomacy aims at both persuading counterparts to introduce measures to advance the implementation of human rights and dissuading them from taking action that is contrary to human rights. In many cases, in particular in inter-state interaction, an element of reciprocity is part of human rights diplomacy. Today, human rights diplomacy can involve a range of actors, not limited to 'classic' diplomats such as representatives of states and inter-governmental organisations. Among them are also non-governmental organisations (NGOs) and other representatives of civil society, national human rights institutions (NHRIs), academic institutions, human rights experts, parliamentarians, religious groups, and even business.

In the analysis of human rights diplomacy it is important to acknowledge that while most actors engage in this pursuit in good faith with the general aim in one way or another to advance the cause of human rights, there are also a variety of ways in which human rights diplomacy can be misused. 'Bad' human rights diplomacy—human rights counter-diplomacy, as it were—assumes a variety of familiar forms: first, engaging in diplomatic action with the intention to undermine established human rights standards; second, the use of diplomatic means by states to minimise and refute criticism of their human rights record; and third, the instrumentalisation of human rights by some actors to achieve foreign policy goals not related to the promotion and protection of human rights.

Human rights diplomacy may moreover be usefully distinguished from humanitarian diplomacy, even though both overlap in some cases. Humanitarian diplomacy is defined more as an emergency policy, involving humanitarian actors in for example negotiating access to vulnerable populations or combating a culture of impunity in armed conflicts where widespread violations of human rights and humanitarian law occur.[1] Human rights diplomacy by contrast has a long-term aim to develop and change laws, policies, practices and systems to ensure the lasting implementation of human rights.

Human rights diplomacy is long-standing in the practice of states and inter-governmental organisations. However, its form has developed considerably in the period since the Vienna World Conference on Human Rights in 1993, and the number of actors involved has increased significantly. There has been a proliferation of diplomatic initiatives at the multilateral, regional and bilateral level, with the aim to promote the implementation of human rights. Above all, the post of United Nations (UN) High Commissioner for Human Rights was established and mandated to carry out a number of functions including some of a diplomatic character. Regional organisations, such as the Council of Europe (CoE) and the Organisation for Security and Co-operation in Europe (OSCE) have established similar high-level posts. In addition, specific human rights-related responsibilities were either attached to or assumed by more generally mandated office-holders such as the UN Secretary-General and commissioners of the European Commission. Experts associated with the UN human rights treaty bodies and special procedures of the UN Human Rights Council (HRC), similarly, now regularly carry out certain functions of human rights diplomacy. At the national level, a number of states have appointed human rights ambassadors, and NHRIs play an ever more active and diversified role in the promotion and protection of human rights.

---

[1] The subject of humanitarian diplomacy is analysed in L. Minear and H. Smith (eds.), *Humanitarian Diplomacy: Practitioners and Their Craft* (New York: United Nations University Press, 2007).

Yet, there is little systematic analysis of the work of these diplomatic initiatives for the promotion and protection of human rights, nor of how their activities forms part of an emerging strategy of human rights diplomacy. Moreover, while the highly formalised modes of interaction of 'classic' inter-state diplomacy are well established,[2] the frame in which human rights diplomacy is carried out is not clearly defined, and the conventions that determine the behaviour of the wide range of actors involved in human rights diplomacy are less well understood. These are among the underlying reasons why the potential of human rights diplomacy is far from being exploited. This, unfortunately, too often results in bypassing the so-called soft stages of addressing human rights problems and in moving directly to more confrontational international and domestic situations. Opportunities for developing long-term strategies to prevent human rights violations, and to build states' institutional capacities to respond when human rights are at risk through human rights diplomacy, are also not taken up to a satisfying extent. The international and domestic systems of human rights protection and ultimately, rights-holders suffer under these circumstances.

The topic of human rights diplomacy has also attracted limited reflective attention at the academic level. Even though some of the issues that are examined in this volume are discussed in existing literature, by and large this literature focuses on the practice and challenges of bilateral and multilateral inter state human rights diplomacy, or the role of human rights in foreign policy more broadly.[3]

Relevant earlier research has been conducted by Müllerson. His monograph "Human Rights Diplomacy"[4] of 1997 contains a valuable chapter on characteristics of states' Cold War human rights diplomacy, or rather on characteristics of human rights counter-diplomacy, some of which still occur in states' contemporary human rights diplomacy, albeit in a changed international context. For instance, not surprisingly, Müllerson holds that 'although human rights diplomacy of that

[2] See 1961 Vienna Convention on Diplomatic Relations, 500 UNTS 95; entered into force on 24 April 1964.

[3] Important publications predating the above-mentioned rash of initiatives in the 1990s include R. J. Vincent (eds.), *Foreign Policy and Human Rights: Issues and Responses* (Cambridge: Cambridge University Press, 1986); and R. P. Claude and B. Weston (eds.), *Human Rights in the World Community* (Philadelphia: University of Pennsylvania Press, 1992).

[4] R. Müllerson, *Human Rights Diplomacy* (London: Routledge, 1997).

[Cold War] period was not exclusively determined by Cold War imperatives, it was certainly rather heavily tainted by the ideological and political clash between the East and the West'.[5] In most cases human rights diplomacy was therefore used for pursuing political purposes other than the promotion and protection of human rights, and in particular the United States' human rights policies lacked consistency and its double-standards were often obvious. The accusation of applying double-standards is still one of the challenges that governmental actors involved in human rights diplomacy face today. Likewise, Müllerson's finding that Western countries' attempts to influence the human rights situation in the Soviet Union by diplomatic means had rather limited effect because the target country was an important actor in international relations, may still be relevant for human rights diplomacy towards current or emerging big powers today. Müllerson also alerts to the fact that when deciding on what 'tools' to rely on in human rights diplomacy towards a particular country, account has to be taken of the characteristics of this country's society, i.e. its political, historical, cultural and religious background; of the concrete causes of particular human rights violations; as well as of the characteristics of the violations.[6] He moreover initially discusses the role of inter-governmental organisations and NGOs in human rights diplomacy[7]—a discussion that will be substantively enlarged upon in this volume.

Other more recent literature highlights additional issues that are further discussed in this volume. Beahr and Casterman-Holleman for example examine different policy instruments states regularly rely on in their efforts to prevent and stop human rights violations in other countries, among them incentives and more confrontational means.[8] Forsythe comprehensively analyses the role of a wide range of actors in the promotion and protection of human rights in international relations, recognising that 'increasingly it is necessary to look beyond not only states and their inter-governmental organizations, but also beyond private groups active for human rights, relief, and development for

[5] *Ibid.*, p.103.
[6] *Ibid.*, ch.5.
[7] *Ibid.*, pp.133–47.
[8] P. R. Beahr and M. Castermans-Holleman, *The Role of Human Rights in Foreign Policy*, 3rd edn, (London: Palgrave Macmillan, 2004), ch.4.

understanding the fate of human rights in the world.'[9] Both books, however, examine the role of human rights in foreign policy/international relations in more general terms than the current volume which focuses on good faith human rights *diplomacy* that, as mentioned above, always involves an element of negotiation or persuasion for the promotion and protection of human rights. A discussion of military intervention as a means to bring an end to gross violations of human rights is, for example, not considered to fall within the notion of human rights diplomacy.[10] Other major publications on the evolving nature of multilateral diplomacy are rather fleeting in their consideration of human rights.[11]

Recognising the gap in the literature in particular in regard to the proliferation of actors involved in contemporary human rights diplomacy, a High-Level Workshop on Human Rights Diplomacy was held in Venice in January 2009. Its aim was to initially explore the notion, components and tools of human rights diplomacy, pooling the high-level experience and expertise of diplomats, scholars and practitioners in the field of human rights. The issues discussed during the workshop included the following:

- the identification of the different actors involved in human rights diplomacy, including their roles and the core tools and instruments they rely on to conduct human rights diplomacy;
- an assessment of the strengths and the weaknesses of the various extant human rights diplomacy mandates at the national, regional and international level;
- a reflection on how the relationship between human rights diplomacy, public advocacy and law-based human rights promotion and protection can be managed best;
- an examination of the role of confidence-building measures within human rights diplomacy as well as the prevention of human rights violation through human rights diplomacy;

---

[9] D. P. Forsythe, *Human Rights in International Relations*, 2nd edn, (Cambridge: Cambridge University Press, 2006), p.258.

[10] Humanitarian intervention is discussed by Beahr and Castermans-Holleman and by Forsythe. They also analyse what was identified above as 'bad' or human rights counter-diplomacy.

[11] For example, J. P. Muldoon *et al* (eds.), *Multilateral Diplomacy and the United Nations*, 2nd edn, (Boulder: Westview Press, 2005); and G. R. Berridge, *Diplomacy: Theory and Practice*, 4th edn, (Basingstoke: Palgrave Macmillan, 2010).

- the identification of the risks and pitfalls in employing diplomatic, negotiation-based means to seek the promotion and protection of human rights; and
- a discussion of the role of international human rights law in human rights diplomacy.

In addition to the 'classical' actors states and inter-governmental organisations, the workshop identified and directly discussed the role of the following actors in bilateral and multilateral human rights diplomacy: inter-governmentally appointed office-holders such as the UN High Commissioner for Human Rights and her Office (OHCHR) and the OSCE High Commissioner on National Minorities; the UN Secretary-General; special procedure mandate-holders of the UN Human Rights Council; UN human rights treaty bodies; UN agencies with the United Nations Children's Fund (UNICEF) as an example; NGOs; and academic institutions.[12] Other actors, such as the UN Security Council, NHRIs, the CoE Commissioner for Human Rights, regional organisations such as the African Union, the Organisation of American States, and the Association of Southeast Asian Nations, parliaments, local government, cities, trade unions, business, health institutions, religious groups, and the legal profession were mentioned during the workshop, and it was concluded that defining their role in an emerging strategy of human rights diplomacy would help to achieve true inclusiveness in the sector. The workshop recognised that the theory of multi-track diplomacy and the multi-stakeholder approach that has been successfully applied in other areas could usefully be relied upon to draw parallels in this regard. Insights from multi-stakeholder and multi-track processes could also enhance the legitimacy, quality and effectiveness of human rights diplomacy.[13]

The tools and instruments the mentioned actors rely on in their engagement in human rights diplomacy vary *inter alia* in accordance with their status and in accordance with the status of their counterpart. To give but one example, while states and inter-governmental organisations like the European Union (EU) can rely on a range of tools, including the cooperative and more confrontational means of 'classical' diplomacy, NGOs have to regularly rely on the outcome of their

[12] Report on the High-Level Workshop on Human Rights Diplomacy, Venice, 30–31 January 2009, annex to the present volume, pp.163–88. (hereinafter Venice Workshop Report).

[13] *Ibid.*, pp.275 and 282.

fact-finding and monitoring results when engaging with other actors behind the scenes or through more public action. They, together with other actors like UN treaty bodies, special procedure mandate-holders and academic institutions, can only to a lesser extent rely on reciprocity. On the other hand, these latter actors are more likely to be recognised as honest brokers since the promotion of human rights is their only aim. The same holds true for inter-governmentally appointed office-holders with a clear human rights mandate. States and intergovernmental organisations often face the challenge to ensure the credibility of their human rights diplomacy as human rights are frequently not the most important interest these actors pursue through diplomatic means, and because they at times demand the implementation of standards by third states that are not met within their own country.[14]

The importance of building networks and to coordinate initiatives of different actors for successful human rights diplomacy was recognised throughout the workshop.[15] One suggestion made during the workshop with a view toward the full exploitation of the potential of multi-layered human rights diplomacy concerned the exploration of strategies for the sequencing of diplomatic initiatives by the various actors.[16]

The risks and pitfalls in employing diplomatic means to seek the promotion and protection of human rights also became clearer during the discussions. Among them is the danger that human rights standards are watered down if compromises found through diplomatic negotiations go too far.[17] While human rights diplomacy can, for instance, involve negotiations about the best means to implement a particular right in a given situation or about a particular interpretation of a human rights norm,[18] it has to always remain grounded in international human rights law. Thus, while in 'classic' diplomacy among states almost everything can be negotiable, human rights diplomacy should avoid compromises on standards set out in international treaties. In particular, the core of international human rights law cannot be

[14] *Ibid.*, pp.268, 274 and 283.

[15] *Ibid.*, pp.268, 272 and 278.

[16] *Ibid.*, p.283.

[17] *Ibid.*, p.266.

[18] See for example the experience of the OSCE High Commissioner on National Minorities, or the reporting procedure before the UN human rights treaty bodies, Venice Workshop Report, annex to the present volume, pp.278 and 281.

negotiable in any diplomatic effort. This also highlights the tension that exists in the notion of 'human rights diplomacy' between on the one hand the requirement for negotiation that is inherent in diplomatic action, and on the other hand the principled (legal) nature of international human rights law.

The contributions in this volume address these and other key issues. The focus is both academic and practice-oriented, to make the findings accessible to a wide range of stakeholders engaged with issues of human rights diplomacy.

The initial chapters by Ulrich and Archer in different ways examine the concept of human rights diplomacy and its relation to other forms of human rights advocacy and diplomatic practice. In Chapter 2 Ulrich presents a general framework for the analysis of human rights diplomacy.[19] He takes his point of departure in a distinction between contexts in which human rights law is accepted and functions as operative norm and contexts in which the applicable standards, and sometimes the very notion of human rights, are being contested. Human rights diplomacy belongs in the latter category and is in this respect similar to yet distinct from a range of other characteristic modes of strategic engagement where the central focus of attention is on legitimising human rights, raising popular awareness, rallying support, advocating a more radical or more consistent application of human rights, and addressing complexities in the interrelation between human rights and other societal priorities. This is true, notably, of public campaigning, political dialogue and dispute, and much scholarly work related to human rights. Where human rights law functions as operative norm, to the contrary, the natural focus of attention is on the correct application of established human rights standards, and practitioners are typically tasked with exercising technical legal competence, be this in judicial settings or in broader contexts of policy making and public administration. Ulrich acknowledges that all of these modes of human rights practice overlap and are closely inter-related. He therefore sees a crucial challenge in building effective coordinated strategies, as is also a central theme in several other contributors to the present publication. Against this background, Ulrich proceeds to an analysis of some of the primary issues at stake in the contestation of human rights.

[19] G. Ulrich, 'Framework for the Analysis of Human Rights Diplomacy', Chapter 2 in the present volume, pp.19–42.

He identifies three salient parameters of contestation in human rights discourse, which are *conflicting values, competing priorities* and *implied status*. All three issues merit careful attention in the exercise of human rights diplomacy, the issue of implied status being perhaps the most sensitive and complicated to address.

In Chapter 3 Archer further reflects on what is meant when we speak about human rights diplomacy, deepening the analysis of specific characteristics of human rights diplomacy in accordance with the provisional 'definition' set out at the beginning of this introduction. Archer's central suggestion is that in its contemporary form "human rights diplomacy' should be thought of less as an activity, and more as a strategy, a way of 'doing' human rights that harnesses people and opportunities together in certain ways'.[20] He identifies elements of 'classical' human rights diplomacy, involving states and intergovernmental organisations following highly formalised procedures. Archer traces more recent developments in the human rights 'movement' and highlights how they resulted in a considerable increase of voices heard and actors involved in a contemporary more hybrid form of human rights diplomacy. He discusses the challenges this brings about for the conduct of human rights diplomacy, for example the need to carefully manage the asymmetry of status of the actors involved which requires creativity and judgement. He furthermore identifies criteria of 'success' of hybrid human rights diplomacy. Among them are a clear and credible status of the actors involved, a clear purpose of the engagement, open-mindedness and mutual trust. He concludes his reflections with an observation on transparency and coherence in human rights diplomacy: due to the complexity of contemporary multi-layered human rights diplomacy, it is unlikely that full coherence can be achieved, in particular in public.

Many of Archer's and Ulrich's observations are confirmed in subsequent chapters of the present volume which give account of the human rights diplomacy by different actors at the bilateral, regional or multilateral (UN) level. Starting with the analysis of the activities of 'classical' actors in human rights diplomacy, in Chapter 4 Escobar shares her experience of engaging in human rights diplomacy as Spanish

[20] R. Archer, 'A Short Reflection on Human Rights Diplomacy', Chapter 3 in the present volume, pp.43–58.

human rights ambassador.[21] Among other things, she discusses missions to third countries that European human rights ambassadors carry out alone or in groups with the aim to examine the human rights situation in the respective country firsthand and, if necessary, to make constructive proposals to governments of how to improve a situation. She thereby extends the list of 'tools' states can rely on in their human rights diplomacy at the bilateral level mentioned during the workshop,[22] among them the sending of confidential or public *demarches*, the calling in of ambassadors, engaging in regular human rights dialogues and consultations with specific countries, supporting human rights defenders, as well as more confrontational means such as suspending or threatening the suspension of cooperation in other fields. Escobar furthermore points out the direct benefit the appointment of human rights ambassadors can provide for conducting effective bilateral human rights diplomacy: due to their rank, they can often engage in substantive dialogue with high-ranking officials in third countries. This privilege that forms part of 'classical' formalised diplomatic interaction can prove very effective to bring about change in some situations. Escobar moreover gives examples of how diplomatic initiatives for the promotion of human rights can be successful if they are firmly led by a state and can count on broad support from inter-governmental organisations as well as civil society actors.

Also adopting a practitioner's perspective, in Chapter 5 Mac Aodha studies the role of small states in human rights diplomacy.[23] He examines broadly the advantages and disadvantages of small states as actors on the international stage, adding to the findings of the Venice report on the strengths and weaknesses of different actors engaged in human rights diplomacy. Key advantages such as the frequent capacity of smaller states to operate as honest brokers are highlighted while possible weaknesses including the absence of possibilities to rely on more confrontational measures (for instance an effective threat of force), are also explored. Specific successes of small states in terms of human rights diplomacy are noted and some positive examples of best practice are surveyed. Among them is the significant contribution of

---

[21] S. Escobar, 'The Role of Human Rights Ambassadors in Human Rights Diplomacy—Perspectives from Spain', Chapter 4 in the present volume, pp.59–68.

[22] Venice Workshop Report, annex to the present volume, p.267.

[23] É. Mac Aodha, 'The Human Rights Diplomacy of Small States', Chapter 5 in the present volume, pp.69–76.

small states to the adoption and implementation of EU guidelines on human rights, and the positive roles small states can play in the universal periodic review (UPR) process of the HRC.

Chapters 6 and 7 examine regional inter-governmental organisations' role in human rights diplomacy, including that of the European Union and independent mechanisms such as the Council of Europe Commissioner for Human Rights.

King explores the nature of the European Union's human rights diplomacy in Chapter 6.[24] He observes that the EU's commitment to promote human rights in its external relations is grounded in the norms that underpin the Union's internal structure and which are fundamental to its own identity. Confirming the instruments that are specific to the EU's human rights diplomacy mentioned in the Venice Workshop Report,[25] King deepens the examination of the EU's regular human rights dialogues with third countries; the conditioning of general EU contractual relationships (EU framework agreements) with all third countries on respect for human rights; the linking of trade policies to human rights; and the EU's support for civil society in third countries. The effectiveness of these instruments is also assessed. King moreover expands the discussion of the challenges the EU is facing when using diplomatic means for the promotion of human rights: the difficulties with meeting the element of reciprocity that is inherent in diplomatic action, as well as preventing compromises in negotiations that undermine established international norms are among them. Just as for states, the promotion of human rights is by no means the only issue that the EU attempts to advance through its foreign policy. King establishes the challenges that follow from this fact in greater detail, including that of ensuring the credibility of the EU's human rights diplomacy. He also explores the role of the European Parliament in human rights diplomacy.

As an independent mechanism with a clear human rights mandate, the CoE Commissioner for Human Rights is more likely to appear as a principled actor in human rights diplomacy than the EU which was not in the first place founded to promote human rights in third states, or states who frequently subordinate human rights to other interests

[24] T. King, 'The European Union as a Human Rights Actor', Chapter 6 in the present volume, pp.77–100.

[25] Venice Workshop Report, annex to the present volume, pp.273–75.

pursued through diplomatic means. With their Chapter 7[26] Hammarberg and Gachet add the experience of the CoE Commissioner for Human Rights to the findings on the practice of human rights diplomacy by other inter-governmentally appointed office-holders summarised in the report on the Venice workshop.[27] They highlight how the Commissioner's regular visits to all member states of the Council of Europe enable him to enter into permanent dialogues on human rights concerns with governments, parliaments, the judiciary, civil society and NHRIs. Among other aspects, they identify regular presence in the field as well as the Commissioner's impartiality and independence as key to the Commissioner's success. Distancing himself from any political considerations and analysing situations exclusively from a human rights point of view ensures the Commissioner's credibility with all actors involved in human rights diplomacy. This allows him to frequently act as an intermediary who commands trust among adversaries and actors of different status, including in highly politicised environments. Hammarberg and Gachet illustrate their observations with examples from the Commissioner's work in Chechnya, the United Kingdom, during the post-electoral events in Armenia in March 2008, and during the human rights and humanitarian crisis in South Ossetia, Georgia, in August 2008. The reliance on well-tested facts as well sas continuous efforts to directly relate to people in the member states of the CoE also contribute substantially to the success of the Commissioner's human rights diplomacy.

Chapters 8–12 bring the examination of human rights diplomacy to the multilateral (UN) level. Salama's Chapter 8 on "Human Rights Diplomacy from a UN Perspective: A Complement to Advocacy"[28] analyses both how human rights diplomacy grounded in international human rights law can complement advocacy for the implementation of human rights, and the role of the UN High Commissioner for Human Rights and her Office in this human rights diplomacy. By focusing on four examples—the Durban Review Conference of April 2009, an OHCHR Expert Seminar on Freedom of Expression and Advocacy of Religious Hatred, the process of

[26] T. Hammarberg and I. Gachet, 'Human Rights Diplomacy and the Council of Europe Commissioner for Human Rights', Chapter 7 in the present volume, pp.101–28.

[27] Venice Workshop Report, annex to the present volume, pp.276–79.

[28] I. Salama, 'Human Rights Diplomacy from a UN Perspective: A Complement to Advocacy', Chapter 8 in the present volume, p.129–54.

strengthening the UN treaty bodies and recent activities of the Working Group on Right to Development and its High-Level Task Force—he shows how highly politicised, seemingly gridlocked debates on certain human rights issues can be brought forward by relying on diplomatic strategies. He identifies two issues as key in this process: persuading actors involved to refocus a politicised debate first on relevant norms of international human rights law, and second on (technical) measures to be taken toward their implementation. He highlights that the documents/statements of UN human rights experts bodies (treaty bodies and special procedures mandate-holders) are important reference points in this process; and that members of these expert bodies can often play an equally important role in it, as they are usually trusted for their expertise by all actors involved. Salama further shows how the UN High Commissioner and her Office can strengthen their central role in fostering a collaborative environment in which these processes can take place by engaging in principled human rights diplomacy with all actors involved. As suggested during the Venice workshop, this could contribute to develop OHCHR into a 'centre of expertise'[29] on human rights issues that states could approach to obtain independent advice on the implementation of human rights.

The role of UN human rights treaty bodies as diplomatic actors is analysed in Chapter 9 by O'Flaherty.[30] In contradistinction to the usual designation of treaty body proceedings as 'quasi judicial' it is argued that the reporting procedure can best be characterised as diplomatic. O'Flaherty observes in this regard that the proceedings are based on dialogues with states in the process of which the treaty bodies develop recommendations proposing specific solutions that states can adopt and implement within the complex task of governance. O'Flaherty analyses how the diplomatic model can aid efforts to strengthen the treaty body system. First, it reinforces suggestions made in the renewed debate about treaty body reform, for instance calls for improved flows of information to and from the treaty bodies, for making them more accessible for NGOs and NHRIs, for enhancing the quality and practicality of the treaty bodies' recommendations, for improved follow-up procedures, and calls to change the composition of government delegations to the treaty bodies as well as the

[29] Venice Workshop Report, annex to the present volume, p.277.

[30] M. O'Flaherty, 'The United Nations Human Rights Treaty Bodies as Diplomatic Actors', Chapter 9 in the present volume, p.155–72.

composition of the treaty body membership itself. Second, understanding the work of treaty bodies as essentially diplomatic can be helpful in other areas, e.g. in regard to clarifying the relationship of the treaty bodies and UPR procedure of the UN HRC.

Another actor engaging in human rights diplomacy at the UN level, is the UN Secretary-General. His role is studied more extensively by Ramcharan in Chapter 10.[31] Ramcharan argues that all UN Secretaries-General should set a few objectives which can be pursued through deploying human rights diplomacy. When making his/her choice, the UN Secretary-General shall take into account the mandates of the UN High Commissioner for Human Rights and the UN HRC. This ensures that the Secretary-General does not duplicate these actors' activities but supports them to the greatest extent possible, contributing to achieve coherence in multi-layered human rights diplomacy that was called for during the workshop.[32] Ramcharan identifies selected areas where the Secretary-General's human rights diplomacy is likely to make a difference, based on both the human rights related activities Secretaries-General have traditionally been involved in, and on the Secretary-General's mandate under Article 99 UN Charter. Among these areas are engaging in humanitarian good offices; the areas of peacemaking, peacekeeping and peacebuilding; the advancement of the responsibility to protect; the strengthening of national protection systems; and the promotion of the principle of justice in support of the International Criminal Court (ICC). Through the authority of his office, the Secretary-General can—openly or behind the scenes—urge other actors to take appropriate measures in regard to certain human rights issues.

Among the actors that the UN Secretary-General can push to take action on human rights is the UN Security Council. Its engagement in human rights diplomacy through adopting resolutions and through other means is examined by Weschler in Chapter 11.[33] In her brief historical overview, she observes that during the Cold War the human rights diplomacy of the Security Council mainly concerned the process of decolonisation and the apartheid regime in South Africa.

[31] B. G. Ramcharan, 'The Human Rights Diplomacy of the UN Secretary General', Chapter 10 in the present volume, pp.173–90.

[32] Venice Workshop Report, annex to the present volume, p.278.

[33] J. Weschler, 'Human Rights Diplomacy and the United Nations Security Council', Chapter 11 in the present volume, pp.191–200.

Only in the 1990s human rights issues became more prominent in the Council's debates, *inter alia* driven by its increased awareness of non-international armed conflicts and the violations of human rights and international humanitarian law that occur in these conflicts. While the references to human rights in the Security Council's debates and resolutions has increased in recent years, Weschler is only cautiously optimistic about the extent to which the promotion and protection of human rights have seized a permanent place in the Council's diplomatic activities. She shows that on the one hand some members of the Security Council remain reluctant to accept the Council's engagement with human rights. On the other hand, Weschler highlights that human rights issues can indeed be taken forward in the Council's diplomacy on the initiative of one or more than one of its members. Determination, diplomatic skill and persistence of UN member states, supported by the UN Secretary-General, are key in this regard—not only for successful human rights diplomacy of the Security Council, but also in other settings.

International human rights conferences are another arena for multilateral human rights diplomacy. Chapter 12 by Kędzia[34] elaborates on the advantages and the risks of holding big conferences on human rights. Focusing on the outcome of the 1993 Vienna World Conference on Human Rights, he shows that many of the statements adopted by the Conference after highly controversial negotiations had a profoundly positive impact on the development of international human rights law and the strengthening of UN human rights mechanisms. For instance, the Vienna Declaration and Programme of Action[35] suggested the creation of the institution of the UN High Commissioner for Human Rights and strongly encouraged the negotiation and adoption of new international human rights treaties, among them the Optional Protocols to the Convention against Torture and the International Covenant on Economic, Social and Cultural Rights. Among the risks involved in conference diplomacy Kędzia mentions their duplicative nature, their discriminatory character, their political bias and their high financial costs. He concludes that these risks have

[34] Z. Kedzia, 'Conference Diplomacy and Human Rights', Chapter 12 in the present volume, p.201–16.

[35] Vienna Declaration and Programme of Action, adopted by the World Conference on Human Rights, UN Doc A/CONF.157/23 (12 July 1993).

to be considered in the context of positive arguments about conference diplomacy when future world conferences are planned by the UN.

Chapters 13 and 14 examine the role of additional actors involved in human rights diplomacy: non-governmental organisations and national human rights institutions. Hicks discusses the diverse roles that NGOs can play in human rights diplomacy.[36] Among them are their roles as catalysts, instigating human rights diplomacy by other actors through exposing abuses; as advocates, pushing for stronger, more effective human rights engagement by governments; as partners in policy-making, for example when NGOs are actively involved in the negotiation of human rights treaties; and as monitors, exposing the hypocrisy of governments engaged in human rights diplomacy. As actors who are able to put forward an 'undiluted case for human rights'[37] because they do not need to consider conflicting interests, the involvement of NGOs in diplomatic processes can contribute greatly to achieving human rights friendly results. Hicks further observes that NGOs can be beneficiaries of human rights diplomacy when they come under pressure.

The Venice Workshop Report identified NHRIs as further important actors in today's hybrid form of human rights diplomacy whose role did not obtain sufficient attention in the discussion during the workshop.[38] Roberts Chapter 14 on "National Human Rights Institutions as Diplomacy Actors" addresses this deficit.[39] Roberts observes that NHRIs today occupy something of a '4th space', as they have taken on hybrid functions in the promotion and protection of human rights that were previously solely the domains of governments, inter-governmental organisations or NGOs. This, and the fact that their independence and impartiality is recognised through a formal procedure at UN level when they are established in conformity with the Paris Principles,[40] gives them unique roles to play in human rights diplomacy. Among them is acting as a link between the national, regional and international systems for the protection of human rights,

[36] P. Hicks, 'An NGO Perspective on Human Rights Diplomacy', Chapter 13 in the present volume, pp.217–22.

[37] *Ibid.*, p.219.

[38] Venice Workshop Report, annex to the present volume, p.282.

[39] K. Roberts, 'National Human Rights Institutions as Diplomacy Actors', Chapter 14 in the present volume, pp.223–50.

[40] Principles relating to the Status of National Institutions (The Paris Principles), annex to UNGA Res 48/134 (1993), UN Doc A/RES/48/134 (20 December 1993).

including ensuring that initiatives at these different levels do not obstruct or duplicate, but reinforce and complement each other. A related role is that of bringing in-depth knowledge about the human rights situation at the national level into discussions in international or regional forums, and ensuring at the same time that decisions of regional and international organisations are implemented by relevant governmental and non-governmental actors at the national level. Roberts further shows that NHRIs can also be engaged in bilateral diplomacy applying peer-centred strategies, which can in some instances be more effective than efforts of governments or NGOs, for example in regard to states with a particular poor-human rights record. Some NHRIs are also in the position to 'mainstream' human rights into the development aid policies of their respective countries, and thereby contribute to ensuring that governmental development agencies become involved in human rights diplomacy as well.

The last Chapter 15 by Benedek[41] draws together the various threads and examines the topic through the prism of multi-track/multi-stakeholder approaches to human rights diplomacy. Benedek explains that the theory of multi-track diplomacy and the multi-stakeholder approach seek to involve all relevant stakeholders and, in contrast to 'classical' inter-state diplomacy, rely on bottom-up approaches that aim to first identify the problems of the people whom the diplomatic action should benefit. Benedek highlights that in particular their reliance on widely ramified networks and open discussions allow that multi-stakeholder approaches/multi-track diplomacy produce widely accepted results and a broad base through which these results can be implemented. As a result, outcomes of multi-track/multi-stakeholder processes can be more sustainable than that of classic inter-governmental diplomacy. Examples of successful multi-track/multi-stakeholder processes give more details to these findings. Challenges remain, however, for instance in regard to the careful preparation, the effective follow-up on results and the managing of hierarchies in multi-track/multi-stakeholder discussions.

During the Venice workshop, two insights emerged prominently in discussions regarding how best to further develop the understanding

[41] W. Benedek, 'The Relevance of the Multi-Stakeholder Approach and Multi-Track Diplomacy for Human Rights Diplomacy', Chapter 15 in the present volume, pp.251–61.

of an emerging strategy of human rights diplomacy:[42] First, criticism and recommendations in regard to the human rights situation in a particular country from outside actors—be they voiced by other states, international or regional human rights bodies or non-governmental actors—are still more often than not taken as something negative that can provoke defensive moves by the respective state (or other actors criticised, for instance transnational corporations). Even among UN agencies that are supposed to 'mainstream' human rights into their work, resistance to human rights seems still common. Skilful diplomatic action, ideally coordinated among the different actors the roles of which are further analysed in this volume, thus seems an essential requirement for pressing ahead with the implementation of human rights. Second, the implementation of human rights in diverse countries around the world is an ongoing process that requires incremental approaches. Concrete measures that are to be taken to further the implementation of a particular human right in a defined situation at a specific point in time have to be established in an on-going process of political and legal debate and review. This highlights the need for continuous dialogues and negotiations among different actors to indentify the best way forward at a time towards the realisation of human rights.

The contributions to this volume demonstrate that human rights diplomacy can become a crucial part of a holistic approach to human rights protection, complementing other means such as legal remedies, public advocacy, political pressure and the provision of technical assistance. In this regard, let our last words be those of Kyung-wha Kang, Deputy UN High Commissioner for Human Rights:

> Governments of countries that share a genuine commitment to human rights, non-governmental human rights organisations on the ground and in the global arena, regional and international human rights entities, and researchers in academic institutions all have a contribution to make in nurturing dialogue and action on human rights toward tolerant and open societies. These are demanding and exciting times for human rights diplomacy.[43]

[42] Venice Workshop Report, annex to the present volume, p.282.

[43] Foreword to the present volume by Kyung-wha Kang, Deputy UN High Commissioner for Human Rights, p.ix.

CHAPTER 2

FRAMEWORK FOR THE ANALYSIS OF HUMAN RIGHTS DIPLOMACY

George Ulrich

Introduction

What do we understand by 'human rights diplomacy'? From a certain point of view, the notion may be regarded as a contradiction in terms, as the cause of human rights arguably has no use for discretion and compromise, which are hallmarks of diplomacy, but rather requires uncompromising and forthright action. In his introduction to the 2011 World Report by Human Rights Watch, polemically entitled "A Façade of Action: The Misuse of Dialogue and Cooperation with Rights Abusers", Kenneth Roth makes a strong case for this position.[1] Ironically, it mirrors in reverse the classical realist conception of diplomacy, on account of which diplomacy is not about promoting universal values like human rights but rather about negotiated self-interest.[2] Nevertheless, the notion makes intuitive sense and resonates quite strongly with the experience of a wide cross-section of practitioners in the field. State representatives and international civil servants, notably high office holders of international organisations, have for decades engaged in a range of practices that can meaningfully be described as human rights diplomacy, and other human rights actors, such as independent experts and civil society representatives, are increasingly

[1] K. Roth, 'A Façade of Action: The Misuse of Dialogue and Cooperation with Rights Abusers', Human Rights Watch World Report 2011, available at: http://www.hrw.org/en/world-report-2011 [last accessed 4 March 2011].

[2] C. W. Freeman, Jr. and S. Marks (primary contributors), 'Diplomacy' in *Encyclopædia Britannica*, accessed online at: http://www.britannica.com/EBchecked/topic/164602/diplomacy [last accessed 4 March 2011], hold: 'The goal of diplomacy is to further the state's interests as dictated by geography, history, and economics. Safeguarding the state's independence, security, and integrity is of prime importance; preserving the widest possible freedom of action for the state is nearly as important. Beyond that, diplomacy seeks maximum national advantage without using force and preferably without causing resentment.'

coming to see this as an important part of their work as well. Indeed this was a central focus of the High Level Workshop on Human Rights Diplomacy in Venice, January 2009, with which the present publication is associated.

Despite widespread interest in the topic, the idea of human rights diplomacy is rarely subjected to sustained conceptual analysis. Somehow the notion is taken for granted and the analytical focus tends rather to be on examining concrete experience, providing examples of successful or unsuccessful human rights diplomacy, pointing to characteristic problems and causes for concern, identifying best practices and making future-oriented recommendations, etc. The aim of the present chapter is not to provide a comprehensive and definitive analysis of the concept of human rights diplomacy, but at least to take a few steps in this direction in the hope that this may help to focus discussions and shed light on certain genuine complexities in the intersection between diplomacy and human rights. This is undertaken with humility as the author is keenly aware that his practical experience in the area in no way matches that of most other contributors to the present volume, and to the discussion in general.

In what follows I shall address the notion of human rights diplomacy from three complementary points of view: first in relation to 20th and 21st century developments in international law and international relations; second, in the broader context of different modalities of human rights practice; and third, from the point of view of (some of) the central parameters of contestation as operative in diplomatic interaction related to human rights.

Schism: Human Rights as Operative Norm and Human Rights in Dispute

In order to establish a general framework for the analysis of human rights diplomacy, and in particular to delineate the role and function of human rights diplomacy in relation to other forms of human rights advocacy, I propose to draw a distinction between contexts in which human rights function as generally accepted operative norm and contexts in which the central focus of interaction has to do with the contestation of human rights. I shall return to this presently but believe it will be helpful to first take a step back and look at certain broader trends in international law and international relations related to human rights.

Almost 50 years ago, Thomas Kuhn famously advanced a notion of periodic paradigm shifts in the sciences.[3] He suggested that periods of 'normal science' are intermittently replaced by periods of 'revolutionary science', which then over time stabilise into new regimes of normal science. A similar analytical framework has since been taken up by scholars in many different disciplines, often with a focus not only on epistemological paradigm shifts but also on related shifts in technology and social practices. While not wishing to push the analogy too far—this would require much more detailed analysis than is possible in the present study[4]—it may be suggested that the rise of international human rights law bears traits of a paradigm shift in international law. The basic features of this shift are familiar. Individuals, as opposed to only states, have standing as subjects of this branch of international law, and human rights law is based not on the conventional principle of reciprocity between states but rather on a common commitment to safeguarding universal values, which have for the first time been codified in the form of internationally binding legal norms. This sets in motion a whole new dynamic of accountability, as states are now accountable for upholding the agreed standards not only towards each other in bilateral relations but also towards the international community generally and towards individuals inhabiting their territories. This in turn entails a certain loosening of the principle of state sovereignty, or perhaps better, a need to rethink the concept of sovereignty so as to also reflect a responsibility to uphold commonly agreed human rights standards.[5] Paragraph 4 of the 1993 Vienna Declaration and Programme of Action, which states that 'the promotion and protection of all human rights is a legitimate concern of the international community', captures

[3] T. Kuhn, *The Structure of Scientific Revolutions* (Chicago: University of Chicago Press, 1962).

[4] A pivotal question in this regard has to do with the degree to which principles of human rights law have come to influence public international law generally. For a comprehensive and interesting discussion of this question, see M. Kamminga, Final Report on the Impact of International Human Rights Law on General International Law, Maastricht University, Faculty of Law, available at: http://ssrn.com/abstract=1150664 [last accessed 4 March 2011].

[5] A classical reference on this topic is D. Rothchild, *et al.*, *Sovereignty as Responsibility: Conflict Management in Africa* (Washington D.C: Brookings Institution Press, 1996). See also J. Hoffmann, 'R2P: A New "Standard of Sovereign Responsibility"?', available at: http://www.thebrokeronline.eu/Online-discussions/Blogs/The-Responsibility-to-Protect/R2P-A-new-standard-of-sovereign-responsibility [last accessed 4 March 2011].

this new orientation in a nutshell.[6] In a similar manner, the introduction of a human rights perspective gives rise to a rethinking of other core concepts of state politics and international relations, such as notably security and development.[7]

These various developments are broadly associated with an 'idealist turn' in international relations, which has been gaining momentum in different waves over more than a century but has also suffered recurrent setbacks, thus leading to the intermittent reassertion of a competing realist paradigm.[8] The fact of increasing global interdependency at multiple levels inevitably leads to a blurring of the distinction between narrowly defined state self-interest and common aspirations related to the environment, global health, peace and security, equitable economical development—and human rights. And yet each of these cosmopolitan policy areas is genuinely complex and fraught with ambiguities.[9] The idealist turn in international relations is thus not a *fait accompli* but has considerable momentum. With specific reference to human rights, one can identify two competing, yet somehow interrelated tendencies. One is characterised by the on-going codification of human rights norms in international treaties, which are widely ratified and

[6] Vienna Declaration and Programme of Action, adopted by the World Conference on Human Rights, UN Doc A/CONF.157/23 (12 July 1993).

[7] Antonio Papisca thus suggests that 'human security and human development [which are] both anchored to the paradigm of human rights … are the new frontiers of global multi-level governance. Both hold the human being as their primary subject.' Papisca further cites G. MacLean for the observation that '[i]n broad terms, human security shifts our focus from traditional "state security to that of the person and of the human communities. Human security recognises that an individual's personal protection and preservation comes, not just from safeguarding by the state as a political unit, but primarily from access to individual welfare and quality".' See A. Papisca, 'Relevance of Human Rights in the Global Space of Politics: How to Enlarge Democratic Practice beyond State Boundaries and Build up a Peaceful World Order' in K. De Feyter, S. Parmentier, C. Timmerman and G. Ulrich (eds.), *The Local Relevance of Human Rights* (Cambridge: Cambridge University Press (forthcoming 2011)). The citation is taken from G. MacLean, *The Changing Perception of Human Security: Coordinating National and Multilateral Responses—The United Nations and the New Security Agenda* (Ottawa: UNAC, 1998).

[8] For an informative overview of the main shifting trends, see: D. B. MacDonald and R. G. Patman, 'Introduction: The Ethical Context of Foreign Policy' in D. B. MacDonald, R. G. Patman and B. Mason-Parker (eds.), *The Ethics of Foreign Policy* (Hampshire: Ashgate, 2007).

[9] The problem of defining precise limits to interventions in the name of human rights and on humanitarian grounds is a case in point. An additional complicating factor in recent years has been the neo-conservative (mis-)appropriation of aspects of the idealist paradigm, whereby democratic ideals have been propagated through the use of force, sometimes involving blatant human rights violations.

accepted by states, and the progressive establishment of a complex architecture of human rights compliance and promotion mechanisms at universal, regional and national level, which to a large extent are functional. The other, concomitant, tendency is marked by a persistent questioning or contestation of human rights norms and mechanisms. Perhaps this is indicative of an unfolding but still incomplete paradigm shift, to once again invoke the Kuhnsian idiom: while an elaborate edifice of new norms and structures is being established, it is at the same time regularly challenged and therefore stands in need of legitimation and sometimes also safeguarding against backlashes. It is on this account that I suggest introducing an analytical distinction between contexts in which human rights law is accepted and functions as operative norm and contexts in which the applicable standards, and sometimes the very notion of human rights, are being contested. In real life the two contexts coexist side by side.

Different Modalities of Human Rights Practice—Pinpointing the Specificity of Human Rights Diplomacy

Against this background, we are now in a position to map a range of key functions related to human rights and seek to pinpoint the specificity of human rights diplomacy in relation to other forms of human rights advocacy and practice. This will be done by introducing a series of rather simple analytical distinctions.

The first important point to note is that the two general contexts identified in the previous section require different modes of engagement. Where human rights law functions as generally accepted operative norm, the all important task for practitioners consists in applying the law correctly. This is typically a matter of exercising technical legal competence. Lawyers and judges involved in trying human rights cases at court may be the most obvious example of practitioners who operate on the premise of a functional human rights law paradigm.[10] Another important example is legislators involved in drafting laws in conformity

---

[10] This is consistent with the general consensus at the Venice Workshop that 'the work of judicial bodies adjudicating human rights should fall outside the definition of human rights diplomacy, with the exception of certain limited aspects of their work. Judicial bodies' function is to apply and interpret the law, and not to negotiate it.' See Report of the High-Level Workshop on Human Rights Diplomacy, Venice, 30–31 January 2009, annex to the present volume, p.266.

with established human rights standards and policy makers tasked with devising wider social policies in a similar fashion. Human rights monitors, fact finders and independent experts tasked with assessing human rights compliance and identifying general patterns of violation mark another important group of practitioners who base their work on the premise of human rights as operative norm.[11] The UN special procedures mandate-holders are particularly important in this regard, and the same can be said of the independent experts associated with UN and regional treaty monitoring bodies, as their express mandate is to form an assessment of whether human rights standards, which have been endorsed by state parties, are in fact being observed. One could point to numerous other relevant examples, the essential point being that in a context where international human rights law is becoming progressively consolidated, it is a primary obligation for the international community and states to ensure its implementation in practice. Human rights work, accordingly, takes on the character of exercising technical competence, juridical or otherwise. The emergence of a plethora of human rights master's programmes and specialised training courses in all parts of the world testifies to the intensity of this general trend.

It may here be relevant to note that some of the abovementioned examples do involve a contestation of norms. This is notably true of legal proceedings, which by their very nature are litigious, but also applies to aspects of human rights monitoring and programming. The important point, however, is that what is being contested is how to correctly apply the operative legal norm in a given situation, not whether it is valid or how it should be defined. It is in other words not the norm itself that is being questioned, but rather its application and practical implications.

Situations where the central focus of interaction is on the contestation of human rights *per se*, on the other hand, bring into play a different set of characteristic practices. These are practices that typically aim

[11] Human rights monitoring in the context of on-going conflicts or post-conflict situations, as is a primary function of human rights field missions organised by the international community with the consent of host states, marks a particular case, as the individual human rights expert will often find him- or herself operating in contexts where human rights norms are being widely contested or ignored, yet one might argue that the central orientation of their work is nevertheless to act as *if* the norms were operative—i.e. in a certain sense act as custodians of a set of values and standards that are temporarily being violated and/or neglected—and report to responsible parties at national and international level, where the validity of the applicable human rights norms is taken for granted.

at legitimising human rights, raising popular awareness, rallying support, advocating a more radical or more consistent application of human rights, and addressing complexities in the interrelation between human rights and other legitimate priorities. Actors enter into dialogue or dispute with the implicit and/or explicit aim to dismiss or defend the validity of human rights as a key reference and source of guidance in international relations. From the side of human rights advocacy, the overriding objective, as I shall argue, is to enlarge the sphere in which human rights function as operative norm, i.e. carve out additional space for the technical application of human rights law as described above. It may be suggested that the skills required to accomplish this aim are predominantly of a strategic rather than technical nature, even if legal competence remains essential at this level of practice as well.

Human rights diplomacy belongs in the latter general context. In a background note prepared for the Venice Workshop in January 2009, O'Flaherty invoked a classical conception of diplomacy as 'the art of persuasion in international affairs' and went on to suggest that human rights diplomacy 'refers to the use of the range of persuasive negotiation-based diplomatic tools available to states and intergovernmental organisations for the specific purpose of promoting and protecting human rights'.[12] This is an apt characterisation, although perhaps subject to expansion with regard to the applicable group of practitioners. What is interesting in relation to the present line of reasoning is the emphasis on persuasion and negotiation, as logically such modes of interaction imply an element of resistance. They are, in other words, only relevant in an underlying context of contestation, which, as we have seen, remains a salient feature of international human rights discourse.

Other forms of human rights practice that in a fundamental sense involve contestation include public campaigning, political action, political dialogue and dispute (either in a parliamentary context or directly targeting public opinion), and much scholarly work related to human rights. In order to pinpoint the specificity of human rights diplomacy in relation to these various other modes of practice, it will be helpful to examine a few additional characteristic features of diplomacy.

---

[12] Report on the High-Level Workshop on Human Rights Diplomacy, Venice, 30–31 January 2009, annex to the present volume, p.265.

Diplomacy, first of all, invariably has a pragmatic orientation. This sets it apart from scholarly pursuits, which in fact often address the same points of contestation but with the aim to enhance our general understanding of a given subject matter rather than effect concrete change. Academic writing, moreover, addresses an anonymous public, whereas diplomacy is in some way or other specifically targeted, i.e. designed to influence the opinion and/or behaviour of identifiable actors. Usually this is approached through interpersonal relations, implicating particular individuals who, however, are engaged in their capacity as institutional representatives or office holders rather than in their purely personal capacity or as members of the general public. In the latter regard, diplomacy can be distinguished from public campaigning, which also has a pragmatic orientation but seeks to accomplish its objectives by mobilising widespread public support for a given cause, typically without need to worry about tact and discretion to the same degree as diplomats. The on-going contestation of values and policy objectives in the political arena differs from human rights diplomacy by being immediately linked to the interests of particular constituencies and by implicating a clash between competing ideologies, but like diplomacy, political debate, notably in a parliamentary context, serves as a primary conduit to channel human rights considerations into legislation and policy making, where their implementation eventually becomes a matter of technical competency. Finally, one should probably also distinguish diplomacy from a range of outright coercive practices that may aim to attain human rights objectives through a threat of negative sanctions (e.g. withdrawal of donor support, trade privileges, or even direct use of force). This point, however, is ambiguous, for while diplomatic persuasion should ideally involve a reciprocal exchange of viewpoints and lead to a voluntary affirmation of a given outcome, real life diplomatic interaction is obviously conditioned by existing power imbalances and the awareness of possible hostile measures and negative consequences, should efforts fail. Some observers openly advocate that instead of making an excuse for or seeking to couch the latent possibility of negative sanctions, they should rather be deliberately leveraged so as to ensure the greatest possible effect of diplomatic action on human rights compliance.[13]

[13] As I understand Roth, this is in fact one of the central implicit recommendations in his introduction to the 2011 Human Rights Watch World Report. See Roth, 'A Façade of Action', 2011, p.1 *et passim*.

Having introduced an analytical distinction between human rights diplomacy and other modalities of human rights practice, it needs to be immediately acknowledged that they are all closely interrelated. The different functions identified above, first of all, feed into each other in intricate ways. An obvious example of this is the way in which public campaigns of a distinctly confrontational nature conducted by one group of actors, typically civil society organisations, may reinforce the prospects of success for discreet diplomatic intervention conducted by other actors in an entirely different tenor. On a variation of the same theme, the then Personal Representative for Human Rights of the Secretary-General/High Representative of the Council of the European Union, Michael Matthiessen, once emphasised in a personal interview how the often strongly worded resolutions of the European Parliament (EP) in the area of human rights helped him in his work. While the EP resolutions may only have had limited direct impact on the intended target groups,[14] they provided an occasion for a diplomat like himself to candidly address sensitive human rights issues in bilateral talks with representatives of third countries.[15] Expert findings, legal analyses or court rulings may similarly serve as a pretext for diplomatic action or may be invoked in the context of diplomatic negotiations so as to support an intended outcome (just as the mere presence of diplomats or other high ranking officials, conversely, may contribute to ensuring the integrity of legal proceedings, in particular with regard to human rights guarantees, in settings where this is otherwise uncertain).

While different functions are often separated by actors, this is not always the case. Sometimes one and the same actor or actor group carries out several different functions, shifting almost imperceptibly between one mode of human rights practice and another. A case in point is the way in which state representatives and high office holders not only engage in conventional diplomatic interaction; as public personae they also have an important advocacy and awareness-raising function, which may involve adopting an entirely different

---

[14] For a detailed analysis of this question, see H. Fischer, S. Lorion and G. Ulrich, *Beyond Activism: The Impact of the Resolutions and other Activities of the European Parliament in the Field of Human Rights outside the European Union* (Venice: Marsilio Editori, 2007).

[15] In the above-mentioned study on the impact of EP resolutions and other activities in the area of human rights, this led my co-authors and myself to the general observation that '[b]ecause the EP can express itself more explicitly and directly than the Council and the Commission, resolutions often serve as useful reference point or even an "alibi" for Council representatives when raising human rights concerns with representatives of third countries.' *Ibid.*, p.236.

voice[16] but which nevertheless needs to be deliberately calibrated so as to also condition the terms of diplomatic interaction and reinforce the possibility of desired outcomes at this level. Elected government officials do something similar when they engage with international and institutional counterparts in a flexible, 'diplomatic' manner while at the same time needing to project strong and uncompromising standpoints in the public media, where the primary addressees are their home political constituencies. UN special procedures mandate-holders and treaty body members may find themselves occasionally shifting from a fact finding and strictly law-based evaluative mode to a more diplomatic mode of interaction related to human rights, for instance in the context of presenting expert findings to the implicated governments or public officials and exchanging views about possible remedial action.[17] Non-governmental organisations' (NGO) representatives also in various ways engage in human rights diplomacy as part of their general advocacy work.[18] This may take the form of lobbying conventional diplomats to take action in relation to a particular human rights cause, or brokering relations between diplomats from different constituencies with such an aim, or civil society actors may become directly involved in diplomatic negotiations with government representatives and decision makers about the drafting and adoption of resolutions, treaty texts and policy documents.[19]

[16] Archer identifies four distinct 'voices' of human rights advocacy, one of which is 'essentially prophetic, the voice of conscience: it appeals to higher values and aspirations, without necessarily having regard for realism or political feasibility.' See R. Archer, 'A Short Reflection on Human Rights Diplomacy', Chapter 3 in the present volume, p.47. Roth associates the 'public voice' of government representatives and high office holders with a capacity for exerting sustained 'public pressure' on violators. His key argument is that this capacity is grossly underused in current international relations to the detriment of human rights diplomacy and of human rights generally. See Roth, 'A Façade of Action', 2011, p.4.

[17] In his chapter below, O'Flaherty goes so far as to argue that 'the dominant task for treaty bodies, the review of periodic reports might better be described as 'diplomatic' rather than as quasi-judicial, in as much as it concerns the engaging of states in dialogue intended to promote treaty compliance - the outcome of such dialogue never being more than recommendatory in nature.' See O'Flaherty, 'The United Nations Human Rights Treaty Bodies as Diplomatic Actors', Chapter 9 in the present volume, p.153.; and the examples given in the Report on the High-Level Workshop on Human Rights Diplomacy, Venice, 30–31 January 2009, annex to the present volume, p.265–66.

[18] See further P. Hicks, 'Human Rights Diplomacy: The NGO Role', Chapter 13 in the present volume, p.217–22.

[19] An interesting case in point is the way in which a broad cross-section of civil society representatives has played a central role in the drafting and advocacy for adoption of the various EU guidelines on human rights.

It is thus not always easy to determine precisely where diplomacy begins and other forms of human rights advocacy end, or vice versa. But then there is no need to draw a hard and fast dividing line. The distinction is primarily of analytical significance. In practice what matters more is to build coalitions and coordinate activities so as to attain the best possible synergy effect. This, in my understanding, is the intention behind the multi-stakeholder approach and notion of multi-track diplomacy advocated by Benedek, and similarly the notion 'hybrid alliances' as elaborated by Archer in the present publication. A common aim of the publication as a whole is, on the basis of high level practical experience, to identify possible contributions to human rights diplomacy on the part of a broad range of different actors and thereby begin to envision effective integrated strategies. This inevitably involves venturing into borderline areas where human rights diplomacy intersects with other modes of human rights practice.

Patterns of Contestation

In turning now to an analysis of some of the primary issues at stake in the contestation of human rights, and therefore by implication in the exercise of human rights diplomacy, it is necessary from the outset to draw a distinction between what may be deemed 'good faith' and 'bad faith' contestation. This is a messy distinction, to be sure, but even so, it is indispensible in so far as it is implicitly operative in virtually all disputes concerning human rights and conditions the manner in which diplomatic interventions and other forms of human rights advocacy are framed.

Good faith contestation revolves around legitimate concerns about aspects or implications of established human rights and aims at achieving a more representative, effective or acceptable normative framework for tackling problems of common concern in a globalised world. This goes beyond the technical question of how best to apply existing human rights norms, as was identified in the previous section as an integral aspect of much human rights work. In one way or another, it involves a contestation of the underlying norm itself, either in terms of its general validity or in terms of its particular articulation (as is always at issue in standard setting). Another possible focus of good faith contestation has to do with the extent to which established human rights norms may be disregarded in view of competing priorities. Good faith contestation invariably involves a certain impetus to reassess existing human rights standards and/or practice without, however, calling the entire edifice of post-World War II accomplishments into question. It may assume the character of a constructive engagement aimed at facilitating a more adequate understanding of universal human rights, or it may be based on more fundamental misgivings. But either way, the important point is that it is based on valid concerns and demands serious consideration. If there is no space for this, then human rights advocacy risks becoming dogmatic and stale.

Bad faith contestation, by contrast, raises questions about human rights for the simple purpose of maintaining power and privilege or out of unwillingness to confront prejudice and bigotry. To confuse matters, this is sometimes articulated in the idiom of good faith contestation, and sometimes is manifested in an inarticulate manner by simply ignoring or blankly refusing to give any consideration to human rights. Either way, bad faith contestation in effect amounts to a radical denial of the notion of human rights as operative norm. In as much as compliance with human rights has come to function as a standard of legitimacy in public affairs and international relations,[20] the charge of deliberate and systematic disregard of human rights is virtually tantamount to brandishing an actor as 'evil', or at least as illegitimate in terms of occupying public office. While it may be difficult to know precisely when manifest opposition to human rights is really a matter of bad faith, the charge is nevertheless constantly imputed, tacitly or expressly, and human rights campaigning, accordingly, assumes the character of mobilising coalitions of likeminded against 'evil' wrongdoers rather than engaging in genuine efforts of persuasion. Clearly, the resolve to mobilise opposition to human rights abuse wherever it is found is not only warranted but also commendable; yet the implied polarisation of good and evil complicates diplomatic relations and stands in danger of degenerating into arrogance.

Where human rights are being challenged in good faith, there are certain general themes that recur with regularity, albeit always in new variations tailored to the given circumstances. These may be described as the *characteristic parameters of contestation* in human rights discourse. Three such parameters have to do with *conflicting values, competing priorities* and *implied status.*

---

[20] J. Habermas, 'Remarks on Legitimation through Human Rights' *Philosophy and Social Criticism* 24 (1998), 157–71.

Conflicting Values

Since the World Conference on Human Rights in Vienna 1993 famously affirmed *both* the universality of human rights *and* the principle of respect for cultural diversity, it has become relatively rare for human rights to be called fundamentally into question within a diplomatic context on account of value differences. In inter-state relations, there is now a general acceptance of the core notion of human rights—at least in terms of what is expressly articulated.[21] But even so, value issues do continue to play a central role in the contestation of human rights. This happens in a variety of different ways.

Having been set aside as cause for a blanket rejection human rights, the issue of cultural relativism, firstly, reappears at the level of the particular. This is evident in disputes about how to interpret particular rights, how to resolve apparent conflicts between different rights, and in a broader sense about which rights count and for how much. A case in point is the question of whether freedom of expression can legitimately be restricted on account of blasphemy prohibitions. Irrespective of what legal experts say, this is highly divisive in the contemporary UN context and so requires careful attention at the level of diplomatic interaction.[22] Value disagreements are also often politically based, such as, e.g., when neo-liberalists manifest a strong opposition to economic, social and cultural rights as expressions of socialist ideology in disguise, or when nationalist factions in the political arena question the

---

[21] Interestingly, the study invoked above on the impact of human rights activities of the European Parliament thus found that states reacting to critical resolutions by the European Parliament almost invariably expressed acceptance of the underlying standards by which they were being judged: 'reactions to EP resolutions almost never question the principles of universal human rights, nor the validity of the international commitments made in this area by the countries named. It is by the same token noteworthy that the argument of cultural relativism is no longer salient. While some Asian officials might note that there is an "Asian manner" to advocate human rights or raise concerns in public, this is rarely, if ever, invoked to reject the idea of universal human rights or the active stance adopted by the EP in this area.' Target countries would, however, take issue with the EP resolutions on other grounds, contending e.g. that 'facts are incorrect', that 'it is difficult to have a perfect record', or that the EU 'applies double standards'. See Fischer, Lorion and Ulrich, *Beyond Activism*, 2007, p.86.

[22] The Human Rights Committee's Draft General Comment 34 on Article 19 of the ICCPR, UN Doc CCPR/C/GC/34/CRP.5 (25 November 2010), expressly addresses this issue in para.50, see: http://www2.ohchr.org/english/bodies/hrc/docs/CCPR.C.GC.34.CRP.4.doc [last accessed 4 March 2011]. See also Salama's analysis of the OHCHR's 2008 Expert Seminar on Freedom of Expression and Advocacy of Religious Hatred. I. Salama, 'Human Rights Diplomacy from a UN Perspective: A Complement to Advocacy', Chapter 8 in the present volume, p.129–54.

legitimacy of international treaties restricting parliamentary powers of autonomous decision making.

Secondly, even if established human rights standards are widely accepted at the level of inter-state relations, this is not necessarily true at other levels of discourse. Various political, cultural and intellectual opinion leaders continue to articulate a deep seated opposition to the very notion of human rights, and this may in fact have considerable resonance in general public opinion. Thus, even while state representatives and high office holders seek to engage in constructive dialogue about the interpretation and application of human rights, they may at the same time be constrained by a need to be, and be seen to be, loyal to their home constituencies—at least up to a certain point. This, I submit, marks an added complicating factor in human rights diplomacy.

Thirdly, one must not underestimate the significance of competing value systems being asserted in the international arena, even if this is not done in explicit opposition to human rights. China has thus under President Hu Jintao forcefully promoted the vision of a 'harmonious society' based on Confucian values.[23] Unlike in earlier 'Asian values' debates, such values are no longer expressly invoked in opposition to human rights, but their resurgence nevertheless clearly marks a reorientation in the direction of a duty based ethos prioritising community interests over individual rights. As value references at this level carry tremendous weight and demand to be treated with respect, the tacit gesture of reasserting traditional values has the capacity to profoundly affect international negotiations concerning human rights, not only in general terms but also with regard to specific applications such as, e.g., in the area of development cooperation, where China is increasingly being seen by countries in the global South to offer a potentially attractive alternative to a rights-based approach.[24]

---

[23] See e.g. 'China's Party Leadership Declares New Priority: "Harmonious Society"' M. Fan for the *Washington Post*, 12 October 2006, available at: http://www.washingtonpost.com/wp-dyn/content/article/2006/10/11/AR2006101101610.html [last accessed 4 March 2011].

[24] Compare Roth, 'A Façade of Action', 2011, p.4.: 'China's economic rise is often cited as reason to believe that authoritarian government is more effective for guiding economic development in low-income countries, even though unaccountable governments are more likely to succumb to corruption and less likely to respond to or invest in people's most urgent needs … '.

Competing Priorities

Another characteristic way of contesting human rights is to express support for human rights in principle, and indeed acknowledge that they embody noble aspirations, but nevertheless stipulate that they are not fully realistic in the given situation. This can be for a multitude of reasons. It may be deemed that they are too expensive, or that they require a level of economic and social development that has not (yet) been fully attained. Society is in other words not yet ready to fully endorse human rights as operative norm, but may be able to do so one day—just as countries in the affluent North have now done, by and large, after centuries of systematically violating the human rights of populations in the global South. Meanwhile it is more reasonable to focus on the progress that has already been made with regard to human rights than on the remaining deficiencies, so the argument goes.

A related argument focuses on the question of competing priorities. On this account it is suggested that while human rights mark a worthy and highly relevant priority for social governance, it is not the only one and therefore needs to be balanced in relation to other legitimate societal objectives. This may entail a certain need to compromise on the compliance with established human rights without for that reason dismissing the notion *en bloc*. Emerging economies may in this way seek to justify sub-standard labour protection in order to ensure competitiveness; coercive policing and prison guard practices may be regarded as necessary to uphold social order and protect the safety of citizens; and the freedom of expression may be suppressed along with a range of other political freedoms on the pretext of safeguarding social cohesion and stability. Further examples can be found in virtually every major policy area. Highly developed industrial societies, which traditionally have assumed the stance as global advocates of human rights, have also in recent decades gone quite far in the direction of restricting human rights on account of other priorities. In the Cold War era, western democracies demonstrated a far-reaching willingness to support repressive regimes in other parts of the world on account of ostensible security interests,[25] and since the attack on the World Trade Centre in September 2001, extensive measures have been put into place to bypass

[25] See D. B. MacDonald, and R. G. Patman, 'Introduction: The Ethical Context of Foreign Policy' in D. B. MacDonald, R. G. Patman and B. Mason-Parker (eds.), *The Ethics of Foreign Policy* (Hampshire: Ashgate Publishing, 2007).

privacy protections, fair trial guarantees, and in notable cases even the prohibition of torture and related norms—all in the name of counter-terrorism. As is evident from recently published memoires, the key actors of the Bush administration, including the President himself, still fully stand behind such policy decisions.[26]

It may be tempting in such cases to dismiss government unwillingness to respect human rights simply as a matter of bad faith in the sense outlined above. While I agree with this assessment in many particular instances, my sense is nevertheless that the underlying pattern of invoking competing priorities is so widespread that it needs to be taken seriously as a legitimate parameter of contesting human rights. In one way or another, the crucial issue at stake is whether indeed it is possible for responsible governments and administrative bodies to manage their full range of social responsibilities while remaining in strict compliance with human rights. The challenge in a nutshell, is thus to demonstrate the *pertinence* of human rights across the full range of concrete contexts in which they are to be applied.[27]

The standard response by human rights advocates consists in taking issue with the premise that certain key societal objectives may not be attainable in compliance with human rights. To the contrary, it is contended that human rights actually provide a more effective vehicle to realise other societal priorities. At the abstract level, this is expressed in the form of a postulation of a general synergy between all of the primary objectives of the international community and its member states. UN Secretary-General Kofi Annan captured this outlook in a nutshell when in his 2005 report "In Larger Freedom: Towards Development, Security and Human Rights for All" he proclaimed that '[w]e will not enjoy development without security, we will not enjoy security without development, and we will not enjoy either without respect for human rights.'[28] Appealing as this vision may be, the challenge remains to

---

[26] G. W. Bush, *Decision Points* (New York: Virgin Books, 2010); D. Rumsfeld, *Known and Unknown* (New York: Penguin Group, 2011). For an advance report on what will be included in Vice-President Cheney's forthcoming memoir, see 'Memoirs to Reveal Dick Cheney Thought Bush had Gone Soft on War on Terror' M. Tran for *The Guardian*, 13 August 2009, available at: http://www.guardian.co.uk/world/2009/aug/13/dick-cheney-george-bush-memoirs [last accessed 4 March 2011].

[27] G. Ulrich, 'Universal Human Rights: An Unfinished Project' in K. Hastrup (ed.), *Human Rights on Common Grounds? The Quest for Universality* (The Hague/London/New York: Kluwer Law International, 2001).

[28] Report of the Secretary-General, In Larger Freedom: Towards Development, Security and Human Rights for All, UN Doc A/59/2005 (21 March 2005), para.17.

continually devise concrete social policies and governance practices in all areas of social life that are in conformity with human rights while at the same time being conducive to attaining other legitimate objectives. This is precisely what the widespread drive to 'mainstream' human rights in contexts where they have otherwise not typically been taken into account is all about. We have thus since the mid 1990s seen intensive efforts to elaborate human rights-based approaches to development cooperation, poverty reduction, military and security practices, and population planning—just to mention some of the key policy areas.

Much of the work required to articulate and implement such rights-based approaches is of a technical nature. It forms part of a broader scheme of human rights cooperation, technical assistance and capacity building which is widely accepted as one of the primary functions of the Office of the High Commissioner for Human Rights (OHCHR) and other intergovernmental human rights bodies, including the recently established Asian Human Rights Commission (AHRC), as well as certain national human rights institutions that are active beyond their own borders (e.g. those of the Scandinavian countries, The Netherlands, Canada, etc.). However, in addition to the characteristic practical challenges, there is also an important challenge of a quintessentially diplomatic nature in preparing the ground for such technical cooperation, and in general in propagating a larger degree of willingness to devise and adopt human rights compliant policy approaches. This, in my view, is one of the key functions of human rights diplomacy. While of relatively limited significance in bilateral diplomatic relations between states, it constitutes a central focal point of negotiations in multilateral settings and between high representatives of international organisations and member states. The background work required to set up representations of the OHCHR in numerous countries around the world is a typical example, as is the diplomatic effort required to establish and carry out structured human rights dialogues between the EU and more than 30 different international counterparts.[29] The issue of asserting human rights in relation to other

[29] For more information on EU human rights dialogues see: http://www.eeas.europa.eu/_human_rights/dialogues/index_en.htm [last accessed 4 March 2011]. See also the EU Guidelines on Human Rights Dialogues with Third Countries, available at: http://www.consilium.europa.eu/uedocs/cmsUpload/16526.en08.pdf [last accessed 4 March 2011].

competing priorities and advocating human rights compliant policy approaches also features prominently in the area of conference diplomacy, as described by Kedzia in his contribution to the present volume. An interesting case in point is the International Conference on Population and Development (ICPD) in Cairo 1994, which in the present perspective can be seen as a sustained, multi-stakeholder effort to build a human rights dimension into global population planning—a policy area which has otherwise been replete with human rights violations. The United Nations Conference on Environment and Development (UNCED) in Rio 1992, by comparison, did not yet give prominence to a human rights perspective,[30] but this has since been incorporated in all high level international negotiations on the environment, as witnessed most recently in the United Nations Climate Change Conferences in Copenhagen 2009 and Cancun 2010.[31]

These are all genuinely complex situations, and there is a continual need to monitor that the impetus to balance different priorities does not turn into a simple excuse for disregarding of human rights—as in some of the initial examples provided above. To this end, different actors have important complementary roles to play: technical experts can help to supply practical solutions to how to reconcile different priorities, uncompromising watchdog organisations hold public actors to account for their obligations and policy choices, and human rights diplomats may help to broker political will to adopt human rights compliant policy approaches.

Implied Status

The third key parameter of contestation to which I wish to draw attention is procedural rather than substantive in character. It has to do with how references to human rights, in particular allegations of lack of human rights compliance, reflect on the parties involved and how this

---

[30] In a background paper prepared for the Joint UNEP-OHCHR Expert Seminar on Human Rights and the Environment, Geneva, 14–16 January 2002, Dinah Shelton notes that 'the 1992 Conference of Rio de Janeiro on Environment and Development formulated the link between human rights and environmental protection largely in procedural terms'. See D. Shelton, Human Rights and Environment Issues in Multilateral Treaties Adopted between 1991 and 2001, available at: http://www2.ohchr.org/english/issues/environment/environ/bp1.htm [last accessed 4 March 2011].

[31] For a general discussion of the interface between human right and environment policy, see A. E. Boyle and M. R. Anderson (eds.), *Human Rights Approaches to Environmental Protection* (Oxford: Oxford University Press, 2003).

positions them vis-à-vis one another. I propose to describe this as a matter of 'implied status'.

Not surprisingly, the parties in the international arena that are alleged to be guilty of human rights violations, or are repeatedly being admonished to pay more attention to human rights, come to experience this as patronising and condescending. The parties commonly making such allegations, on the other hand, in effect project a superior image of themselves, irrespective of whether this is intended or not. There is an undeniable asymmetry in international relations in this regard. For decades the characteristic pattern has been for liberal Western democracies to occupy the position as advocates of universal human rights, while less developed countries have been pegged in a position as human rights violators. Whether warranted or not, this general pattern is widely found to be unacceptable, not least in view of the perception that Western power and wealth is to some degree premised on a historical legacy of oppression and outright exploitation, leading to structural underdevelopment and impoverishment, of populations in other parts of the world. This is undoubtedly an important contributing factor behind the reluctance of many African nations to join forces with their Western counterparts in the attempt to mobilise human rights charges against African leaders who are blatantly abusive of their own people.[32] One may similarly speculate that concerns about implied status play a central role in China's characteristic unwillingness to be lectured by the West on human rights, as was noticeable in what might otherwise be regarded as a disproportionately strong reaction to the awarding of the 2010 Nobel Peace Prize to the imprisoned Chinese dissident and human rights defender Liu Xiaobo.

A peculiar feature of diplomatic interaction surrounding implied status is that it is difficult to openly state the relevant concerns. It may be awkward, in other words, to complain about not being treated with respect in diplomatic relations, but much easier to articulate reservations at the two other levels of contestation outlined above. On this account one sees a characteristic tendency towards 'displacement', almost in a Freudian sense, whereby concerns about discursive positioning or implied status are being articulated in a different idiom as

[32] Compare Roth, 'A Façade of Action', 2011, p.4: 'For example, some African governments complain that the International Criminal Court's current focus on Africa is selective and imperialist, as if the fate of a few African despots were more important than the suffering of countless African victims.'

concerns about the values underlying human rights or about the pertinence of human rights in a given situation in view of other competing priorities. It is in this perspective telling that China in implicit response to the awarding of the Nobel Peace Prize to Liu Xiaobo immediately instituted a parallel Confucius Peace Prize, which on 9 December 2010, i.e. one day before the official Nobel awarding ceremony, was awarded to a moderately controversial yet system friendly recipient, the former Taiwanese Vice President Lien Chan. Similar displacements take place on a regular basis in diplomatic relations albeit usually on a less prominent scale. This significantly complicates diplomatic interaction and points to a pressing need for sensitivity to the issue of how human rights discourse reflects on the parties involved—not necessarily in the sense that every misgiving related to implied status should be accepted as justified, but simply because it will help to better understand the operative dynamics in the contestation of international human rights.

In ethical terms, what is essentially at stake in such situations is the quality of inter-subjective and inter-institutional relations, i.e. the quality of how parties interact as opposed to the more tangible question of what parties do to and for one another. This in my view is a fundamental parameter of ethical concern,[33] which is under-recognised in some ethical theories, e.g. utilitarianism, but salient in Kantian ethics[34] and in certain contemporary schools of thought such as notably the theory of discourse ethics.[35] The key operative concepts at this level of ethical interaction are claims to recognition, autonomy, reciprocity and respect. It may well be, paradoxically, that the 'idealist turn', which places ethical considerations high on the agenda of international relations, at the same time complicates the ethical dimension of diplomatic interaction in the sense identified here. For whereas

---

[33] See, e.g., G. Ulrich, 'Towards an Ethical Base for the Work of Human Rights Field Operations' in M. O'Flaherty (ed.), *The Human Rights Field Operation: Law, Theory and Practice* (Aldershot: Ashgate, 2007).

[34] Witness the second formulation of Kant's categorical imperative which enjoins us to 'act in such a way that you treat humanity, whether in your own person or in the person of any other, always at the same time as an end and never merely as a means to an end'. See I. Kant, *Groundwork of the Metaphysics of Morals*, in P. Guyer and A. W. Wood (eds.), *Works of Immanuel Kant* (Cambridge: Cambridge University Press, 1996), p.429.

[35] See J. Habermas, *Moral Consciousness and Communicative Action* (Cambridge: Polity Press, 1990); and J. Habermas, *Justification and Application: Remarks on Discourse Ethics* (Cambridge Massachusetts: MIT Press, 1994).

the classical (realist) notion of diplomacy, which is framed as the reciprocal interaction between sovereign equals united in a common pursuit of negotiated self-interest, may involve extreme power imbalances, it positions all parties on a level plane from an ethical point of view. Diplomacy in pursuit of a universal normative codex introduces a different element, namely an absolute standard of right and wrong by which all parties in international relations are unwittingly being measured. This introduces a dimension of disparity which can easily degenerate into paternalism and condescension, in particular in contexts where virtually any resistance to established human rights leads to a latent suspicion of acting in bad faith. The ability to negotiate this paradox and forge constructive, reciprocal and mutually respectful alliances in common pursuit of universal values may well account for one of the most important parameters of success in human rights diplomacy.

A ubiquitous contemporary trend in international relations, which is closely related to the abovementioned ethical complication, consists in seeking to rebalance accumulated disparities. This is noticeable, e.g., in recruitment policies in international organisations as well as in recurrent demands within the UN system to revise regional representational quotas so as to better reflect exiting geopolitical realities.[36] A notable shift in regional quotas was applied in 2006 when the UN Human Rights Council was established out of the ashes of the Commission on Human Rights. Evidently this has set in motion a new dynamic within the Council revolving precisely around the issue of implied status. The Universal Periodic Review (UPR) has thus been deliberately established as a balancing mechanism whereby all state parties are subject to review irrespective of their perceived human rights record,[37] and this in turn may signal a wider tendency for traditional human rights friendly nations to be increasingly subjected to

---

[36] In a commentary on the on-going review of the Human Rights Council, the International Service for Human Rights thus notes: 'On the issue of the selection of mandate holders, States argued [that] the selection and appointment process of special procedures needed to be improved and strengthened to avoid any discrimination and manipulation. In this context several States stressed the need for respect for the principle of equal geographical balance in the selection and appointment of mandate holders.' See: http://www.ishr.ch/council/952-review-of-human-rights-council-gets-underway [last accessed 4 March 2011].

[37] In a statement on human rights diplomacy delivered before a congregation at Harvard University in October 2009, UN High Commissioner Navi Pillay points out that '[c]rucially, the new Universal Periodic Review of the Human Rights Council,

criticism on an equal footing with all others. In a medium or long term perspective one may hope that the quest to reinforce traditionally marginalised voices within the international community and ensure a more even handed application of human rights evaluations may help to generate a more widespread sense of ownership of the underlying human rights idiom, but a concomitant concern is that the dominant focus on procedural matters and implied status risks shifting the focus away from what must always be the core substantive priority, to advance global respect for human rights.

Conclusion

In the exercise of human rights diplomacy, there is always an inherent risk that well meaning attempts to engage in constructive dialogue and cooperation comes to serve as an excuse for failure to take concrete action and 'stand up firmly against abusive governments'.[38] This is the charge levelled by Kenneth Roth in his scathing critique, cited by way of introduction, of an impressive line up of powerful actors in the international arena who ought to take a stand on the side of human rights, ranging from UN Secretary-General Ban Ki-moon, EU High Representative for Foreign Affairs and Security Policy Catherine Ashton, the UN Human Rights Council, and current North American and European governments to leading democracies in the South such as Brazil, India and South Africa (which themselves have benefitted from international solidarity in their struggle to end dictatorship, colonisation, and apartheid[39]). All have it in common, according to Roth, that they fail to speak out in the face of scandalous human right abuses, fail to apply public pressure on abusive governments, and instead profess a preference for dialogue and cooperation as the most suitable means to engage abusive governments and effect change. Roth attributes this to a combination of cowardice, opportunism and loss of moral

designed to examine the human rights record of all States, seeks to overcome the perceived selectivity and regional confrontations of the former Commission on Human Rights.' Statement by Navanethem Pillay, United Nations High Commissioner for Human Rights, 'Human Rights Diplomacy: An Oxymoron?', Cambridge, Massachusetts (28 October 2009), p.3, available at: http://www.ohchr.org/EN/NewsEvents/Pages/DisplayNews.aspx?NewsID=9569&LangID=e [last accessed 4 March 2011].

[38] Roth, 'A Façade of Action', 2011, p.1.

[39] *Ibid.*, p.19.

confidence and argues that without firm public pressure and principled action in defence of human rights, 'the quest for dialogue and cooperation becomes a charade designed more to appease critics of complacency than to secure change, a calculated diversion from the fact that nothing of consequence is being done.'[40]

When taken to its logical conclusion, this line of argument would seem to collapse the distinction between good and bad faith contestation and in effect render every impetus to contest human rights illegitimate. Roth may not intend to go quite that far—he repeatedly affirms that diplomacy and cooperation have their place and even cites positive HRW experiences in this regard[41]—but he comes close. My own sense is that recurrent sceptical questions raised about human rights on account of value differences, competing priorities or repercussions with regard to discursive positioning and implied status demand to be taken seriously, and that this places a need for skilful diplomatic intervention centred around dialogue and negotiation high on the international agenda—with all the ambiguities and complications that this involves. The concrete cases examined by Ibrahim Salama in his contribution to the present publication from an inside UN perspective bear clear testimony to this. However, Salama is at the same time cognisant that human rights diplomacy needs to be undertaken as part of a wider integrated strategy and with a clear view to safeguarding 'the hard-won normative foundation on which human rights stand'.[42] To avoid the type of set-backs that would occur, e.g., if freedom of expression should become formally restricted on account of a reinforced prohibition against the defamation of religion, Salama emphasises the crucial importance of including solid normative analysis and high level expert input into the diplomatic process, going so far as to propose a notion of 'of expertise-based human rights diplomacy'.[43] In the same spirit one could—and should, fully in keeping with Roth—emphasise the need to exercise diplomacy in such a way that it builds on and reinforces rather than replaces forthright human rights advocacy.

---

[40] *Ibid.*, p.2

[41] *Ibid.*, p.8; see also P. Hicks, 'Human Rights Diplomacy: The NGO Role', Chapter 13 in the present volume, pp.117–22.

[42] I. Salama, 'Human Rights Diplomacy from a UN Perspective: A Complement to Advocacy', Chapter 8 in the present volume, p.146.

[43] *Ibid.*, p.145 *et passim.*

I wish to suggest, in conclusion, that the ultimate test of whether human rights diplomacy achieves its aim has to do with whether it contributes to enlarging the domain in which human rights law functions as operative norm. An apt analogy can be found in the fight against impunity. While in specific conflict and post-conflict situations there may be strong arguments for granting an amnesty or on other grounds not taking direct action against perpetrators of human rights abuse (such as, e.g., the possible cessation of on-going hostilities and concern that protracted high profile legal proceedings may jeopardise a future-oriented reconciliation process amongst the conflicting parties), such arguments are invariably met with opposition by human rights advocates on the ground that a failure to see justice done will effect long term damage both by facilitating a continued sense of impunity on the part of would-be perpetrators and by demoralising the general population. The decisive consideration, in other words, is that any decision to forego criminal proceedings, even if opportune in the immediate situation, risks undermining the very foundation for future human rights enforcement and compliance. Only if this foundation can be reliably ensured, preferably strengthened, can alternative approaches to justice, truth and reconciliation conceivably be justified.

Similarly with regard to human rights diplomacy: whatever compromises may seem opportune in a given situation in pursuit of particular objectives are only justifiable if ultimately they contribute to strengthening the rule of law and application of human rights in all spheres of public life. Conversely, however, it may well be that the prospect at the current juncture of history for strengthening the global status of human rights law as operative norm depends precisely on the ability to address deep seated reservations and concerns through reciprocal and open-minded diplomatic engagement. For more than half a century since the end of the Second World War, diplomacy has played a decisive role in human rights standard setting, institution building and policy making. The international community needs to stay cognisant of this legacy so as to maintain the momentum of the on-going paradigm shift placing human rights and human dignity at the centre of international law and international relations.

CHAPTER 3

A SHORT REFLECTION ON HUMAN RIGHTS DIPLOMACY

Robert Archer

When people speak of human rights diplomacy, the model they usually have in mind is a private, reasoned discussion between states of human rights principles and their relevance, in a specific political context that is understood to condition policy outcomes. In this form, we think of human right diplomacy as an alternative (or precursor, in case of failure) to forceful intervention or the rupture of relations. Sometimes we think also of more specific interventions, as when a state intervenes (often on behalf of another state) in a disinterested manner to negotiate the release or physical protection of individuals who are held hostage or have been imprisoned.

In a larger frame, the different UN and regional processes for negotiating human rights norms and monitoring adherence to them (through treaty bodies, etc.) may also be brought inside the tent of human rights diplomacy.

This paper asks whether, in practice as well as theory, we should widen the notion, to take account of the much richer range of cooperative or complementary activities that states and different kinds of human rights organisation engage in. The paper suggests that many kinds of human rights activity can be considered forms of 'diplomacy'. If so eclectic and catholic an approach might clearly devalue the notion of 'human rights diplomacy', it has the merit of suggesting new ways in which different actors might collaborate or act in complementary ways to achieve human rights outcomes. Some at least of those forms of cooperation might usefully be explored more often and more consciously.

The paper does not claim to be based on extensive research. On the contrary, it is better considered as an individual's reflection, triggered by the two day discussion at the European Inter-University Centre for Human Rights and Democratisation in Venice on this subject in January 2009.[1] Unlike the author, many of the participants at that

[1] This essay is based on a short presentation to the same meeting.

meeting have considerable personal experience of human rights diplomacy as it has classically been understood. I would not wish my remarks to be interpreted as putting that knowledge or its value in question; this is rather an outsider's comment on the wider possibilities of imaginative dialogue.

The central suggestion is that 'human rights diplomacy' should be thought of less as an activity, and more as a strategy, a way of 'doing' human rights that harnesses people and opportunities together in certain ways.

Elements of Human Rights Diplomacy in Its 'Classical' Form

What are the basic elements of what we usually consider to be 'human rights diplomacy'?

- Two or more parties, usually States, meet to exchange views or negotiate regarding human rights.
- The parties attend voluntarily: the talks normally avoid explicit conditionality and displace use of force (or may be its precursor in case of absolute failure).
- At least one party is normally an advocate of human rights, and at least one party is presumed to be less comprehensively committed to (certain) human rights norms.
- Outcomes are often open-ended; a specific outcome is not necessarily expected. Human rights diplomacy is often part of a larger process, involving larger state interests.

An obvious example of such a dialogue is the series of meetings between the EU and China over human rights. The dialogue covered a range of subjects, was extended over time, and involved a range of representatives (officials and experts) on both sides. Both sides entered into the discussions because they were curious, for different reasons, to explore issues associated with law and rights (China and the EU having very different traditions in this regard). No specific outcome was presumed. EU governments (and the Chinese government) clearly understood from the start that China's political culture and history would constrain the range of possible outcomes of any discussion of human rights. And many wider interests (no doubt more important issues for the states concerned) were at play alongside. The human rights dialogues might at best be described as a distinctive voice in a large choir of discussions and negotiation. It is not surprising, given the above mix, that it becomes difficult, either from outside or from inside, to judge whether such processes have been 'successful', or to agree on criteria for measuring success, which is not at all to say that these or similar discussions failed or were not useful.

International human rights standard-setting perhaps provides an even better paradigm of what we mean. The negotiation of international human rights standards is of interest in this context because states employ very formal procedures of negotiation to produce (when they are successful) explicit outcomes in the form of legal standards and treaties. But the evolution of these procedures in real time is idiosyncratic and unpredictable, and depends a great deal on the play of personalities and opportunity; while, alongside, human rights actors have generated a penumbra of less formal processes in their efforts to proclaim and spread human rights ideas. Declarations clearly, but also a variety of other 'soft law' documents, have had considerable influence, even though they do not have the legal standing of treaties. Study of the emergence of new international standards, in all their forms and in the various regional and global forums that produce them, reveals that success usually involves a combination of dogged purpose, opportunism, a genius for alliance, expertise, and luck. Procedure, order and reason do not explain very well what happens in practice.[2] Here too, it is arduous to describe good practice or identify replicable indicators associated with success.

The Evolving Environment

Before looking at new opportunities for exploring and developing 'human rights diplomacy', let us briefly consider how the environment has changed and evolved, particularly in the last 15 years.

The human rights 'movement' has made a long journey since its formal inception some 65 years ago. Especially since the 1990s, human rights have gradually moved from the edge towards the centre of political affairs. Though they still by no means determine national and international political decisions, today human rights have become a reference that numerous organisations, from the UN to governments

[2] See for example, International Council on Human Rights Policy, 'Human Rights Standards: Learning from Experience', 2006.

and civil society organisations, feel bound to take account of as a matter of course.

At the same time, the range of application of human rights principles has broadened. There is deeper engagement with economic and social rights; the rights of new groups have been recognised in international treaties (human rights defenders, persons with disabilities, indigenous peoples); and it has become necessary to consider human rights in many areas where they are still contested—in the sphere of business, in relation to armed groups and other private actors, and with regard to culture and sexuality.

Indeed, the influence of human rights has been such that many Western governments that promoted and affirmed human rights in the context of foreign policy have started to push back against their penetration in domestic affairs, echoing the resistance of numerous states that continue to challenge the universality of human rights or their application to local cultural practices.

The larger political environment in which human rights are evolving has changed, too, as global power relations have been shifted by the emergence of new regional and global powers. The replacement of the G-8 by the G-20 symbolises the weakening authority of the United States and Western Europe, historically the most explicit advocates of human rights, relative to new emerging states, including China, India, and South Africa, whose diplomacy has historically taken much less account of human rights or has opposed the extension of human rights norms.

At the same time, albeit unevenly and with important exceptions, most governments have taken steps towards recognising at least some elements of human rights in national law; and, where this has occurred, civil society organisations have increasingly helped to implement reforms (by working with official monitoring organisations and participating in training programmes for judicial, police and prison officials, for example), extending their activities beyond independent monitoring and reporting, even if these continue to be central to their work. A long wave of institutional reform is very gradually transforming the organisation of many societies, even if progress in many can scarcely be discerned in the short term, and human rights values and rule of law principles are central to this process.

In parallel, finally, human rights have become academically established, with the result that important new resources of expertise exist, influencing and informing policy, while the dissemination of human rights ideas across a range of disciplines, from development to governance, from environment to health, has generated a slow transfer of ideas which is beginning to influence the evolution of human rights as much as human rights is influencing other disciplines.

This very brief summary suggests some of the ways in which we might adjust how we think about 'human rights diplomacy'. Though human rights law, and much human rights discussion, remains essentially state-led, there are far more actors in play than was the case even a few years ago. The agenda is richer and more varied. Even at multilateral and intergovernmental level, the 'mainstreaming' of human rights has created many new spaces to explore dialogue and interchange. Not only are more state processes hybrid; many other new forms of alliance are available for the discussion and promotion of human rights; and they involve a wider range of institutions and professional groups. The emergence of new powers like China and India, which do not promote human rights norms, will also influence how human rights norms are implemented. The rest of this short essay considers in bullet form some of the ways in which we might widen the horizon, and enrich the menu of activities associated with the notion of 'diplomacy'.

Voice

One might begin by considering the different expressions or 'voices' of diplomatic advocacy. In some cases, the emphasis is on consistent reiteration of essential (legal) principles. This is commonly the voice of some of the UN special procedures mandate-holders, whose job it is to remind the international community, and in particular governments, of their duties in relation to specific human rights standards. It is classically the voice of the many annual and country reports produced by organisations such as Amnesty International, the US State Department, the British Foreign Office etc.

In other cases, advocacy is essentially prophetic, the voice of conscience: it appeals to higher values and aspirations, without necessarily having regard for realism or political feasibility. In some instances, this voice has been at the foundation of essential progress. The Universal Declaration might itself be considered prophetic in this sense; as could the demand for an International Criminal Court which languished for several decades as an abstraction until it suddenly came alive in the 1990s.[3]

Documented advice is a third register: this technical voice provides factual and objective input, grounding policy. The legal analysis that underpins much human rights discussion falls in this category. Use of language of this kind has spread particularly quickly in recent years, as human rights have been mainstreamed into the programmes of international and national organisations and have therefore been integrated as a technical vocabulary, among others, that is relevant to health, environment, education, agriculture, development etc. It is closely associated with work that defines a 'human rights approach'.

A fourth voice would be exemplified by the classical form of human rights diplomacy: rational discussion of values embedded in a specific political context, which has the intention or purpose of conditioning policy outcomes.

With respect to new expressions of diplomacy, it is interesting to ask to what extent these 'voices' (and more could be identified) are complementary or incompatible. The question has particular relevance in two areas. First, it may be asked whether single institutions can successfully adopt all of them simultaneously. The UN High Commissioner for Human Rights and her Office, for example, are frequently exhorted to be the UN's 'conscience' (prophetic voice), to be rigorously objective (legal principle voice), and to provide practical pragmatic advice and guidance on the implementation of national policy (policy advice voice). It is hard for the Office to speak in all these tongues successfully, just as it is hard for an organisation like Amnesty International, which historically has spoken prophetically and with the voice of legal principle, to adopt simultaneously a policy advice voice (or engage in some of the more open-ended forms of human rights diplomacy).

[3] Much NGO advocacy is naturally of this form. However, it is useful to note that adversarial or confrontational forms of advocacy also imply dialogue between an authority (usually a government) and its critics, even if it is mediated through the international community of states. The efficacy of peer pressure and persuasion, as well as a foundation of common values, are assumed. Even judicial processes (involving the ICC, for example, or the Inter-American Court) have an exemplary dimension: they seek to inform and influence by example. Indeed, this is probably an essential objective, since it is unlikely ever to be the case that all violators of rights can be prosecuted. To this extent, prosecutorial and 'shame and blame' strategies eventually lie also within the sphere of political diplomacy.

Secondly, some 'voices' evidently complement one another. The availability of sound evidence-based policy advice is clearly likely to assist many state discussions of human rights. But others may work against one another. Bringing the voice of conscience into bilateral government discussions, or into documents that provide evidence-based policy advice, may or may not be helpful.

This is not a theoretical issue. At many levels, human rights advocates and officials are struggling to find a coherent voice and message, and one reason for this is that they are engaged at so many levels. It is no accident that the prophetic voice—the voice of human rights in its earliest days—is heard in the desert, or outside the city walls. Even the voice of reasoned legal principle is inherently abstract in many respects; indeed its force lies in the fact that it is invariable and gives no ground to political pragmatism or realism. Yet, human rights actors are now being asked to deliver practical programmes that produce tangible benefits at reasonable cost, and that can be integrated into existing programmes by institutions that have different intellectual traditions—and all this, without forfeiting principle. It is not surprising that human rights officials (and their organisations) are increasingly being accused of being aspirational (impractical) and at the same time diluting their principles, if not actually selling out.

A first challenge then, is to understand what forms of voice can be combined; what forms and mixtures of voice can be sustained by different organisations; and what elements of voice are essential to preserve moral integrity and intellectual coherence.

This immediately raises other issues, notably questions of confidentiality and trust. The voice of prophecy and the voice of legal principle lend themselves to uncompromising transparency. Questions of ambiguity scarcely arise. By contrast, pragmatic policy advice is all about making practical compromises (even if these are progressive) that take account of competency, capacity and a range of financial and political constraints. Public transparency on such matters is invariably difficult to sustain; and this is even more the case for classic forms of human rights diplomacy, which may occur on the specific condition that 'Chatham House' or stricter rules of confidentiality apply.

This raises complicated issues for actors who may wish, or have a common interest, to join in alliance, but who have asymmetrical transparency requirements.

Actors

A bewildering array of actors is now active in the field of human rights. To the non-governmental organisation (NGO) activist, the human rights lawyer, the national and international official with human rights responsibilities, one must add a vast range of NGOs and NGO networks that operate North and South and South-South, faith organisations and trades unions, national human rights institutions (NHRIs) and Ombuds offices, local government officials, city officials, and a much wider range of officials in government and international organisations that have undertaken to engage with human rights—in health, education, development, the environment etc.

Several comments may be suggested here. The first is to remember that some of the most effective diplomatic actions have been undertaken by hybrid alliances of civil society and official organisations. The anti-landmines campaign, which involved cooperation between a remarkably wide swathe of institutions—from the International Committee of the Red Cross (ICRC) and governments, to military representatives and civil society organisations—and ran an 'inside-outside' strategy of public campaigning and private negotiation, is an often-cited example. But modern policy-making is replete with examples that are similar. In the field of development, the British Government has positively encouraged NGOs to campaign aggressively for higher aid, in order to create public pressure in support of issues that it would otherwise find difficult to support. 'Make Poverty History' brought a vast alliance of civil society organisations together around simple policy demands, timed to peak as key governments met in Scotland. The current climate change negotiations are evolving along similar lines.

In relation to human rights, it may be useful to ask how far such campaigns influence in specific ways the decisions that are made (they clearly have other positive impacts), and to reflect more consciously on the possibilities of developing regional or local hybrid alliances, with the same 'inside-outside' character, to achieve human rights policy goals. The Amnesty campaigns on violence against women were of this character.

In some cases the creation of hybrid alliance can occur co-operatively. Horizontal forms of collaboration, between cities, local governments, health authorities, education ministries, etc., clearly have much potential in this respect.

In other cases, co-operation is better described as highly conditional or stressed. Much of the work that has been done on corporate responsibility is of this kind. Governments, UN bodies, corporations, trade unions and human rights NGOs have been persuaded to sit together in a number of forums, in the UN Global Compact, for example, or to regulate conflict diamonds; but the groups involved consider that they share interests only to a very limited extent. Maintaining 'non-consensual co-operation' of this kind is extremely difficult to do: this is one reason why the Ruggie initiative can be considered a rather remarkable achievement.[4]

In such instances, and to a considerable extent in all cases of hybrid alliance, the challenges of 'voice' and trust and the issues of transparency and confidentiality that have already been noted clearly arise, often in sharp terms. Where this is so, it is evidently important to think about conditions of effectiveness and criteria for 'success'.

Access and Hierarchy

This is highly relevant to discussion of human rights diplomacy, particularly in its classical form. The latter presumes a peer-to-peer relationship between the states involved, at least as 'peer' is understood by international diplomats. However unequal in power, the diplomatic presumption is that the states in question meet as sovereign equals (meaning that they are equal in status with each other and higher in status than any other actors except international institutions that the same states create). This has practical importance because, in their relations, states share essential presumptions and apply codes of comportment that govern their exchanges. These include the exclusion (as desired) of other actors, such as NGOs and other civil society representatives. States are in a position (and in some respects compel

[4] Professor John Ruggie has been the Special Representative of the UN Secretary-General on Business and Human Rights since 2005. During his term, he produced a sequence of punctiliously-calibrated papers, based on wide consultation with businesses, governments and NGOs, which gradually enlarged the space available for negotiation of the application of human rights norms to business activities. His work is comprehensively documented by the Business and Human Rights Resource Centre: See: http://www.business-humanrights.org/SpecialRepPortal/Home [last accessed 9 November 2010].

themselves) to discuss human rights matters in certain ways, ways they consider make discussion of rights possible, but which at the same time limit the range of possible outcomes, and exclude voices that are not state voices from (certain) deliberations.

Among the core assumptions that states share is an understanding that they have multiple interests and obligations that each state must accommodate and balance. Human rights may lie higher or lower on a particular state's list of priorities; and they may be considered a legal and international obligation rather than a moral and domestic one. In all cases, however, human rights are one interest to be accommodated: they are never the 'pre-emptive norm', the overriding value that they are for human rights lawyers and NGO advocates. They cannot be, to the extent that a state's direct interest is not advanced by full and complete implementation of the right in question. For the state itself, human rights are always relatively important; and between states the management of human rights matters is always a question of negotiation—to be considered in principle, but also, and essentially, in relation to other considerations (trade, political relations, security).

It follows from this that the characteristics of classical human rights diplomacy that make it useful—its ability to permit states to engage in a discussion of human rights in a realistic and pragmatic manner—also generate the familiar criticisms of it. States are inevitably considered to be flirting with compromise; are inevitably accused of lacking frankness; are almost always criticised for setting goals that are too low and timetables that are too slow. NGOs in particular press states to take up matters that are sensitive and politically difficult, to divulge more information publicly, and to make progress more quickly; and if these things cannot be achieved, they tend to argue that diplomacy should cease, and be replaced by more forthright action.

This leads to a point that is dumbly self-evident but is nevertheless central to the success (even the possibility) of hybrid forms of institutional co-operation: managing asymmetry of status. In any negotiating process, proximity determines the quality of access that individuals enjoy, not just to information and to people who have influence, but to the elements of political chemistry and nuance that determine a negotiation's direction and outcome. In this respect, diplomats are in a qualitatively different relationship of proximity to even privileged observers (such as international NGOs) and both observers and international NGOs have a quality of access that is literally unimaginable to human rights actors (such as many national

NGOs) who lack standing to participate and are physically distant from the place of discussion.

The consequences are predictable. Speaking schematically, senior diplomats and officials in multilateral institutions tend to highlight leadership, partly because they take for granted (indeed are gifted) their standing and entitlement to participate. They are certainly conscious of the importance of knowledge and sound analysis (and acutely conscious of their absence); but they are in the room with their peers, and leadership (willingness to take risks, show imagination, and carry responsibility) is naturally crucial to their perception of the success of what they are doing. As a result, diplomats will often analyse diplomatic processes against highly personal indicators, because they do indeed conduct much of their business in a personal face-to-face manner. They know the people with whom they negotiate, both in the forums of Geneva, and in their own capitals.

By contrast, the staffs of international human rights NGOs tend to look up at those above them in the hierarchy and also down, at those they work with and for. Their perspective is partly personal, because they too know some of the decision makers, but they also tend to speak in broader terms (of governments and institutions as if they were persons, for example). They speak distinctively as insiders, nevertheless, compared with those who are distant from the rooms in which discussion occurs, and who have no standing. This group (the vast majority in terms of number), having no access to nuance or detail, put very little faith in leadership, speak happily of institutions as if they were single coherent persons, and tend to emphasise popular organisation and public advocacy (change from below).

The point is so obvious that one hesitates to make it. Yet public discussion at every moment is being catalysed by such differences of perspective. In the case of classical human rights diplomacy, for example, it is not possible for diplomats who are directly involved in processes of negotiation to provide a complete explanation of their work to those who are not present. They are prevented from doing so by rules of confidentiality, but in addition by the fact that most negotiations are diffuse and unspecific until they conclude. The diplomat can only ask the NGO expert to trust her (or her judgement) that an exercise is worth pursuing; and the same is true if she believes a discussion is stuck and requires some external advocacy. To explain the veracity and inertia of such processes to people who know none of those involved, are unfamiliar with diplomatic procedures, and have never visited their capitals (let alone Geneva or New York) is clearly impossible. Described, diplomatic processes more resemble forms of myth or mystification, fairy tales or tales of deception. And they are indeed described, often, in such terms.

Management of asymmetrical access is therefore fundamental to the success of hybrid diplomacy (as it is to democracy more generally).

Conditions of Effectiveness, Criteria of 'Success'

At least six conditions probably need to be in place before it is likely that what we are calling hybrid human rights diplomacy can be successful.

- The actors directly involved need to have a clear and credible status: other parties directly involved must recognise that they have standing.
- The authority, mandate and capacities of different actors need to be understood by all parties involved. This is particularly important in the case of hybrid alliances, where some parties have standing, others are proximate, and still others are distant. Misunderstandings are much more likely to occur in such situations than where relationships are horizontal or between peers.
- The purpose(s) of the exercise should be clear: it needs to be understood in broad terms what the parties are meeting to discuss and what those involved (inside and outside) expect to achieve. (It is allowed that inside and outside parties may have different purposes, and that 'clear purpose' can include discussions that have no clear outcome in mind.)
- Open-mindedness: assuming that the parties are not of one mind to start with, there must be some readiness to engage and in principle to change position.
- Trust: there must be enough trust to proceed (or at least discuss with a degree of honesty).

If these conditions are broadly in place, the range of possibilities for hybrid co-operation is virtually unlimited. Indeed it is essentially constrained only by the parties' capacity to manage institutional asymmetry; and the limits of imagination. Both are considerable constraints.

Managing Asymmetry

Managing networks, let alone asymmetrical ones, is demanding and time consuming, requiring energy and diplomatic skills from those involved.

Success is also likely to be dependent on the work of key intermediaries—individuals and sometimes institutions who command trust up and down the network's range of vertical relationships. Only certain individuals and institutions are in a position to act as such intermediaries. Individual politicians can sometimes do so. In the field of human rights, a sprinkling of individuals have acquired the moral authority to create the conditions of co-operation between institutions that mistrust one another but need or want to negotiate or co-operate. Some special procedures mandate-holders are also able to play such a role.

Among institutions, international NGOs are probably best equipped to act as intermediaries in vertical networks; indeed, this may be one of their most essential functions. It might be said that international NGOs gain (or lose) value and influence to the extent that they successfully communicate the views of 'distant publics' they represent to those who have powers of decision (or fail to do so); and communicate effectively to those distant publics the higher processes of decision-making that they are privileged to observe (or fail to do so).[5]

Creativity

The challenge here is that, whereas diplomatic processes are conducted according to well-established rules and conventions, hybrid coalitions and processes are *ad hoc* almost by definition: they succeed when they bring together groups that have a coincidence of interest, and making this coincidence productive is largely a matter of social and political invention. Numerous real life cases illustrate this—both ones where failures of invention or flexibility have led to the collapse of co-operation, and ones where an inspired willingness to invent has discovered ways to exploit opportunities that were never foreseen.

[5] On this, see also K. Roberts, 'National Human Rights Institutions as Diplomacy Actors', Chapter 14 in the present volume, p.234. who suggests that national human rights institutions could also take on the role of intermediaries.

A second challenge, in this context, is to invent while working with the grain of contrasting institutional cultures. Here too, the presence of trusted intermediaries who are comfortable with a range of environments is likely to be a critical factor in success. This amounts once more to saying the obvious: that judgement is an essential element in the success of all such work.

Final Remarks

A first insight into the future of effective human rights diplomacy (in the broader sense that we have been using it here) is that at least some formal processes are likely to be most effective when complemented by other forms of operational activity or advocacy. Even if diplomats and officials are pre-eminent in certain areas, including the legal adoption of human rights standards (and the conduct of classical human rights diplomacy), they are increasingly not able to work alone and need the contributions of other actors to define, legitimise and implement the decisions they reach.

A second insight may be that organisations involved in human rights diplomacy (or other forms of persuasion) should probably focus on functions that are compatible with one another, allowing other actors to supply elements they cannot themselves provide. There are lessons here for the Office of the UN High Commissioner for Human Rights, but also for other UN agencies, such as the United Nations Development Programme (UNDP).

What this really says is that political decisions and policies are the product of negotiation and contest that involve an ever-widening range of increasingly interdependent institutions and actors. This in turn means that, as the Venice discussion showed, to visualise a broader, more inclusive palette for human rights diplomacy it will be helpful to evaluate not just the *forms of process* that might be available, but the *variety of actors* who might participate in them, indirectly or directly.

In doing this, it is important to recognise the character, and strengths, of diplomatic processes: these differ from most others in the clarity of their rules of engagement, which are both formally articulated and transparent to those with diplomatic standing.

It is equally important, wherever attempts are made to create wider or hybrid alliances or conversations across institutional cultures, to manage asymmetry. The attention which NGOs and social movements give to participation, consultation and access to information, are too often considered as rhetorical or politically correct, but may best be understood as attempts to engage with asymmetry—even if it is clear that transparency and full disclosure are incompatible with most negotiation and the actual practice of most diplomacy.

The outcomes of classic human rights diplomacy are uncertain: serendipitous, unpredictable almost by definition. This implies that we should not judge their value by any simple measure of success. In particular we should probably not test for performance against the hardest cases, but rather look for models of useful good practice where conditions for success are reasonably favourable. That would mean, for example, not using China, Uzbekistan or Russia as test cases of performance.

When assessing outcomes in the context of hybrid alliances, it is worth thinking about both long-term value and immediate value. Some forms of human rights diplomacy, or hybrid alliance, aim to achieve specific short-term goals. Whether these are achieved or not, it is worth also taking into account collateral, longer-term benefits.

This is a particularly relevant consideration when relations with other institutional cultures are considered. Human rights are being mainstreamed or explored in a wide variety of policy contexts: climate change, poverty, institutional reforms, health, corruption, etc. This work involves engaging with professionals from different institutional cultures. Few people working on development or climate change, or issues such as governance, are familiar with human rights, and there is an enormous job to be done to communicate with them in a language that they can respond to. This is likely to be a dimension of any hybrid form of human rights diplomacy, and means that human rights actors need to develop a listening diplomacy that is designed not just to influence others but to engage, understand and communicate with other disciplines in their own terms.

The role of intermediaries is crucial in both vertical relationships and hybrid initiatives. Some individuals and institutions are better equipped than others to create bridgeheads between institutions or institutional cultures that have reason to co-operate but also a predisposition to mistrust one another. Some UN special rapporteurs are able to play this role; international human rights NGOs are often well-equipped to do so as well, because the trust they inspire gives them unusual vertical access across society—richer and wider than most governments or official institutions can achieve (though the delivery capacity and influence of governments is obviously incomparably greater than that of NGOs).

At the Venice meeting the participants were asked whether human rights actors should set some standards of good practice in relation to human rights diplomacy. In this context, the discussion highlighted a range of questions regarding consistency and effectiveness, and also transparency.

These are clearly important values in principle. However, the Venice discussion suggested (to this author at least) that they may not be achievable, and might not even be desirable in practice. Much of the discussion suggested that particular initiatives need to be assessed politically against what is likely to work; that chance and opportunity are likely to be factors in success; and that human rights diplomacy, and hybrid forms of collaboration even more so, rely on the establishment of trust which in turn depends on confidentiality. This suggests that, if consistency is desirable in private, it may not always be achievable in public; and that full disclosure (transparency) may not be a realistic or appropriate goal. In a complex negotiation, involving many interests, it is not always possible to explain to every actor what has been done.

All through, we are faced by the importance of judgment in this area: the need to make complex political judgements and the challenge of doing no harm, both in relation to principles of human rights and in relation to efforts that other institutions are making to promote rights. The discussion in Venice suggested that excellent human rights diplomacy will often fail, will not always be uncontested, and won't look transparent.

In short, if it is true that the more interesting future of human rights diplomacy will involve managing large complex asymmetrical alliances and dialogues, requiring ingenuity, careful translation, and the exercise of subtle political judgement (not to speak of skills in responding to serendipitous circumstances), can one seek coherence? Should it even be an objective?

CHAPTER 4

THE ROLE OF HUMAN RIGHTS AMBASSADORS IN HUMAN RIGHTS DIPLOMACY—PERSPECTIVES FROM SPAIN

Silvia Escobar

A number of member states of the European Union (EU) have appointed human rights ambassadors today. Among them are Austria, Denmark, Finland, France, Germany, Hungary, the Netherlands, Spain and Sweden. There are also human rights ambassadors in Norway and Japan and several South American countries.

Informal meetings and coordination among the European human rights ambassadors has proved very useful since 2006, as the European ambassadors share values and fulfil tasks which do not differ in their essentials. Yet, each European ambassador represents his or her own individual ministry of foreign affairs. Accordingly, the priorities of their work depend on the specific mandate they are entrusted with by their respective ministries, on the role their country takes on in the area of human rights, and on the way in which human rights are integrated into the structures and activities of their ministry. In Spain, the human rights ambassador is located at the Spanish Ministry of Foreign Affairs and Cooperation. The Ministry also has a human rights desk. Both report to the Ministry's Director-General of Multilateral Affairs and work in close cooperation.

In my understanding, human rights ambassadors are spokespersons for a certain view of international relations. His or her appointment constitutes a very important step in the promotion of human rights through diplomatic means. Their rank as ambassadors frequently allows them to engage in substantive dialogue with high-ranking officials of third countries—a privilege that can prove effective to bring about change in different situations. The appointment of a person directly responsible for human rights issues at the rank of an ambassador in different European countries also conveys a strong message to third countries that human rights have attained an important status in European states' foreign policy. In this contribution, I will attempt to further explain a few aspects of the added value of the appointment of human rights ambassadors for the framing of foreign policies in different areas.

Renowned professor Stanley Hoffmann of Harvard University once made the following statement: 'I have taught international relations for 58 years and have arrived at the following dichotomic conclusion: First, everybody knows what should be done, and second, everybody knows that what should be done cannot be done.'[1] Persuading people that something can and should be done to further the implementation of human rights around the world is one of the most important tasks of human rights ambassadors. Without being naïve, human rights ambassadors believe in people's capacity to seek solutions to the big challenges the world is facing today, among them widespread poverty, armed conflicts, pandemics and environmental damage.

We believe that we can build a better world—a more democratic world with responsible and accountable governments. Human rights ambassadors and other professionals who work towards the realisation of human rights have the hope that progress can be made even though it cannot always be seen on the near horizon.

The 1993 United Nations (UN) Vienna World Conference on Human Rights established that the promotion and protection of human rights is the responsibility of all governments.[2] Promoting human rights through diplomatic action is also justified and required by their universality and the related rejection of the position that human rights are strictly matters of states' internal affairs. Both the individual and inter-state complaint mechanisms that form part of most international and regional human rights mechanisms, and the concept of universal jurisdiction, are manifestations of this recognition. It has been acknowledged that human rights are a vital element on the international agenda. Ensuring respect for human rights is crucial when it comes to cementing peace and security and to establishing improved conditions for social and economic development.

---

[1] Stanley Hoffmann, Paul and Catherine Buttenweiser University professor of international relations at Harvard University and founder of the Centre for European Studies in Harvard University, addressing students during the celebrations of the 50th Anniversary of the Institut of International Relations of Harvard University in 2007 [on file with author].

[2] Vienna Declaration and Programme of Action, adopted by the World Conference on Human Rights, UN Doc A/CONF.157/23 (12 July 1993), para.1. On the important role of civil society in implementing human rights see below.

As a matter of fact, ensuring universal respect for and observance of human rights and fundamental freedoms for all is a foundational objective of the United Nations.[3] Diplomats in charge of promoting human rights rely on classical tools such as mediation, representation and negotiation. Human rights ambassadors can act as commissioners for and observers on human rights in diplomatic action. They usually head their countries' diplomatic delegations in regional and international human rights fora, be it at the UN, the Organisation for Security and Co-operation in Europe (OSCE), the Council of Europe, or at bilateral meetings. Their main mission is the promotion of human rights as a fundamental element in the foreign policy and international cooperation of their countries, both in their bilateral and multilateral relations.

Among other tasks of European human rights ambassadors are: First, to ensure the coordination and cooperation of different actors involved in developing and implementing their country's human rights policies. This includes coordination with civil society. Second, ambassadors contribute to shaping their country's diplomacy on human rights at the bilateral, regional and international level, including through setting of priorities. Third, they carry out visits or missions to third countries for the promotion and protection of human rights. And fourth, they work to strengthen human rights policies of the European Union. These tasks shall be elaborated on in more detail in the following sections. The focus is placed on my own country, Spain.

Coordination and Cooperation with National and International Actors

To ensure coherence in and effectiveness of Spain's human rights policies, the Spanish human rights ambassador has to coordinate her work with other actors at the national and international level. She works in close cooperation with other governmental authorities, ministries and state institutions, such as the ombudsman and the national and European parliaments. As in other countries, the ambassador is also in contact with special procedures mandate-holders of the UN Human Rights Council, other UN experts, with national and international personalities visiting the Spanish Ministry of Foreign Affairs, with her

[3] Articles 1(3) and 55(c) UN Charter.

European peers, with the Human Rights Commissioner of the Council of Europe, with the European Council, with the European Agency for Fundamental Rights, and with the OSCE. Establishing good contacts for cooperation and coordination with these actors is key for the human rights ambassador to fulfil many of her other tasks at the national and international level.

For example, within Spain the human rights ambassador took part in extensive discussions with different ministries to draft Spain's first national human rights plan of action in 2008. She also cooperates with relevant national departments to help ensuring compliance with the judgements of the European Court of Human Rights, for following up on the implementation of concluding observations of the UN human rights treaty bodies and of the recommendations of the Council of Europe's organs and bodies. The ambassador is furthermore involved in the elaboration of education and outreach strategies to promote the understanding of human rights and the role of national and international institutions that work towards their implementation in Spanish society. She also cooperates with others towards the creation of a Spanish national human rights protection system, involving all relevant ministries and covering all Spanish territory.

At the international level, coordination is important for preparing Spain's contributions to the universal periodic review (UPR) process of the UN Human Rights Council. It is also essential for appraising different international treaties and agreements on human rights, and, if necessary, for taking or supporting initiatives to increase the level of protection envisaged in them. Last but not least, coordination is required for the effective and visible introduction of human rights into Spanish foreign policy.

Coordination and Cooperation with Civil Society

Her coordinating function also involves the very important issue of establishing contact and cooperating with civil society. Non-governmental organisations (NGOs), universities, trade unions and foundations are among the civil society actors that play an ever more important role in human rights diplomacy today.

For example, human rights ambassadors take part in university forums in their countries and abroad. Among them are forums organised by European Inter-University Centre for Human Rights and Democratisation (EIUC) in Venice, including attending the diploma-awarding ceremony of the European Master's Programme in Human Rights and Democratisation. The Spanish Foundation "Tres Culturas" has also organised a seminar on the topic of 'new diplomacy' in Spain.[4] The human rights ambassador and other civil society actors participated in this seminar.

Cooperation with civil society and other human rights ambassadors has also proven fruitful in the framework of the Asia-Europe Meetings (ASEM).[5] ASEM has provided a forum for dialogue between Asians and Europeans since 1966, and consultations include different human rights topics.[6] The Community of Democracies[7] is another forum for human rights ambassadors' cooperation with different actors involved in human rights diplomacy.

Shaping Spain's Human Rights Diplomacy

The ambassador contributes to the formulation of his or her country's position on human rights in foreign policy, and to decisions on how diplomatic means can best be used to communicate and implement this position.

The constructivist theory of international relations makes it clear that the idea a country has of itself, as well as the idea that other countries have of it, is of great importance. The well-known question *'How many divisions does the Vatican have?'* shows convincingly that military strength is not a prerequisite for having a presence and for exerting influence in international relations. It is in this domain where the power and potential success of the human rights ambassadors' work lies. On this basis, human rights ambassadors form an essential part of

---

[4] For more details see: http://www.tresculturas.org/index.asp?idioma=es [last accessed 20 January 2011].

[5] For more details see: http://www.aseminfoboard.org/ [last accessed 20 January 2011].

[6] See also W. Benedek, 'The Relevance of the Multi-Stakeholder Approach and Multi-Track Diplomacy for Human Rights Diplomacy', Chapter 15 in the present volume, p.256, discussing the successful participation of civil society representatives in ASEM.

[7] The Community of Democracies is an intergovernmental organisation with a stated commitment to strengthening and deepening democratic norms and practices worldwide. The Community of Democracies was founded in June 2000 during a Ministerial Conference in Warsaw. For details see: http://community-democracies.org/ [last accessed 20 January 2011].

their country's capacity to launch debates and take the lead on current human rights topics.

For instance, the human rights desk of the Spanish Ministry of Foreign Affairs and the human rights ambassador have promoted the system-wide UN Action Plan on the implementation of UN Security Council resolution 1325 on Women, Peace and Security.[8] Another priority is taking part in most of the UN and Council of Europe meetings on trafficking in human beings, one of the great challenges of the 21st Century. This topic has become a very important one on the international agenda. The Spanish human rights ambassador is also actively involved in issues related to the reform of the UN and the Council of Europe, and the future of the OSCE. As mentioned, the ambassador regularly represents the Spanish Ministry of Foreign Affairs or the Government in these and other international and regional human rights fora.

Spain and the Spanish human rights ambassador are furthermore particularly active in regard to the abolition of the death penalty. Spain continues to urge countries which retain the death penalty in their penal codes to place a moratorium on this punishment with a view of its abolishment. This is in line with the resolution adopted in November 2007 by the UN General Assembly that was promoted by the European Union.[9] There is also a Spanish initiative by which an International Commission against the Death Penalty was established in October 2010 in Madrid as part of the celebrations of World Day against the Death Penalty.[10] The International Commission is chaired by former UNESCO chief Federico Mayor Zaragoza[11] and has the support and

[8] UNSC Res 1325 (2000) on Women, Peace and Security, UN Doc S/RES/1325 (31 October 2000). For the latest report of the UN Secretary-General on progress regarding the Action Plan see: Report of the UN Secretary-General, Women Peace and Security, UN Doc S/2010/498 (28 December 2010).

[9] UNGA Res 62/149, Moratorium on the Use of the Death Penalty, UN Doc A/RES/62/149 (26 February 2008).

[10] For the 'Statement on the Constitution of the International Commission against the Death Penalty' see: http://www.academicsforabolition.net/repositorio/ficheros/223_121.pdf [last accessed 20 January 2011].

[11] Other members of the Commission are Giuliano Amato (Former President of the Council of Ministers of Italy), Louise Arbour (Former UN High Commissioner for Human Rights), Robert Badinter (Former Minister of Justice of France), Mohammed Bedjaoui (Former Foreign Minister of Algeria), Ruth Dreifuss (Former President of the Swiss Confederation), Michèle Duvivier Pierre-Louis (Former Prime Minister of Haiti), Asma Jinali Jahangir (President of the Human Rights Commission of Pakistan), Ioanna Kuçuradi (UNESCO Chairperson of the Philosophy and Human Rights

advice from the following countries: Argentina, the Dominican Republic, France, Italy, Kazakhstan, Mexico, Mongolia, Philippines, Portugal, South Africa, Spain, Switzerland and Turkey. Spain took the initiative to found the International Commission at a time where there is a strong and continuing trend towards the abolition of the death penalty in all regions of the world, as highlighted in the latest report of UN Secretary-General of 15 August 2010 on "Moratoriums on the Use of the Death Penalty".[12] The Commission was created to join all the efforts in favour of abolishing the death penalty carried out by civil society, the UN, other international and regional organisations and political leaders of the world. The International Commission will work with all of them in close cooperation with the ultimate goal of achieving the total abolition of this punishment.

Missions to Third Countries

One of the main tools of human rights diplomacy relied on by European human rights ambassadors are visits to third countries. Visits are carried out individually or in groups. Their aim is to examine the human rights situation firsthand and, if necessary, to make constructive proposals to governments of how to improve a situation. Among other countries, human rights ambassadors have visited Bangladesh, Belarus, Cambodia, Colombia, the Democratic Republic of Congo (DRC), the Philippines, Sri Lanka and Turkmenistan.

How are these missions planned and conducted? Based on the preparatory work of our regional directorates and embassies, a common programme is drafted. In general terms, the mission then consists of a number of interviews with government officials at the highest level, with officials from the most important state institutions and with members of civil society. Human rights ambassadors communicate their reasons for visiting the country to the respective government, as well as their main concerns about different human rights issues. For example, in the DRC the ambassadors brought up the issue of violence against women. In the Philippines, they focussed on the issue of the death penalty, which was still in force when they visited the country.

Department), Rodolfo Mattarollo (Former Deputy Secretary for Human Rights in Argentina) and Bill Richardson (Governor of New Mexico, USA).

[12] Report of the Secretary-General, Moratoriums on the Use of the Death Penalty, UN Doc A/65/280 (11 August 2010).

Missions often include visits to prisons, hospitals, schools and universities. At the end of each mission, the human rights ambassadors usually hold a press conference while still in the country, and sometimes they issue a public statement. They also directly inform the respective government of the findings of their visit. Once the European ambassadors return to their countries, they draft a COREU (*Correspondance Europenne*)[13] to communicate the results of their mission to EU member states and the European Commission.

Human Rights Ambassadors' Work at the European Level

Like the other European countries, Spain takes active part in the EU Council Working Group on Human Rights (COHOM), where EU human rights policies are drafted. Spain participates in developing new and refining the content of existing EU guidelines on human rights. The main aim of these guidelines is to strengthen the EU's and its member states' activities in seven human rights priority areas on which guidelines currently exist. There are guidelines on the abolition of the death penalty, the prevention of torture and inhuman or degrading treatment or punishment, on children and armed conflict, on human rights defenders, on the promotion and protection of the rights of the child, on violence against women and girls, and on international humanitarian law.[14] The guidelines structure EU human rights dialogues and consultations, and are the basis for *demarches* to third countries as well as campaigns and action plans. Likewise, the EU guidelines are regularly included in diplomatic meetings at the bilateral level, and are disseminated to authorities, civil society and local institutions of third countries.

Spain took over the Presidency of the EU (January-June 2010) at an important time for Europe and the international community, in a context of rising unemployment rates and the fight against climate change. Spain's intention during the Presidency was to make full use of and strengthen well-established policies and tools in the area of human

[13] The COREU (*Correspondance Europenne*) is an EU communications network between the member states and the EU Commission in the field of foreign policy. It facilitates swift decision making in emergencies and abides by the rules of confidentiality.

[14] The EU guidelines on human rights are available at: http://www.consilium.europa.eu/showpage.aspx?id=1681&lang=EN [last accessed 20 January 2011].

rights that are forming the basis of the human rights work of the EU and its member states. Among them are the guidelines mentioned above. The Spanish Presidency's human rights priorities were the following:

1. the fight against the death penalty;
2. the fight against torture and other inhumane, cruel, or degrading treatment and punishments;
3. the fight to end the plight of child soldiers within the framework of the promotion and protection of children's rights;
4. supporting gender equality and the promotion and protection of women's rights;
5. the promotion and protection of the rights of lesbians, gays, bisexuals and transsexuals (LGBTs);
6. the promotion of access to drinkable water and sanitation as a human right;
7. the promotion and protection of rights of people with disabilities; and
8. the protection of human rights defenders.

Another priority of the Spanish Presidency was to work towards providing strong momentum for the 2011 review of the work and functioning of the UN Human Rights Council five years after it has come into existence. The review process will hopefully turn the Council into a stronger and more efficient organ for the analysis and condemnation of the most serious human rights violations around the world.

During the Spanish Presidency, as during the previous Swedish Presidency, human rights ambassadors chaired most of the EU-third country human rights dialogues and consultations. Among others, dialogues and consultations were held with Armenia, Canada, Georgia, Indonesia, Japan, Mexico, Moldova, the Russian Federation, Turkmenistan and the candidate countries (Croatia, Iceland, the former Yugoslav Republic of Macedonia, Montenegro and Turkey).

At the time of writing, the EU human rights policy has been reinforced and promises to become more consistent. A permanent Chair of the Human Rights Working Group (COHOM) has been established, and the new European External Action Service has been launched with an important human rights unit. Moreover, coordination of human rights initiatives among EU member states in other fora is stronger than ever before, especially in the Human Rights Council and the Third Committee of the General Assembly of the United Nations.

The Spanish Presidency has contributed to the reflection among the 27 EU member states on how to strengthen and invigorate the effectiveness of the EU's work in the area of human rights. This promises to make human rights an ever more central aspect of the EU's external relations—in the political dialogues it holds with third countries, through its action in international fora such as the UN, and through its development policies. Ultimately, rights-holders around the world will benefit from this. European human rights ambassadors, and undoubtedly civil society, will continue to do their utmost in this direction.

CHAPTER 5

HUMAN RIGHTS DIPLOMACY OF SMALL STATES

Éamonn Mac Aodha

Introduction

The aim of this chapter is to examine some of the key aspects of the human rights diplomacy of small states. How do small states use the tools of human rights diplomacy? What is the track record of small states in this regard? What are the particular advantages and disadvantages of small states in working on human rights issues?

These and other related questions are examined from a practitioner's perspective with a view to ascertaining whether there are clear examples of best practice which, in particular, might provide a template for others working in the area? The chapter which takes an admittedly Eurocentric approach is intended more to point out some key issues rather than to address them comprehensively and draws significantly on the author's experience of managing Ireland's human rights foreign policy.

Definitions

By necessity, definitions of what constitutes a small state will be somewhat arbitrary. Possible quantitative definitions include land area, gross national product, per capita income or population size.

The Commonwealth Secretariat for example offers a definition for small states as countries with a population of 1.5 million or less.[1] For the purposes of this exercise population will also be used as a measure. However it is proposed that the focus should be on states with a population of less than ten million people. While at the upper end of what might reasonably be considered small this will allow for a wider

[1] See: http://www.thecommonwealth.org/Internal/190628/190656/faqs/ [last accessed 11 February 2011].

canvass as, on current estimations, there are 192 countries in the world of which 108 have populations below this threshold.[2]

Again, various options for a definition of human rights diplomacy present themselves. One broad approach considers that all humanitarian work could be said to advance human rights diplomacy. By this yardstick a number of small states play a very important role. In similar mode overseas development assistance, certain forms of military intervention and other foreign policy interactions could be said to offer opportunities for the advancement of a state's human rights diplomacy goals. It could also be argued that work on climate change where, for example, the Maldives has taken a progressive stance[3] could be described as human rights diplomacy. Again, mediation or peace talks facilitation/honest broker activity can in some senses be described as human rights work, for example that undertaken by Norway in respect of the Oslo Middle East accords, on the Sudanese Comprehensive Peace Agreement and in relation to peace efforts in Sri Lanka.

However for present purposes human rights diplomacy is taken to mean the advancement by states, through their foreign policy, of what have been described as 'internationally agreed values, standards or rules regulating the conduct of states towards their own citizens and non-citizens'.[4] In this context the main prism will be actions by states in multilateral diplomacy, in particular at the United Nations (UN).

Tools for Human Rights Diplomacy

All states, large or small, have access to at least some of the well established tools for advancing human rights foreign policy goals. Viewing the toolbox through the specific example of Ireland is instructive and will be pursued below. These tools can include public diplomacy, policy partnerships, outreach programmes, *demarches*, human rights guidelines, dialogues and resolutions. Smaller states may be limited in

---

[2] See: http://www.worldatlas.com/aatlas/populations/ctypopls.htm [last accessed 11 February 2011].

[3] See, for example, the content of the address by President Gayoom to the United Nations General Assembly 1987, available at: http://www.un.org/wcm/content/site/chronicle/cache/bypass/home/archive/Issues2009/pid/8409?ctnscroll_articleContainerList=1_0&ctnlistpagination_articleContainerList=true [last accessed 11 February 2011].

[4] P. R. Baehr and M. Castermans-Holleman, *The Role of Human Rights in Foreign Policy*, 3rd edn (The Hague: Palgrave Macmillan, 2004), p.3.

what they can do either by an absence of resources or by restrictions on their freedom of political manoeuvre (for example in relation to public diplomacy). It may be that their very size assists in effective engagement (for example, through policy partnerships). Some relative advantages and disadvantages of small states are set out below.

Advantages of Small States

Smaller states enjoy some or all of the advantages referred to in the following passage in terms of prioritising human rights diplomacy if that is what they choose to do.

Many smaller states are neutral or non-aligned and thus can be seen to have greater credibility for their activities across regional and other groupings, especially at the UN.

Several states have a history of having to work alongside dominant neighbours which can also build a capacity to work well with a wide range of competing ideologies or perspectives from other states. Finland, Ireland and Austria might all be said to fall into this category.

Regional integration, for example, in Europe through the European Union (EU), can also afford smaller states the opportunity for a larger role in global affairs. However, it also runs the risk that larger states within a regional grouping can stymie the natural instincts of smaller ones. The corollary is that smaller states can sometimes hide behind the reluctance of larger regional partners to engage in human rights questions.

It is, however, notable that of the four thematic sets of human rights foreign policy guidelines adopted by the European Union over the past two decades small states have been prominent either at the outset in having these adopted or subsequently in contributing to their more effective implementation. These separate sets of key guidelines focus on Human Rights Defenders, Torture, the Death Penalty and Children in Armed Conflict.[5] Essentially these guidelines request EU member states, and the Union acting collectively, to highlight the issues covered by them in relevant foreign policy contexts.

[5] The EU guidelines on human rights are available at: http://www.consilium.europa.eu/showpage.aspx?id=1681&lang=EN [last accessed 11 February 2011].

As in other aspects of foreign policy, decision-making loops in smaller national systems and foreign ministries on human rights questions can involve fewer players and thus policy initiatives and innovation can be easier to achieve. Opportunities for informal policy progression are also probably greater in smaller systems.

In addition, in smaller states links between national administrations and civil society can be closer and consequently political lobbying of government can be more effective. One clear example of this is the work done by Frontline, an international human rights non-governmental organisation (NGO) based in Ireland, which successfully lobbied the Irish EU Presidency in 2004 to pursue adoption by member states of Guidelines on Human Rights Defenders. In this regard the NGO concerned enjoyed considerable access, including at ministerial level, to make their case.

While the range of means available to states to develop and maintain a profile on human rights is wide, smaller countries may find it easier to adapt their foreign ministries to human rights foreign policy goals. Again, Ireland is a case in point. Three significant structural changes followed the publication of its first White Paper on foreign policy in 1996.[6] These three innovations were the creation of a Human Rights Unit within the Department of Foreign Affairs, the establishment of an NGO Standing Committee on Human Rights chaired by the Department and the convening of an annual open and participative public Forum on Human Rights. Proceedings from the latter reveal discussion of a broad range of issues by a wide variety of participants.[7]

It is also important to note here that the range of foreign and economic interests of smaller states can often be more limited thus sometimes allowing for a less inhibited focus on human rights.

Smaller states can also prompt and/or collaborate on reflective writing or discussion involving a multiplicity of stakeholders on key or evolving thematic human rights issues. One leading example of the latter is the work done by Switzerland on human rights and business.[8]

Switzerland has also been actively involved in developments aimed at renewing the international human rights machinery. This work has

---

[6] Government of Ireland White Paper on Foreign Policy: Challenges and Opportunities Abroad, Dublin, Government Publications, 1996.

[7] For details see: http://www.dfa.ie [last accessed 11 February 2011].

[8] For more details see: http://www.eda.admin.ch/eda/en/home/topics/humri/humcon.html [last accessed 11 February 2011].

encompassed supporting important publications on the UN human rights architecture, including an impressive work on the first year of the UN Human Rights Council (HRC).[9] Switzerland—working in tandem with Norway—has also cooperated with the United Kingdom Foreign and Commonwealth Office (FCO) to support a series of important gatherings on the HRC at the FCO-supported conference facility of Wilton Park.[10]

The HRC—with its less confrontational universal periodic review (UPR) system for country review—may offer some positive aspects for smaller states. In particular it affords smaller states the opportunity to question larger states—even when the respective states may be on friendly terms—on their domestic human rights situation. Again, Ireland is a notable example and has asked questions during a range of UPR sessions including those of larger countries with whom it has traditionally had good relations.[11] This form of diplomacy assists in drawing attention to specific human rights gaps but is less confrontational than traditional methods. This is true not only in relation to UPR itself but also in respect of the greater importance of side-events and other means of highlighting human rights issues afforded directly or indirectly by the new structures.

It is worth noting in this context that of the forty-seven member states of the UN HRC listed for 2010–2011[12] fifteen are states with a population of less than 10 million people.[13]

Finally, smaller states have a range of other means available to them to highlight human rights issues. Again, a clear example of this has been the manner in which Ireland has sought to raise its profile in other significant ways consistent with its traditional foreign policy values. Its profile was greatly enhanced when former President Mary Robinson assumed the role of United Nations High Commissioner for Human Rights in 1997.

Doyle and Connolly have noted other examples of Irish activism indicated by the state's election to the United Nations Commission on

---

[9] L. Müller (ed.), *The First 365 Days of the United Nations Human Rights Council*, Swiss Federal Department of Foreign Affairs, Political Affairs Division IV, 2007.

[10] See: http://www.wiltonpark.org.uk/en/conferences/policy-programmes [last accessed 11 February 2011].

[11] See: http://www.ohchr.org/en/hrbodies/upr/pages/uprmain.aspx [last accessed 11 February 2011]. Ireland has posed questions in the UPR examinations of *inter alia* several of its European partners and of the United States of America.

[12] See: http://www2.ohchr.org/english/bodies/hrcouncil/membership.htm [last accessed 11 February 2011].

[13] See: http://www.data.worldbank.org/country [last accessed 11 February 2011].

Human Rights (CHR) for the period 1997–1999 and 2003–2005 and the election of an Irish Judge to the International Criminal Court in 2003.[14] Ireland also used its period on the Security Council in 2001–2002 to promote human rights.[15] Ireland is a member of the cross-regional group of states known as the Human Security Network (HSN) and chaired the group in 2008–2009. The HSN is often described as the nexus of human rights, humanitarian action and disarmament. Ireland will seek election to the United Nations Human Rights Council in 2012 and meanwhile continues an activist role as an observer on the Council—and elsewhere—with regard to human rights defenders and other issues such as treaty body strengthening.

Disadvantages of Small States

Baehr and Castermans-Holleman point out that 'small states usually exert limited influence in international politics while major powers may have dominant influence'.[16] Small states tend to have limited territory, limited wealth and lack military strength. In general, the opposite can be said both of the current major players and of the emerging dominant players of recent years. As has been pointed out with regard to larger states, in the end 'they have the power to use force'.[17]

Aside from the threat of military strength smaller states also often lack the economic and other soft power that might assist in advancing human rights foreign policy. This is not universally the case and can depend on resource availability. For example, small states such as Switzerland and Norway have been very effective in particular in terms of multilateral engagement on human rights.[18]

One aspect of human rights diplomacy where small states traditionally tended not to be active was in relation to resolutions condemning

[14] J. Doyle and E. Connolly, 'La Politica Exterior Irlandesa a l'ONU i a la UE: Influencia e Participacio', *DCIDOB* 111 (2010), 11–27, available at: http://www.cidob.org/es/publicaciones/revistas/dcidob/irlanda_de_l_euforia_al_desencis [last accessed 11 February 2011].

[15] J. Doyle, 'Irish Diplomacy on the UN Security Council 2001–2002: Foreign Policy Making in the Light of Day', *Irish Studies in International Affairs* 15 (2004), 73–102.

[16] Baehr and Castermans-Holleman, *The Role of Human Rights in Foreign Policy*, 2004, p.20.

[17] *Ibid.*, p.21.

[18] Norway has been a lead player in the creation and subsequent maintenance of a United Nations Special Representative on Human Rights Defenders.

the rights records of individual states. At the now defunct UN CHR few small states (other than acting as EU Presidency) took the lead on country resolutions. One exception was Denmark which sponsored an unsuccessful draft resolution on China in the 1990s and found this to be a bruising experience. Another exception is Switzerland which worked on resolutions at CHR in relation to Nepal but this can be distinguished from the Danish example in that the Nepalese authorities assented to engagement on the draft resolution.

The tendency for smaller countries has, in fact, often been to involve themselves on somewhat less contentious issues. The work done by Ireland on the human rights of persons with disabilities in Geneva in the early years of the last decade is a case in point or, more recently, its focus on human rights defenders. Other notable examples include Austria's work on internally displaced persons or Portugal's efforts in respect of economic and social rights (it is acknowledged that the population of the latter country marginally exceeds ten million). It is not that these examples are entirely uncontroversial—indeed in some respects they are highly political—but rather that they tend not to expose their proponents to quite the same degree of exposure as a 'finger-pointing' country resolution might occasion.

Finally, one issue worth touching on in the multilateral context is that the new increase in the meeting time of the HRC has to some extent favoured larger delegations, and has led to smaller states in the EU and in other regional contexts (e.g. Africa) relying on the analysis and leadership offered by the larger entities. This has been one of the factors in the disappointing tendency for 'bloc dynamics' to persist.

Conclusion

While this chapter focuses primarily on the role of some European countries, it is suggested that many of the points made are of general application to smaller states across the world.

There are significant benefits to being small and, as described, these can include decision-making and organisational adaptability, proximity to grass-roots human rights concerns and opportunities to profit from emerging structures in the multilateral human rights system.

Disadvantages may include an over-reliance on unsupported moral persuasion and an unwillingness to engage in country-specific human right work.

As the foregoing suggests, small states—despite operating with some clear disadvantages—can be well placed to avail of opportunities to play a progressive role on human rights internationally. The degree of success in this regard will depend as much on political willingness as on systemic adaptability to engage with the possibilities afforded by the international system.

CHAPTER 6

THE EUROPEAN UNION AS A HUMAN RIGHTS ACTOR

Toby King

The European Union Treaties place human rights at the heart of the European Union's (EU) external relations. Article 21(1) of the Treaty on European Union (TEU) provides:

> The Union's action on the international scene shall be guided by the principles which have inspired its own creation, development and enlargement, and which it seeks to advance in the wider world: democracy, the rule of law, the universality and indivisibility of human rights and fundamental freedoms, respect for human dignity, the principles of equality and solidarity and respect for the principles of the UN Charter and international law.[1]

The pre-Lisbon legal framework contained similar, albeit slightly less comprehensive, provisions.[2] The EU Annual Report on Human Rights demonstrates the enormous range of actions undertaken by the EU to promote human rights worldwide, ranging from *demarches* and public statements to the holding of human rights dialogues to the insertion of human rights clauses in agreements with third countries to extensive financial support for human rights projects all over the world.[3] The range and ambition of EU human rights diplomacy reflect the fact that

[1] Article 205 of the Treaty on the Functioning of the European Union (TFEU) provides that the Union's action on the international scene shall be guided by the principles, pursue the objectives and be conducted in accordance with the general provisions laid down in *inter alia* Article 21 TEU.

[2] In the Treaties before the amendments introduced by the Treaty of Lisbon, Article 11 TEU provided that one of the objectives of the Common Foreign and Security Policy was to 'develop and consolidate democracy and the rule of law, and respect for human rights and fundamental freedoms'. So far as first pillar actions were concerned, Article 177(2) of the Treaty establishing the European Communities provided that European Community development co-operation 'shall contribute to the general objective of developing and consolidating democracy and the rule of law, and to that of respecting human rights and fundamental freedoms', while Article 181(a) made similar provision concerning Community economic, financial and technical co-operation measures with third countries.

[3] 'Human Rights and Democracy in the World', report on EU action July 2008 to December 2009, available at: http://ec.europa.eu/external_relations/human_rights/docs/hr_report_2010_en.pdf [last accessed 15 December 2010].

> the EU has gone further towards making its external relations informed by, and conditional on, a catalogue of norms which come closer to the European Convention of Human Rights and the Universal Declaration of Human Rights than most other actors in world politics.[4]

The purpose of this paper is not to analyse systematically the tools used and results obtained by EU human rights diplomacy, which have already been examined in several recent academic studies, but rather to offer some observations on the nature of human rights diplomacy, its possibilities and its limitations, as observed through the prism of EU practice.[5]

The Nature of EU Human Rights Diplomacy

The EU's commitment to the promotion of human rights in external relations is conceived as a reflection of the norms which underpin the Union's internal structure and which are fundamental to its own identity.[6] However, the European Community and its member states were for many years reluctant to tackle the issue of human rights promotion.[7] The Treaty references to the promotion of human rights in external relations were introduced only by the Treaty of Maastricht in 1992 as the European Union sought to seize the post-Cold War *zeitgeist* in which liberal democracy underpinned by civil and political rights and the rule of law seemed to have become the dominant worldwide model.[8] Almost twenty years later, the worldwide

---

[4] I. Manners, 'Normative Power Europe: A Contradiction in Terms?', *Journal of Common Market Studies* 40 (2002), 241.

[5] Recent studies of human rights in EU external relations include: U. Khaliq, *Ethical Dimensions of the Foreign Policy of the European Union* (Cambridge: Cambridge University Press, 2008); L. Bartels, *Human Rights Conditionality in the EU's International Agreements* (Oxford: Oxford University Press, 2005); P. Leino, 'European Universalism? The EU and Human Rights Conditionality', *Yearbook of European Law* 24 (2005), 329; K. Smith, *European Union Foreign Policy in a Changing World* (Cambridge: Polity Press, 2008), ch. 5 (human rights), pp.111–41.

[6] Article 2 TEU: 'the Union is founded on the values of respect for human dignity, freedom, democracy, equality, the rule of law and respect for human rights, including the rights of persons belonging to minorities. These values are common to the Member States in a society in which pluralism, non-discrimination, tolerance, justice, solidarity and equality between men and women prevail'.

[7] For an analysis of the European Community's dogged resistance to promoting human rights in external relations until 1991, see T. King, 'Human Rights in the Development Policy of the European Community' *Netherlands Yearbook of International Law* 28 (1997), 51.

[8] The best-known exposition of this analysis remains F. Fukuyama, *The End of History and the Last Man* (New York: Free Press, 1992).

triumph of human rights, democracy and the rule of law looks much less assured.[9] The evident economic success of many Asian States, most notably China, which largely reject Western interpretations of human rights and democracy, coupled with the perception that the global financial crisis is a product of the Western model, leads other states to question both the legitimacy and usefulness of human rights. Moreover, while it has often been assumed that economic development will over time lead to the growth of a middle class which will demand greater political freedoms and participation in decision-making, as in Europe, some states which are experiencing rapid economic growth seem to be pursuing a different path of development; the so-called authoritarian capitalist countries (or 'managed democracies') permit the greater part of the population substantial economic freedom while severely restricting access to information and harshly suppressing anyone who challenges the *status quo* and the position of the ruling elite.[10] At the same time, the credibility of Western discourse on human rights has been gravely undermined by flagrant violations of human rights under the guise of counter-terrorism activities ranging from the treatment of prisoners in Guantanamo and Abu Ghraib to detention in secret prisons and 'renditions', coupled with an almost complete failure to hold anyone responsible for these abuses. At the same time, growing racism and xenophobia in European societies reinforce still further perceptions of double standards. Human rights thus remains a far more contested, and hence far more challenging, issue in foreign relations than may have been foreseen when the far-reaching provisions on human rights were added to the Treaty of Maastricht.[11]

The EU has made clear that human rights are promoted not just for altruistic ethical reasons but because the EU believes that, just as the promotion of human rights within Europe has been indispensable to the creation of enduring peace and stability, in the long term the Union's security is best assured through a world composed of states which respect human rights. As the European Security Strategy notes:

---

[9] See generally S. Dennison and A. Dworkin, 'Towards an EU Human Rights Strategy for a Post-Western World', European Council on Foreign Relations Policy Brief (2010).

[10] See generally J. Kampfner, *Freedom for Sale* (London: Simon and Schuster, 2009).

[11] The Finnish Foreign Minister, Alexander Stubb, has recently expressed doubts as to whether EU human rights policy is either effective or credible, and called for the EU to display greater humility and understanding of third countries. A. Stubb, 'Adopting a Dignified Foreign Policy', *European Voice* 16(34) (2010), 13.

> Spreading good governance, supporting social and political reform, dealing with corruption, and abuse of power, establishing the rule of law and protecting human rights are the best means of strengthening the international order.[12]

The EU thus claims that realist and liberal foreign policy objectives are compatible rather than competing. However, even if in the long term the European Union would derive enormous benefits from promoting human rights, in the short term human rights remain in practice an inherently disruptive issue in relations with many countries.

Traditional diplomacy is based on the promotion of the national interest, while human rights diplomacy transcends the national. It is seen as normal diplomatic practice for any state to promote its own national interests in its external relations, even when these interests conflict with the national interests of other states. Hence when the EU wishes to negotiate a trade agreement with a third country, that third country will recognise that the EU has certain interests which it will, quite naturally, seek to promote in the negotiations; by the same token, the third country will fight for its own interests during the negotiations. Both parties recognise the other's interests as legitimate. In contrast, when the EU seeks to raise a human rights issue, the third country will usually not view the EU as pursuing its 'national' interests in the normal way.

Human rights concerns can be very roughly divided into two types. The first are issues where the EU challenges traditional, and widely-held, views in the third country. Examples include women's rights, sexual orientation and the death penalty. When these issues are raised, third countries frequently ground their arguments on cultural relativism and respect for the popular will, claiming that the EU is attempting to impose alien values on a society which does not want them. In some cases, interlocutors in third country Ministries of Foreign Affairs may even express guarded sympathy with the EU's aims on these issues but argue that popular feeling makes it impossible for them to make progress on these issues. Moreover, third countries may use these issues to warn the EU against pushing for democratic reform, claiming that any moves that the government might want to make to introduce an unpopular human rights reform supported by the EU, such as

[12] Council of the European Union, A Secure Europe in a Better World: European Security Strategy (12 December 2003).

abolition of the death penalty, would be undermined if the government were simultaneously made more accountable to the people.

The second category comprises issues which question the legitimacy of a third country government. As Conor Gearty has noted:

> The idea of human rights is a radical, emancipatory one. It should always be on the side of the underdog, perpetually trying to force an invisible individual or group of individuals into public view, giving them a language with which to shout for attention, and then having secured it to demand an end to suffering and a better set of life-chances.[13]

The EU's interlocutors are well aware of the radical implications of implementing human rights. When the EU calls on an authoritarian regime to allow greater freedom of expression or freedom of assembly for its political opponents, the EU is perceived by the regime of that country as making common cause with its own citizens who are opposed to the way in which the regime exercises its powers. The normal tools of diplomatic persuasion are of little use in such cases. In general, the best forms of persuasion are to show that the suggested course of action lies in the interests of the third country or to offer reciprocity for a concession. Unfortunately, this is often impossible in human rights diplomacy, as there is little scope to persuade a totalitarian regime that reducing the restrictions it places on its opponents would be in its best interests, nor is there much room for the EU to offer reciprocity in return for the elimination of human rights violations. In the most difficult countries, human rights diplomacy consists of advocacy of measures which both the EU and its interlocutor know would, if implemented, be fatal to the regime's survival. At worst, the EU when acting as a human rights advocate may be perceived as attempting to stir up domestic forces against the government, at best, as tiresomely self-righteous. In any event, the third country will view raising human rights issues as a form of meddling in affairs which are not the legitimate concern of the EU and which run directly counter to the interests of the ruling elite.

Human rights are also disruptive to international relations because of their principled nature. Diplomacy in general makes much use of compromise, ambiguity and secrecy, while human rights represent legal claims. The principled and rigid nature of human rights

---

[13] C. Gearty, *Can Human Rights Survive?* (Cambridge: Cambridge University Press, 2006), p.157.

arguments makes many diplomats view them with considerable suspicion. Writing in 1986, R. J. Vincent's summary of the reasons underpinning reluctance by states to raise human rights issues holds good today:

> Human rights are a subject taken up by losers as well as on behalf of them. [...] Human rights are perceived as a problem not a solution. They get in the way of ordinary diplomacy. They inhibit the flexibility necessary for operation in the world of states. They are enormously complex. Any successes are better not claimed, while failures make the front page.[14]

Many diplomats fear quite rightly that the quickest way to sour a meeting that might otherwise be cordial and productive is to put human rights issues on the agenda. Peter Baehr has noted that although the creation of departments tasked with the promotion of human rights within foreign affairs bureaucracies is intended to ensure that human rights issues are consistently fed into the formulation of policy, human rights departments in national ministries of foreign affairs (MFA) often face considerable challenges in trying to ensure that their concerns are taken on board by colleagues in geographic units in the ministry as well as by other relevant ministries, such as trade or justice.[15] Similar challenges arise at the European level. Within the Council of the European Union, the main forum for developing and implementing the EU's external human rights policy is the Council Working Group on Human Rights—generally known by its acronym COHOM–which meets at the level of heads of the human rights department of the ministries of foreign affairs of the member states. As a body composed of human rights specialists, COHOM faces the same challenge at the European level which confronts MFA human rights departments at the national level, namely how to ensure that its concerns are reflected in the decisions taken by the Council's geographic working groups which are primarily responsible for the formulation of policy towards particular countries.

If at the level of a national administration it is difficult to achieve consensus on the correct weight to give human rights in the formulation

---

[14] R. J. Vincent, *Human Rights and International Relations* (Cambridge: Cambridge University Press, 1986), pp. 136–37.

[15] P. Baehr, *The Role of Human Rights in Foreign Policy* (Basingstoke: Macmillan, 1996), pp.26-28. For discussion of the challenges faced by the Human Rights Bureau in the US State Department, see generally J. Mertus, *Bait and Switch: Human Rights and US Foreign Policy* (New York/London: Routledge, 2008).

of policy, the difficulties in achieving consensus are naturally magnified when it is also necessary to achieve agreement between the 27 member states. The degree of importance which any member state attaches to the promotion of a human rights issue with a particular third country naturally varies, depending on issues such as the member state's particular links with the third country concerned, national economic and strategic interests in the third country and the degree of pressure on human rights exerted by the domestic electorate (including diaspora communities) and civil society. This can make both achieving the initial agreement on a particular action and ensuring that all member states support the implementation of that action extremely challenging. Since EU foreign policy decisions are taken by consensus, the EU's human rights policy can proceed only at the pace of the most cautious member state. On the other hand, a collectively-decided foreign policy acts as a shield, and can enable member states to act more assertively on sensitive issues, as a member state which might be reluctant to criticise a third country if it had to act alone may be far more willing to support measures taken by the European Union as a bloc. A further difficulty is that gaps sometimes open between EU policy positions and the actions of the member states.[16] Such inconsistencies do not pass unnoticed by third countries, and do not contribute to the reputation of the EU as either a serious or a principled actor.

However, if the decision-making processes of the EU make it difficult both for the EU to adopt policy lines and to implement them consistently, these processes also provide considerable opportunities for human rights advocates to seek to influence the formulation of policy. While diplomats responsible for political or trade relations with third countries may continue to view human rights issues with some trepidation, at the same time there is sustained and vociferous external pressure on the EU institutions from European civil society and the European Parliament to pursue a more vigorous human rights policy.

[16] E.g. in advance of the 2007 elections to the Russian Duma, the EU Presidency issued a statement condemning the fact that Russian obstruction had prevented the deployment of an OSCE election observation mission, yet at the same time, at least one member state sent a message of congratulations to Russia on the elections. EU Presidency Statement on the OSCE/ODIHR Election Observation Mission to the Russian Duma Elections, 16 November 2007; and Reuters, 'EU Split on Vote after Sarkozy Calls Putin' (4 December 2007), available at: www.reuters.com [last accessed 15 December 2010].

Human rights non-governmental organisations (NGOs) such as Amnesty International, Human Rights Watch and *Federation Internationale de Droits de l'Homme* devote substantial resources to advocacy at the EU level.[17] For their part, the Commission and Council have a general policy of openness and transparency towards NGOs, which may find it significantly easier to bring their concerns to the attention of officials at the EU level than at the national level.[18] The EU has established various mechanisms for consulting NGOs, such as arranging for NGOs to brief Council working groups from time to time and holding meetings or seminars with NGOs in the margins of official human rights dialogues with third countries, which give NGOs an opportunity to make their case to EU and member state officials. Moreover, NGOs produce a continuous flow of reports and policy papers designed to influence EU policy, ranging from investigations into human rights violations in particular third countries to Amnesty International's biannual human rights recommendations to the incoming EU Presidency. Although some studies have expressed scepticism concerning the impact of NGO lobbying on EU external policy, in practice NGO activism is highly influential in ensuring that human rights concerns are constantly brought to the attention of policy-makers and constitute an important part of the decision-making process.[19]

In addition to civil society, the European Parliament, which views itself as the human rights champion among the EU institutions, both exerts continual pressure on the member states and Commission to raise human rights issues more forcefully, and also conducts its own human rights diplomacy as an independent actor.[20] In general, in national parliaments, the governing party and the majority of

[17] An informal grouping of NGOs, the Human Rights and Democracy Network, has been established to lobby the EU institutions and member states on human rights issues. For details, see: http://www.act4europe.org/code/en/about.asp?Page=41 [last accessed 15 December 2010].

[18] European Commission, An Open and Structured Dialogue between the Commission and Special Interest Groups, 93/C 63/02 (1992); General Principles and Minimum Standards for Consultation of Interested Parties by the Commission, COM (2002) 704, 11 December 2002.

[19] For a recent study of NGO influence, see C. Hansen, 'Non-Governmental Organisations and the European Union's Promotion of Human Rights in China: NGO Influence or No Influence?', *EU Diplomacy Papers* 4 (2010), College of Europe, Bruges.

[20] See generally H. Fischer, S. Lorion and G. Ulrich (eds.), *Beyond Activism: The Impact of the Resolutions and other Activities of the European Parliament in the Field of Human Rights outside the European Union* (Venice: Marsilio Editori, 2007).

members of parliament come from the same political party, which will to some extent inhibit their willingness to criticise actions of the government; in the European Parliament, there is no identity of political party interest between the Commission and the Members of the European Parliament (MEPs), who consequently feel little need to restrain their criticisms of Commission or member state actions. Moreover, the Parliament, composed of democratically-elected members, naturally sees the promotion of human rights as a fundamental part of its own identity. The Parliament has established a Sub-Committee on Human Rights which holds regular debates on the human rights situation in particular countries and the promotion of particular human rights goals, such as death penalty abolition, worldwide. MEPs submit frequent written questions to the Commission concerning particular human rights issues. Urgency debates at the Parliament's plenary session frequently concern human rights and lead to resolutions. The Parliament awards the annual Sakharov Prize for Freedom of Thought to a prominent human rights activist. Parliament adopts an annual report on human rights in the world and EU policy which is usually considerably more forthright in its criticisms of human rights violations—and of the EU's response—than the equivalent annual report issued by the Commission and Council.[21] Delegations of MEPs visiting third countries sometimes—though not always—raise human rights concerns. Parliament, whose assent is required to agreements between the European Union and third countries, has made clear that it will refuse this assent if agreements do not contain adequate safeguards for human rights.[22]

The potency of these tools varies. In 2008, the Parliament awarded the Sakharov Prize to the Chinese dissident Hu Jia; while this award had considerable symbolic value, it did not succeed in securing Mr Hu's release. On the other hand, Parliament's declaration that it will refuse its assent to any EU agreement with a third country which does not contain a human rights clause has significantly strengthened the Commission's negotiating position with third countries, as it enables the Commission to make clear that no matter how much the third country concerned may object to the inclusion of references to human

[21] E.g. European Parliament, Resolution on the Annual Report on Human Rights in the World 2008 and the European Union's Policy on the Matter (7 May 2009).

[22] European Parliament, Resolution on the Human Rights and Democracy Clause in European Union Agreements (14 February 2006), para.10.

rights in the agreement, without such references the agreement will certainly be rejected by the Parliament.[23]

The Possibilities of EU Human Rights Diplomacy

The general Treaty provisions on human rights have been fleshed out by a series of detailed guidelines adopted by the Council of the European Union on certain human rights issues, such as the death penalty or prevention of torture.[24] The guidelines set out in some detail the EU's policy goal and the possible means to achieve it. The guidelines reflect issues where there is a high degree of internal consensus between the member states, and represent an attempt to define a public strategy for how and when the EU will take steps to address a particular human rights issue. However, these guidelines do not cover many key human rights issues, such as freedom of expression, freedom of assembly or economic, social and cultural rights in general. Despite the absence of guidelines in these fields, the EU nevertheless undertakes a wide range of actions in these areas; the absence of guidelines, however, necessarily makes such actions rather more *ad hoc* than where guidelines exist.

In implementing actions under the guidelines or otherwise, the EU has much the same range of tools at its disposal to promote human rights as a state: confidential *demarches*; the summoning of an ambassador; public declarations or Council conclusions; sponsoring resolutions at the United Nations (UN) or in other international organisations such as the Organisation for Security and Co-operation in Europe (OSCE); raising human rights issues in political dialogue with third countries; linking trade incentives to human rights; conditioning certain exports upon respect for human rights; targeting financial assistance to promote human rights; criticism in the EU's annual report

[23] Parliament's insistence on the inclusion of a human rights clause has become even more significant following the entry into force of the Treaty of Lisbon. Article 218 of the revised TFEU significantly extends the range of external agreements which now require the consent of Parliament.

[24] The Council has adopted guidelines on: the death penalty; torture and other cruel, inhuman or degrading treatment or punishment; human rights dialogues with third countries; children and armed conflict; human rights defenders; promotion and protection of the rights of the child; and violence against women and children, and combating all forms of discrimination against them. Council of the European Union, Guidelines on Human Rights and International Humanitarian Law (2009).

on human rights; or—in the most extreme cases—the imposition of sanctions, possibly through suspending an EU agreement with a third country. These tools can roughly be broken down into three types: measures of criticism (e.g. *demarches*, statements, UN resolutions), persuasion (e.g. political dialogue meetings, trade conditionalities) and support for grass-roots actions (e.g. financial support for civil society).

Public criticism by the EU of human rights violations in third countries, though often barely noticed by the European media, is generally profoundly resented by third countries, who devote substantial resources to engaging in public refutations as well as vigorous private protests. From the EU's point of view, public condemnation of third countries is sometimes inevitable, particularly in response to especially egregious, shocking or persistent violations of human rights or when a third country turns a resolutely deaf ear to confidential protests. However, where human rights violations are concerned, it is far easier to make a point than a difference. Public criticism, while it may cause considerable irritation to the country condemned, is in itself not likely to promote genuine changes in behaviour. Accordingly, as far as possible, the EU prefers to make use of various forms of dialogue, persuasion and incentive when addressing human rights issues.

The EU's most notable innovation in human rights diplomacy is that it has established some forty human rights dialogues and consultations with third countries, which makes it the clear leader among like-minded countries in the use of such dialogues. Human rights dialogues are established in line with detailed Council Guidelines on Human Rights Dialogues. Human rights dialogues, which are usually held once a year at the level of senior officials, allow the EU to raise all human rights issues, ranging from freedom of expression to the death penalty to freedom of religion with the dialogue partner, to enquire what steps are being taken to address any human rights violations and to offer advice and assistance. Dialogues are held on a basis of equality, with the dialogue partner having the opportunity to raise human rights concerns within the EU.

The Guidelines on Human Rights Dialogues provide that, before a dialogue is established, an assessment must be made of the extent to which the government of the country concerned is willing to improve the human rights situation, the degree of commitment shown by the government in respect of international human rights conventions, the government's willingness to co-operate with United Nations human rights mechanisms and the government's attitude towards civil society.[25] Although these criteria indicate that dialogues should be established only with countries that show at least some willingness to address human rights problems, in practice human rights dialogues have been established even with countries where the human rights situation is extremely difficult. Moreover, the benchmarks for measuring progress in the dialogue remain confidential, as do the EU's periodic evaluations of the dialogues.[26] Analysis of the human rights dialogues has often been critical. Karen Smith has argued that 'it is difficult not to view them [EU human rights dialogues] as a cover for inaction',[27] while the European Parliament has called for more transparency to enable a better assessment of whether the dialogues are actually producing changes in the behaviour of the partner countries.[28] In particular, the Parliament has called for benchmarks to be made public, for the Council and Commission to identify more clearly the objectives of each dialogue and for clear criteria to be set for the termination of a dialogue when it is not producing results.

As a rule of thumb, whether an EU human rights dialogue is productive depends simply upon the extent of political will on the other side of the table. At their best, human rights dialogues allow officials from the ministries of the dialogue partner to meet EU counterparts to exchange best practice, to listen to EU questions and to identify possible solutions to which the EU can contribute through technical assistance, training or projects. Human rights dialogues can act as a useful forum in which to expose officials from ministries other than foreign affairs, such as ministries of interior, security, justice, health or women, who in general will have limited contact with international bodies, to EU concerns and thus to increase the pressure for legislative or administrative change. In some cases, officials may be disarmingly frank about the challenges they face—frequently financial ones—in attempting to improve respect for human rights, and request EU assistance.

[25] EU Guidelines on Human Rights Dialogues, 2001, para.4.

[26] In contrast, an assessment of the Canada-China human rights dialogue, which led to the discontinuation of the dialogue, has been made public. See 'Assessment of the Canada-China Bilateral Human Rights Dialogue', available at: http://spartan.ac.brocku.ca/~cburton/ [last accessed 15 December 2010].

[27] Smith, *European Union Foreign Policy*, 2008, p.135.

[28] European Parliament, Resolution on Human Rights Dialogues and Consultations with Third Countries (6 September 2007).

Human rights dialogues represent a particularly useful forum for identifying EU technical assistance projects to improve human rights. In response to requests made by third countries, the Commission has, for example, been able to programme projects to support police training with a view to improving interrogation and detention practices or developing investigative techniques based on forensic science with a view to reducing torture.

On the other hand, at their worst, human rights dialogues can consist of stonewalling, long-winded presentations in minute detail of national legislation (which both sides know is not implemented in practice) and vociferous attacks on human rights violations—some real, some imaginary—in the European Union. Yet—with the exception of Iran—not even the most unconstructive dialogue partner has ever sought to bring to an end a human rights dialogue with the EU. The willingness of even countries which are largely deaf to the EU's human rights concerns to persist in holding annual human rights dialogues indicates that even the most authoritarian states feel the need at least to appear to take human rights seriously. Moreover, given the EU's very clear public commitment to human rights, third countries are aware that the EU will inevitably attempt to raise human rights with them in some form of political dialogue and may calculate that it is preferable to concentrate discussion of human rights in one annual human rights dialogue with the EU in order to prevent human rights from 'contaminating' other political dialogue meetings. The resilience of human rights dialogues even with difficult partner countries thus demonstrates the extent to which human rights has become an unavoidable component of EU foreign policy. For its part, the EU strenuously attempts to avoid discussion of human rights becoming confined to human rights dialogues. The Guidelines on Human Rights Dialogues make clear that even when a human rights dialogue has been established, the EU will continue to raise human rights issues in other political dialogue meetings.[29] Third countries may also claim that the establishment of a dialogue with the EU means that they no longer need to co-operate with the various UN human rights mechanisms. This is an argument which the EU firmly refutes, as in its view an EU human rights dialogue is intended to encourage and support

[29] EU Guidelines on Human Rights Dialogues, 2001, para.9.

co-operation between third countries and the UN, and certainly not to supplant such co-operation.

While the EU has established human rights dialogues with some forty countries, it conditions its general contractual relationship with all third countries on respect for human rights. Since 1995, it has been EU policy that all EU framework agreements (such as Association Agreements or Partnership and Co-operation Agreements) concluded with third countries should include a human rights clause, which provides that respect for human rights, democracy and the rule of law constitutes the basis for the agreement and represents an essential element of the agreement.[30] This policy has considerable symbolic value, as no like-minded state so consistently inserts human rights references into its treaties with third countries. So far, the EU has obtained agreement to a human rights clause from 134 countries.[31] Such a policy has its costs. In order to secure the inclusion of the human rights clause, the EU often has to make concessions during negotiations on other important clauses in the agreement, while in other cases the EU's insistence on the human rights clause has entirely prevented the conclusion of an agreement with a third country. In the late 1990's, for example, negotiations for an agreement with Australia broke down as a result of Australia's refusal to accept the human rights clause.[32] On the other hand, as the EU does not require that a country meet a minimum standard of respect for human rights before an agreement containing a human rights clause can be signed, this policy is open to the criticism that it can give a spurious legitimacy to third countries which in reality are far from ensuring respect for human rights. The conclusion of agreements containing human rights clauses which commit the parties to respect for human rights with countries which are well known, at the time of concluding the agreement, to have a deplorable human rights record has led the European Parliament to call for the EU to conclude such agreements only with countries which respect

[30] European Commission, Communication on the inclusion of respect for democratic principles and human rights in agreements between the Community and third countries, COM (95) 216 (23 May 1995). The standard wording of the clause is: 'Respect for human rights, democratic principles and the rule of law, which underpin the Partnership, shall underpin the domestic and international policies of the Parties and constitute the essential elements of this Agreement.'

[31] A database of EU agreements containing the human rights clause is available at: http://ec.europa.eu/world/agreements/default.home.do [last accessed 15 December 2010].

[32] See King, *Human Rights in EU Development Policy*, 1997, p. 97.

human rights in practice at the time of signature.[33] The potential for the human rights clause to be misinterpreted was illustrated in *Saadi v Italy*, when Italy argued before the European Court of Human Rights that because the EU had concluded an Association Agreement with Tunisia containing a human rights clause, it could be assumed that Tunisia respected human rights and thus a person deported to Tunisia could be certain that he would not face torture or cruel, inhuman or degrading treatment; this interpretation of the clause was rightly rejected by the Court.[34]

Although the human rights clause constitutes the legal basis for sanctions in the case of serious violations of human rights in the partner country, it has been invoked only sparingly. The EU has relied on the clause twenty times as the basis for sanctions—usually after a *coup d'etat*, severely flawed elections or widespread and egregious human rights violations—and only in respect of African, Caribbean and Pacific countries under the Cotonou Agreement.[35] The European Parliament has criticised the Commission for a timorous approach to the application of the human rights clause in practice, arguing that clear criteria should be set to assess whether a third country is meeting its obligations under the clause and that sanctions should be imposed when countries fall short.[36] For its part, the Commission has taken the view that the principal value of a human rights clause is to demonstrate the shared commitment of the parties to human rights, and that sanctions under the clause should be reserved only for the most extreme and flagrant violations of human rights.

As the world's largest trading bloc, the EU evidently has enormous but as yet unfulfilled potential to use trade policy to promote human

[33] European Parliament, Resolution on the Human Rights and Democracy Clause in European Union Agreements (14 February 2006), para.3.

[34] ECtHR, *Saadi v Italy*, Application No 37201/06 (28 February 2008), para.112: 'Tunisia had also signed an association agreement with the European Union. A precondition for implementation of that agreement was respect for fundamental freedoms and democratic principles. The European Union was an international organisation which, according to the Court's case-law, was presumed to provide a level of protection of fundamental rights "equivalent" to that provided by the Convention. In the Government's submission, it could be presumed that Tunisia would not default on its obligations under international treaties.'

[35] See generally European Parliament, Directorate-General for External Policies of the Union, Policy Department, 'Political Dialogue and Human Rights in the Framework of the Cotonou Agreement', (2007).

[36] European Parliament, Resolution on the Human Rights and Democracy Clause in European Union Agreements (14 February 2006), paras.2, 4 and 12.

rights. The main instrument used to link human rights to trade policy is the Generalised System of Preferences (GSP).[37] Under the GSP Regulation, access to the basic GSP scheme may be withdrawn from beneficiary countries in the case of serious and systematic violation of principles laid down in the core UN human rights treaties and International Labour Organisation (ILO) Conventions, even if the state concerned is not party to those instruments. The Commission has used this power very rarely, and only in response to grave violations of ILO standards rather than human rights more generally. Two countries have been suspended from access to the GSP, namely Burma/Myanmar in 1997 for systematic use of slave labour, and Belarus in 2006 for serious breaches of the right to freedom of association.[38]

While withdrawal of access to the GSP is thus a sanction reserved for exceptionally grave abuses in countries which are not amenable to dialogue, the GSP Regulation also establishes an incentive scheme, known as the GSP+ scheme, whereby countries that ratify and undertake effectively to implement the core ILO and UN human rights conventions are eligible to benefit from supplementary reductions in import tariffs. The Regulation makes clear that the financial benefits flowing from access to GSP+ are an incentive intended to compensate the beneficiary country for the costs it incurs through its implementation of obligations under the human rights conventions.[39] Should it become clear that a beneficiary country is in fact not effectively implementing its obligations under the core UN human rights conventions, the EU can, following an investigation to ascertain the facts, withdraw access to GSP+ benefits. The effect of withdrawal of GSP+ benefits has proven variable. In 2009, the Commission opened an investigation into El Salvador, following a judgment of the El Salvador Supreme Court that El Salvador's ratification of ILO Convention No 87 was

[37] Regulation (EC) No 732/2008 of 22 July 2008 applying a scheme of generalised tariff preferences for the period from 1 January 2009 to 31 December 2011, OJ L 211/2008, p.1.

[38] Regulation (EC) No 1933/2006 of 21 December 2006 temporarily withdrawing access to the generalised tariff preferences from the Republic of Belarus, OJ L 4056/2006, p.35.

[39] Recital 8 to the Regulation provides: 'Consequently, additional tariff preferences should be granted to those developing countries which, due to a lack of diversification and insufficient integration into the international trading system, are vulnerable while assuming the special burdens and responsibilities resulting from the ratification and effective implementation of core international conventions on human and labour rights, environmental protection and good governance.'

unconstitutional. The prospect of loss of access to GSP+ benefits appears to have been instrumental in persuading the El Salvadorian government to take steps to amend the Constitution so as to render ratification of the Convention constitutional.[40] On the other hand, a Commission proposal to withdraw access to the GSP+ from Sri Lanka, following an investigation which had found widespread violations of the International Covenant on Civil and Political Rights (ICCPR),[41] the Convention against Torture (CAT)[42] and the Convention on the Rights of the Child (CRC),[43] was not sufficient to persuade the Sri Lankan Government to take adequate steps to address the violations identified by the investigation. In consequence, Sri Lanka was temporarily suspended from the GSP+ scheme in August 2010.[44]

The EU has adopted a number of other measures which link trade and human rights, such as adopting a regulation prohibiting the export or import of goods which have no other use than the imposition of capital punishment or torture or cruel, inhuman or degrading treatment, and conditioning the export of military equipment upon respect for human rights in the country of destination.[45] However, these rather piecemeal measures fall well short of a comprehensive policy linking trade and human rights, even though Article 207(1) Treaty on the Functioning of the EU (TFEU) provides that the common commercial policy shall be conducted in the context of the principles and objectives of the EU's external actions, which include the promotion of human rights. A comprehensive approach to linking trade and human

[40] European Commission, Report of the Investigation pursuant to Article 18(2) of Council Regulation (EC) No 980/2005 with respect to the protection of the freedom of association and the right to organise in El Salvador, C(2009) 7934 (2009).

[41] 1966 International Covenant on Civil and Political Rights (ICCPR), UNGA Res 2200A (XXI) (1966), UN Doc A/RES/2200 XXI (A) (16 December 1966), 999 UNTS 171; entered into force 23 March 1976.

[42] 1984 Convention against Torture and Other Cruel, Inhuman or Degrading Treatment or Punishment (CAT), 1465 UNTS 85; entered into force 26 June 1987.

[43] 1989 UN Convention on the Rights of the Child (CRC), 1577 UNTS 3 (CRC); entered into force 2 September 1990.

[44] Implementing Regulation (EU) No 143/2010 of 15 February 2010 temporarily withdrawing the special incentive arrangement for sustainable development and good governance provided for under Regulation (EC) No 732/2008 with respect to the Democratic Socialist Republic of Sri Lanka, OJ L 45/2010, p.1.

[45] Regulation 1236/2005 concerning trade in certain goods which could be used for capital punishment, torture or other cruel, inhuman or degrading treatment or punishment, OJ L 200/2005, p.1. Council Common Position 2008/944/CFSP of 8 December 2008 defining common rules governing control of exports of military technology and equipment, OJ L 335/2008, p.99.

rights would have to cover issues as diverse as considering to what extent all EU trade agreements (and not merely GSP+) should be made conditional upon the partner country ratifying and implementing core human rights conventions, developing a methodology (sometimes known as human rights impact assessments) to analyse to what extent EU trade agreements may undermine human rights in the partner country (for example, economic liberalisation measures may endanger access by the poor to basic services such as water or sanitation), establishing a policy to regulate the export of goods which can be used for repressive purposes (such as data mining technology or CCTV cameras) from the EU to authoritarian countries and establishing a coherent approach to regulating imports of goods made by prison, slave or child labour or from conflict zones. Although these issues are gaining greater prominence, not least due to sustained pressure from the European Parliament, the EU is still quite some way from designing all aspects of its trade policy so as to promote human rights in third countries.[46]

The EU complements its efforts directed at official interlocutors with a range of activities to support civil society in third countries, which reflects the EU's general policy of working with civil society partners both internally and externally. The EU holds an annual NGO forum, bringing together both EU and non-EU NGOs, which produces recommendations—often highly critical—concerning the role of human rights in EU foreign policy.[47] Human rights dialogues, which are confidential meetings held between officials, are usually accompanied by public civil society seminars held in the margins of the dialogue.[48] These seminars bring together representatives of civil society from the EU and the partner country to discuss a particular human rights issue, such as children's rights or the prevention of torture. Civil society seminars are intended to create a more open and informal forum for discussion of sensitive issues than the official dialogue itself and also to enable civil society activists from the EU and the third

---

[46] E.g. European Parliament, Committee on International Trade, Report on human rights and social and environmental standards in international trade agreements (2009/2219(INI)) Rapporteur: Tokia Saïfi, (26 October 2010).

[47] A summary of the annual NGO Forum is available at: http://www.humanrightsngoforum.eu/ [last accessed 15 December 2010].

[48] EU Guidelines on Human Rights Dialogues, para.7 reads: 'Civil society could become involved […] in the conduct of the dialogue itself (particularly by organising meetings with civil society at local level in parallel with the formal dialogue)'.

country concerned to forge links. In practice, involving civil society representatives in the margins of human rights dialogues is fraught with difficulty as civil society representatives are able and willing to speak far more forthrightly than normal diplomatic practice allows. Officials from authoritarian third countries—naturally unused to being the targets of blunt criticism from civil society—are not always entirely at ease in meetings where their country's policies are subject to vigorous denunciation, which has led in some cases to the cancellation or postponement of civil society events.[49]

A particularly innovative feature of the EU's support for civil society in third countries is the European Instrument for Democracy and Human Rights (EIDHR), under which each year the EU provides some € 130 million of financial support to civil society organisations working outside the EU to promote human rights.[50] Unlike almost all of the EU's external financial assistance which is provided directly to governments, the EIDHR provides financial grants direct to NGOs without the intervention in any way of the government of the country concerned.[51] In the Commission's words:

> The EIDHR builds on the work being done with and through civil society organisations aimed at defending the fundamental freedoms which form the basis for all democratic processes and helping civil society to become an effective force for political reform and defence of human rights.[52]

The EIDHR is intended to complement the financial assistance provided directly to governments for projects to promote human rights—such as the projects for police reform mentioned above—with smaller projects implemented by grass-roots organisations. The Commission has argued that human rights cannot be promoted solely through

[49] In 2007, the Chinese delegation walked out of the civil society seminar held in the margins of the EU-China human rights dialogue in protest at the presence of 'anti-government organisations'. China Labour Bulletin, 'Chinese delegation walks out of human rights dialogue meeting with the European Union over the participation of China Labour Bulletin and Human Rights in China', available at: http://www.china-labour/org.hk/public/contents/news [last accessed 15 December 2010].

[50] Regulation (EC) No 1889/2006 establishing a financing instrument for the promotion of democracy and human rights worldwide, OJ L 386/2006, p. 1. See generally, EIDHR Strategy Paper 2011-2013, C(2010)2432 (21 April 2010).

[51] The EIDHR also provides limited funding to international human rights mechanisms such as the International Criminal Court and funds EU election observation missions.

[52] EIDHR Strategy Paper 2011-2013, para.2.

dialogue with governments; financial support for civil society is essential 'to help empower citizens, to allow them to claim their rights and to sustain momentum for change and political reform'.[53]

Authoritarian regimes in third countries, however, often view financial support for national civil society organisations rather differently; the EU is seen as providing financial support for their principal domestic opponents. Recent years have seen increasing efforts in many countries to restrict the activities of NGOs. These restrictions take the form of introducing extremely onerous registration and reporting requirements for NGOs, establishing very restrictive rules controlling foreign funding for NGOs, prohibiting NGOs from engaging in political activities or 'supporting an ideological tendency', placing limitations on NGOs' contacts with foreigners, aggressive use of criminal defamation laws against NGOs or simply not allowing NGOs to operate at all.[54] Increasing constraints on independent NGOs in many countries have been accompanied by a growth in the number of organisations which are ostensibly NGOs but which in reality are controlled by, or are highly sympathetic to, the government (sometimes known as GONGOs). Authoritarian third countries deploy these organisations strategically to burnish the image of the government at home and abroad. GONGOs are encouraged to praise their government's human rights achievements in international forums, such as the UN Human Rights Council's Universal Periodic Review or the OSCE Human Dimension Implementation Meeting. Their activities give the impression that domestic civil society applauds the government's human rights record, so undermining the legitimacy of criticisms made by genuinely independent domestic or Western NGOs and by the EU. Both the tightening of restrictions on genuinely independent NGOs and the growth of GONGOs may, in part, be seen as a reaction to the success of schemes such as the EIDHR in supporting effective and vigorous grass-roots movements worldwide.

---

[53] *Ibid.*, para.13.

[54] A summary of measures worldwide against NGOs can be found in: 'Restrictions on Foreign Funding of NGOs', *International Journal of Not-for-Profit Law* 11(4) (2009), 5; and *International Journal of Not-for-Profit Law* 12(3) (2010), 6; and in 'Barred from the Debate; Restrictions on NGO Public Policy Activities' *Global Trends in NGO Law* 1(3) (2009).

The Limitations of EU Human Rights Diplomacy

The EU's sheer size and its weight as a trading partner and financial donor give it great potential as a human rights actor. But any value-based foreign policy is vulnerable to charges of inconsistency. All states face difficulties in ensuring consistency in three ways: between internal and external policies; between external policy areas; and between actors. These challenges are magnified at the level of the EU.

Any international actor which preaches values to others must, to be credible, ensure that its own house is in impeccable order. The fact that responsibility for accession to, and implementation of, international human rights conventions rests with the member states rather than with the EU as an international organisation gives rise to inconsistencies, as policies agreed at EU level are not always fully reflected at the national level. The various EU guidelines on human rights task the EU to call on third countries to accede to certain UN human rights instruments to which not all member states are themselves party; the Optional Protocol to the UN Convention against Torture[55] is a notable example.[56] A particularly sore point with third countries is that while the EU repeatedly emphasises the universality of human rights standards, no EU member state has acceded to the UN Convention on the Rights of All Migrant Workers,[57] even though the United Nations considers this a core human rights convention. Implementation by the EU member states of the recommendations of international human rights monitoring bodies also shows a mixed picture. To take only two examples, when confronted with allegations of torture or extra-judicial killing by state authorities in third countries, the EU frequently urges the holding of an independent investigation. Yet, despite repeated recommendations by UN monitoring committees and judgments of the European Court of Human Rights, many member states have not

[55] 2002 Optional Protocol to the Convention against Torture and Other Cruel, Inhuman or Degrading Treatment or Punishment (OP-CAT), UNGA Res 57/199 (2003), UN Doc A/RES/57/199 (9 January 2003), 2375 UNTS 237; entered into force 22 June 2006.

[56] EU Guidelines on Torture, section III: 'The EU will urge third countries to [...] give favourable consideration to accession to the OP-CAT'.

[57] 1990 Convention on the Protection of the Rights of All Migrant Workers and Members of Their Families (CMW), UNGA Res 45/158 (1990), UN Doc A/RES/45/158 (18 December 1990), 2220 UNTS 3; entered into force 1 July 2003.

established independent bodies to investigate complaints against the police. The deaths of numerous migrants in the Mediterranean as they attempt to reach Europe in small boats raises considerable doubts as to how actively the member states have sought to safeguard the right to life. Demonstrable failure by the EU member states to meet the standards they urge on others naturally blunts the EU's international credibility.

The second difficulty that the EU faces in its human rights diplomacy is ensuring coherence across policy areas. Although states face similar difficulties, the enormous range of policies conducted at EU level creates a particular challenge. Despite the importance given in the Treaties to the promotion of human rights in external relations, the Commission's Work Programme for 2010, which includes a substantial section on external relations, makes no mention of human rights in this context.[58] Policies in the area of Justice, Freedom and Security pose especially significant human rights dilemmas. The EU clearly has legitimate interests in strengthening co-operation with third countries on fighting organised crime, on controlling illegal migration and on developing judicial co-operation. Yet how far can the EU go in forging links with police forces and judiciaries in authoritarian countries? There is always a danger, for example, that technical assistance provided to help detect sophisticated organised criminals could, in the wrong hands, be turned against human rights defenders or that reinforcing co-operation on border management with authoritarian countries could make it impossible for human rights defenders in danger to flee the country. The Stockholm Programme, adopted by the Council in December 2009, which sets out the framework for policies in the area of Justice, Freedom and Security for the next five years, demonstrated growing awareness of these dilemmas by calling for the EU to adopt an action plan on human rights issues in the external dimension of these policies.[59]

---

[58] European Commission, Commission Work Programme 2010 - Time to Act, COM(2010) 135 (31 March 2010).

[59] Council of the European Union, The Stockholm Programme—An Open and Secure Europe Serving and Protecting the Citizens, 17024/09 (2 December 2009). The Programme called for the establishment of a Human Rights Action Plan to promote its values in the external dimension of Justice, Freedom and Security policies. This Plan should be examined by the European Council and should take into account that internal and external aspects of human rights are interlinked, for instance as regards the principle of *non-refoulement* or the use of the death penalty by partners that the Union cooperates with.

The third danger for human rights diplomacy is that it can become the victim of its own success, as there is a risk that exchanges on human rights issues become the preserve of specialists and thus distanced from the mainstream of foreign relations. The EU and its member states have established an extensive range of diplomatic tools with which to promote human rights and a group of human rights specialists has developed, within the EU institutions and the member state foreign ministries, as well as within third country foreign ministries and international organisations. The challenge for the EU is to ensure that human rights issues do not remain the exclusive preserve of these human rights specialists but are raised consistently with third countries, including at the highest political level. Confining discussion of human rights to exchanges between specialists has the potential to send the message to third countries that the EU's interest in human rights abroad is rather limited. If the EU makes a *demarche* to the ministry of foreign affairs of a third country protesting at the unjustified trial and imprisonment of a human rights defender, and the same point is not raised at subsequent foreign minister meetings or at summits, the country concerned may well form the view that in reality the EU attaches little importance to the issue. Human rights may thus become a technical issue for discussion between specialists, with third countries calculating that in reality there are few political costs for violations of human rights.

The EU attempts to avoid these pitfalls through pursuing a strategy of 'mainstreaming' human rights, that is, developing 'a strategic pro cess of incorporating human rights considerations into processes and structures that are not explicitly mandated to deal with human rights'.[60] This process was launched by the Commission's 2001 Communication on Human Rights in External Relations, and subsequently the Council has adopted ambitious guidelines designed to ensure that human rights are taken into account across the EU's external relations.[61] The Council identified fifty-two ways in which promotion of human rights should be mainstreamed, including the need to raise human rights at the highest political levels and not only at expert meetings,

[60] European Parliament, DG for External Policies, Human Rights Mainstreaming in the EU's External Relations, EXPO/B/DROI/2008/6 (6 September 2009), p.4.

[61] European Commission, The European Union's Role in Promoting Human Rights and Democratisation in Third Countries, (2001); Council of the European Union, Mainstreaming Human Rights across CFSP and other EU Policies, 10076/06 (7 June 2006).

establishing stronger links between EU financial assistance to third countries and the promotion of human rights and intensifying still further contacts with civil society in third countries. A recent study of the effectiveness of mainstreaming has concluded that while 'the Commission and Council have a solid understanding of the concept', much remains to be done in implementation.[62] In particular, the study argued that while many EU official documents support mainstreaming and a human rights-based approach to external relations polices, these declarations were frequently not accompanied by operational measures.

Apart from these difficulties, the most frequent and obvious criticism made of EU human rights diplomacy is that the EU often chooses to promote its economic or strategic interests with third countries at the expense of human rights or that it is selective in its approach. Such criticism may partly reflect the fact that the EU's own rhetoric, which repeatedly emphasises the EU's attachment to human rights but more rarely mentions the EU's strategic or economic interests, has inflated public expectations of how much the EU can or will influence human rights developments in third countries. Moreover, human rights diplomacy is an inherently paradoxical concept, mixing together the absolutes of legal claims to rights with the nuances and ambiguities of diplomacy. As a diplomatic actor, the EU will never be able to pursue a policy based solely on human rights concerns; the most that can be expected is that policy-makers will take human rights into account as an important and legitimate aim to be weighed carefully in the balance when deciding on external policies.

[62] European Parliament, Human Rights Mainstreaming in the EU's External Relations, 2009.

CHAPTER 7

HUMAN RIGHTS DIPLOMACY AND THE COUNCIL OF EUROPE COMMISSIONER FOR HUMAN RIGHTS

Thomas Hammarberg and Isil Gachet

When the Council of Europe celebrated its 50th Anniversary in May 1999 it decided to set up a new and independent institution: a Commissioner for Human Rights.

The main objectives were defined in a resolution by the Committee of Ministers:[1]

- foster the effective observance and enjoyment of human rights;
- assist member states in the implementation of Council of Europe human rights standards;
- identify possible shortcomings in the law and practice of member states concerning the compliance with human rights as embodied in the instruments of the Council of Europe, promote the effective implementation of these standards by member states and assist them, with their agreement, in their efforts to remedy such shortcomings;
- promote education in and awareness of human rights in member states;
- facilitate the activities of national ombudspersons and other human rights structures; and
- provide advice and information regarding the protection of human rights.

The Mandate

In discussions when this decision was being prepared, the intergovernmental steering committee on human rights noted that the

[1] Committee of Ministers, Resolution (99)50 on the Council of Europe Commissioner for Human Rights (7 May 1999). The text of the resolution is appended to this article.

Commissioner would not assume a judicial role, but rather pay attention through other means to problems of compliance with the human rights standards of the Council of Europe.

When identifying possible shortcomings, the Commissioner would be able to draw on the findings of the various treaty organs of the Council of Europe, but the basis of his/her action would not be limited to those. The Commissioner would have sufficient flexibility to play an early warning role if need be.

The advisory role of the Commissioner was to be a key element. The resolution stipulates that the Commissioner 'shall provide advice and information on the protection of human rights and the prevention of human rights violations'.[2] This provision does not specify to whom such advice might be addressed in order not to restrict unnecessarily the work of the Commissioner. However, it is clear that both the public authorities, including governments and parliaments, and the public are among the potential addressees of advice and information.

Another important feature of the agreed mandate was that the Commissioner should *not* deal with individual complaints. When the draft terms of reference were submitted to the Parliamentary Assembly for its opinion the latter proposed that the Commissioner be allowed to deal exceptionally with individual cases provided that they were not already before the Court or likely to be the object of an application before it.[3] However, because of the importance of the 'non-interference principle' this amendment was not confirmed by the Committee of Ministers.

The need for *independence* and *impartiality* was to be a key element for the effective action of the Commissioner. The election by the Parliamentary Assembly and the requirements in the resolution about the personal qualities of the candidates as well as the non-renewable term of office correspond to this priority.[4]

In light of the promotional, preventive and flexible nature of the institution, publicity would be an important feature. The Commissioner would be able to issue reports and to provide recommendations or opinions.

---

[2] *Ibid.*, Article 3(d).

[3] Parliamentary Assembly, Council of Europe Commissioner for Human Rights: Draft Terms of Reference, Opinion 210 (1999) of 29 January 1999.

[4] Committee of Ministers, Resolution (99)50 on the Council of Europe Commissioner for Human Rights (7 May 1999), Articles 10 and 11.

Due to the personalised character of the institution and the wide and fairly vague terms of reference, it was clear from the beginning that the mandate in practice would depend upon the interpretation of the post holder. These issues will be explored in the following sections. However, one can immediately note that the actual interpretation of the mandate by the two office holders so far—as demonstrated by their activities—has been broadly supported by both the Parliamentary Assembly and the Committee of Ministers. For instance, the response to the annual reports submitted by the Office has been overwhelmingly positive.

Without interfering with the independence of the Office, the Committee of Ministers and the Parliamentary Assembly later recommended to the Commissioner to take on some further tasks. In January 2004, the Committee of Ministers adopted a Declaration on the protection of human rights during armed conflicts, internal disturbances and tensions in which it commended the activities already undertaken and

> encourage[d] the Commissioner to continue to pay particular attention to situations where there is a threat or where there are allegations of serious and massive violations of human rights, notably by further developing fact-finding and the formulation of targeted recommendations to which appropriate follow up should be given.[5]

Likewise, the Commissioner was asked by the Committee in February 2008 to take the role as the main regional mechanism to strengthen the protection of human rights defenders and to promote their activities.[6]

Relations between the Commissioner and Governments

The main focus of the Commissioner's work is placed on assisting governments in their implementation of human rights standards. Member states have undertaken to respect a wide range of human rights through their adhesion to European and international instruments. The Commissioner builds on these standards, the case-law of the European

---

[5] Committee of Ministers, Declaration on the Protection of Human Rights During Armed Conflict, Internal Disturbances and Tensions (21 January 2004), para.12.

[6] Committee of Ministers, Declaration on Council of Europe Action to Improve the Protection of Human Rights Defenders and Promote Their Activities (6 February 2008), para.4.

Court of Human Rights, and the general comments and concluding observations of United Nations (UN) human rights treaty bodies, in seeking dialogue with all European governments with the objective of assisting them in fully complying with the agreed standards. Although human rights are ingrained in the European experience, the Commissioner has found that there is still a gap between political rhetoric and reality when it comes to implementing the agreed rights.

The impartiality and independence of the Commissioner are crucial preconditions to his dialogue with governments. The Commissioner avoids negative politicisation and any kind of ranking of governments. On the basis of well-tested facts, he provides constructive advice to all governments on how to improve the human rights situation in their country. It is equally important that the Commissioner be ready to voice criticism where necessary. The purpose of such criticism is to help identify the actual problems in order for them to be addressed.

The Commissioner encourages the governments of member states to address structural aspects in a systematic and sustainable manner. Some countries have sought to review all aspects of human rights implementation in a comprehensive way by means of a consultative process leading up to a national action plan on human rights adopted by their parliament. This is a practice which the Commissioner has supported.

The Commissioner's permanent dialogue with member states has taken the form of country visits for a comprehensive assessment of the human rights situation in each member state of the Council of Europe. The assessment visits typically last one week or more, and include meetings with the highest representatives of government, parliament and the judiciary, as well as with leading members of human rights protection institutions and civil society.

The Commissioner also visits institutions and sites with particular human rights relevance such as prisons, police stations, shelters for victims of violence, facilities for accommodating asylum-seekers, psychiatric institutions and schools. An element of fact-finding is, therefore, also an integral part of these country visits. The visits enable the Commissioner to assess local realities and exchange good practice, while entering into direct contact with national authorities.

In 2008, the current Commissioner completed the full cycle of broad assessment missions which were begun by his predecessor. During the past decade all 47 member states have been visited for the purpose of a comprehensive human rights appraisal.

Assessment visits have led to the drafting of an assessment report which contains both an analysis of the human rights situation in the country in question and detailed recommendations about possible means of improvement. The governments may submit comments on the final report to the Commissioner, which are then appended to the report when it is published on the Commissioner's website.[7]

The assessment reports were presented to the Council of Europe's Committee of Ministers and the Parliamentary Assembly. The Committee of Ministers has held a discussion on each report and the Commissioner has published the reports on the day of their presentation to the Committee of Ministers. The reports have been widely circulated in the policy-making and non-governmental organisations (NGO) community, as well as to the media.

Yet there is also a need for a more continuous dialogue with the governments of member states and other stakeholders to ensure that the Commissioner's recommendations are followed up and that sufficient attention is paid to acute human rights problems. When not travelling to member states, the Commissioner regularly receives visiting national officials to discuss the implementation of the report's recommendations.

Where appropriate, the Commissioner has also made visits with a more focused agenda to maintain contact or address specific concerns, such as the special visit to Bosnia and Herzegovina in December 2006 to look into the issue of the rights of police officers who had been 'decertified' by the UN without a genuine possibility of appeal.

In addition, the Commissioner's Office has carried out follow-up visits to member states in order to report on the progress made in implementing the Commissioner's recommendations. The Commissioner has issued follow-up reports as a result of such visits for a number of member states.

Upon the completion of the full cycle of comprehensive assessment visits to every member state in 2009, the Commissioner developed an approach of focused visits with the aim of defining key problems and issuing more precise recommendations. Reporting has been adapted to the new approach: it is shorter, more focused and the reports are published soon after the visit. While the Commissioner continues to

---

[7] Available at: http://www.coe.int/t/commissioner/Activities/countryreports_en.asp [last accessed 8 March 2011].

assist all member states in their endeavours to implement human rights standards, the new approach also allows for a more flexible schedule of visits including more frequent and prompt visits to countries where needs and expectations for assistance may be higher.

Moreover, the Commissioner has enhanced his capacity to react rapidly to developments which may affect human rights in member states, thus functioning increasingly as a rapid response mechanism. His work in crisis and conflict situations is a case in point, and is discussed later on in this paper.

In addition to a bilateral human rights dialogue with individual member states, the Commissioner actively contributes to the shaping of human rights policies in Europe more generally. Through the presentation of his quarterly and annual reports to the Committee of Ministers, the Commissioner encourages multilateral debate on shared human rights concerns and various national responses to them.

Such an approach facilitates peer review of human rights questions and promotes shared strategies for progress. Moreover, the Commissioner's thematic reports, recommendations, opinions, issue papers and viewpoints, as well as his participation in debates during the Council's ministerial conferences are tools for providing advice and indicators to all member states for the implementation of human rights standards. The Commissioner's advice is also often sought by expert committees working under the authority of the Committee of Ministers.

Relations with Other Key Actors at National Level

Resolution 99(50) requests that the Commissioner 'shall, wherever possible, make use of and co-operate with human rights structures in the member states'[8] and where such structures do not exist, the Commissioner will encourage their establishment. The Commissioner shall also 'facilitate the activities of national ombudsmen or similar institutions'.[9] National ombudsmen and human rights institutions have become obvious partners for the Commissioner at national level.

---

[8] Committee of Ministers, Resolution (99)50 on the Council of Europe Commissioner for Human Rights (7 May 1999), Article 3(c).

[9] *Ibid.*, Article 3(d).

From the very beginnings of the institution, the Commissioner has endeavoured to work closely with ombudsmen. In his first annual report in 2001, the Commissioner underlined that his

> main concern, at this early stage, has been to establish the necessary links with the structures working in the domain of the protection and promotion of human rights... To this end I have [he has] organised meetings with Ombudsmen with the intention of establishing the necessary cooperative ties.[10]

Meetings with groups of ombudsmen became a standard and regular fixture in the Commissioner's annual calendar. Due to the equal importance of regional ombudsmen, the Commissioner proposed to organise separate meetings with these institutions that focused specifically on their concerns.

Co-operation with national human rights structures, which were beginning to play an increasingly important role in the promotion of human rights at national level, was also developed during the course of the first Commissioner's mandate.

This co-operation has proved to be particularly important in the light of the many individual complaints addressed to the Commissioner, but which he is unable to pursue. Serious complaints may be referred to a national ombudsman where the Commissioner feels that this would be appropriate. In effect, the first-hand experience of national ombudsmen makes them essential interlocutors for the effectiveness of the Commissioner's visits.

The Commissioner has been particularly active in the promotion of ombudsmen offices, national human rights centres or institutes and equality bodies where these do not yet exist. For example, in 2002, the Commissioner co-operated with the Venice Commission in the organisation of seminars on ombudsman institutions in Armenia and Azerbaijan to assist in the setting-up of institutions there. In 2003, the Commissioner started an ambitious project to help establish ombudsmen institutions in the regions of the Russian Federation. For the promotion of the ombudsman institution in South-Eastern Europe, the Commissioner received generous support from the 'Eunomia' Project, supported by the Greek government.[11]

---

[10] Commissioner for Human Rights, Annual Report to the Committee of Ministers and the Parliamentary Assembly, CommDH(2001)9 (23 April 2001), para.3.

[11] For more details see: http://www.synigoros.gr/eunomia/en_index.htm [last accessed 8 November 2010].

The starting point for the work with ombudsmen and human rights structures is that all ombudsmen have an important role to play in the defence of human rights, even if this is not specifically set out in their respective mandates. The Commissioner has, at the same time, been concerned with encouraging close ties between ombudsmen and organised civil society.

Another key non-governmental actor with whom the Commissioner collaborates is civil society. The Commissioner's mandate recognises the important role of civil society in the defence of human rights and places particular emphasis on his co-operation with NGOs. He is, in effect, encouraged both to take advantage of the experience of NGOs in his own activities and to assist them, in turn, in the fulfilment of theirs.

NGOs have also played an important analytical and promotional role in the numerous seminars the Commissioner has organised. The Commissioner has, in turn, sought to promote the role of NGOs in his dialogue with national authorities by encouraging transparency and co-operation with these partners in the defence of human rights.

The Commissioner systematically meets with NGOs during his official visits to hear first hand of the human rights situation in the country before his meetings with government officials. The information received is then tested in official meetings and during on-site visits around the country. In addition to meeting NGOs while on missions, the Commissioner regularly receives visits from NGO representatives in Strasbourg, particularly at the time of the Parliamentary Assembly sessions.

The institution of the Commissioner is arguably unique in that the Commissioner holds close ties with both NGOs and national authorities. This experience has enabled the Commissioner to understand fully and thereby promote the role of civil society in Europe.

In addition to national civil society representatives, the Commissioner co-operates with international human rights organisations. There are regular contacts with international NGOs such as Amnesty International, Human Rights Watch and the International Federation for Human Rights. These and other NGOs (many of them have a participatory status within the Council of Europe) tend to come to Strasbourg at the time of the Parliamentary Assembly sessions when they would often see the Commissioner. International NGOs also contribute to the Commissioner's thematic workshops, roundtables of human rights defenders and other events.

The Commissioner attaches great importance to working effectively with the media to highlight human rights concerns and communication activities have steadily increased over recent years. Interviews, articles, opinion editorials, press releases and statements on major human rights issues have been regularly published and broadcasted by major national and international media, in particular on the occasion of reports, visits and thematic publications.

The second Commissioner has published a fortnightly communiqué ('Viewpoints'), on topics of specific human rights relevance.[12] On some occasions, journalists, photographers and camera crews have accompanied the Commissioner during country visits. This has resulted in an increased knowledge of the Commissioner's work and human rights visibility in the media. The Commissioner's website has been kept up-to-date and is accessible both to the media and the public. New sections and tools, such as an RSS feed and a multimedia section, have also been created, and are being developed further.

Relations with Other Key Actors at European and International Level

While the Commissioner must protect the independence of his institution, he also seeks common cause with many others, both within the Council of Europe and outside it. Within the Council of Europe, the other institutions of the organisation are natural partners. In addition to the Committee of Ministers discussed above, these include the Parliamentary Assembly, the Congress of Local and Regional Authorities and the independent human rights monitoring bodies.[13] There also are regular exchanges of information between the Commissioner and the European Court of Human Rights.

The Parliamentary Assembly has assumed an increasingly active role in monitoring the implementation of human rights standards and debating human rights concerns. One specific example of this has been

---

[12] The Commissioner's 'Viewpoints' are available at: http://www.coe.int/t/commissioner/Viewpoints/default_en.asp [last accessed 8 November 2010].

[13] Among them are the European Committee for the Prevention of Torture and Inhuman or Degrading Treatment or Punishment (CPT); the European Committee of Social Rights (ECSR); the Advisory Committee on the Framework Convention for the Protection of National Minorities; the European Commission against Racism and Intolerance (ECRI); the Group of Experts on Action against Trafficking in Human Beings (GRETA).

the Assembly's recent work in monitoring the human rights compliance of member states' counter-terrorism measures. The Commissioner has welcomed this development as he is of the opinion that human rights should be the subject of regular political debate and follow-up.

The Commissioner regularly addresses plenary sessions of the Parliamentary Assembly and presents his annual report to it. The Commissioner, or his Office, also participates in the work of the Assembly's specialised committees. Information is regularly exchanged on the country monitoring activities of the Assembly. Moreover, meetings with national parliamentarians are an important part of the Commissioner's visits to member states, and during Parliamentary Assembly sessions in Strasbourg.

The pivotal role of local and regional authorities in implementing human rights standards has often been overlooked. The Congress of Local and Regional Authorities has supported efforts by the Commissioner to mainstream human rights work into the ordinary work of local and regional authorities. This co-operation is reflected in the Commissioner's recommendation on systematic work for implementing human rights published in February 2009.[14] The Commissioner and the Congress have also organised workshops to explore the possibilities for setting up local and regional ombudsman structures.

Since one of the principal tasks of the Commissioner is to promote the observance by member states of the organisation's human rights instruments, co-operation with above-mentioned human rights monitoring mechanisms is necessary to ensure the complementarity of roles. It is evident that any conflicting recommendations issued by the monitoring bodies and the Commissioner must be avoided through co-operation. The Commissioner's role in promoting all human rights instruments of the Council is also fundamentally different from the specific and defined competence of the other monitoring mechanisms. Nevertheless, the Commissioner seeks to benefit from the accrued specialised expertise of these monitoring bodies. He maintains direct contact with these bodies, supported by a more continuous exchange of information at the level of their secretariats and his advisers.

Furthermore, the Commissioner relates constructively to other European and international organisations with human rights

[14] Commissioner for Human Rights, Recommendation on Systematic Work for Implementing Human Rights at the National Level, CommDH(2009)3 (18 February 2009).

mandates. Active co-operation with the European Union (EU), the Organisation for Security and Co-operation in Europe (OSCE) and the UN is essential for ensuring coherent human rights messages to member states. The human rights impact of international organisations can be enhanced all over Europe through rational co-ordination which builds on the strengths of each organisation.

The Commissioner supports the mainstreaming of human rights into EU policies and choices. In recent years, the Council of the EU has also adopted specific EU guidelines on human rights, albeit mainly with reference to third countries.[15] As for the EU Council, the Commissioner maintains contact with the High Representative for the Common Foreign and Security Policy, his Personal Representative for Human Rights in the Area of Foreign and Security Policy as well as the EU Counter-Terrorism Coordinator. The Commissioner has also discussed human rights issues with the Political and Security Committee (COPS) and the EU Council Working Group on OSCE and Council of Europe (COSCE). Actions with the EU Council have often been co-ordinated. The Commissioner has also highlighted the importance of the European Union's planned accession to the European Convention on Human Rights (ECHR).[16] Accession would subject all of the EU institutions to external monitoring of compliance with fundamental rights.

The Commissioner maintains regular contact with several EU Commissioners to review EU legislation and policy implementation with human rights ramifications.[17] The agenda of the Commissioner's meetings with EU Commissioners have included the EU's asylum and migration policy, human rights in crisis situations, procedural rights within the EU, criteria for EU accession and children's rights. The Commissioner has often consulted the EU Commission's representatives during his country visits and in Strasbourg during liaison meetings.

[15] For example on the death penalty, torture, children and armed conflict, human rights defenders and International Humanitarian Law. For details see: http://www.consilium.europa.eu/showPage.aspx?id=1681&lang=EN [last accessed 8 November 2010].

[16] European Convention on Human Rights (ECHR), 213 UNTS 221; entered into force 3 September 1953.

[17] For example with the Commissioner for Justice, Freedom and Security; the Commissioner for External Relations and European Neighbourhood Policy; the Commissioner for Enlargement; and the Commissioner for Employment, Social Affairs and Equal Opportunities.

The Commissioner has established regular contacts with the European Parliament's Committee on Civil Liberties, Justice and Home Affairs as well as the Sub-Committee on Human Rights. The Commissioner has also met with the President of the European Parliament and held exchanges of views with other committees and rapporteurs on specific human rights questions. Draft EU legislation, counter-terrorism measures and crisis situations have often figured among the discussions between the Commissioner and the European Parliament. Moreover, the Commissioner has maintained close contacts with the European Ombudsman (EU).

The Commissioner liaised early on with the Director of the EU's Fundamental Rights Agency and a regular schedule of meetings has since been established. In addition to joint activities, the Commissioner's Office participates regularly in the implementation of the Agency's research programmes.

He maintains contact with the Chairman of the OSCE Permanent Council and the Director of OSCE's Office for Human Rights and Democratic Institutions. He is a regular speaker at the OSCE Human Dimension Implementation Meetings in Warsaw. Crisis situations, the protection of human rights defenders and the rights of Roma have been regular themes of co-operation and exchanges of information. The OSCE High Commissioner on National Minorities and the Representative on Freedom of the Media are further key players for the Commissioner's co-operation activities. Moreover, the Commissioner usually consults OSCE field missions during his country visits.

The Commissioner has a close working relationship with the UN network, in particular with the High Commissioner for Human Rights and her Office (OHCHR), the High Commissioner for Refugees (UNHCR) and the UN Children's Fund (UNICEF).

In addition to regular meetings with the UN High Commissioners for Human Rights and Refugees, the Commissioner often meets with UN special rapporteurs working under the special procedures of the UN Human Rights Council. The Commissioner's country reports are brought to the attention of the Universal Periodic Review (UPR) process carried out by the Human Rights Council. During country visits, the Commissioner often meets with the UN resident co-ordinator, OHCHR's field representatives or heads of UN peacekeeping missions as well as the UN humanitarian co-ordinator or OCHA representative in countries affected by conflict or in crisis situations.

Co-operation and information exchanges between the OHCHR and Commissioner have covered a wide range of themes. With UNICEF, the Commissioner's Office has collaborated on the realisation of the rights of the child throughout the European continent. In particular, joint activities are being developed on the reform of juvenile justice systems, human rights indicators and the setting-up of special ombudsmen for children's rights and the adoption of national action plans targeting children and juveniles.

Assessment of Impact

From the very beginning, the Commissioner's action has always aimed to be concrete and result-oriented. The principle goal of the substance-based work of his Office is to have a real impact on problems in the field of human rights in member states. It is, therefore, necessary to ask about the extent to which this goal has been achieved during its first years of existence.

Given the nature of the Commissioner's mandate, attempting to measure its impact is not easy. Even in cases as clear as that of legislative reforms following precise recommendations from the Commissioner, it is difficult to evaluate the extent to which the reform is directly linked to the request from the Commissioner, since it could also come following a series of different national and international pressures.

There can also be cases where the Commissioner has played an important role in the turnaround of a situation, but where it is preferable to accord the credit for this change to a national body. The Commissioner has in effect obtained concrete results in a certain number of cases, but the Office prefers to remain modest in the attribution of merit for these changes and the proof of tangible achievements. Having said this, the four examples which follow illustrate the concrete significance of the Commissioner's contribution—and some of the problems.

Example 1: Chechnya

The Russian Federation—and, more particularly, the Northern Caucasus region (Chechnya, Dagestan and Ingushetia)—was the first member state to be visited by the first Commissioner, Álvaro Gil-Robles, in December 1999. This coincided with the armed conflict in the region and the Commissioner could only visit the northern areas in Chechnya which were under the control of the Russian federal authorities.

However, he could discharge his visit effectively, which was no simple matter bearing in mind the major internal armed conflict taking place. He met authorities and ordinary people and could report on the actual situation.[18]

One of the main threads of the Commissioner's message to the Russian authorities (and the public)—and one of the most challenging to convey under the circumstances—was that 'the ends cannot justify the means'. In other words, while a state has the right to defend its territorial integrity and to react strongly against groups or individuals who attempt to overthrow the established order through the use of violence, the response should never be allowed to degenerate into gross violations of human rights.

The Commissioner urged for a political solution to the conflict as soon as possible and clearly stated his opposition to the bombing of areas where there was a mix of armed groups and civilian populations, even though such operations were strongly supported by the majority of public opinion in Russia at the time.

The establishing of the Office of a Chechen Ombudsman was one of the concrete results which were achieved following the advice of Commissioner Gil-Robles.

The second Commissioner visited Chechnya four times during 2006-2009 and pursued a dialogue with the federal and regional authorities, the judiciary, the Ombudsman and with representatives of civil society. For part of that period the Office had a staff member located in Grozny, and this facilitated communications.

The Commissioner made public his concern about torture and abductions and urged that the fate of the more than three thousand persons missing since the two wars be clarified through the opening of identified graves and modern DNA technique testing.

Regrettably, progress has been slow on these issues; the work will have to continue. When the Commissioner visited Grozny in September 2009 he was approached by a couple of women whose sons were missing. After having reported what they knew about their cases, they said:

[18] For example Report by Mr Álvaro Gil-Robles, Commissioner for Human Rights, on his Visit to the Russian Federation (in particular Chechnya, Daghestan and Ingoushetia), 7-10 December 1999, CommDH(1999)1 (10 December 1999).

'It is so important that you are coming here—and are coming back. Thank you'.

Example 2: The United Kingdom
Both the first and second Commissioners have visited the United Kingdom during their respective mandates. The first visit took place in November 2004 leading to a report published in early 2005.[19] The report raises concerns over the United Kingdom's anti-terrorism legislation, changes to the asylum system, prison conditions and the juvenile justice system. Regarding anti-terror legislation, the Commissioner's views on UK anti-terror measures were quoted in judgments of the House of Lords—in particular, the indefinite detention without charge of foreigners suspected of involvement in terrorist activity and who could not be expelled under the Anti-terrorism, Crime and Security Act 2001.[20] The Commissioner regarded these detentions as discriminatory and disproportionate. The House of Lords agreed with the Commissioner's view that the reliance on evidence obtained by third parties through torture in the determination of the suspicion of involvement in terrorism-related activity could not be reconciled with the absolute nature of the prohibition of torture in Article 3 of the ECHR.[21]

But even before the 2004 visit, the Commissioner had released two Opinions related to the United Kingdom in 2002. The first Opinion focused on the UK's derogation from Article 5 of the ECHR.[22] The second Opinion dealt with the review of powers of the Northern Ireland Human Rights Commission.[23] These Opinions were requested, respectively, by the Joint Committee on Human Rights of the Parliament of the United Kingdom of Great Britain and Northern Ireland (issued in respect of a legislative initiative) and the Northern Ireland Human Rights Commission.

---

[19] Report by Mr Álvaro Gil-Robles, Commissioner for Human Rights, on his Visit to the United Kingdom, 4-12 November 2004, CommDH(2005)6 (8 June 2005).

[20] *A and others v Secretary of State for the Home Department*; *X and another v Secretary of State for the Home Department*, [2004] UKHL 56.

[21] *A and others v Secretary of State for the Home Department (No 2)*, [2005] UKHL 71.

[22] Opinion of the Commissioner for Human Rights, Mr Álvaro Gil-Robles, on Certain Aspects of the United Kingdom 2001 Derogation from Article 5(1) of the European Convention on Human Rights, CommDH(2002)7 (28 August 2002).

[23] Opinion of the Commissioner for Human Rights, Mr Álvaro Gil-Robles, on Certain Aspects of the Review of Powers of the Northern Ireland Human Rights Commission, CommDH(2002)16 (3 November 2002).

The impact of these Opinions is illustrated by the fact that the first one was cited in a Court of Appeal judgment of 25 October 2002 and the second one (on the competencies of the Northern Ireland Human Rights Commission) was referred to in a review procedure initiated by the UK government.

During the second and third visits to the UK of Commissioner Hammarberg, in February and March 2008, some of the issues discussed in 2001 and 2004 were still on the agenda: counter-terrorism measures, immigration policies and juvenile justice. As during the visit in 2004, the Commissioner paid special attention to the conditions of detention of asylum seekers and young offenders in a Young Offenders Institution. In addition to meeting with several ministers and ombudspersons he also met with members of the newly-established Equality and Human Rights Commission. Moreover, the Commissioner was invited for an exchange of views on pressing human rights issues by the Joint Committee on Human Rights of the UK Parliament.

Based on the two visits in 2008, three thematic Memoranda on Asylum and Immigration,[24] Corporal Punishment[25] and Juvenile Justice[26] were published. Drafts were sent to the government for comments before publication and the government responded within a couple of weeks with constructive comments (which were then appended to the Memoranda).

Regarding the issue of 'corporal punishment' for children, a concern for the Commissioner in all Council of Europe member states, the correspondence between the Commissioner and the UK Government shows fundamentally different views. The Commissioner considers, in referring to international human rights law, including the UN

[24] Memorandum by Thomas Hammarberg, Council of Europe Commissioner for Human Rights, Following his Visits to the United Kingdom on 5-8 February and 31 March–2 April 2008. Issues Reviewed: Asylum and Immigration, CommDH(2008)23 (18 September 2008).

[25] Memorandum by Thomas Hammarberg, Council of Europe Commissioner for Human Rights, Following his Visits to the United Kingdom, 5-8 February and 31 March–2 April 2008. Issues Reviewed: Corporal Punishment, CommDH(2008)28 (9 October 2008).

[26] Memorandum by Thomas Hammarberg, Council of Europe Commissioner for Human Rights, Following his Visits to the United Kingdom, 5-8 February and 31 March–2 April 2008. Issue Reviewed: Juvenile Justice, CommDH(2008)27 (17 October 2008).

Convention on the Rights of the Child,[27] that corporal punishment is a form of violence against children. The UK Government however 'does not accept that the term violence is appropriate for the level of physical punishment for which the defence of reasonable punishment is available in English or Northern Irish law or for which the defence of justifiable assault is available in Scots law'.[28] The UK has so far not accepted the Recommendations of the Commissioner to remove the 'reasonable punishment' defence and 'justifiable assault' from the law.

The Commissioner's Memorandum on Asylum and Immigration had, however, some concrete impact. One of the issues raised in the Memorandum was the situation of the Sri Lankan Tamils whose asylum claims had been rejected in the UK, where a significant number of applications had been lodged before the European Court of Human Rights. The Commissioner recommended in his Memorandum that the UK authorities declare a moratorium on these deportations until the Court had had an opportunity to rule on the merits of one of these cases.[29] This was eventually followed by the UK Government.

In the same Memorandum, the Commissioner recommended that the UK promptly withdraws its 'immigration reservation' to the UN Convention on the Rights of the Child by which refugee or immigrant children, despite their special vulnerability, were subject to exclusion from the protective ambit of this Convention. Following the Commissioner's visit and Memorandum, the UK announced the removal of the above reservation.

The Commissioner also engaged during his 2008 visits to the UK in ongoing discussions on proposals to detain suspects of terrorism for up to 42 days without charge. The Commissioner referred to this as an 'excessive' measure.[30] The UK Government eventually dropped its plan to introduce the 42-day detention.

---

[27] 1989 UN Convention on the Rights of the Child (CRC), UNGA Res 44/25 (1989), UN Doc A/RES/44/25 (20 November 1989), 1577 UNTS 3; entered into force 2 September 1990.

[28] Comments by the Government of the United Kingdom, Appendix to the Commissioner's Memorandum on Corporal Punishment, CommDH(2008)28, para.3.

[29] Memorandum on Asylum and Immigration, CommDH(2008)23, para.86.

[30] 'Brown Told Detention Excessive and out of Step', A. Travis and P. Wintour for *The Guardian*, 2 June 2008, available at: http://www.guardian.co.uk/politics/2008/jun/02/terrorism.uksecurity [last accessed 8 November 2010].

All three published Memoranda received good media coverage in the UK press, and the Memorandum on Juvenile Justice was quoted in parliamentary debates.[31] The UK Parliamentary and Health Service Ombudsman referred to the Commissioner in her annual report.[32]

Example 3: Armenia

The Commissioner visited Armenia shortly after the post-electoral events in March 2008 which resulted in ten deaths (eight civilians and two law enforcement officials), injuries to many others, and what has been termed 'a one-sided pursuit of accountability' through arrests and prosecutions of opposition representatives. The Commissioner's visit took place in the middle of the 20-day declared state of emergency and in a polarised atmosphere. The different sides—i.e. the authorities represented by the incumbent President Robert Kocharyan and the opposition, primarily represented by the country's previous (first) President, Levon Ter-Petrosyan—saw the events through diametrically opposed lenses and blamed each other for bearing all 'moral responsibility' for the violence.

The Commissioner sought to obtain a complete picture of the situation, gathering information from a variety of sources about human rights issues and sought to provide advice about the way forward. He published a report rapidly after his visit,[33] and pursued a continuous dialogue with the Armenian authorities and other actors on two main issues: firstly, the need to carry out a thorough, independent and credible inquiry into the March 2008 events, and secondly, the principle that no one must be detained or convicted, even with non-custodial sentences—solely on the basis of their beliefs or non-violent political activities.

The mechanism for an inquiry, as initially established by the Armenian Parliament in the form of an *ad hoc* parliamentary committee of inquiry, was politically-oriented and one-sided. Representatives of the opposition, both parliamentary and extra-parliamentary, refused

[31] 'Youths in Custody: Our Duty of Care', Letter by Professor P. Scraton in *The Guardian*, 27 January 2009, available at: http://www.guardian.co.uk/society/2009/jan/27/youth-custody [last accessed 8 November 2010].

[32] Parliamentary and Health Service Ombudsman, Annual Reports 2007-08, available at: http://www.ombudsman.org.uk/__data/assets/pdf_file/0002/1010/Annual-Report-2007-08.pdf [last accessed 8 November 2010].

[33] Report by the Commissioner for Human Rights, Mr Thomas Hammarberg, on his Special Mission to Armenia, 12–15 March 2008, CommDH(2008)11REV (20 March 2008).

to take part in this committee, thereby reducing the chances that it would be seen as credible by society as a whole. To overcome this deadlock, the Commissioner advised the authorities to separate the process of establishing the facts from the political conclusions which could be drawn.

After considerable discussions, and with the support of international expert advice, the authorities accepted to establish a 'fact-finding group' of local independent experts tasked with examining the facts of the March 2008 events and reaching a common account or reading of those events, with the final purpose of delivering a report to the *ad hoc* parliamentary committee and the public in general.

The exercise of establishing such a group had no previous model in Armenia, and proved to be a difficult one. Nevertheless, it did have moderate initial success in that it helped to defuse the tensions which prevailed in the months following the violent events.

Following the sustained efforts by the Commissioner and other Council of Europe institutions (notably the monitoring committee of the Parliamentary Assembly) as well as their effective interaction and co-ordination, which maximised the impact of the common message, an amnesty was declared in June 2009, which covered most of the opposition representatives who were deprived of their liberty in connection with the March 2008 events. They included a former Foreign Minister, members of Parliament who had been stripped of their immunities shortly after the March events, and many other lower-ranking members of the political movement affiliated with Levon Ter-Peterosyan.

Example 4: The South Ossetia Conflict

The Commissioner was one of the first international and Council of Europe figures to react to the human rights and humanitarian crisis created by the South Ossetia conflict in August 2008. The Commissioner visited various areas affected by the conflict shortly after the five-day war, and held meetings with the relevant authorities at various levels, including with the Georgian President, Mr Saakashvili. The work of the Commissioner in this area has been complicated due to the highly charged and politicised environment and unprecedented situation within the Council of Europe. It has also involved close co-ordination with other international institutions and actors in the field.

The Commissioner formulated six principles for urgent human rights and humanitarian protection, which covered the right to return of the displaced persons; the provision of adequate aid and living conditions for the displaced until their return home; demining efforts; law and order in the war affected areas; humanitarian exchanges of prisoners of war, other detainees and stranded persons as well as ensuring an international presence and assistance in the affected areas to address human rights and humanitarian issues.[34] The foregoing six principles received wide support and have served as a reference framework for various Council of Europe and other international institutions as well as NGOs.

The question of ensuring humanitarian access and human rights support to the people in the areas affected by this conflict has been a difficult one, with obstacles and conditions being placed on such access by the different sides. One of the Commissioner's main messages has been that people must not be held hostage to political processes and kept in isolation.

One of the major achievements of the Commissioner in the aftermath of the active hostilities was the facilitation of exchanges of prisoners, detainees and the bodies of those who died during the conflict. The Commissioner encouraged such exchanges as being important humanitarian acts to save lives, to protect the human rights of those victimised by the conflict and to start rebuilding mutual confidence between the parties. More than a hundred detainees were exchanged through the good offices of the Commissioner.

An adviser to the Commissioner was deployed to the Council of Europe Office in Tbilisi to help assess the implementation of the Commissioner's six principles and to enhance the effectiveness of co-ordination and synergies with other international actors.

Dilemmas and Lessons Learned

Despite the fact that the institution is still relatively young, and that the means for the Office have been limited during the first ten years of its existence, the rapid development of the Commissioner for Human Rights' action and its tangible productivity already allow us to see certain dilemmas which it faces in the framework of human rights diplomacy.

[34] The principles were set out in the Commissioner's report on his mission to Georgia and the Russian Federation: Human Rights in Areas Affected by the South Ossetia Conflict, Special Mission to Georgia and Russia, by Thomas Hammarberg, Council of Europe Commissioner for Human Rights (Vladikavkaz, Tskhinvali, Gori, Tbilisi and Moscow), 22–29 August 2008, CommDH(2008)22 (8 September 2008).

The Commissioner's credibility relies above all upon his independence and his impartiality. Their preservation requires that he extract himself from any considerations of a political nature and approach situations exclusively from a human rights point of view. The Commissioner focuses only on the human rights situation. This approach—based exclusively on respect for human rights, and exempt from any considerations of a political nature—allows him to make progress which would not be possible had he integrated political aims into his approach.

However, the dilemma itself resides in the fact that the Commissioner's action often takes place within a highly politicised environment. This is when the question of how to deal with politicised situations is raised. How should the Commissioner extract himself from this politicisation, often deliberate and forced by the parties present in order to further their own point of view?

The most evident example in this domain is that of areas in dispute or post-conflict situations. Up until now, the Commissioner has managed to work on these complex cases and has received in return constructive support from the parties involved even when his reports were critical rather than offering support to a particular political description. The fact remains, however, that it is difficult to work for human rights in such areas because diplomatic and political sensitivities are such that they can take precedence over everything else.

Certain governments show great caution—if not to say an obsession—relating to the issue of status/recognition. The fact is that an important part of the Commissioner's task is to relate to people living in areas that are politically disputed. His action in this domain hinges on all of the political actors accepting that the Commissioner's action is, above all, destined to help people living in these territories and that his contacts do not signal political or diplomatic recognition.

Multilateral human rights diplomacy sometimes makes use of the threat of sanctions or actual sanctions, and this comes with another dilemma. In the case of the Council of Europe, such threats or sanctions are of course dealt with by the political organs, which are the Parliamentary Assembly and the Committee of Ministers. But they also have direct repercussions on the Commissioner's action in that they can be put forward by these political organs with reference to massive violations of human rights or non-respect of certain human rights principles.

Are these threats effective and should they be actively supported? One case in point is the threat by the Parliamentary Assembly to suspend the right to vote of the members of the parliamentary delegation of countries where there are problems relating to the respect of the principles defended by the Council of Europe, which are the respect for democracy, the rule of law and human rights. But does the threat of removing the right to vote of a parliamentary delegation because of the actions of the government of its country not in itself contradict the principle of the rule of law and the separation of powers? Why punish a delegation of the legislative organ for the errors committed by the executive branch in its country? The national parliamentary delegations within the Parliamentary Assembly of the Council of Europe are made up of elected members from all political groupings of the national parliaments, including the opposition. Some members of the national opposition are sometimes on the front lines in their country against the actions of the government, and there is a certain ambiguity in threatening them with the withdrawal of their right to vote and holding them almost responsible for the very actions they are combating. In any case, there is much to reflect on in this dilemma.

Another dilemma, directly linked to the work of the Commissioner, is that of the extent to which he should limit himself to the existing standards and norms agreed by the member states. Of course, when he analyses the situation in a member state, the Commissioner relies on international and European human rights treaties, in the first instance the ECHR. He takes the case-law of the European Court of Human Rights into account and a large part of his work consists of advising governments to effectively apply the existing standards. The Commissioner concentrates his efforts on filling the existing gaps between the European standards agreed by states and their effective implementation at national level.

This raises the question of whether in certain cases he should go further, and demand more, and if so, on what basis. There are new human rights problems which are not always covered by the existing texts. In such cases, should the Commissioner keep quiet and ignore these threats on the grounds that they are not covered by existing conventions? Or should he light the way, or at least give directions? In other cases, standards exist but are not sufficient or do not go far enough. Again, this raises the question of whether the Commissioner should ask for more, act as a catalyst for insufficiencies, and point out what is missing for the full protection of human rights in the member states.

Finally, another dilemma: how to make use of the media. The mediatisation of the standpoints of the Commissioner is both helpful and a source of potential risk for the effectiveness of his actions. The two Commissioners who have held office since the creation of the institution have each enjoyed a good level of presence in the media and significant press coverage of their action. Exposure to the media has certainly contributed to make the institution known and raise its profile over the years. It has also helped to further certain particularly important issues which have been the subject of a lively public debate, thanks to the media who exposed the Commissioner's analysis and recommendations.

But there are also cases where the media have, voluntarily or not, been the instrument of a distortion of the Commissioner's message. There have been cases where journalists have used quotes taken out of context on the occasion of the publication of important reports and ruined their immediate impact in public opinion.

Another important issue in this context is when, how and why certain facts and considerations should be made public. Here, the approach of the Commissioner will be dictated by what is the best option in order to obtain concrete results. If he deems that this requires discretion and silence for some time, the Commissioner will not hesitate to apply 'silent diplomacy'. However, he also has the obligation to account for his work and to be as transparent as possible. His quarterly and annual reports offer a possibility to provide information which had to be kept confidential at earlier stages.

Over the years, and by building on acquired experience, the Commissioner has accumulated a sum of knowledge which has guided his action in order to make better use of all of the resources available in a context of multilateral diplomacy at the service of the defence of human rights. This knowledge guides his action and will be enriched by future experience.

To date, and very succinctly, the lessons learned by the Commissioner and which could be of general interest for others in the field of human rights diplomacy can be summarised by six main guidelines and one overarching rule:

- Firstly, ensure a good knowledge of the facts and base actions on solid and verified data.
- Secondly, avoid stereotypes concerning countries and any hasty conclusions about them.

- Thirdly, be present in the field, visit countries and see things personally *in situ*.
- Fourthly, make contact with and refer to other actors in the country, such as ombudsmen and equality bodies, and welcome them as sources of information.
- Fifthly, co-ordinate with other actors of the international community.
- Sixthly, always respect the basic rules of fair play in procedures and contacts with governments.
- The overarching rule: to be principled.

APPENDIX

RESOLUTION (99) 50

ON THE COUNCIL OF EUROPE COMMISSIONER FOR HUMAN RIGHTS

(adopted by the Committee of Ministers on 7 May 1999 at its 104th Session)

The Committee of Ministers,

Considering that the aim of the Council of Europe is the achievement of greater unity between its Members and that one of the methods by which that aim is to be pursued is the maintenance and further realisation of human rights and fundamental freedoms;

Having regard to the decisions taken by the Heads of State and Government of the Member States of the Council of Europe at their Second Summit (Strasbourg, 10-11 October 1997);

Considering also that the 50th Anniversary of the Council of Europe provides an occasion to enhance further the work undertaken since its creation,

Decides to institute the office of Council of Europe Commissioner for Human Rights ("the Commissioner") with the following terms of reference:

Article 1

1. The Commissioner shall be a non-judicial institution to promote education in, awareness of and respect for human rights, as embodied in the human rights instruments of the Council of Europe.
2. The Commissioner shall respect the competence of, and perform functions other than those fulfilled by, the supervisory bodies set up under the European Convention of Human Rights or under other human rights instruments of the Council of Europe. The Commissioner shall not take up individual complaints.

Article 2

The Commissioner shall function independently and impartially.

Article 3

The Commissioner shall:

a. promote education in and awareness of human rights in the member States;
b. contribute to the promotion of the effective observance and full enjoyment of human rights in the member States;
c. provide advice and information on the protection of human rights and prevention of human rights violations. When dealing with the public, the Commissioner shall, wherever possible, make use of and co-operate with human rights structures in the member States. Where such structures do not exist, the Commissioner will encourage their establishment;
d. facilitate the activities of national ombudsmen or similar institutions in the field of human rights;
e. identify possible shortcomings in the law and practice of member States concerning the compliance with human rights as embodied in the instruments of the Council of Europe, promote the effective implementation of these standards by member States and assist them, with their agreement, in their efforts to remedy such shortcomings;
f. address, whenever the Commissioner deems it appropriate, a report concerning a specific matter to the Committee of Ministers or to the Parliamentary Assembly and the Committee of Ministers;
g. respond, in the manner the Commissioner deems appropriate, to requests made by the Committee of Ministers or the Parliamentary Assembly, in the context of their task of ensuring compliance with the human rights standards of the Council of Europe;
h. submit an annual report to the Committee of Ministers and the Parliamentary Assembly;
i. co-operate with other international institutions for the promotion and protection of human rights while avoiding unnecessary duplication of activities.

Article 4

The Commissioner shall take into account views expressed by the Committee of Ministers and the Parliamentary Assembly of the Council of Europe concerning the Commissioner's activities.

Article 5

1. The Commissioner may act on any information relevant to the Commissioner's functions. This will notably include information addressed to the Commissioner by governments, national parliaments, national ombudsmen or similar institutions in the field of human rights, individuals and organisations.
2. The gathering of information relevant to the Commissioner's functions shall not give rise to any general reporting system for member States.

Article 6

1. Member States shall facilitate the independent and effective performance by the Commissioner of his or her functions. In particular, they shall facilitate the Commissioner's contacts, including travel, in the context of the mission of the Commissioner and provide in good time information requested by the Commissioner.
2. The Commissioner shall be entitled, during the exercise of his or her functions, to the privileges and immunities provided for in Article 40 of the Statute of the Council of Europe and in the agreements made thereunder.

Article 7

The Commissioner may directly contact governments of member States of the Council of Europe.

Article 8

1. The Commissioner may issue recommendations, opinions and reports.

2. The Committee of Ministers may authorise the publication of any recommendation, opinion or report addressed to it.

Article 9

1. The Commissioner shall be elected by the Parliamentary Assembly by a majority of votes cast from a list of three candidates drawn up by the Committee of Ministers.
2. Member States may submit candidatures by letter addressed to the Secretary General. Candidates must be nationals of a member State of the Council of Europe.

Article 10

The candidates shall be eminent personalities of a high moral character having recognised expertise in the field of human rights, a public record of attachment to the values of the Council of Europe and the personal authority necessary to discharge the mission of the Commissioner effectively. During his or her term of office, the Commissioner shall not engage in any activity which is incompatible with the demands of a full-time office.

Article 11

The Commissioner shall be elected for a non-renewable term of office of six years.

Article 12

1. An Office of the Commissioner for Human Rights shall be established within the General Secretariat of the Council of Europe.
2. The expenditure on the Commissioner and the Office of the Commissioner shall be borne by the Council of Europe.

CHAPTER 8

HUMAN RIGHTS DIPLOMACY FROM A UN PERSPECTIVE: A COMPLEMENT TO ADVOCACY

Ibrahim Salama[1]

Introduction

Human rights diplomacy is a strategic approach that should be grounded in human rights law and applied for enhancing human rights advocacy. It can also be described as an important missing link between the codification of human rights in international law and public advocacy for human rights that can lead to more effective progressive development and implementation of human rights norms and standards.

The importance of human rights diplomacy for furthering the implementation of human rights cannot be overstated. However, the role of human rights diplomacy is often poorly understood and at times contested. Defined as the art of persuasion in international affairs, diplomacy is frequently viewed as falling under the purview of international relations as opposed to international law, wielded and shaped by power, not by norms. In this chapter I hope to question such boundaries and assumptions. Human rights diplomacy does not mean and should indeed never lead to compromising on human rights. I will make a renewed call for human rights diplomacy which is not power-centric, but is instead grounded in norms, and reliant on—albeit different from—the work of judicial and expert human rights mechanisms. At the United Nations (UN) level, among these expert human rights mechanisms are human rights treaty bodies and the special procedures mandate-holders and working groups established by the UN Human Rights Council (HRC).

[1] The views expressed in this article do not necessarily reflect the views of the Office of the High Commissioner for Human Rights (OHCHR), and are made entirely in the author's personal capacity.

Human rights diplomacy does not only mean building relationships and lines of communication among governments and other stakeholders with a view to exchanging information, anticipating developments and building confidence. The above is only one component of human rights diplomacy, namely the routine functioning and pro-active performance of all relevant actors, including the UN Secretariat. One of the main particularities of human rights diplomacy is the huge potential that it holds for widening states' policy options due to the important role of human rights expert mechanisms in human rights diplomacy. In this regard, a key aim of human rights diplomacy is to ensure that actors with competing political objectives, often pursuing legitimate concerns, use the appropriate legal entry points and tools compatible with international human rights law.

Human rights expert mechanisms not only play a leading role in progressively developing international human rights law, but also provide innovative policy options for governments on a wide range of human rights issues, including controversial and politically sensitive matters. Independent human rights experts mechanisms are in this sense both actors in and 'tools' of human rights diplomacy, which is an underutilised resource of the human rights protection system.

In this article, I will address some of the key challenges of engaging in human rights diplomacy; but also discuss opportunities hidden in relying on diplomatic means for the promotion and protection of human rights that should not be squandered or neglected by the human rights community. In laying out the case for a pro-active approach to human rights diplomacy, I will rely on selected examples and recent milestones such as the Durban Review Conference that took place in Geneva in April 2009, an expert seminar held in 2008 on Freedom of Expression and Advocacy of Religious Hatred that Constitutes Incitement to Discrimination, Hostility or Violence (Articles 19 and 20 of the International Covenant on Civil and Political Rights (ICCPR)[2]), the ongoing process of strengthening the UN human rights treaty body system, and innovations within the Intergovernmental Working Group on the Right to Development, a subsidiary body of the HRC. I will also attempt to shed more light on the role of the UN High Commissioner for Human Rights (High

[2] 1966 International Covenant on Civil and Political Rights (ICCPR), UNGA Res 2200A (XXI), UN Doc A/RES/2200 XXI (A) (16 December 1966), 999 UNTS 171; entered into force 23 March 1976.

Commissioner) and her Office in facilitating and leading diplomatic strategies for the promotion and protection of human rights.

The above-selected examples illustrate the shift from a focus on law-making in earlier decades to implementation and mainstreaming with a view to fulfil the protection needs of rights-holders. These examples also have the common feature that they all indicate a greater reliance on the expert knowledge and observations generated by the mentioned expert human rights mechanisms. The universal periodic review (UPR) process, soon entering its second cycle, also provides a privileged opportunity to compile the findings of expert human rights mechanisms and enhance their implementation through peer review. This is how a political process can augment and complement—but hopefully not alter nor weaken—the role of expert human rights mechanisms. A better understanding of human rights diplomacy will display to all actors that their respective roles provide much higher potential and complementarity for ensuring the implementation of human rights around the world than has been achieved so far.

The Need for Human Rights Diplomacy

The human rights arena has changed substantially in the past two decades. Its increasingly multi-actor nature has altered the dynamics in which negotiations and the implementation of human rights obligations take place. While states continue to play a principal role and carry the primary responsibility for the protection of human rights, the human rights diplomacy theatre also sees a host of other actors, among them regional mechanisms, national human rights institutions (NHRIs), the UN Secretariat and various UN agencies, civil society groups, grassroots organisations and the media.[3] Also, the Office of the High Commissioner for Human Rights (OHCHR) is a *sui generis* institution with no comparable mandate and unique authority within and outside the UN system. The OHCHR operates in an intergovernmental environment but its work cannot be seen in light of political parameters only. OHCHR's work goes to the heart of human rights and is frequently inspired by expert knowledge generated by the independent human rights mechanisms that OHCHR supports.

[3] See B. G. Ramcharan, *The International Law and Practice of Early Warning and Preventive Diplomacy: The Emerging Global Watch* (Dordrecht: Martinus Nijhoff, 1991), p.10.

These various actors are of a different political nature. They do not have much in common in terms of institutional parameters and political dynamics, and yet are all operating in the same human rights sphere. Allowing effective collaboration among these different actors and ensuring outcomes of this interaction that is compatible with international human rights standards is one of the main challenges of both the concept and practice of human rights diplomacy.

The role of the OHCHR is naturally central in this respect given that it constitutes a convergence point and institutional hub for the international human rights system in its entirety. OHCHR supports various UN human rights bodies and mechanisms while retaining its own distinct mandate for the promotion and protection of human rights.[4] The UN High Commissioner for Human Rights plays an autonomous role, relying on dialogue and diplomacy in her own right. Diplomacy, in other words, is also at the heart of the OHCHR and the High Commissioner's mandate.

Indeed, recent experiences indicate the need for something more than outreach or advocacy by the High Commissioner and her Office and other actors. For the purposes of this article, I assert that beyond raising human rights issues with a view to promoting and mainstreaming human rights, human rights diplomacy provides a toolbox of methods that can usefully be applied to obtain certain outcomes conducive to furthering the implementation of human rights. For example, human rights diplomacy can prove essential for overcoming misperceptions within or among different stakeholders on certain thematic issues. It may also be required to address urgent protection needs of either a thematic or case-specific nature. Also, with a view to bridging divides and building consensus, human rights diplomacy often promises to pay greater dividend than just relying on outreach and advocacy activities. I should stress here, however, that outreach or public advocacy and human rights diplomacy should always go hand in hand, as both approaches complement and mutually reinforce each

[4] B. G. Ramcharan, *A UN High Commissioner in Defence of Human Rights* (The Hague: Martinus Nijhoff, 2005), p.73, observing that 'in the contemporary world, the mantle of human rights is worn by the United Nations High Commissioner for Human Rights'. He also holds at p.50 that 'the High Commissioner for Human Rights is expected to engage in leadership, advocacy and trouble-shooting in such a politically turbulent world and it is not hard to see that the position of the High Commissioner is a difficult one'.

other. In the following section, I will shed light on some of the tools of human rights diplomacy as applied in recent practices.

Characteristics of Human Rights Diplomacy and the Dynamic Role of the UN High Commissioner for Human Rights

Human rights diplomacy is underpinned by the principle of engagement with persuasion, and is more than the unspoken threat of public exposure as its primary tools.[5] Analysing implementation challenges is often more constructive than conceptual controversies and political accusations. Needs assessment and capacity building, at least in the long-term, can achieve better results than merely exerting pressure. It should be noted that public advocacy can work independently of or in tandem with quiet diplomacy, as well as with judicial and quasi-judicial human rights mechanisms.

As outlined above, human rights diplomacy could usefully be applied, for example, to address urgent protection needs, to overcome obstacles to implementation or to bridge divides between key players. The tools used to achieve such objectives are underpinned by the recognition of the importance of the following factors: coordination, communication, integrity, transparency, using a multi-pronged approach, adopting confidence building measures, ensuring confidentiality, optimising each stakeholder's comparative advantage, and implementing an incremental strategy. With these factors in mind, five characteristics of human rights diplomacy shall be identified in the following, and some of the challenges highlighted.

First, in light of the multitude of stakeholders that are active players in the human rights arena, the main challenge for a successful human rights diplomacy by any concerned actor (governments, OHCHR, human rights expert mechanisms, NHRIs and non-governmental

[5] See e.g. the observation by H. Smith, 'Humanitarian Diplomacy: Theory and Practice' in L. Minear and H. Smith (eds.), *Humanitarian Diplomacy: Practitioners and their Craft* (New York: United Nations University Press, 2007), p.48: 'Diplomatic methods rely on what in other circumstances would be considered social and personal activities, which assume a political significance in terms of the communication and negotiation functions of the diplomat'; and further: 'Humanitarians as diplomats are not political advocates but political negotiators. In carrying out their negotiating role, humanitarian actors, consciously or not, use the paraphernalia of diplomatic methods, procedures and instruments' (p.50).

organisations (NGOs)) is often to obtain a meaningful and human rights compatible outcome of multi-stakeholder discussions. The key solution is to raise awareness and deepen understanding of the issues under consideration. Panel discussions in the margins of the Human Rights Council are a good example of one of the tools human rights diplomacy can rely on.

Second, human rights issues often fall victim to their political context which nourishes generalisation, creates stereotypes and provokes divides. Human rights being perceived as a 'Western invention', as an instrument of foreign policy thus discredited by the accusation of applying double standards, is only one of such negative perceptions that often reduce the power and impact of human rights advocates. In order to dispel such negative perceptions, the adoption of confidence building measures is key. Credibility is also very important for collaborative action. Even if a given human rights situation cannot be redressed, it should never be overlooked. Confidence building measures are not a prescribed set of instruments that can be used regardless of the specific context. Rather, they are measures tailored to various situations with a view to enhance genuine dialogue and create a common ground for action to be identified. Specific issue-based or constituency-based briefings and consultations are examples of confidence building measures which should be standard procedures applied on a periodic basis by and among all groups of stakeholders.

Third, linked to the previous point is the fact that human rights diplomacy combines confidential contacts with public action. Protecting and promoting human rights is essentially about confronting power with truth. It therefore comes to no surprise that the general perception about human rights advocacy is often reduced to mobilising shame. While this is true at times, it is not always the case. Civil society organisations will of course by definition favour public action and visible pressure, while on the other end of the spectrum, intergovernmental bodies tend to adopt a more incremental approach. As outlined above, the High Commissioner for Human Rights is situated at the nexus of the various players in the human rights movement, and is therefore required, almost on a daily basis, to balance quiet diplomacy and public advocacy, and to judge what is most conducive to obtaining the best possible result.[6] This is further complicated by the

[6] As observed by Ramcharan, *A UN High Commissioner*, 2005, p.50.

need of the High Commissioner and her Office to limit their sphere of action to the human rights dimension of the situation, and to refrain from interfering in the wider political context.[7]

Fourth, the main specificity of 'human rights' diplomacy resides in the fact that it builds on the *acquis* of international human rights law, including the output of expert mechanisms mandated to oversee the implementation of human rights norms and standards. OHCHR supports these mechanisms—the custodians of international human rights norms—and houses all of the UN human rights mechanisms. Given this role, it is clear that OHCHR has both a duty and a comparative advantage for advancing the human rights framework through supporting and promoting the realisation of the findings of expert human rights mechanisms established by states themselves.[8] This is why the legal framework and expert findings of independent mechanisms are part and parcel of OHCHR's programmes and activities.[9] A case in point is the degree to which the High Commissioner relies on such findings for preparing and conducting numerous challenging missions, including to the countries of the Gulf Cooperation Council in 2010. The positive interaction between the High Commissioner and the Gulf countries during her first visit of its kind proves that the findings of expert human rights mechanisms constitute a privileged and politically acceptable tool of engagement and of human rights diplomacy.[10] Just as the Organisation for Security and Co-operation in Europe's (OSCE) High Commissioner on National Minorities, the UN

---

[7] L. Minear, 'The Craft of Humanitarian Diplomacy' in Minear and Smith (eds.), *Humanitarian Diplomacy*, 2007, p.9.

[8] See Ramcharan, *A UN High Commissioner*, 2005, p.50, holding that: 'The High Commissioner of the future must consciously seek to develop and apply a diplomacy of human rights protection. This concept is an important one. It does not imply the timidity of traditional diplomacy; rather it involves a quality of diplomacy that is up to the challenge of helping to bring protection and relief to those in need.'

[9] W. A. Kemp (ed.), *Quiet Diplomacy in Action: The OSCE High Commissioner on National Minorities* (Boston: Kluwer Law International, 2001). This piece on the role of the previous OSCE High Commissioner on National Minorities can be referred to draw some analogies. On pp.25–26 Kemp observes: 'While seeing himself as a political instrument, Van der Stoel also interpreted his role as having a solid basis in international standards… The challenge is to explain to the parties the logic and possibility of internalizing and applying the norms under discussion. The key is to move from the abstract to the concrete, to get States to take measures—legal and political—to create the types of conditions foreseen in the standards concerning minorities'.

[10] 'Human Rights and the Gulf Region', address by Ms Navanethem Pillay, UN High Commissioner for Human Rights, at the King Abdullah University for Science and Technology in Jeddah, Saudi Arabia (19 April 2010), available at:

High Commissioner for Human Rights can also be seen 'as a "normative intermediary"—an agent dispatched by a norm-concerned community with the authority and tools to communicate norms and persuade states to comply with them'.[11]

Last, in the face of human rights violations and victims thereof, the human rights system is likely to produce an instinctive reaction geared towards applying maximum pressure so as to secure the quickest result. Fundamental as this may be, the toolbox should be larger than simply applying more pressure. Indeed, a long-term perspective should always be born in mind, in particular because in many instances cultural barriers lie at the core of certain practices that contradict international human rights law. Sustainable institutional and cultural developments should therefore genuinely emerge from within societies. This requires time. Tailoring a strategy for the improvement of a human rights situation in an incremental fashion allows to combat cultural relativism while also tactically accommodating context-specific concerns with a view to introduce acceptable and lasting changes. The debate around 'defamation of religions' and the artificial divide between enhancing freedom of expression and combating hate speech, constitutes a good example of a strategy combining short- and long-term aims and measures.[12] The key issue in this example is how to transcend both terminological and perception traps to deal with the legitimate underlying concerns of all parties with respect to a complex matter.

---

http://www.ohchr.org/EN/NewsEvents/Pages/DisplayNews.aspx?NewsID=9997&LangID=E [last accessed 24 November 2010]. In her keynote speech, the High Commissioner referred to reservations to the 1979 Convention on the Elimination of All Forms of Discrimination against Women (CEDAW), UNGA Res 34/180 (1979), UN Doc A/RES/34/180 (18 December 1979), 1249 UNTS 13; entered into force 3 September 1981, and to obligations under the 1990 Convention on the Protection of the Rights of All Migrant Workers and Members of Their Families (CMW), UNGA Res 45/158 (1990), UN Doc A/RES/45/158 (18 December 1990), 2220 UNTS 3; entered into fore 1 July 2003. See also the press conference by High Commissioner Pillay, Abu Dhabi (24 April 2010), opening statement, accessible at: http://www.ohchr.org/EN/NewsEvents/Pages/DisplayNews.aspx?NewsID=9983&LangID=E [last accessed 24 November 2010].

[11] S. Ratner, 'Does International Law Matter in Preventing Ethnic Conflict?' *New York University Journal of International Law and Politics* 32 (2000), 668. The OSCE High Commissioner on National Minorities came to be seen as an important standard-bearer regarding compliance with international provisions protecting the rights of national minorities.

[12] For further details see the discussion below on the 2008 Expert Seminar on Freedom of Expression and Advocacy of Religious Hatred that Constitutes Incitement to Discrimination, Hostility or Violence.

In a lecture entitled "Human Rights Diplomacy: An Oxymoron", the High Commissioner for Human Rights, Ms Navanethem Pillay, dispels some myths on what human rights diplomacy means and how she defines her role in these evolving diplomatic spaces.[13]

The decades from 1960s to the 1980s can be loosely categorised as the decades of human rights law-making and the creation of international human rights institutions and bodies, including both the UN Charter-based and independent human rights treaty-based bodies.[14]

The 1990s witnessed the end of the Cold War, astonishing technological advances, further unleash of the market forces, and a stronger impact of non-state actors in various fields. These years saw large-scale humanitarian and human rights-oriented advocacy campaigns launched by civil society organisations—and reinforced or supported by like-minded states and international organisations—in response to numerous atrocities in many parts of the world. Such campaigns included the movement to ban landmines, to stop the use of child soldiers, and to limit and control the proliferation of small arms and light weapons. At the same time, with the adoption of the Rome Statute in 1998,[15] a permanent system for the enforcement of international criminal law was established. It is also against this background that the post of the High Commissioner for Human Rights was created in 1993, much as a result of public human rights advocacy which culminated at the Vienna World Conference on Human Rights. Since then the OHCHR has progressively expanded responding to fundamental needs and protection gaps. As the High Commissioner clearly puts it, 'with regard to diplomacy, OHCHR's efforts have unfolded both "internally" and "externally"; both proactively and reactively; both publicly and quietly; and both as a stand-alone outreach strategy and in partnership'.[16]

OHCHR also played a pivotal role in mainstreaming human rights within the UN system. However, this progress has not been without its

[13] Statement by Navanethem Pillay, United Nations High Commissioner for Human Rights, 'Human Rights Diplomacy: An Oxymoron?', Cambridge, Massachusetts (28 October 2009), available at: http://www.ohchr.org/EN/NewsEvents/Pages/DisplayNews.aspx?NewsID=9569&LangID=e [last accessed 24 November 2010].

[14] Ramcharan, *Early-Warning and Preventive Diplomacy*, 1991, p.1.

[15] 1998 Rome Statute of the International Criminal Court (ICC Statute), 2187 UNTS 3; entered into force 1 July 2002.

[16] Statement of the High Commissioner, 'Human Rights Diplomacy: An Oxymoron?', 2009.

challenges. The main challenges as identified by the High Commissioner are that

> from the Security Council to the UN Country Teams that operate on the ground, there is an ongoing reluctance to embrace human rights mainly driven by the perceived need to accommodate the sensitivities of governments. We must address this head on if we are to make significant progress.[17]

Two recent developments contributed to both the creation of a more conducive environment and bigger space for human rights diplomacy, and a greater need for human rights diplomacy. The first development is the establishment of the Human Rights Council in 2006. Since it is virtually a standing body, the HRC creates further opportunities for human rights diplomacy which in turn should allow for progress toward better protection of human rights through enhanced international cooperation. Second, as also highlighted in the High Commissioner's lecture, the new UPR process of the Human Rights Council, designed to examine the human rights record of all states, seeks to overcome the selectivity and regional confrontations of the former Commission on Human Rights when considering specific human rights situations. As a result of this process, various countries under review firmly pledged to strengthen the implementation of human rights standards at the national level, as well as their cooperation with other states and different UN human rights bodies and agencies to this end. Theoretically at least, human rights diplomacy should see brighter horizons in the newly established HRC.

The role of the High Commissioner could be viewed as a bridge between different actors and mechanisms, and also as the anchor for streamlining and harmonising the activities of the various bodies created by the international human rights system.[18] However, the High

---

[17] *Ibid.*

[18] D. Chigas, 'Preventive Diplomacy and the Organisation for Security and Co-operation in Europe: Creating Incentives for Dialogue and Co-operation' in A. Chayes and H. Chayes (eds.), *Preventing Conflict in the Post-Communist Wold. Mobilizing International and Regional Organizations* (Washington: Brookings Institute, 1996), p.39. Chigas refers to the 'insider third party'. She explains: 'the role combines some of the basic characteristics of traditional mediation by international organizations with those of an 'insider' to the conflict working for change within the governmental and political processes in the state concerned, and in some cases actually becoming part of the governing process. It maintains two essential characteristics of an outside mediator of the conflict: impartiality and lack of vested interests in the substantive issues at

Commissioner also commands a leadership role in blazing the path forward as regards human rights, being first and foremost its key champion.

Selected Illustrations of Human Rights Diplomacy in Action

The Durban Review Conference

The Durban Review Conference was decided upon by the UN General Assembly and held in Geneva in April 2009. The process of facilitating a successful outcome of this conference by the OHCHR is a unique illustration of how human rights diplomacy can work and should continue to work in practical terms. This illustration also highlights the risks that characterise certain human rights negotiations: that sensitivities and misperceptions can overshadow the real issues and exacerbate the divergences among the actors involved. As often the case, and indeed also in this instance, the Outcome Document of the Review Conference[19] may not be perfect to any of the concerned parties. Yet, finding a consensual mid-point on the difficult issues at stake with clear added value is in itself a successful illustration of human rights diplomacy from which lessons for the future can be drawn.

The Durban Review Conference was a highly complex endeavour for all actors, including OHCHR, given the controversial history of the 2001 World Conference against Racism, Racial Discrimination, Xenophobia and Related Intolerance and the minefield of political and diplomatic controversies that erupted in the post-September 11 era. Because of unacceptable excesses in its parallel NGO Forum, the 2001 World Conference outcome document itself—the Durban Declaration and Programme of Action (DDPA)[20]—had been wrongfully depicted

stake. This allows the third party to move easily back and forth among the parties. The 'insider third party' role also maintains the traditional function of the international organization as watchdog and monitor of the conflict, while ensuring transparency and providing an impartial analysis of the situation, as well as exerting by its very presence pressure on the government to modify its behaviour.'

[19] The Outcome Document of the Durban Review Conference is available at: http://www.un.org/durbanreview2009/pdf/Durban_Review_outcome_document_En.pdf [last accessed 24 November 2010].

[20] The 2001 Durban Declaration and Programme of Action is accessible at: http://www.un.org/durbanreview2009/pdf/DDPA_full_text.pdf [last accessed 24 November 2010].

as containing anti-Semitic language. Moreover, despite the unfounded nature of such allegations, the DDPA was met with opposition from some governments and civil society organisations ever since its adoption. The Durban Review Conference had therefore to navigate through a minefield of stereotypes and misrepresentations. This was further compounded by negative media coverage and yet further deterioration of the situation in the Middle East with the end of December 2008 - early January 2009 Gaza armed conflict taking place during the preparations for the Review Conference. All of the above overshadowed the wider scope and valuable objectives of the Review Conference, as well as the fact that many issues to be discussed at Review Conference were of a technical nature.

The Review Conference provides an insight into how OHCHR can engage with politically sensitive issues both with governments and civil society, and how key lessons can be learned from the experiences gained during this complex and difficult process. Even if some issues are sensitive to handle in the eyes of one or more than one group of states, this does not absolve OHCHR from its responsibility to implement its mandate of promoting and protecting human rights in the most impartial and objective manner possible.[21] What is essential for assuming this responsibility is the development of a careful strategy underpinned by an in-depth analysis of the framework of international law, the international obligations entered into by states, and the duties and responsibilities resulting from such a framework for all parties concerned.

The main factors for an effective role of OHCHR were the timing and the substance of the High Commissioner's written contribution of 24 February 2009 containing various proposals.[22] Results show that it is through leadership, anticipation and concrete suggestions by the High Commissioner for Human Rights that the entire process was brought back on track.[23] The lesson here is that bridging divides and

---

[21] B Dickson, 'Law, Diplomacy and Conflict: State Crises and the Role of the European Convention on Human Rights' (unpublished paper delivered at a conference on The Diplomacy of Human Rights, 7 December 2007, co-organised by the Irish Centre for Human Rights and University of Paris II) [on file with author].

[22] Report of the UN High Commissioner for Human Rights on the Organization of the Work of the Durban Review Conference and Other Matters, UN Doc A/CONF.211/PC.4/5 (24 February 2009).

[23] For an exposition on how the diplomacy of the High Commissioner and her aides paid off, see: 'Et "Durban II" fut sauvée', A. Duparc for *Le Monde* (25 April 2009).

effective leadership can only be credibly demonstrated through the courage of submitting concrete suggestions based on substantive human rights grounds, orchestrated with a human rights diplomacy based on a finely crafted political analysis, to facilitate the acceptance of such suggestions.

One very important element of human rights diplomacy that emerged from the Durban Review Process—and which can also be applied more widely—is the active engagement with governments. A proactive UN Secretariat needs to be vigilant about not to overstep its mandate, and should avoid at all costs to show biases or the perception thereof. Nevertheless, as a legitimate player in the human rights arena, the High Commissioner and OHCHR have the capacity to usefully enrich the intergovernmental processes with a view to furthering the implementation of human rights. This can be done through clarifying technical matters and by offering the results from comparative analyses which may widen the scope of policy options available to governments. When applied strategically, i.e. in a timely, substantive and constructive fashion, these activities will reinforce the position of the High Commissioner as a trustworthy point of reference, and is thereby also likely to strengthen her and her Office's independence with respect to the main stakeholders who have the primary responsibility to respect, protect and fulfil human rights: states.

Another lesson learned from the Durban Review Process is that anticipation is crucial. This is proven by the strategic decision that was made public early in process to replace the suggested NGO forum with a programme of meetings (so-called 'side events') in the margins of the 2009 Review Conference itself. Organising a range of smaller activities instead of one major event facilitated a more focused contribution from the widest possible spectrum of civil society organisations, and helped to avoid the excesses, manipulations and polemics that had characterised the NGO Forum in Durban in 2001. Because of the objective and transparent criteria that had been set for the running of these events, the initiative proved successful and empowered civil society organisations to express their views, experiences and expectations.

The success of the Durban Review Conference clearly demonstrates that a clear strategy, pro-active diplomacy, and courageous leadership by the High Commissioner for Human Rights are key factors for a healthy development of the human rights movement at large.

The Role of Treaty Bodies and Special Procedures: The Example of the 2008 Expert Seminar on Freedom of Expression and Advocacy of Religious Hatred

The role of the ten human rights treaty bodies and the various procedures of the Human Rights Council, including special rapporteurs, independent experts and working groups is crucial not only for the progressive development of human rights law, but also in the conduct of human rights diplomacy. Special procedures mandate-holders are entrusted with the examination, investigation and monitoring of human rights issues and situations worldwide. They produce public reports to the HRC and advise all relevant stakeholders on how to address a particular situation or thematic human rights issue. The treaty bodies are independent mechanisms, each with a mandate to monitor the implementation of states' obligations under one of the core human rights treaties. The body of general comments, concluding observations, statements and 'jurisprudential' outputs created by the treaty bodies clarify and develop existing human rights law through interpretation. They constitute a strong normative basis on which countries can plan the implementation of human rights at the national level, and on which states can be held to account.

Given their independent status and collective nature, these mechanisms are well-placed to conduct human rights diplomacy—something that I would like to call an 'expertise-based diplomacy'. For example, it can take the shape of the inclusion of experts in discussions, meetings or negotiations to inject objective analysis and deeper understanding of complex human rights issues. The other very important role that treaty bodies and special procedures mandate-holders can play in human rights diplomacy lies in the substance of their findings—their concluding observations, general comments, views and reports to the HRC. Human rights diplomacy relies on these outputs when striving to further the realisation of human rights.

One of the main challenges for optimising the powerful potential of independent human rights expert mechanisms in human rights diplomacy concerns the preservation of their independence. This main virtue should be fully respected. The treaty bodies, for instance, are composed of experts with various legal backgrounds, coming from different cultural traditions of the world; and the special procedures mandate-holders are appointed by the President of the HRC after extensive consultation among the Council's members. In addition, coordinated human rights diplomacy requires a minimum level of coherence in the approach used, and in the shared vision towards the pursued objectives. This is why internal coordination structures such as the Coordination Committee of Special Procedures and the Meeting of Chairpersons of Human Rights Treaty Bodies are crucial innovations with promising potential for human rights diplomacy.

The greatest fear in regard to using diplomatic means for furthering the implementation of human rights is that, if not applied within the proper parameters of human rights law, it could erode the hard-won normative foundation on which human rights stand.[24] To prevent this from taking place and to build a case for the legitimacy for human rights diplomacy, a normative analysis should remain central and not be left at the margins. This precaution can be facilitated by the function of the independent human rights mechanisms to interpret and develop international human rights law progressively. This function, and the resulting international 'jurisprudence' should provide the backdrop for human rights diplomacy that strives to find creative and implementable solutions based on human rights norms, without undermining them through negotiations.[25]

A recent example demonstrates how this can work in practice. In October 2008 OHCHR held an expert seminar in Geneva on the links between Articles 19 and 20 of the ICCPR, on freedom of expression and advocacy of religious hatred that constitutes incitement to discrimination, hostility or violence. This was initiated in anticipation of major controversies that might arise on this issue during the Durban Review Conference of 2009. In the new millennium, freedom of expression has at times become a topic of contention on the world's stage. Those who regard freedom of expression as one of the highest values felt it to be under attack by those who allegedly have yet to fully respect this freedom. Some actors also saw the scope of protection given to freedom of expression as excessive in some areas, to the detriment of other human rights, including the rights of certain minority communities. In the context of the Human Rights Council, this political tension is reflected in the controversial debates on the topic of the 'defamation of religions'. Indeed, some assert that religions as such, including their symbols and practices, should receive protection under international law. Others, however, fear that this would open the door

---

[24] As observed by Minear in the context of 'humanitarian diplomacy', see Minear, 'The Craft of Humanitarian Diplomacy', 2007, p.14

[25] Obviously, there is 'a greater chance for success [for human rights diplomacy] if it is clear to all parties that there are things that are not negotiable', see *ibid.*, p.31.

for the imposition of disproportionate limitations to freedom of expression, and indeed also to the freedom of religion or belief, including the right to not hold any belief.

To a greater or lesser extent, these positions reflect legitimate political concerns and objectives. Indeed, the High Commissioner herself indicated in her report to the Human Rights Council that

> there are legitimate concerns about an increase in manifestations of intolerance and discrimination based on religion or belief as well as acts of violence, including attacks against places of worship, which are threatening the enjoyment of human rights and fundamental freedoms.[26]

With this in mind, the principal goal of OHCHR is to ensure that arguments reflecting competing political objectives use the appropriate legal entry points and that the tools relied on are compatible with international human rights law. The purpose of the above-mentioned expert seminar organised by OHCHR in 2008 was therefore to present an approach based on human rights law which, in this example, aimed to ensure a sound legal interpretation of Articles 19 and 20 of the ICCPR. It underlined the need to first fully understand what was necessary to fully promote freedom of expression before examining permissible restrictions.[27]

This example points to the mutually supportive roles of expert mechanisms (treaty bodies and special procedures) on the one hand, and the High Commissioner for Human Rights on the other hand, that can lead to positive results. The work of treaty bodies and special procedures mandate-holders was instrumental for analysing the legal and normative framework relevant to the issues under discussion, and this provided a platform for innovative solutions. Through holding the

---

[26] Study of the United Nations High Commissioner for Human Rights Compiling Existing Legislations and Jurisprudence Concerning Defamation of and Contempt for Religions, UN Doc A/HRC/9/25 (5 September 2008), para.81. In that same report (para.82), the High Commissioner indicated that 'further clarity is needed with regard to the legal contours of the demarcation line between freedom of expression and incitement to religious hatred. In order to protect individuals and groups, a better understanding of the permissible limitations to freedom of expression in accordance with international human rights law needs to be developed'.

[27] See the Report of the OHCHR on the Expert Seminar on the Links between Articles 19 and 20 of the ICCPR, Freedom of Expression and Advocacy of Religious Hatred that Constitutes Incitement to Discrimination, Hostility or Violence, UN Doc A/HRC/10/31/Add.3 (16 January 2009), para.34. Other related information can be found at: http://www2.ohchr.org/english/issues/opinion/articles1920_iccpr/2008_seminar.htm [last accessed 24 November 2010].

seminar, OHCHR furthermore created space for civil society organisations to also express their views and to thereby ground the discussions in the reality of contemporary challenges. This is also at the heart of human rights diplomacy: to listen to other voices[28] outside of formal meetings that usually do not provide enough space for them to be heard. This example of expertise-based human rights diplomacy strengthened OHCHR's proactive profile, confirming the autonomy and right to initiative of the High Commissioner. It revealed the benefits of the independence of the High Commissioner and highlighted the role she can play in building bridges.

At the time of writing OHCHR is building upon this precedent and the support it generated for its work in this field by organising a series of expert workshops on the prohibition of incitement to national, racial or religious hatred to be held in various parts of the world. The mapping undertaken in the context of these follow-up workshops will enable OHCHR to continuously apply human rights diplomacy by presenting country-specific technical information and expert knowledge with a view to unblock difficult political debates regarding freedom of expression, as well as regarding new human rights challenges faced by increasingly multicultural societies around the world.[29]

A major recent achievement has been the adoption by consensus of the milestone HRC resolution 16/18, embodying a paradigm shift from 'defamation of religions' to the 'prohibition of incitement to national, racial or religious hatred'. This timely achievement, which offers ample possibilities for concrete collaborative action, is mainly due to two important factors: first, the internal expert-based reviews within the Organisation of Islamic Cooperation (OIC), and second, the creative thinking and diplomatic skills of IOC representatives in

[28] See R. Archer, 'A Short Reflection on Human Rights Diplomacy', Chapter 3 in the present volume, p.47.

[29] See the concept paper on this initiative which indicates the following as one of the objectives of the regional seminars to be held in 2011: 'By grounding the debate around incitement to hatred in international human rights law the objective of the series of expert workshops is to gain a better understanding of legislative patterns, judicial practices and policies in the different regions of the world with regard to the concept of incitement to national, racial, or religious hatred while ensuring full respect for freedom of expression as outlined in articles 19 and 20 of the ICCPR.' Concept Paper on OHCHR's Expert Workshops on the Prohibition of Incitement to National, Racial or Religious Hatred - Follow-up to the Expert Seminar on Articles 19 and 20 of the ICCPR with Regard to Freedom of Expression and Incitement to Hatred, available at: http://www2.ohchr.org/english/issues/opinion/articles1920_iccpr/docs/Incitement_Workshops_Concept_Paper.pdf [last accessed 24 November 2010].

New York and Geneva and their interlocutors from different regional groups. The role of US diplomacy was also instrumental, as most recently demonstrated by the high-level event in Istanbul, in July 2011, co-chaired by the US Secretary of State and the Secretary-General of the OIC.[30] It is also important to note the role of the leadership within Secretariats of international organisations in this context, namely the clear vision of the United Nations High Commissioner for Human Rights expressed in her numerous public statements and reports, including her report to the Durban Review Conference in 2009, as well as the enlightened leadership of the Secretary-General of the OIC. This positive result may have been facilitated by the substantive discussions within the above-mentioned expert workshops organised by OHCHR.

The main lesson here from a human rights diplomacy perspective is the importance of ensuring that all actors involved deepen their understanding of the relevant complex legal issues in relation to the subject under discussion so that further politicisation, not to say manipulation, of serious matters for advancing narrow political agendas can be avoided. We might call this the 'anticipatory function' with regard to areas of tension surrounding religion and freedom of expression.

A second point to be emphasised as a useful feature of human rights diplomacy—which was already be referred to as expertise-based diplomacy—is the ability to generate comparative analysis of different solutions to the same problem. Indeed, analysing and compiling good practices can only stimulate creative thinking, fill knowledge gaps and promote international cooperation to further the cause of human rights.

The room for 'expert diplomacy' in this particular example is widened by the fact that international human rights law only prohibits certain forms of advocacy of hatred; it does not define this prohibition clearly. While it is not up to international human rights law to provide detailed prohibitions, there is insufficient clarity on what the most efficient means of combating hate speech are in its increasingly changing modes and facets. There are many problems with different facets around the world, and the same solution cannot fit everywhere. This is exactly one of the major areas where human rights diplomacy can add

[30] The Joint Statement by the Co-Chairs can be accessed at: http://www.oic-oci.org/topic_detail.asp?t_id=5545 [last accessed 6 August 2011].

value. It is not always about adding or enforcing norms, but about understanding how they apply to different situations in ever-changing environments. The role of human rights and expert diplomacy is to safeguard the existing norms, to think creatively and to add new options for their implementation. Inviting civil society to a meaningful, constructive dialogue with both governments and expert mechanisms is part of the process. Such positive and cross-fertilising interaction is hardly achievable in traditional inter-governmental settings.

The Process of Strengthening the Human Rights Treaty Bodies

When the first human rights treaty body was established in 1969 (the Committee on the Elimination of Racial Discrimination), there was no master plan or even an intention to build a treaty body system as such. Over 40 years later, the now ten treaty bodies have evolved into a demanding, complex and heavy-to-maintain system. Obviously, the creation of these new mechanisms is extremely positive as they increase the protection of human rights. However, its success and growth poses new challenges to the entire treaty body system, and to all actors involved.

In order to address these challenges facing the treaty body system, in 2005 the then High Commissioner for Human Rights, Ms Louise Arbour, presented a proposal for the creation of a unified standing treaty body.[31] This initiative did not gain acceptance. However, the experience provides valuable lessons with respect to applying human rights diplomacy.

The treaty body system includes many stakeholders, ranging from state parties, civil society organisations and NHRIs to the treaty body experts themselves. Each of these constituencies constitutes a heterogeneous group in its own right. The challenge of strengthening the treaty body system lies in finding a common vision leading to a harmonised, more user-friendly and efficient system beneficial to all concerned. For this to happen, treaty bodies should first understand themselves more as a common system for the promotion and protection of human rights, even though individual treaty bodies were created as separate entities over the last four decades. The High Commissioner is

[31] Concept Paper on the High Commissioner's Proposal for a Unified Standing Treaty Body, UN Doc HRI/MC/2006/2 (22 March 2006).

ideally positioned to facilitate a meaningful outcome of a multi-stakeholder discussion to this end, and to act as a catalyst in the process of strengthening the treaty body system. As I have outlined earlier in this article when discussing the characteristics of human rights diplomacy, for the role of the High Commissioner to be effective, she and her Office need to ensure a multi-pronged approach that consists of providing space where activities are tailored to the needs of specific stakeholders, but where these spaces are also incorporated in a wider strategy that is geared towards reaching a meaningful outcome of the over-arching process. The 2005 proposal on establishing one unified standing treaty body had the best intentions and was certainly coherent in its own merit. However, more time and space were needed to analyse and address the concerns of the various parties involved.

In a renewed attempt to strengthen the treaty body system in 2009, the present High Commissioner for Human Rights requested all stakeholders, including state parties to human rights treaties, civil society organisations and NHRIs, treaty body members and other parties involved, to initiate a process of reflection on how to streamline and strengthen the system. This time around the need for reform was pressing. The system is struggling, even though only 30 percent of states comply with their reporting obligations. In the words of the High Commissioner: 'the system [...] reached its limits both in terms of coherence and sustainable functioning within [...] available resources'.[32] Following this call, OHCHR has enhanced its outreach activities vis-à-vis these constituencies with a view to stimulate debate, generate ideas and mobilise all players to contribute to this process.[33]

Treaty body experts are the best placed constituency to take the lead on matters related to treaty body strengthening. It is therefore not surprising that the first response to the High Commissioner's call came from this constituency. A number of former and current members of the treaty bodies convened in Dublin in November 2009 and adopted a statement outlining some principles that should govern the reflection

[32] See the opening address by Ms Navi Pillay, United Nations High Commissioner for Human Rights to an informal technical consultation meeting on treaty body strengthening for state parties in Sion, Switzerland, on 12 May 2011, available at: http://www2.ohchr.org/english/bodies/HRTD/docs/consultation/Sion/HC12052011.pdf [last accessed 6 August 2011].

[33] For detailed information please consult the following link: http://www2.ohchr.org/english/bodies/HRTD/index.htm [last accessed 6 August 2011].

process.[34] Subsequently, a similar initiative was organised for and by NHRIs in June 2010 in Marrakech,[35] as well as a meeting of treaty body experts and NGOs took place in Poznan at the end of September 2010. These meetings were followed by a technical consultation for States parties in May 2011 in Sion, Switzerland, focusing mainly on the preparation of state reports, the 'constructive dialogue' and the implementation of treaty body recommendations. Two more consultations were held for civil society in Seoul (April 2011) and Pretoria (June 2011), both resulting in innovative statements.

This new approach combines both formal and informal tracks while nonetheless upholding full transparency of the process. Indeed, transparency, inclusiveness and bottom-up approaches are key ingredients for successful multi-stakeholder negotiations and for human rights diplomacy.[36] Following the public call by the High Commissioner, a number of stakeholders have come forward and have organised formal events that serve as a catalyst for reflection by their constituencies. These initiatives have at the same time provided the opportunity for OHCHR to intensify its outreach activities; and to draw from its extensive expertise on the work and role of treaty bodies to inject substantive ideas for reflection into these processes. Such a multi-pronged, inclusive and incremental strategy, underpinned by substantive human rights expertise and geared toward finding common ground for the enhancement of the human rights treaty body system, no doubt qualifies as a good example of intelligently applied human rights diplomacy.

Working Group on Right to Development and Its High-Level Task Force on the Implementation of the Right to Development

Another area where human rights diplomacy has often seen bitter bloc struggles and raging rhetorical battles is in regard to the right to

[34] The Dublin Statement on the Process of Strengthening of the United Nations Human Rights Treaty Body System (19 November 2009), available at: http://www.nottingham.ac.uk/hrlc/documents/specialevents/ dublinstatement.pdf [last accessed 24 November 2010].

[35] The Marrakech Statement on Strengthening the Relationship between NHRIs and the Human Rights Treaty Bodies System (10 June 2010), available at: http://www.nhri.net/2010/Marrakech_Declaration_(EN).pdf [last accessed 24 November 2010].

[36] This is not to say that full transparency can be guaranteed in all processes involving human rights diplomacy. See for example the observations by R. Archer, 'A Short Reflection on Human Rights Diplomacy', Chapter 3 in the present volume, p.58.

development (RtD). I would again like to illustrate how the dynamics of the discourse on an issue as divisive as the RtD[37] can be transformed and de-politicised through the integration of expert knowledge into the process, in a similar way as outlined above in regard to the 'defamation of religion'.

The RtD has raised many expectations and controversies over the past 25 years. For some the RtD is the 'missing link' between trade, development and human rights—the 'parent of all rights'. For others it is just rhetoric, a political attempt to shift human rights from its normal course, and a drift away from national obligations to the vague notion of responsibility of the international community.[38] It is nevertheless not a miracle that was needed in order to reconcile those two camps and to reach a shared, workable vision for the realisation of the RtD. What was required was a new approach, a combination of political will, sustained commitment, conceptual clarity, creative thinking, collaborative action through partnerships involving all relevant stakeholders, and finally sound combined expertise informing the political discussions. This encapsulates the essence of human rights diplomacy as evidenced so far in this article.

At the beginning of the new millennium, the negotiating process on the RtD had reached a diplomatic crossroad. On the one hand, the international community committed itself in the Millennium Declaration in 2000—at the highest political level—to the inspiring slogan of 'making the right to development *a reality for everyone*'.[39] On the other hand, inter-governmental negotiations involving the RtD continued to be blocked by the well-known obstacles to the RtD, grounded in the fear that a new binding instrument would be adopted creating obligations of developed countries, and undercutting the primary responsibility of states to ensure the protection of human rights at the national level. While these obstacles cannot be eliminated, a new approach seemed to emerge that allows furthering the realisation of the RtD nonetheless.

---

[37] See UNGA Res 41/128 (1986), Declaration on the Right to Development, UN Doc A/RES/41/128 (4 December 1986), Article 1.

[38] I. Salama, 'Les Droits de l'Homme Sont-ils Solubles dans la Gouvernance?' in S. Bellina, H. Magro and V. de Villemeur (eds.), *La Gouvernance Démocratique: un Nouveau Paradigme pour le Développement* (Paris: Editions Karthala, 2008), p.206.

[39] UNGA Res 55/2 (2000), United Nations Millennium Declaration, UN Doc A/RES/55/2 (8 September 2000), para.11 (emphasis added).

The debate about the RtD as embodied in the 1986 Declaration of the Right to Development has undergone a renewal in recent years with a clear focus on implementation. This has led to cautious optimism as to the future of the RtD. Among the key factors that have triggered this renewal were those that were instrumental for the success of other experiences detailed above, for instance the use of technical information and expert knowledge to advance ideologically and politically motivated debates. From a human rights diplomacy perspective, the novelty with respect to the RtD was first the creation of institutional mechanisms that provide space for sustainable expert advice to counter the obstacles that had blocked progress in this area. The second novelty was the development of pilot projects with the aim to comprehend how the RtD could possibly be implemented in practice.[40]

As set out in resolution 1998/72 of the former UN Commission on Human Rights, since 1998 the debate on the RtD has exclusively been conducted by an inter-governmental Working Group on the Right to Development.[41] This led nowhere, simply because one cannot expect political discussions alone to settle highly technical issues related to the actual implementation of the RtD. In a later resolution 2004/7,[42] the former Commission on Human Rights endorsed the establishment of a High-Level Task Force (HLTF) on the Implementation of the Right to Development within the framework of the Working Group. In the view of the Commission, the HLTF was to assist the working group to fulfil its mandate. The Task Force was composed of high-level representatives from trade, finance and development institutions/organisations, in addition to five experts with diverse backgrounds, but with practical experience related to the implementation of the RtD. The UN HLTF on the RtD represented an innovative approach inspired by lessons learned from past attempts to negotiate the realisation of the RtD.

---

[40] See F. Kirchmeier, M. Lüke and B. Kalla, *Towards the Implementation of the Right to Development: Field-testing and Fine-tuning the UN Criteria on the Right to Development in the Kenyan-German Partnership* (Friedrich Ebert Stiftung and GTZ, August 2008).

[41] UN Commission on Human Rights, Res 1998/72 on the Right to Development, UN Doc E/CN.4/RES/1998/72 (22 April 1998).

[42] UN Commission on Human Rights, Res 2004/7 on the Right to Development, UN Doc E/CN.4/RES/2004/7 (13 April 2004).

The main added value of the HLTF—demonstrated already at its first meeting in Geneva in December 2004—was that it created a space for a structured dialogue between the human rights community, the worlds of trade rule-makers and development practitioners. It also contributed to addressing discrepancies in vocabulary used by different actors. These discrepancies sometimes stem from divergent concepts and approaches masking the true links between development, trade and human rights. Furthermore, it structured the discussion around a limited number of issues which allowed the most focused debate on the RtD since the Working Group had been established in 1998.

Up until the last meeting of the HLTF in January 2010, the Working Group and the HLTF focused on Millennium Development Goal 8 (MDG 8) on global partnerships for development. It elaborated criteria to monitor the implementation of the RtD, and tested these criteria in pilot projects with a view to refining and eventually finalising them. In its most recent 6th session, the HLTF provided the Working Group with the final criteria and sub-criteria, as well as with a number of suggestions relating to further action to be taken towards the implementation of the RtD.[43]

The work of the HLTF did not proceed without its problems and obstacles. However, the fact that the Working Group and the Human Rights Council have been able to adopt many of the conclusions, recommendations and resolutions on the RtD by consensus, endorsed pilot projects, and encouraged a wide range of partners to participate in the activities of the HLTF, has to be viewed as a substantial and most welcome departure from the past. The pilot projects included the examination of eleven global partnerships implemented within the context of MDG 8 from the right to development perspective. The work on the RtD criteria, sub-criteria and indicators is the result of considerable efforts undertaken by the HLTF and OHCHR. They will undoubtedly both deepen the discussion about the RtD and open promising horizons for its concrete implementation. This was only possible by focusing on the 'technical' side of the debate, pushing 'political' issues to the background. These achievements would have

[43] See the Report of the High-level Task Force on the Implementation of the Right to Development on its Sixth Session (14–22 January 2010), UN Doc A/HRC/15/WG.2/TF/2 (24 February 2010); and Report of the Working Group on the Right to Development on its Tenth Session (22–26 June 2009), UN Doc A/HRC/12/28 (30 July 2009).

been unthinkable without relying on expert knowledge and careful diplomacy.

Conclusion

I have asserted that engaging in human rights diplomacy is different in nature but complementary in practice to advocacy for human rights. Independent expert human rights mechanisms are at the heart of human rights diplomacy, both as actors and as tools. It has been demonstrated that bringing independent expertise into intergovernmental processes can have positive effects in situations where there is a need to overcome obstacles, to bridge divides, to build consensus, or to ensure specific protection needs.

Human rights diplomacy is an emerging concept and strategic approach, which has unique characteristics and, as a consequence, relies on a specific toolbox. The selection of these tools is determined by the need to form a multi-pronged strategy which aims to play out each actor's comparative advantage in an incremental fashion.[44] As an illustration of this, I have analysed the examples of the Durban Review Conference, the OHCHR Expert Seminar on Freedom of Expression and Incitement to Religious Hatred, the ongoing effort to strengthen the treaty body system and the RtD process. These case studies illustrate how expertise-based human rights diplomacy can bring innovative ideas to the fore and, in doing so, can create common ground for action. It can also optimise the central and autonomous role of the High Commissioner for Human Rights and her Office in fostering a collaborative environment. OHCHR can offer technical advice, highlight policy options, and produce comparative analyses in a manner that helps widening the choice of governments who bear the ultimate responsibility with respect to ensuring sustainable implementation and protection of all human rights.

[44] For a different take and also to note the importance of diplomacy working in tandem with other human rights tools, see H. Smith, 'Humanitarian Diplomacy: Theory and Practice' in Minear and Smith (eds.), *Humanitarian*, 2007, p.49.

CHAPTER 9

THE UNITED NATIONS HUMAN RIGHTS TREATY BODIES AS DIPLOMATIC ACTORS

MICHAEL O'FLAHERTY

Introduction

The United Nations (UN) human rights treaty bodies play a central role in the international framework for the supervision of implementation by states of their treaty obligations. In the literature this role is commonly described as being a quasi-judicial one. As a matter of fact, the dominant task for treaty bodies, the review of periodic reports might better be described as 'diplomatic' rather than as quasi-judicial, in as much as it concerns the engaging of states in dialogue intended to promote treaty compliance—the outcome of such dialogue never being more than recommendatory in nature. The diplomatic aspect of treaty body work has been brought into new prominence by the extent to which treaty body findings play a role in the application of the Human Rights Council's (HRC) new procedure of universal periodic review (UPR). The present chapter explores this dimension of treaty body work and reflects on how they might be strengthened in their important diplomatic function.

The Treaty Body System: An Overview

Ten treaties are generally considered to comprise the core of the UN human rights treaty system: the International Covenant on Civil and Political Rights (ICCPR),[1] the International Covenant on Economic, Social and Cultural Rights (ICESCR),[2] the International Convention

[1] 1966 International Covenant on Civil and Political Rights (ICCPR), UNGA Res 2200A (XXI) (1966), UN Doc A/RES/2200 XXI (A) (16 December 1966), 999 UNTS 171; entered into force 23 March 1976.

[2] 1966 International Covenant on Economic, Social and Cultural Rights (ICESCR), UNGA Res 2200A (XXI) (1966), UN Doc A/RES/2200 XXI (A) (16 December 1966), 933 UNTS 3; entered into force 3 January 1976.

on the Elimination of All Forms of Racial Discrimination,[3] the Convention on the Elimination of All Forms of Discrimination against Women (CEDAW),[4] the Convention on the Rights of the Child (CRC),[5] the Convention against Torture and Other Cruel, Inhuman or Degrading Treatment or Punishment (CAT),[6] Optional Protocol to the Convention against Torture (OP-CAT),[7] International Convention on the Protection of the Rights of All Migrant Workers and Members of Their Families (ICRMW),[8] the Convention on the Rights of Persons with Disabilities (CRPD),[9] the International Convention for the Protection of All Persons from Enforced Disappearance (CPED).[10] With regard to each of them a monitoring body has been established (by treaty in all but the case of the Committee on Economic, Social and Cultural Rights—which was established by the UN Economic and Social Council). These bodies are known interchangeably as the 'committees' and as 'treaty bodies'. They each meet for two or three sessions of some one to four weeks duration *per annum*. They comprise from 10 to 25 (depending on the treaty in question) members all of whom serve in an independent expert and voluntary capacity. The committees carry out their responsibilities by means of a number of functions. Six of them have the capacity to receive and consider complaints from

---

[3] 1965 International Convention on the Elimination of All Forms of Racial Discrimination (ICERD), UNGA Res 2106 (XX) (1965), UN Doc A/RES/2106 XX (21 December 1965), 660 UNTS 195; entered into force 4 January 1969.

[4] 1979 Convention on the Elimination of All Forms of Discrimination against Women (CEDAW), UNGA Res 34/180 (1979), UN Doc A/RES/34/180 (18 December 1979), 1249 UNTS 13; entered into force 3 September 1981.

[5] 1989 UN Convention on the Rights of the Child (CRC), UNGA Res 44/25 (1989), UN Doc A/RES/44/25 (20 November 1989), 1577 UNTS 3; entered into force 2 September 1990.

[6] 1984 Convention against Torture and Other Cruel, Inhuman or Degrading Treatment or Punishment (CAT), UNGA Res 39/46 (1984), UN Doc A/RES/39/46 (10 December 1984), 1465 UNTS 85; entered into force 26 June 1987.

[7] 2002 Optional Protocol to the Convention against Torture and Other Cruel, Inhuman or Degrading Treatment or Punishment (OP-CAT), UNGA Res 57/199 (2003), UN Doc A/RES/57/199 (9 January 2003), 2375 UNTS 237; entered into force 22 June 2006.

[8] 1990 International Convention on the Protection of the Rights of All Migrant Workers and Members of Their Families (CMW), UNGA Res 45/158 (1990), UN Doc A/RES/45/158 (18 December 1990), 2220 UNTS 3; entered into force 1 July 2003.

[9] 2006 Convention on the Rights of Persons with Disabilities (CRPD), UNGA Res 61/106 (2006), UN Doc A/RES/61/106 (13 December 2006); entered into force 3 May 2008.

[10] 2006 International Convention for the Protection of All Persons from Enforced Disappearance (CPED), UNGA Res 61/177 (2006), UN Doc A/RES/61/177 (20 December 2006); entered into force 23 December 2010.

rights-holders and to adopt views on the matter of whether the state in question has violated the treaty. Five treaty bodies may undertake investigative activities, including by means of country visits. All but one (the Subcommittee on Prevention of Torture and other Cruel, Inhuman or Degrading Treatment or Punishment) review reports submitted periodically by state parties indicating the state of their compliance with the treaty.[11] The review of periodic reports, in terms of time devoted to it, is the dominant work area for treaty bodies.[12] For instance, in a typical session of the Human Rights Committee, that scheduled for March 2011, some 50% of meeting time is devoted to it, with some 25% of meeting time devoted to consideration of individual complaints.[13] In some other committees, such as the Committee on Economic, Social and Cultural Rights, the proportion of time devoted to the reporting procedure is even greater. The development and application of the reporting procedure provides the context for the reflections in this chapter.

The origins of the reporting procedure are to be found in the practice of the International Labour Organisation where it is applied as a typical oversight tool for that organisation's conventions.[14] Commentators have observed that, whatever its utility in the specific context of labour issues, its importation into human rights treaties was intended to ensure that oversight of latter treaties would be of a relatively mild form which, in the avoidance of binding jurisdiction, of formal legal assessment and judgement, or of otherwise intrusive external review, was respectful of state sovereignty.[15] Certainly, any examination of the *travaux preparatoires* of the human rights treaties makes clear

---

[11] OHCHR, 'The United Nations Human Rights Treaty System: An Introduction to the Core Human Rights Treaties and Treaty Bodies', (Fact Sheet No 30), 2005, available at: http://www.ohchr.org/Documents/Publications/FactSheet30en.pdf [last accessed 19 December 2010].

[12] M. O'Flaherty, 'The Concluding Observations of United Nations Human Rights Treaty Bodies', *Human Rights Law Review* 6 (2006), 27.

[13] See Human Rights Committee, Programme of Work, 101th Session, 14 March to 1 April 2011, available at: http://www2.ohchr.org/english/bodies/hrc/docs/PoW_CCPR101.doc [last accessed 19 December 2010].

[14] M. Nowak, *UN Covenant on Civil and Political Rights: CCPR Commentary*, 2nd revised edn (Kehl: N. P. Engel, 2005), p.713; M. Scheinin, 'International Mechanisms and Procedures for Implementation' in R. Hanski and M. Suksi (eds.), *An Introduction to the International Protection of Human Rights: A Textbook* (Turku/Åbo: Institute for Human Rights, Åbo Akademi, 1997), p.356; M. Kjærum, 'State Reports' in G. Alfredsson *et al.* (eds.), *International Human Rights Monitoring Mechanisms: Essays in Honour of Jakob Th. Möller*, 2nd revised edn (Leiden: Martinus Nijhoff, 2009), p.18.

[15] Nowak, *CCPR Commentary*, 2005, p.731.

that there was little appetite among states for the design of sturdy mechanisms of oversight.[16] What is more, for over a decade following the adoption of the first of the treaties, the committees themselves implemented the reporting procedure in a formulaic and non-intrusive fashion whereby it demonstrated very little utility in the identification and response to situations of concern. These practices only came to change with the de-escalation and eventual demise of the Cold War when various UN human rights mechanisms came to seize opportunities to be more effective in the discharge of their responsibilities. As a result, in a process dating from the late 1980s and in continuous development since, the treaty bodies have engaged in a more rigorous substantive assessment of country situations. They take into account not only government-sourced information, but also that of civil society and other actors, entering into frank debate with government delegations that come before them, and issuing increasingly detailed commentary and recommendations as to how the human rights situation might be improved.[17]

Today, the precise procedures for the review of reports vary from committee to committee, albeit the core elements are common to all.[18] By way of illustration, the practice of the Human Rights Committee (the Committee) may be described.[19] States are obliged to submit a report on ratification of the ICCPR and thereafter according to a schedule established by the Committee. All reports other than those of an initial nature are intended to furnish the Committee with updates on the treaty-related human rights situation. In so doing they are expected to take account of the outcome of previous dialogue with the Committee, the state of implementation by the state of any recommendations that have been put to it previously and to reflect on any relevant changes in national circumstances. Following an initial confidential

[16] M. J. Bossuyt, *Guide to the "Travaux Préparatoires" of the International Covenant on Civil and Political Rights* (Dordrecht: Martinus Nijhoff, 1987), p.617; I. Boerefijn, *The Reporting Procedure under the Covenant on Civil and Political Rights* (Antwrep: Intersentia, 1999), pp.20–22.

[17] O'Flaherty, 'Concluding Observations', 2006, 29-30; T. Buergenthal, 'The UN Human Rights Committee', *Max Planck Yearbook of United Nations Law* 5 (2001), 352.

[18] OHCHR, The United Nations: Human Rights Treaty System, 2005, pp.17–25.

[19] Report of the Human Rights Committee on its 97th—99th sessions, UN Doc A/65/40 (Vol.I) (2010). In 2009, the Committee decided to implement a new procedure whereby, in most circumstances, states would be invited to submit responses to a list of questions in place of a periodic report. This, as yet un-implemented, procedure, which is similar to that already being implemented by the Committee against Torture, is not further addressed in this chapter.

review of the report by a group of members of the treaty body, a 'task force' chaired by a committee member designated as 'country rapporteur', the state receives a set of questions, the 'list of issues'. The list of issues, typically comprising some 25–30 questions, addresses what are considered to be the most important matters in need of further examination by the Committee. This list, like the report itself, is a public document. States are invited, though not required, to submit answers in writing. Some six to eight months after transmittal to the state of the list of issues, the Committee schedules an oral dialogue with the state, which, for now, takes place either in Geneva or New York. That exchange of views normally takes place over six hours of Committee meeting time. It is held in public. Civil society is strongly encouraged by the Committee to be present.[20] Non-governmental submissions are paid close attention to by committee members and there are numerous opportunities for these organisations to undertake oral and written briefings to members. The Committee also has access to such other sources of information as the proceedings of other treaty bodies, of the HRC and its special procedures and reports by UN specialised agencies. States are encouraged to send high level delegations for dialogue with the Committee. Practice varies, with most states fielding representatives of all relevant offices of state and headed by either a senior official or member of government, with others—particularly poorer states, sending diplomatic delegations from their UN permanent missions. The dialogue takes the form of the delegation presenting the report and either orally responding to the list of issues or otherwise drawing attention to what it considers to be the most pertinent aspects of the country situation. This presentation is followed by questions and commentary by Committee members. The interjections of members are dominated by those of the country rapporteur and members of the task force. These normally take the form of queries for further information in order to better understand the country situation, expressions of concern regarding human rights problems, highlighting of what appears to be good practice by the state, reference to good practice elsewhere that may be relevant for the country situation and suggestions as to how situations might be improved. The delegation responds orally

[20] Centre for Civil and Political Rights, 'UN Human Rights Committee Participation in the Reporting Process: Guidelines for Non-Governmental Organisations', 2nd edn, pp.17–19, available at: http://www.ccprcentre.org/doc/CCPR/Handbook/CCPR_Guidelines%20for%20NGOs_en.pdf [last accessed 19 December 2010].

to such commentary in an exchange that may go back and forth with Committee members. States may also submit written responses with a very tight deadline of one or two days. Following the oral exchanges the Committee debates an outcome document, known as 'concluding observations', taking into account the dialogue and any written responses that may have been received. The document is adopted on a consensus basis. The concluding observations are delivered to the state and put in the public domain at the conclusion of the session of the Committee, that is within one to two weeks of the dialogue with the delegation.

The concluding observations comprise a succinct assessment of the state of implementation of the ICCPR in the country in question, with reference to positive aspects, areas of concern and recommendations for action by the state (typically some 20 to 30 in number).[21] The document concludes with reference to a small number of the recommendations with regard to which the state party is requested to provide an implementation up-date to the Committee within a period of six months, as well as the stipulation of the date when the next report is due. For now, the Committee indicates a due date of three, four or five years hence, with the greater imminence of that date serving as an indication of the extent to which the Committee considers the human rights situation to be problematic.

The Committee has a follow up procedure to concluding observations.[22] A member, designated as 'follow-up special rapporteur' is tasked with assessing the implementation up-dates and reporting accordingly to the Committee. The special rapporteur has the discretion to enter into correspondence with the state, to meet with its representatives and to take whatever other action may be appropriate to promote implementation of the designated recommendations. On advice of the special rapporteur, the Committee may choose either to consider a country-file to be closed or to maintain a state of 'ongoing dialogue' with the state.

The reporting procedure is considered to promote country-level human rights compliance in multiple ways.[23] Studies persistently

---

[21] O'Flaherty, 'Concluding Observations', 2006, 31.

[22] Report of the Human Rights Committee on its 94th–96th sessions, UN Doc A/64/40 (Vol.I) (2009), Annex VI, pp.232–33.

[23] P. Alston, 'The Purposes of Reporting' in OHCHR, *Manual on Human Rights Reporting under Six Major International Human Rights Instruments* (Geneva: United

indicate that the very act of writing a report is often a catalyst to make governments more sensitive to human rights considerations and to encourage various ministries to engage with each other on human rights.[24] Findings also demonstrate how engagement by civil society in the reporting process can greatly strengthen the non-governmental organisations (NGOs), promote the development of strong coalitions and, more generally, promote human rights debate in society.[25] It is also considered that the publication of the reports and other materials serves a useful function.[26] Recent studies point in particular to the value of widely disseminating the treaty body findings—they can be considered as authoritative analysis of the human rights situation, sometimes providing a fresh perspective on what may be longstanding problems.[27]

These are of course what can be termed as peripheral merits of the reporting procedure. The key question is that of assessing the actual impact of treaty body recommendations—do they change things on the ground. Here our information sources are limited. The follow-up procedures indicate that a majority of states at least claim to partially implement recommendations.[28] Academic studies come to similar conclusions. For instance, a recent study of African countries indicated a higher level of implementation than might have been expected.[29] Some country studies, many focussing on the rights of the child, have

Nations, 1997), p.20; *General Comment 1*, Committee on Economic, Social and Cultural Rights (Third session, 1989), Compilation of General Comments and General Recommendations adopted by Human Rights Treaties Bodies, UN Doc HRI/GEN/1/Rev.9 (Vol.I) (27 May 2008), p.1.

[24] L. Theytaz-Bergman, 'State Reporting and the Role of Non-Governmental Organizations', in A. F. Bayefsky (ed.), *The UN Human Rights Treaty System in the 21st Century* (The Hague: Kluwer, 2000), p.45.

[25] J. Karp, 'Reporting and the Committee on the Rights of the Child', in *ibid.*, p.36; R. Brett, 'State Reporting: an NGO Perspective', in *ibid.*, p.57.

[26] C. Shalev, 'State Reporting and the Convention on the Elimination of All Forms of Discrimination against Women', in *ibid.*, p.29; M. O'Flaherty, *Human Rights and the UN Practice before the Treaty Bodies*, 2nd edn (The Hague/London: Kluwer Law International, 2002), p.2.

[27] O'Flaherty, *Human Rights and the UN Practice before the Treaty Bodies*, 2002, p.2.

[28] M. Schmidt, 'Follow-up Activities by UN Human Rights Treaty Bodies and Special Procedures Mechanisms of the Human Rights Council—Recent Developments' in Alfredsson *et al.* (eds.), *International Human Rights Monitoring Mechanisms*, 2009, pp. 30-31.

[29] S. Goonesekere, 'Law Reform and Children's Rights in Plural Legal Systems: Some Experiences in Sub-Saharan Africa', in UNICEF, *Protecting the World's Children: Impact of the Convention on the Rights of the Child in Diverse Legal Systems* (Cambridge/New York: Cambridge University Press, 2008), pp.209–62.

suggested that important improvements were triggered by findings of the relevant monitoring body, the Committee on the Rights of the Child.[30] Studies by United Nations Children's Fund (UNICEF) and others indicate that these findings relate to all regions of the world and to all legal systems.[31] Other UN reports demonstrate the extent to which treaty body findings are reflected in its own capacity building programmes and are taken account of in the development work of many states and international organisations.[32]

Of course, the reporting procedure can only bring benefit if it is actually engaged by states. As a matter of fact, and across all of the treaty bodies, a substantial minority of states either do not submit reports or are seriously in arrears.[33] More generally, it is considered by the preponderance of observers that the procedure could be strengthened greatly with a view towards its having a greater impact for human rights compliance at the national level.[34] Elsewhere, the present author has identified a number of general challenges confronting the treaty body system. Each of these has direct relevance for the reporting procedure.[35]

In the first place there are what may be termed the 'input challenges'. These are the issues of how to ensure that committees have jurisdiction as well as access to all the necessary information. In this context we can locate the problem of non-reporting states and of the submission of seriously overdue and/or poor quality reports. Another problem concerns the need to further enhance the role played in the process by civil society, such as by means of ensuring a better participation of national-level NGOs that may be poorly resourced.

---

30 UNICEF, The State of the World's Children: Celebrating 20 Years of the Convention on the Rights of the Child, Special Edition, 2009, pp. 26 and 54, available at: http://www.unicef.org/rightsite/sowc/pdfs/SOWC_Spec%20Ed_CRC_Main%20Report_EN_090409.pdf [last accessed 19 December 2010].

31 *Ibid.*

32 Karp, 'Reporting and the Committee on the Rights of the Child', 2000, p.43.

33 OHCHR, Recent Reporting History: Submission of Reports by States Parties to the Seven International Human Rights Treaty Bodies, available at: http://www2.ohchr.org/english/bodies/docs/RRH.pdf [last accessed 19 December 2010].

34 C. Heyns and F. Viljoen, 'The Impact of the United Nations Human Rights Treaties on the Domestic Level', *Human Rights Quarterly* 23 (2001), 531–34.

35 M. O'Flaherty, 'The Strengths and Weaknesses of the UN Human Rights Treaties System', keynote address, Promoting Human Rights in Japan through UN Treaties Conference, Waseda University, Tokyo, 4 November 2010, available at: http://www.euij-waseda.jp/common/pdf/101104O%27FlahertyScript.pdf [last accessed 19 December 2010].

A second category of issues is that of 'analysis challenges'. Here one may locate the problem that the procedure can only be as good as is allowed by the quality and the capacity of the committees themselves. Committee members come from a wide range of backgrounds and disciplines and are of varying levels of expertise. It is evident that treaty body work would be enhanced by the more systematic identification and election of the best possible specialist members. Resources also are insufficient and there can be no doubt of the sharp limitations on the capacity of bodies of part-time volunteers, meeting for just a few weeks a year, to realise all of the potential of the reporting procedure.

The third category is that of 'output challenges'—how the committees can deliver better results, including in the form of more targeted recommendations within the concluding observations. The next category is that of 'impact challenges', embracing the myriad concerns of how to ensure that committee makes a difference for the rights holders. Among the most important issues that arise in this context is that of the building up of awareness of the work of the committees at the national level. Another consideration with direct relevance for impact is that of the formal nature of the outputs and whether a more obligatory form, such as judicial findings, might be considered.

Finally, there are the 'environment challenges'—this odd designation is intended to capture the many issues of how the committees must better interact with each other and with other parts of the international human rights system. The relationship of the reporting procedures with the HRC and its UPR procedure is of particular interest.

UPR is the HRC's procedure for periodic peer review by states of each other's human rights record.[36] At time of writing of this chapter it has been in place for four years and by the end of 2011 the record of all UN member states will have been reviewed. UPR comprises five distinct elements:[37] the (recommended) convening by the state under review of a national consultative process as a step in the preparation of its report; the submission of the state report; preparation by the Office of the UN High Commissioner for Human Rights (OHCHR) of compilations of civil-society and national human rights institution- sourced

[36] UNGA Res 60/251 on the Human Rights Council, UN Doc A/RES/60/251 (3 April 2006), para.5(e).

[37] Human Rights Council Resolution 5/1 (2007), Institution-building of the United Nations Human Rights Council, UN Doc A/HRC/RES/5/1 (18 June 2007), Annex, paras.15–25.

information, and of the relevant findings of treaty bodies and other relevant UN actors; dialogue between a government delegation and the HRC and its relevant working group; and, the issuance by the Council of a report on the process that includes the recommendations that may have been put to the state under review by other states. A sixth element, that of follow up, is gradually emerging and taking shape in the present period.

Treaty body findings figure largely in all of the UPR elements:[38] they lie behind much of the national level commentary in national consultations; they are frequently referred to in state reports; they are the dominant source for one OHCHR compilation (on UN actors) and they are frequently cited in the other (on civil society); they underlie a great many of the comments and questions put to states by their peers in the dialogue; and, they lie behind many if not most UPR recommendations. More generally, UPR is serving to throw new and somewhat unexpected light on the treaty bodies and their reporting procedures. That light is not always favourable since, as we have already observed, treaty body work is not of consistently high quality. Furthermore, there have been instances of UPR recommendations that directly contradict specific treaty body findings.[39] Finally, if one looks at the treaty body-UPR relationship from the other perspective—that of its impact for treaty body practice—there is as yet little to show, with only a few modest references to the procedure in the committees' review of reports.[40]

---

[38] Exploring Complementarity between the Treaty Monitoring Bodies and the Universal Periodic Review Process, side-event panel discussions report by Ireland and the Netherlands, UN Doc A/HRC/12/G/1 (4 September 2009), Annex, pp.3–4.

[39] Human Rights Watch, Curing the Selectivity Syndrome: The 2011 Review of the Human Rights Council, p.14, available at: http://www.hrw.org/sites/default/files/reports/hrc0610webwcover.pdf [last accessed 19 December 2010].

[40] E.g., CAT took note of the state party's commitment made in the context of UPR when considering reports submitted by Cameroon (UN Doc CAT/C/CMR/CO/4, para.32), Yemen (UN Doc CAT/C/YEM/CO/2/Rev.1, para.35), Chad (UN Doc CAT/C/TCD/CO/1, para.36) and Indonesia (UN Doc CAT/C/IDN/CO/2, para.12). CEDAW also noted the state party's participation in the URR in the Concluding Observations of reports submitted by Turkey (UN Doc CEDAW/C/TUR/CO/6, paras.11 and 42), Botswana (UN Doc CEDAW/C/BOT/CO/3, para.17), Japan (UN Doc CEDAW/C/JPN/CO/6, para.24), Switzerland (UN Doc CEDAW/C/CHE/CO/3, para.45), Tuvalu (UN Doc CEDAW/C/TUV/CO/2, para.14), Bahrain (UN Doc CEDAW/C/BHR/CO/2, para.16) and Finland (UN Doc CEDAW/C/FIN/CO/6, para.16). In particular, CERD referred to specific recommendations by the UPR Working Group in the Concluding Observation of China's report (UN Doc CERD/C/CHN/CO/10-13, paras.15, 22 and 24).

The Diplomatic Nature of the Reporting Procedure

There is no precise and globally accepted understanding of the term 'diplomacy'. Nevertheless, at its core it is generally considered in the words of Marshall Green, to comprise, 'the art of persuasion in international affairs'.[41] Constitutive of its persuasive nature, are such activities as negotiation and the seeking of common ground. Diplomacy may be undertaken by states and various other forms of groups engaged at the international level. Diplomacy is distinguished from other types of intervention, such as judicial proceedings, by the extent to which its success rests on persuasive power and strength rather than on legally obligatory or other forms of coercive jurisdiction. That said, it is not inconsistent with the diplomatic function for any one or more interlocutors to operate on the basis of an agreed mandate that may have the force of law, such as, for example, the diplomatic function of the UN Secretary-General as established in the UN Charter. Turning to one specific form of diplomacy, 'human rights diplomacy', the present author adopts the usage that is employed in the present volume, whereby it consists of the use of the range of persuasive negotiation-based diplomatic tools available to states, inter-governmental organisations, international civil society and other actors with a public role or function at the international level, for the specific purpose of promoting and protecting human rights.[42] Writing on the topic of an analogous discipline, that of humanitarian diplomacy, Lakhdar Brahimi added that, to be effective, it required of the protagonist such skills and capacities as a keen knowledge and understanding of the interests of the interlocutor, an ability for empathy and clarity regarding one's own interests and objectives.[43]

Thus defined, it is suggested that the reporting procedures of the treaty bodies can be understood as tools for human rights diplomacy. The actors certainly are appropriate to the designation: states, treaty bodies and civil society. The activity they engage in—the exchange of views, what the Committee on the Elimination of Discrimination

[41] Report of the High-Level Workshop on Human Rights Diplomacy, Venice, 30–31 January 2009, annex to this volume, p.265.

[42] *Ibid.*

[43] L. Brahimi, 'Foreword' in L. Minear and H. Smith (eds.), *Humanitarian Diplomacy: Practitioners and Their Craft* (New York: United Nations University Press, 2007), p.xiv.

against Women terms, 'constructive dialogue'[44], on implementation of treaties has an inherently persuasive and negotiation-related quality. That activity, if it is to be effective, requires of the treaty bodies that they undertake a wide-ranging and detailed survey of the national situation. The outcome of the process, concluding observations, consists in the main of recommendations that should propose specific solutions that states can adopt and implement within the complex task of governance. These recommendations are adopted within the treaty bodies in an exercise of the seeking of consensus and, non-binding by definition, their only force rests in their persuasive force and evident utility. The shared goal of all the protagonists is the promotion and protection of human rights as set out in the treaties.

The categorisation of the reporting procedure as an inherently diplomatic one carries with it some interesting insights as to how this important area of treaty body work can be strengthened. Before addressing those it is necessary to confront the concern that what 'is' need not necessarily constitute what 'ought', or, in other words, whether the diplomatic nature of the reporting procedure is an impediment to its effectiveness and that efforts should be made instead to move it closer towards a judicial model. The present author is of the view that this would be an unfortunate approach. The diplomatic rather than the judicial model best suits the reporting function. This is in large part due to the very wide scope of the report-related review that a committee must undertake, whereby it seeks an all-encompassing overview of a state's human rights infrastructure and of its regime to promote and protect an entire category of human rights. As such, it cannot be constrained by such judicial conventions as those that restrict the forms of information that can be relied on. The exchange with the state, if it is to be successful, must not be hampered and formalised by the threat of negative judgement or by the combative nature of adversarial communication. The outcome document, concluding observations, comprises recommendations, including those that concern policy and programming. The latter are not the stuff of binding judgements. For instance, treaty bodies will frequently recommend that treaties be ratified,[45]

[44] E.g. Report of the Committee on the Elimination of Discrimination against Women on its 24th and 25th sessions, UN Doc A/56/38(SUPP) (2001), p.51 (Consideration of combined initial report submitted by Andorra).

[45] E.g. Committee on Economic, Social and Cultural Rights, Concluding Observations: Chile, UN Doc E/C.12/1/Add.105 (1 December 2004), p.5.

reservations be withdrawn[46] and the conclusions of international conferences be implemented[47]—such suggestions can never have legal force. Furthermore, a treaty body, may and often does suggest that a state chose between identified policy options—again a context in which an insistence on legal obligation does not seem appropriate.[48] Finally, as a practical consideration, it would be unhelpful to characterise as binding the outcome of a proceeding that is undertaken over just a few hours and within which there is limited opportunity for claim, counterclaim and the implementation of the various steps of review and due process that would be appropriate to the judicial function.

How then can the diplomatic model aid efforts to strengthen the treaty body system? In the first instance this assistance takes the form of a validation of a range of current reform initiatives. Since late 2009, there has been a newly-invigorated debate on how the system might be strengthened.[49] The insights of the discussion are contained in a number of statements agreed by treaty body members, national human rights institutions, civil society and other experts. The statements (Dublin, November 2009;[50] Marrakesh, June 2010;[51] Poznan, September 2010;[52] the NGO Statement, December 2010[53]) all emphasise

[46] E.g. Committee on the Rights of the Child, Concluding Observations: New Zealand, UN Doc CRC/C/15/Add.216 (27 October 2003), p.2.

[47] E.g. Report of the Committee on the Elimination of Discrimination against Women on its 28th and 29th Sessions, UN Doc A/58/38(SUPP) (2003), p.17 (Consideration of combined initial and second periodic reports submitted by Albania).

[48] E.g. Committee on Economic, Social and Cultural Rights, Concluding Observations: Ireland, UN Doc E/C.12/1/Add.77 (5 June 2002), p.4.

[49] M. O'Flaherty, 'Reform of the UN Human Rights Treaty Body System: Locating the Dublin Statement', *Human Rights Law Review* 10 (2010), 327–29.

[50] The Dublin Statement on the Process of Strengthening of the United Nations Human Rights Treaty Body System, 19 November 2009, available at: http://www.nottingham.ac.uk/hrlc/documents/specialevents/dublinstatement.pdf [last accessed 19 December 2010], reprinted in *Netherlands Quarterly of Human Rights* 28 (2010), 121–27.

[51] Marrakech Statement on Strengthening the Relationship between NHRIs and the Human Rights Treaty Bodies System, 10 June 2010, available at: http://bangkok.ohchr.org/files/NHRICSOs-Consultation/Marrakesh.doc [last accessed 19 December 2010].

[52] The Poznan Statement on the Reforms of the UN Human Rights Treaty Body System, 28–29 September 2010, available at: http://www.nottingham.ac.uk/hrlc/documents/projectsummaries/pdfs/poznanstatement.pdf [last accessed 19 December 2010].

[53] Dublin Statement on the Process of Strengthening the United Nations Human Rights Treaty Body System: Response by Non-governmental Organizations, November 2010, available at: http://www.ishr.ch/document-stuff/browse-documents/doc_download/1082-response-by-ngos-to-the-dublin-statement-on-the-process-of-strengthening-the-un-treaty-body-system [last accessed 19 December 2010].

improvements that are constitutive of and necessary to the diplomatic function. These include calls for improved flows of information to and from the treaty bodies, a stronger role in the proceedings for national and other NGOs and for national human rights institutions, concluding observation recommendations that are better crafted to take account of how governments carry out their function and improved systems for the follow-up of findings.[54]

The diplomatic perspective also provides added detail for many of the proposals that are being discussed. For instance, there are calls for states to send better delegations to meet with the committees.[55] The diplomatic approach suggests that this should be interpreted to mean, not that the state would necessarily send more human rights lawyers or simply more senior delegates, but that its team be constituted of officials with the necessary technical competence across the whole range of relevant government departments and agencies. Similarly, calls for the election of better qualified treaty body members can be taken to refer to candidates who are better qualified to undertake human rights diplomacy. In this regard it is evident that committees need more members with direct experience of the implementation of human rights by the state. This insight has interesting implications. For instance, it suggests that it is not necessarily a good thing for all or for the preponderance of treaty body members to be lawyers.[56] It also challenges the commonly stated view that government officials should not be put forward for treaty body membership.[57] The diplomatic model suggests that we should have more such experts rather than less—albeit the argument that they should not currently be in the service of their governments does have merit.

Another area of practice in the review of reports that might usefully be re-examined in light of the diplomatic perspective is that of the procedures for the dialogue. For example, in consideration of the extent to

---

[54] O'Flaherty, 'Reform of the UN Human Rights Treaty Body System', 2010, 333–35.

[55] E.g., A. F. Bayefsky, Report: The UN Human Rights Treaty System - Universality at the Crossroads, 2001, p.75, available at: http://www.bayefsky.com/report/finalreport.pdf [last accessed 19 December 2010].

[56] Among 18 members of the Human Rights Committee, 17 hold legal background.

[57] Amnesty International, Membership of Treaty Bodies, available at: http://www.amnesty.org/en/united-nations/treaty-bodies/membership [last accessed 19 December 2010]; Bayefsky, Report: The UN Human Rights Treaty System, 2001, 108–12.

which diplomacy may at times require discretion and confidentiality, it may be argued that at least some elements of the exchanges between treaty bodies and states be undertaken in private. Again, this is a sensitive topic and would have to be addressed in a manner that does not undermine the important attribute of the procedure as a form of public accountability tool and the more general value of transparency. However, the present writer can see merit in a limited scope for confidentiality such as for confidential exchange of views between committees and states on a preliminary draft of concluding observations, or for the concluding observations themselves pending the publication of a response by the state (albeit delay in preparing such a response must not block timely publication of the concluding observations).

The diplomatic approach also throws light on areas of reform that have not yet been highlighted in the current debates. For instance, it suggests that more attention might be paid in the reporting procedures to the identification and highlighting of national good practices, since effective dialogue conducive to understanding and agreement should address both successes and the failures and, more generally, the identification of good practice may be of assistance for both the state under review and other state parties. As the system is configured currently, reference to such practices is not precluded and, indeed, there is a relatively modest section of the concluding observations of some treaty bodies that identifies achievements by states.[58] Nevertheless, there is scope for improvement, whereby good practice is actively sought out, acknowledged and reported. This suggestion is, of course, coloured by the consideration that precious and limited treaty body time should focus on issues of greatest concern and avoid a time-wasting exchange of compliments.

There is one further area of contemporary debate where the diplomatic perspective is of assistance—the relationship of the treaty bodies and the HRC, in particular with regard to its UPR procedure.[59] In the first instance it suggests that it is unhelpful to characterise the relationship between the committees (in their reporting function) and the Council as being that of (quasi-) judicial bodies and a political one. Thus any attempt to draw an analogy with the relationship of the European Court of Human Rights and the Committee of Ministers of

[58] O'Flaherty, 'Concluding Observations', 2006, 31.

[59] Exploring Complementarity between the Treaty Monitoring Bodies and the Universal Periodic Review Process, UN Doc A/HRC/12/G/1 (2009), Annex.

the Council of Europe (for instance for 'enforcement' of treaty body findings through UPR) is inappropriate. It also suggests that contradictions between treaty body and UPR recommendations need not necessarily give cause for concern, at least where they are on matters of policy and programming rather than law. That said, both the treaty bodies and the Council share a common diplomatic function in the promotion of human rights. It is incumbent on them to ensure the best possible cooperation and complementarity in working methods and outputs. As has already been noted, the issue is in receipt of some attention with regard to the practice of the Council.[60] As yet this reflection has not addressed possibilities for action at the level of individual states. The present writer considers that it would be worthwhile for states to explore how best to relate the UPR and treaty body procedures at the national level. For instance, it would be of interest to seek to integrate discussion of both forms of reporting when undertaking UPR-related national consultations. It would also be helpful for states to integrate programmes for the follow up and implementation of recommendations emerging from both the UPR and treaty body report-review procedures.

Treaty bodies, too, need to determine how best to relate to UPR. In the first instance, they should consider what use to make, if any, of UPR recommendations. At a more systemic level they might re-examine certain of their working methods in light of UPR innovations. In this regard, the constitutive text for UPR, the Council's 'institution-building' resolution,[61] in describing the purpose of UPR, includes some elements that may invite a review of the purpose and form of the treaty body report-review procedure—such as, for example, the injunction that the procedure is a cooperative one, comprising an assessment undertaken in an objective and transparent manner, including positive developments and the challenges faced by the country; that it is intended to permit the sharing of good practice; and, that it should facilitate the provision of technical assistance and capacity-building.[62] Treaty bodies might also consider the manner by which state reports under UPR are characterised as 'national' rather than 'government' reports[63] and that it is recommended that they should emerge from a

[60] F. D. Gaer, 'A Voice Not an Echo: Universal Periodic Review and the UN Treaty Body System', *Human Rights Law Review* 7 (2007), 121–35.
[61] Human Rights Council Resolution 5/1 (2007).
[62] *Ibid.*, paras.3-4.
[63] *Ibid.*, para.15(a).

process of consultation with all relevant stakeholders.[64] This is quite different to the practice whereby reports to treaty bodies are considered to be government texts—with the prevailing view being that NGOs should not participate in their formulation but should rather submit their own alternative or 'shadow' reports.[65] It is suggested that the UPR-form of report, which in no way precludes the submission of additional reports from non-governmental sources, is the more useful model.

Conclusion

Treaty bodies play a distinct role in the promotion of human rights. Their specialised and detailed function is integral to the implementation of the treaty system. The independence of the expert members as well as the manner in which they undertake highly detailed examination of situations in lights of the provisions of the treaties are dimensions that cannot be replicated in such other oversight frameworks as those of the Human Rights Council. They carry out the function by way of a range of distinctive tools and methods. One of these, the consideration of individual communications, and such attendant actions as the issuing of requests for interim measures, is clearly of a quasi-judicial character.[66] The issuance of general comments is of a similar nature, at least to the extent that the treaty bodies consider the general comments to constitute authoritative legal analysis of the treaties.[67] As we have seen, the review of periodic reports has a quite different diplomatic character. Rather than being perceived as a weakness, this character affords to the treaty bodies considerable scope to further refine and strengthen the work area. It has been the purpose of this chapter to draw attention to this neglected perspective and to identify some current related opportunities, such as in the context of the operationalisation of the UPR. Ultimately, it is hoped that recognition and bolstering of the diplomatic dimension it will contribute to efforts for the strengthening of the treaty body system as a bulwark for the international protection of human rights.

---

[64] *Ibid.*

[65] O'Flaherty, *Human Rights and the UN Practice before the Treaty Bodies*, 2002, ch.1.

[66] Nowak, *CCPR Commentary*, 2005, pp.668–89.

[67] M. Schmidt, 'United Nations' in D. Moeckli *et al.* (eds.), *International Human Rights Law* (Oxford: Oxford University Press, 2010), pp.408–09.

CHAPTER 10

THE HUMAN RIGHTS DIPLOMACY OF THE UN SECRETARY-GENERAL

Bertrand G. Ramcharan

Introduction

This essay on human rights diplomacy by the United Nations (UN) Secretary-General will focus on the future, while bearing in mind experiences of the past. It will argue that each Secretary-General should set his or her sights on selected human rights objectives and deploy diplomacy for the achievement of those objectives. In identifying these objectives the Secretary-General should keep in mind the mandates of the UN High Commissioner for Human Rights and the UN Human Rights Council and will not seek to duplicate their efforts. Yet, the Secretary-General should make a personal choice of areas on which he or she wishes to place a personal stamp and should call human rights diplomacy in aid for this purpose. As we see it, policy and diplomacy, while closely related, are not identical. A Secretary-General might indicate policy choices. Human rights diplomacy, however, is marshalled for the achievement of selected policy initiatives. Before offering a selection of goals for the deployment of human rights diplomacy, we first take a look at experiences of the past.

A Historical Perspective

While one could refer to strands of human rights diplomacy or policy by previous Secretaries-General it would probably be accurate to say that no UN Secretary-General to date has had a human rights diplomacy as such.[1] The incumbent, Mr Ban Ki-moon has so far not yet

[1] See, generally, B. G. Ramcharan, *Humanitarian Good Offices in International Law. The Good Offices of the UN Secretary-General in the Field of Human Rights* (The Hague: Martinus Nijhoff, 1983), ch.I; D. P. Forsythe, 'The UN Secretary-General and Human Rights: The Question of Leadership in a Changing Context' in B. Rivilin and

developed one either. Secretary-General Trygve Lie professed his allegiance to the 'free world' and, in his proposed action programme, which never took off, included the promotion of human rights. He, like his successors until Secretary-General Pérez de Cuéllar, did engage in humanitarian good offices to help some individuals or groups in need.

According to John Humphrey, the first Director of the UN Division of Human Rights and prominent drafter of the Universal Declaration of Human Rights, Secretary-General Dag Hammarskjold wanted the human rights programme kept at 'minimum flying speed'.[2] Hammarskjold is credited with being the father of preventive diplomacy, but he saw it mainly in the political and security fields, rather than in the area of human rights. Hammarskjold left no lasting imprint on human rights—but he did attach high priority to development, which has since been declared a human right by the UN General Assembly.

Secretary-General U Thant was a great humanitarian and it was he who called for attention to man-made humanitarian crises and who established the UN Disaster Relief Office, which is nowadays part of the Office for the Coordination of Humanitarian Affairs. Secretary-General U Thant engaged in significant humanitarian good offices, which he recorded in his memoir, "View from the UN".[3] U Thant was a professed believer in preventive diplomacy.

Secretary-General Kurt Waldheim was a cautious Secretary-General for whom human rights were not a priority. He did, however, continue the exercise of humanitarian good offices and acknowledged the importance of preventive diplomacy, again in the political and security areas.

Secretary-General Pérez de Cuéllar was an even colder fish when it came to human rights issues, but he did engage in humanitarian good offices and also professed belief in preventive diplomacy. His "Perspectives on the Work of the United Nations in the 1990s", an enclosure to the draft UN medium-term plan issued in 1987,[4]

L. Gordenker (eds.), *The Challenging Role of the UN Secretary-General* (Westport, Connecticut: Praeger, 1993), pp.211-32; J. D. Livermore and B. G. Ramcharan, 'Purposes and Principles. The Secretary-General's Role in Human Rights', in *ibid.*, pp.213–48; and B. G. Ramcharan, *Preventive Diplomacy at the UN* (Indiana: Indiana University Press, 2008), ch.4.

[2] See J. Humphrey, *Human Rights and the United Nations: A Great Adventure* (New York: Transnational Publishers, 1984).

[3] S. U Thant, *View from the UN* (Newton Abbot: David and Charles, 1978).

[4] Some Perspectives on the Work of the United Nations in the 1990s, enclosure to Programme Planning - Preparation of the Next Medium-Term Plan, Note by the Secretary-General, UN Doc A/42/512 (2 September 1987).

made the case for the maintenance of a 'global watch' over human security. One of the central pillars of this 'global watch' was the promotion and protection of human rights.[5] However, this did not lead to any significant uplift in the human rights activities of the UN.

Of the Secretaries-General before Boutros Boutros-Ghali, David Forsythe, an eminent authority on human rights and on the human rights policies of the Secretaries-General (or lack thereof), wrote in 1993:

> While one can perhaps make comparative judgments about activism in relative historical terms, none of the five Secretaries-General has really been very active about protecting human rights in the sense of trying to make systematic use of the full weight of the office. None has sought to interject systematically the presence of the office of the Secretary-General into situations of potential or actual gross violations of human rights. None has been very personally committed to taking risks to advance the practice of those rights.
>
> ...
>
> The fact that none of the five Secretaries-General has been deeply interested in human rights, despite making public speeches in favour of the subject, may stem mostly from views about the United Nations as a whole. If the primary purpose of the United Nations is the maintenance and restoration of international peace and security, then this issue-area may preoccupy the Secretary-General. Unless he believes that some human rights issue is directly and immediately linked to that peace and security, he may be inclined to sacrifice human rights initiatives on the altar of inter-state stability.[6]

One could also add, in fairness, that during the period of the Cold War, the Secretaries-General had to operate in very limited and controlled space. However, things did not improve much after the end of the Cold War. Boutros-Ghali, the first post-Cold War Secretary-General, could have claimed more operating space for human rights, but he chose not to. Yet, the World Conference on Human Rights, held in 1993, adopted the Vienna Declaration and Programme of Action[7] which sought to inject more dynamism in the UN's human rights programme—even if the Secretary-General continued to operate in classical mode.

---

[5] See on this Ramcharan, *Preventive Diplomacy*, 2008, pp.37–42.

[6] Forsythe, 'The UN Secretary-General and Human Rights', 1993, p.236.

[7] Vienna Declaration and Programme of Action, adopted by the World Conference on Human Rights, UN Doc A/CONF.157/23 (12 July 1993).

Secretary-General Boutros Boutros-Ghali, whose Agenda for Peace[8] is rightly considered to be one of the foundation documents in the development of preventive diplomacy, was very much statist in his approach to international politics and had a distinctly dismal view of the place of human rights at the UN. He was against the establishment of the post of UN High Commissioner for Human Rights and, after the post was established, sought to contain it.

With the arrival of the High Commissioner in 1994, humanitarian good offices appeared to cease in the Office of the Secretary-General and the buck was passed to the Office of the High Commissioner. There is, however, little evidence that High Commissioners have engaged in much humanitarian good offices.

Of all the Secretary-Generals up to his time, Secretary-General Kofi Annan was certainly the most active on human rights issues. He regularly addressed the annual sessions of the Human Rights Commission/Council and he actively championed the cause of humanitarian intervention. He made the Office of the High Commissioner for Human Rights a member of the four Executive Committees he had created and he successfully sought to use his influence to increase the human and financial resources of the Office of the High Commissioner. There is no evidence available that he engaged in humanitarian good offices on behalf of individuals or groups in need, but he expressed support for preventive diplomacy in the political and security areas.

Overall, Secretary-General Annan certainly had strong human rights policies. But did he have human rights diplomacy? We think not. His championship of humanitarian intervention was well-meant, but it was the anti-thesis of human rights diplomacy. The majority of UN members rose up in revolt against humanitarian intervention and remains suspicious of the successor concept, the responsibility to protect.[9] This was a failure of diplomacy on the part of the Secretary-General, pure and simple, and it was certainly not human rights diplomacy. Getting the membership riled up over humanitarian intervention was not diplomacy, even if the intentions were laudable. Working behind the scenes and seeking to rally consensuses on human rights policies might have been more helpful.

[8] Report of the Secretary-General, An Agenda for Peace, Preventive Diplomacy, Peacemaking and Peace-keeping, UN Doc A/47/277 - S/24111 (17 June 1992).

[9] Discussed further below.

As of the time of writing, Secretary-General Ban Ki-moon has given no evidence of the practice of a defined human rights diplomacy. Like his predecessors, he professes belief in preventive diplomacy to head off crises and conflicts and expresses support for the human rights programme of the UN. He has also occasionally made public comments in support of human rights in particular situations. His political efforts on Darfur, at the beginning of his term, sought to deal with a political/humanitarian situation but did not make much headway. His leadership on issues such as climate change and water shortages have involved significant diplomacy. To the extent that these are partly human rights issues, he may be credited with some elements of human rights diplomacy.

Against this background, we may, before proceeding to examine possibilities for the exercise of human rights diplomacy by the Secretary-General, first note the context that needs to be taken into account.

The Context

In considering opportunities and options for the exercise of human rights diplomacy by the Secretary-General, one should keep in mind that at any point in time the United Nations as an organisation has in place a medium-term human rights programme decided upon by the UN General Assembly and a biennial budget programme in this area, both of which are based on proposals first put forward by the Secretary-General. The UN also include the policies and programmes of the UN Human Rights Council and its subsidiary organs, the operations of the principal human rights treaty bodies, the activities of principal organs such as the General Assembly, the Security Council and the Economic and Social Council in the area of human rights, and the activities of the UN High Commissioner for Human Rights and her Office.

There is thus a great deal of activity going on and the Secretary-General, as the principal administrative officer of the UN, is required to support all these activities. The Secretary-General also has his responsibilities pursuant to Article 99 of the UN Charter that allows him to 'bring to the attention of the Security Council any matter which in his opinion may threaten the maintenance of international peace and security'.[10] Since the establishment of the post of the High Commissioner

[10] Charter of the United Nations, 26 June 1945.

for Human Rights the High Commissioner sometimes reacts to situations that might otherwise have called for attention from the Secretary-General under Article 99 of the Charter. It therefore seems to be helpful to place some markers around the respective competences of the High Commissioner and the Secretary-General.

The Secretary-General and the High Commissioner

In broad terms, one could say that the UN Secretary-General should first engage in facilitative diplomacy to take forward the Charter's vision of a world of peace and justice grounded in respect for human rights and in economic and social progress. The promotion of the universality of human rights and the advancement of a universal culture of human rights through human rights education would be examples of such efforts. Diplomatic engagement of the Secretary-General with key governmental leaders in support of universality seems particularly useful.

Second, the UN Secretary-General should also lead on preventive strategies for dealing with new threats and challenges such as climate change. The current Secretary-General, Ban Ki-moon has given good leadership on this.

Third, the UN Secretary-General should deploy diplomatic efforts in support of the High Commissioner for Human Rights. In situations where the High Commissioner might need the behind-the-scenes backing of the Secretary-General, the latter, in his judgment, could act to support the High Commissioner.

Fourth, the UN Secretary-General should use diplomatic efforts behind the scenes to rally support for the implementation of the responsibility to protect. The national responsibility to protect is particularly important, because it is at home in each country that the protection of human rights must be built up.

Fifth, the UN Secretary-General should use diplomatic efforts behind the scenes in support of justice, nationally, regionally, and internationally. While maintaining a discreet posture, the Secretary-General should support the International Criminal Court (ICC).

Beyond these general objectives, we shall discuss later in this chapter some additional areas where the human rights diplomacy of the Secretary-General might be considered.

The UN High Commissioner for Human Rights, for her part, is the principal actor for the promotion and protection of human rights within the UN system, and her roles and responsibilities, under the leadership of the Secretary-General, are much wider than the exercise of human rights diplomacy.[11] Nevertheless, it is useful to have a sense of where the diplomacy of the High Commissioner should be particularly considered.

First, like the Secretary-General, the High Commissioner should also engage in facilitative diplomacy to take forward the Charter's vision of a world of peace and justice grounded in respect for human rights and economic and social progress.

Second, the High Commissioner should be the spearhead and coordinator of the human rights community and should deploy diplomacy for this purpose.

Third, the High Commissioner is the voice of human rights and could use diplomatic means to identify and highlight the human rights dimensions of new threats and challenges such as biological experimentation and human cloning.

Fourth, the High Commissioner for Human Rights should deploy diplomacy to support the strengthening of national protection systems in each country of the world. The High Commissioner should call on the diplomacy of partnership with governments, regional organisations, and non-governmental organisations.

Finally, the High Commissioner, as the defender of human rights, should deploy diplomacy to head off and help prevent gross violations of human rights.

Against this general background, one should be selective in one's expectations of the Secretary-General when it comes to the exercise of human rights diplomacy. What one should be looking for is diplomacy that can make a true difference when it comes to the protection and promotion of human rights, in support of the High Commissioner's action. How can one help to identify areas that the Secretary-General might usefully consider?

The following criteria might help to answer this question: first, it has been a long-established practice that Secretaries-General may use their humanitarian good offices to help individuals or groups at risk.

---

[11] See generally, B. G. Ramcharan, *The UN High Commissioner for Human Rights and the Challenges of International Protection* (The Hague: Martinus Nijhoff, 2002); B. G. Ramcharan, *A UN High Commissioner in Defence of Human Rights* (The Hague: Martinus Nijhoff, 2005); and M. Robinson, *A Voice for Human Rights* (Philadelphia: University of Pennsylvania Press, 2006).

Second, the Secretary-General could rely on diplomacy when discharging his responsibilities under Article 99 of the UN Charter. Third, diplomacy could play a role in the Secretary-General's activities in relation to peacemaking, and fourth, in relation to his role in the areas of peacekeeping and peace-building. Fifth, the Secretary-General could use diplomatic means to draw support for the responsibility to protect. Sixth, he could rely on diplomacy in support of justice, nationally and internationally. Seventh, the Secretary-General could deploy diplomatic means towards the strengthening of national protection systems. And eighth, the advancement of a universal culture of human rights through human rights education and information could be promoted through diplomatic action. We discuss each of these areas in turn.

Humanitarian Good Offices

Going back to the earliest days of the United Nations, the earlier Secretaries-General had sought to help people through discreet diplomacy exercised on humanitarian grounds.[12] This continues to be the case today. There are occasions when the Secretary-General may issue a public comment calculated to express concern or to help nudge governments or parties to a humanitarian resolution of a situation. On 2 January 2008, for example, Secretary-General Ban Ki-moon issued a public statement "Secretary-General Troubled by Escalating Kenyan Tensions" in which he urged that all efforts be made to avoid provocations and violence during planned demonstrations in Kenya. The statement continued:

> The Secretary-General is also concerned with the deteriorating humanitarian situation, as large numbers of people have been displaced by the violence. He calls on all concerned to allow safe access for relief workers helping those affected by recent events. [...]
>
> The Secretary-General is in the process of contacting the leadership in Kenya, the African Union and other concerned parties on how to address the crisis. A solution is urgently needed, through a spirit of dialogue and by making full use of constitutional and legal rules and mechanisms.[13]

---

[12] See Ramcharan, *Humanitarian Good Offices*, 1983.

[13] Statement attributable to the spokesperson for the Secretary-General on the situation in Kenya, UN Press Release, UN Doc SG/SM711356-AFR71641 (2 January 2008).

There is another strand in the practice of humanitarian good offices by the Secretary-General that seems to have fallen in disuse since the establishment of the Office of High Commissioner for Human Rights but which, in our submission, should be revived and retained by Secretaries-General in the future. For many years until the term of office of Secretary-General Pérez de Cuéllar, Secretaries-General visiting countries would ask for some appropriate cases that they might raise with their hosts and seek humanitarian relief and this had a successful outcome in many instances. Similarly, when Secretaries-General met visiting heads of state or other national leaders during the high-level segment of the annual sessions of the General Assembly, they would similarly be provided with appropriate cases that might be raised in a good offices format. We do not have direct information about what is taking place at the present time but we know from our own experience and that of other colleagues that these practices have fallen into disuse for some time. We urge that they be retained for future use.

A related part of this practice of which use is no longer made concerns the communications or petitions procedures within the human rights programme. In the past, letters received by the UN Secretariat were screened by an experienced officer and cases selected for the exercise of good offices by the leadership of the human rights programme, by other UN leaders, and by the UN Secretary-General. We know from personal experience that because of staff cuts this no longer takes place, except in respect of the procedure of interim measures of protection under human rights treaties, or correspondence reaching the special procedures mandate-holders of the UN Human Rights Council. But it is in the nature of discreet humanitarian diplomacy that efforts behind the scenes, without fanfare, might be able to save lives or lessen human suffering—and the Secretary-General has a part to play in this. However, to enable him to do so, those processing petitions within the Office of High Commissioner for Human Rights and relevant parts of the UN Secretariat should have the experience, aptitude and training to spot cases for the exercise of humanitarian good offices.

Going beyond particular cases, there are situations that might merit the attention of the Secretary-General under Article 99 of the UN Charter.

Article 99 of the UN Charter

As mentioned earlier, Article 99 provides that the Secretary-General may bring to the attention of the Security Council any matter which, in his opinion, may threaten the maintenance of international peace and security. Three features of the practice of Secretaries-General concerning Article 99 might be noted: First, from the outset, Secretaries-General have claimed and established the right to engage in fact-finding in respect of particular situations with a view to determining whether to exercise their competence under Article 99. Second, Secretaries-General have been sparing in their formal invocations of Article 99 and there have hardly been a dozen situations in which this has been done. However, the practice of informal briefings of the Security Council has made it less necessary to invoke Article 99 formally. Third, Secretaries-General have always exercised their own judgment whether they would invoke Article 99.

Since the arrival of the High Commissioner in 1994 and the establishment of the Human Rights Council in 2006, with the latter making use more and more of special sessions to deal with emergencies and special situations or issues, one could say that the first-line actors in dealing with human rights emergencies should be the Human Rights Council and the High Commissioner. The Human Rights Council has an explicit mandate to deal with human rights emergencies. It would be appropriate for the Secretary-General to leave the lead to these entities.

Nevertheless, the Secretary-General always retains his mandate under Article 99 and it would be useful for the Secretary-General to keep under review situations where he might call upon diplomacy for fact-finding, representations, and informal briefings of the Security Council. The Secretary-General now has a Special Representative for Children and Armed Conflict,[14] a Special Adviser on the Prevention of Genocide and a Special Adviser on the Responsibility to Protect.[15] With its agreement, they may all brief the UN Security Council in respect of situations where they consider this necessary. This might lead the Secretary-General to think that he could be even more selective when calling on his competence under Article 99 of the Charter.

However, in the end the Secretary-General is the office-holder with the mandate under Article 99, and this can never be overtaken by the

[14] For more information on the mandate and activities of the Special Representative of the Secretary-General see: http://www.un.org/children/conflict/english/index.html [last accessed 11 February 2011].

[15] For more details on the role of both Special Advisers see: http://www.un.org/en/preventgenocide/adviser/index.shtml [last accessed 11 February 2011].

role of his Special Representatives or Advisers. It would therefore be our submission that the Secretary-General should keep in focus the role of fact-finding, representations, and briefings of the Security Council in cases involving the four issues included by the General Assembly and the Security Council when endorsing the responsibility to protect concept: genocide, ethnic cleansing, war crimes and crimes against humanity.

Even in respect of these four issues, one should not expect the Secretary-General to jump in. As mentioned, he has his Special Adviser on the Prevention of Genocide. One could also expect the High Commissioner to be particularly alert in respect of threats of ethnic cleansing and crimes against humanity. Then there is the role of the International Committee of the Red Cross in relation to war crimes and crimes against humanity.

It would be appropriate to look to the Secretary-General to use his diplomacy behind the scenes in support of these other actors and, where he considers that it might be useful, to consider the deployment of fact-finders, the designation of representatives on the spot, and briefings of the Security Council. One cannot, however, prescribe for the Secretary-General because, at the end of the day, judgment is called for whether the Secretary-General becomes engaged or not. But one can indicate areas that the Secretary-General might have in mind which he might reflect on periodically.

There is also a role for human rights diplomacy by the Secretary-General in the area of peacemaking, which we discuss next.

Peacemaking

In principle, all United Nations peacemakers act on behalf of, or in the name of the Secretary-General. There is much contestation about the extent to which peacemakers should take human rights considerations into account in crafting peace agreements.[16] As a general proposition they should, but it should be left to each peacemaker to chart the course to peace, keeping in mind human rights considerations. One thing is clear, however: a United Nations-brokered peace agreement should never provide for amnesties for international crimes.

---

[16] See generally, C. Bell, *Peace Agreements and Human Rights* (Oxford: Oxford University Press, 2000).

When it comes to the Secretary-General, it would be our submission that, supported by the Department of Political Affairs and the Office of the High Commissioner for Human Rights, he should be particularly attentive to the human rights provisions of peace agreements, and should deploy diplomatic efforts, as needed, to secure the following:

- that peace agreements provide a solid blueprint for the promotion and protection of human rights in the country in the future;
- that, as needed, peace agreements provide for wise plans on issues of truth, reconciliation and justice;
- that peace agreements provide for the establishment of national human rights institutions;[17] and
- that peace agreements provide for human rights education in schools and universities.

If it becomes known that these are issues in which the Secretary-General is taking a personal interest, peace negotiators and parties will pay particular attention to them and the profile of human rights will thereby be raised. It shall be emphasised that what we are suggesting here is discreet diplomacy by the Secretary-General, if needed. We are not suggesting lecturing or hectoring by the Secretary-General, but are calling precisely for the exercise of human rights *diplomacy*, the subject of this essay and this book.

Peacekeeping and Peacebuilding

Like peacemaking, peacekeeping and peacebuilding take place under the authority of the Secretary-General following mandates from the UN Security Council or the UN Peace-building Commission. It has now become standard practice that all peacekeeping and peacebuilding operations should have solid human rights components, and the Office of the High Commissioner for Human Rights is in the lead on this. But it is our submission that the Secretary-General still has room for the exercise of human rights diplomacy on selective issues.

A category of issue that would warrant special attention from the Secretary-General, on which he should be appropriately briefed by the

[17] See on this, B. G. Ramcharan (ed.), *The Protection Roles of National Human Rights Institutions* (Leiden: Martinus Nijhoff, 2005).

relevant departments and offices, relates to human rights grievances that might be the cause of breakdown in peace agreements or peace-building processes. Peacekeeping or peacebuilding operations involving ethnic communities, nationalities or minorities would merit the attention of the Secretary-General and, at his direction, his senior representatives.

The identification of sensitive situations, the devising of preventive blueprints, the deployment of representatives and, if necessary, observers or peacekeepers would be issues deserving of the attention of the Secretary-General and his senior staff.

Responsibility to Protect

The responsibility to protect is one of the leading policy planks of the United Nations and of the UN Secretary-General. On 12 January 2009, Secretary-General Ban Ki-moon issued his first Report on the Responsibility to Protect.[18] He recalled the 2005 World Summit Outcome document which had stated that:

> Each individual State has the responsibility to protect its populations from genocide, war crimes, ethnic cleansing and crimes against humanity. This responsibility entails the prevention of such crimes, including their incitement, through appropriate and necessary means.[19]

The strategy put forward in the report stressed the value of prevention and, when it fails, early and flexible response tailored to the specific circumstances of each state. It discusses the role of early warning and assessment and outlines a broad-based approach to the prevention and protection responsibilities of member states, the UN, regional and sub-regional organisations and civil society partners.

Pillar one of the strategy presented in the report is the enduring responsibility of the state to protect its populations from genocide, war crimes, ethnic cleansing, and crimes against humanity. The responsibility of the state is critical to effective and timely prevention strategies.

---

[18] Report of the Secretary-General, Implementing the Responsibility to Protect, UN Doc A/63/677 (12 January 2009). A second report was issued in 2010: Report of the Secretary-General, Early Warning, Assessment and the Responsibility to Protect, UN Doc A/64/864 (14 July 2010).

[19] UNGA Res 60/1 (2005), World Summit Outcome, UN Doc A/RES/60/1 (24 October 2005), para.138.

Pillar two is the commitment of the international community to assist states in meeting their obligations. Pillar three is the responsibility of member states to respond collectively in a timely and decisive manner when a state is manifestly failing to provide such protection.

The Secretary-General recommended that member states may wish to review what more they could do, individually and collectively, to implement their obligations under human rights law. He urged that states should become parties to the relevant international instruments, including the Statute of the ICC.

He called for efforts to help build the capacities of regional and sub-regional organisations to prevent crimes and violations relating to the responsibility to protect, which he thought could be a wise investment. Noting that there had been a host of proposals for creating a standing or standby rapid-response civilian and police capacity for emergencies, he encouraged further creative thinking about such options. He urged that member states be provided with assistance in respect to

- conflict-sensitive development assistance;
- indigenous mediation capacity;
- consensus and dialogue, i.e. capacities for carrying out inclusive and participatory processes of dialogue;
- local dispute resolution capacity; and
- capacity to replicate capacity.[20]

He considered that the UN system should increase its rule of law assistance to member states. Furthermore, in a rapidly unfolding emergency situation, the UN, regional, sub-regional and national decision makers must remain focused on saving lives through 'timely and decisive' action.[21] He called upon the General Assembly to consider whether and, if so, how a periodic review of what member states have done to implement the responsibility to protect could be produced and reviewed. In this regard, he aired the possibility that the Secretary-General could submit an annual or biennial report for the next several years on implementation steps relating to the responsibility to protect.

In an annex "Early Warning and Assessment" to his 2009 Report on the Responsibility to Protect he also asked the relevant line departments, programmes, agencies and inter-agency networks to incorporate

---

[20] Report of the Secretary-General, Implementing the Responsibility to Protect, UN Doc A/63/677 (12 January 2009), para.45.

[21] *Ibid.*, para.50.

consideration and perspectives relating to the responsibility to protect into their ongoing activities and reporting procedures. In his 2010 follow-up report, the Secretary-General reiterated that the United Nations need to develop 'world class early warning and assessment capacities'[22] to implement the responsibility to protect, and made further suggestions of how this capacity could be increased.[23]

There are many things of value in the reports. The question that is pertinent in this essay is to ask where the Secretary-General might be able to deploy human rights diplomacy to advance the responsibility to protect. We believe that the strengthening of national protection systems is the area where the Secretary-General can make a distinctive contribution.

The primary responsibility for the prevention of violations of human rights lies with the national protection system of each state. As has been correctly noted,[24] the first obligation of a government is to respect and to ensure to all individuals within its territory and subject to its jurisdiction the rights recognised in the International Covenant on Civil and Political Rights (ICCPR)[25] and the International Covenant on Economic, Social and Cultural Rights (ICESCR).[26] A state complies with the obligation to respect the recognised rights by not violating them. The duty to ensure imposes an affirmative duty on the state and calls for specific activities by the state to enable individuals to enjoy the recognised rights.[27]

The second obligation is for the state to take the necessary steps, in accordance with its constitutional processes and with the provisions of international human rights treaties it has ratified to adopt such legislative or other measures as may be necessary to give effect to these rights and freedoms.[28] The third obligation is to ensure that any person whose

---

[22] Report of the UN Secretary-General, Early Warning, Assessment and the Responsibility to Protect, UN Doc A/64/864 (14 July 2010), para.19.

[23] *Ibid.*, paras.10-13.

[24] N. Jayawickrama, *The Judicial Application of Human Rights Law: National, Regional and International Jurisprudence* (Cambridge: Cambridge University Press, 2002), p.46.

[25] 1966 International Covenant on Civil and Political Rights (ICCPR), UNGA Res 2200A (XXI) (1966), UN Doc A/RES/2200 XXI (A) (16 December 1966), 999 UNTS 171; entered into force 23 March 1976.

[26] 1966 International Covenant on Economic, Social and Cultural Rights (ICESCR), UNGA Res 2200A (XXI) (1966), UN Doc A/RES/2200 XXI (A) (16 December 1966), 933 UNTS 3; entered into force 3 January 1976.

[27] Jayawickrama, *The Judicial Application of Human Rights Law*, 2002, p.48.

[28] *Ibid.*, p.49.

rights or freedoms are violated shall have an effective remedy, notwithstanding that the violation has been committed by persons acting in an official capacity; to ensure that any person claiming such a remedy shall have his/her right thereto determined by competent judicial, administrative, or legislative authorities, or by the legal system, and to develop the possibilities of judicial review; and to ensure that the competent authorities shall enforce such remedies when granted.[29]

The concept of the national protection system is one of the most strategic for the universal realisation of human rights. It is thus understandable that the summit of world leaders, meeting on the occasion of the sixtieth anniversary of the United Nations in 2005, highlighted the right to be protected at the national level, and that Secretary-General Kofi Annan, in his last report on conflict prevention, emphasised the responsibility to prevent gross violations of human rights.[30] National human rights plans of action can also help reinforce a national protection system.

The introduction of the Universal Periodic Review (UPR) process as part of the reforms brought in with the establishment of the Human Rights Council would allow the Secretary-General to discuss governments' efforts to strengthen their national protection systems and to participate in the system of the UPR when visiting their countries. This could be done through discreet diplomacy, complementing the efforts of the High Commissioner for Human Rights.

Justice

The pursuit of justice internationally can be a tricky one, as we have seen recently with the indictment of the President of Sudan and the reaction to it in some countries. Nevertheless, that the Secretary-General can marshal diplomacy discreetly behind the scenes in support of the ICC and in favour of further ratifications of the Statute of the Court. Many countries would listen to the voice and counsel of the Secretary-General presented discreetly and in a confidence-building manner.

---

[29] *Ibid.*, pp.49–50.

[30] Report of the Secretary-General, Progress Report on the Prevention of Armed Conflict, UN Doc A/60/891 (18 July 2006).

A Universal Culture of Human Rights

Likewise, the Secretary-General can use his efforts behind the scenes to promote ratifications of the principal human rights treaties, particularly the Optional Protocol to the Convention against Torture.[31] That instrument provides for a system of regular visits to prisons and places of detention by national and international bodies. Keeping in mind that many abuses take place in places of detention and in prisons, a system of regular visits can help prevent abuses. The Optional Protocol has, at the time of writing, been ratified by 57 states.[32] That leaves almost another 140 to go. This is an area on which the Secretary-General can make a mark through discreet diplomacy behind the scenes.

The spread of human rights education in schools and universities would be a practical way of taking forward the promotion and protection of human rights and would be an area where the Secretary-General could deploy diplomatic efforts in support of the work of the Office of the High Commissioner. We should emphasise that we are not advocating that the Secretary-General duplicates the activities of the High Commissioner. Rather, we are suggesting that if the Secretary-General were to use his authority and prestige in support of efforts for human rights education that could indeed make a difference.

Finally, the courts have a decisive role to play in the protection of human rights in every country. An approach that could assist the courts immeasurably would be for them to be provided with selected compilations of international norms and jurisprudence in local languages so that they may have access to these norms and jurisprudence in their daily work. Very little of this kind of support is given at the present time. The Secretary-General could help a great deal by letting it be known to all concerned discreetly that he attaches importance to such efforts, and by using his influence and authority to help stimulate efforts in this area as well.

---

[31] 2002 Optional Protocol to the Convention against Torture and Other Cruel, Inhuman or Degrading Treatment or Punishment (OP-CAT), UNGA Res 57/199 (2003), UN Doc A/RES/57/199 (9 January 2003), 2375 UNTS 237; entered into force 22 June 2006.

[32] See: http://treaties.un.org/Pages/ViewDetails.aspx?src=TREATY&mtdsg_no=IV-9-b&chapter=4&lang=en [last accessed 11 February 2011].

Conclusion

In this essay we have sought, keeping in mind insights from the past, to make a case for the deployment of the human rights diplomacy of the UN Secretary-General in selected areas. One should always be careful about making suggestions to a sitting Secretary-General because one never knows what actually is taking place at any particular time and what the priorities and demands are. Nevertheless, as a matter of policy reasoning we think that the Secretary-General can exercise diplomacy for the relief of human suffering, in the exercise of his responsibilities under Article 99 of the UN Charter, in the areas of peacemaking, peacekeeping and peacebuilding, for the advancement of the responsibility to protect, for the strengthening of national protection systems, for the advancement of the principle of justice and in support of the ICC, and in favour of the entrenchment of a universal culture of human rights in all societies. The promotion of ratification of the principal human rights treaties, the spread of human rights education, and human rights support for the judiciaries around the world would be suitable ways of moving further towards the emplacement of a universal culture of human rights in practice.

CHAPTER 11

HUMAN RIGHTS DIPLOMACY OF THE UNITED NATIONS SECURITY COUNCIL

JOANNA WESCHLER

The United Nations (UN) Security Council is the world's highest political body and the most important actor and facilitator of high-level multilateral diplomacy. It can be argued that virtually all activities of the Security Council involve diplomacy—i.e. an element of negotiation and persuasion. The questions to answer here will thus be about the extent to which the Security Council's work concerns human rights; about how willing the Security Council has been to actively pursue human rights issues in its work; about the impact the Council has had on human rights overall; and whether there is potential for the Security Council to achieve more in regard to the promotion and protection of human rights. Before these questions are addressed it shall be noted that this contribution focuses on the human rights diplomacy of the UN Security Council as such, that is diplomatic action taking place at the UN Headquarters in New York. It does not attempt to analyse the impact of UN operations established by the Security Council on the promotion and protection of human rights in a particular country; nor does it discuss the impact of institutions created by the Council, such as the *ad hoc* international criminal tribunals.

Historical Background

During the first decades of its existence, the Security Council very rarely addressed human rights. Historically, human rights were considered separate from peace and security issues, with most governments, in particular the Communist bloc, being very reluctant about the Council entering an area that was perceived as a matter of strict state sovereignty. For over four decades, human rights were something of a taboo at the Council. However, even during the Cold War period they were not entirely absent from the Council's diplomacy. Rights language was included in some of its resolutions, for example on the Congo in 1961[1] and the Dominican Republic in 1965.[2] Particularly interesting for that period and therefore worth some attention is Security Council resolution 120 of 1956 on the situation in Hungary.[3] It is an example of how diplomatic creativity can be used to address human rights issues in politically difficult situations. It would seem obvious that any Council action in response to the Soviet invasion of Hungary following the popular uprising of 1956 would be vetoed by the USSR. Yet, the resolution was adopted because essentially it only decided to call an emergency special session of the General Assembly 'to make appropriate recommendations concerning the situation in Hungary'.[4] While raising human rights concerns, the decision as such was considered procedural and, according to Council rules, the Soviet 'no' vote did thus not count as a veto.

From the early 1960s onwards, resolutions adopted by the Council in the context of decolonisation often included strong human rights language. Above all, several resolutions addressing South Africa between 1963 and the late 1980s had human rights as their main focus, and called on the apartheid government to take specific measures in relation to the protection of human rights.[5] Among them were calls to end detentions without charges and to ensure that detainees had access to a counsel; to grant amnesties to political prisoners; to commute death sentences or allow for stays of execution of specific prisoners; and to allow exiles back into the country. Four resolutions of the Security Council mentioned Nelson Mandela by name. These pronouncements complemented the sanctions imposed by the Council, and collectively they certainly contributed to the eventual dismantling of the apartheid regime.

The most important development, however, that led to the gradual acceptance of human rights issues as relevant to the work of the Security Council was the changing nature of armed conflicts from international to predominantly internal conflicts. In internal conflicts human rights violations have almost always been at the core of the events—they have been linked to the causes of conflict, and civilian

---

[1] UNSC Res 161 (1961) on the Congo, UN Doc S/RES/161 (21 February 1961).

[2] UNSC Res 203 (1965) and UNSC Res 205 (1965) on the Dominican Republic, UN Docs S/RES/203 (14 May 1965) and S/RES/205 (22 May 1965).

[3] UNSC Res 120 (1956) on Hungary, UN Doc S/RES/120 (4 November 1956).

[4] *Ibid.*

[5] For more details see S. Bailey, *The UN Security Council and Human Rights* (New York: St. Martin's Press, 1994).

populations are often directly targeted by combatants in this type of conflict. Through their link to the maintenance of international peace and security, it was gradually accepted that human rights issues are a necessary factor to be considered by the Security Council. The fact that the change in the nature of armed conflict coincided with the end of the Cold War helped this process along, though not without strong resistance from some members of the Security Council.

For example, on 11 August 1992 when the Security Council got set to hear one of the special rapporteurs of the then UN Commission on Human Rights for the first time ever, the Indian representative warned against dire consequences. He suggested that:

> A deviation from the Charter, in which the nations of the world have reposed their faith and support, could erode that confidence and have grave consequences for the future of the Organization as a whole. [...] The Council [...] cannot discuss human rights situations per se or make recommendations on matters outside its competence.[6]

The words of the Indian ambassador reflect the attitudes of many diplomats towards the Council's involvement with human rights prevalent at the time. Interestingly, during that same debate, one of the diplomats who strongly argued against inviting UN special rapporteurs to speak to the Security Council was Ecuador's representative on the Council, José Ayala-Lasso. In 1993, he became the first UN High Commissioner for Human Rights.

Gradually the resistance decreased and human rights became more present in the Council's discourse and decisions. Human rights components were increasingly included in the mandates of peacekeeping operations established by the Council. Human rights were also more often referred to in the Council's resolutions and presidential statements. While in 1994 five percent of resolutions and seven percent of presidential statements mentioned human rights, by 2000 these percentages had risen to about 30, and in 2010 reached 51 and 53 percent respectively.

The acceptance of the need to address human rights did not, however, develop along straight, ascending lines. The reluctance of the Council's members lingered on, and after the establishment of the Human Rights Council in 2006 some governments argued that by

[6] UNSC Provisional Verbatim Record of the 3105th meeting, UN Doc S/PV.3105 (11 August 1992).

considering human rights issues, the Security Council would encroach on the mandate of the Human Rights Council. This rhetoric was used as an excuse for not taking up some human rights issues at the Council, or in explanation of a negative vote on a resolution. For example, in January 2007 during the vote on a US/UK sponsored resolution on Myanmar[7] which was ultimately rejected due to a double Chinese/Russian veto, several other governments voted against the adoption of the resolution or abstained. Explaining their vote, they argued that they believed that the issue should be dealt with by the Human Rights Council rather than the Security Council. South Africa in addition questioned the overall validity of the Security Council addressing human rights violations, holding that the issues covered in the draft resolution did 'not fit with the Charter mandate conferred upon the Security Council'.[8]

It seems useful to look at some of the tools the Council developed over the years to address various situations with human rights implications. Among them are the imposition of sanctions, field visits, informal human rights briefings, the establishment of the Council's Working Group on Children and Armed Conflict, public debates, the involvement of the UN High Commissioner for Human Rights in the Council's work, and reference to the responsibility to protect. These can be described as the Council's means of conducting human rights diplomacy, and shall be discussed briefly in turn.

Sanctions

Whether imposed on an entire country's economy, on a commodity such as oil or diamonds, or on individuals (as has been the case in several countries in the last decade or so), sanctions are an important means at the Council's disposal to force some actors to change their behaviour. Once decided by the Council, the implementation of sanctions has been uneven, and sanctions are often criticised as purely symbolic. However, it can be argued that despite their symbolic nature, they constitute a very important diplomatic measure. Indeed, on several occasions the Council based its decision to target individuals with

[7] UNSC Draft Resolution, UN Doc S/2007/14 (12 January 2007).

[8] UNSC Provisional Verbatim Record of the 5619th meeting, UN Doc S/PV.5619 (12 January 2007).

measures such as travel bans or the freezing of their assets *inter alia* on the fact that the respective individual had committed serious human rights violations.[9] Even if the measures as such do not affect the respective individual's life very much—when the person operates from the jungle and/or does not care about visas and bank accounts, for example—the fact that targeted sanctions are applied to individuals who are involved in committing human rights violations sends an important message about what clearly amounts to an internationally unacceptable conduct.

Missions

In the early 1990s, the Council began undertaking field visits to conflict or post-conflict areas, and has conducted several dozens of such missions over the years.[10] With a few exceptions, human rights concerns have been among the issues raised with interlocutors on the ground, including sometimes those in a position to reduce the level of human rights violations. Thus, Security Council missions provide examples of direct human rights diplomacy. In at least one case, in East Timor in 1999, the Council's visit resulted in an immediate reduction of the level of violence and the number of rampant human rights violations.[11]

Informal Briefings Known as the 'Arria formula'

An interesting tool that has been used with varying success and frequency to give a range of human rights actors access to the Security Council are the so-called 'Arria formula' briefings. These briefings allow human rights experts, representatives of non-governmental

[9] See e.g. UNSC Res 1572 (2004) on Cote d'Ivoire, UN Doc S/RES/1572 (15 November 2004); UNSC Res 1591 (2005) on Sudan/Darfur, UN Doc S/RES/1591 (29 March 2005); UNSC Res 1698 (2006) and 1807 (2008) on the DRC (in particular concerning violations of children's rights and sexual violence), UN Docs S/RES/1698 (31 July 2006) and S/RES/1807 (30 March 2008); and UNSC Res 1970 (2011) on Libya, UN Doc S/RES/1970 (26 February 2011).

[10] The Reports of Security Council's Missions are available at: http://www.un.org/Docs/sc/missionreports.html [last accessed 8 March 2011].

[11] For details see the Council's report on its Mission to East Timor and Indonesia: Report of the Security Council Mission to Jakarta and Dili, 8 to 12 September 1999, UN Doc S/1999/976 (14 September 1999).

human rights organisations and private individuals to provide witness testimonies to members of the Council. While the briefings are not exclusively reserved to address human rights, their roots go firmly back to human rights issues. In March 1992, the then President of the Council, Venezuelan ambassador Diego Arria, was contacted by a Croat priest who had just come out of the Balkan conflict zone. Ambassador Arria wanted the priest to convey his eyewitness account to other members of the Council, and not being able to find a formal way, he simply invited his fellow ambassadors to meet with the priest in the delegates' lounge. The ten or eleven ambassadors who attended were shaken by the testimony and highly appreciative of the first-hand eyewitness information.[12] Several similar briefings soon followed, and while most were held in conference rooms and were provided with interpreting services, they have remained informal. Over the years, several special rapporteurs of the (former) UN Commission on Human Rights, a former UN High Commissioner for Human Rights, representatives from numerous human rights organisations, celebrities involved in the protection of human rights, and private individuals who had been eye-witnesses to human rights violations participated in the 'Arria formula' briefings. Several meetings afforded a good opportunity for substantive discussions of human rights issues among the members of the Security Council.

Working Group on Children and Armed Conflict

The Working Group on Children and Armed Conflict is one of the Council's most effective human rights tools. Without going into a more detailed analysis, an aspect worth mentioning is how the Group has overcome some of the considerable difficulties in applying pressure on non-state actors who recruit child soldiers. A large proportion of the violations of children's rights addressed by the Working Group is perpetrated by non-state armed groups. As the Council does not have direct diplomatic channels of communication with non-state actors, it developed a practice whereby the chair of the Working Group issues public statements that function as messages to non-state actors. Several

[12] For more details see J. Weschler, 'The Security Council and Human Rights' in M. Malone (ed.), *The UN Security Council: From the Cold War to the 21st Century* (Boulder: Lynne Rienner Publishers, 2004).

such messages have been sent, among them to the Lord's Resistance Army, the Sri Lankan Tamil Tigers and various groups active in the Great Lakes region.

Public Debates

Public debates of the Security Council can also facilitate human rights diplomacy and provide a venue for its conduct. Over the years, the number of Council debates in which human rights were mentioned grew considerably: from about 22 percent in 1994 to 46 percent in 2010. Several debates on specific situations and thematic issues have had a strong human rights focus and provided, both figuratively and literally, a means of broadcasting human rights views from the top political body to the world at large.[13] So-called open debates in which all UN members states can participate, have on some occasions been used very effectively by states not on the Council to condemn human rights violations and to make recommendations concerning rights issues. Public debates of the Council have also afforded the UN High Commissioner for Human Rights an opportunity to establish a presence within the Security Council.

Involvement of the UN High Commissioner for Human Rights

Direct access of the High Commissioner to the Security Council has been a politically sensitive issue, and for years several governments strongly resisted any formal interaction. Even though the post had been created in late 1993, it was not until 16 September 1999 that the High Commissioner was allowed to address the Council. That it happened at all was due to intense diplomacy by several actors, foremost by former Secretary-General Kofi Annan, but also by human rights non-governmental organisations. After several setbacks, the High Commissioner was allowed to address the Council during an open debate on the protection of civilians in armed conflict. This was a breakthrough, and for the next few years the High Commissioner was

[13] Public debates of the Security Council can be watched live on UN webcast, and archives dating back as far as 2003 are available at: http://www.un.org/webcast/sc.html. For debates from 17 September 2010 onwards, see: http://www.unmultimedia.org/tv/webcast/ [last accessed 8 March 2011].

invited several times to speak at the Council. The periodic debates on the protection of civilians in armed conflict were among the debates attended by the High Commissioner. In addition, the Commissioner participated in the first ever Council retreat on human rights in March 2001, and in some closed country-specific consultations, for example on events in the Democratic Republic of Congo.

But as with all human rights related activities of the Security Council, the participation of the High Commissioner remained controversial, and acceptance of the High Commissioner's valuable contribution to the Council's work has been far from universal. From 2005 onwards, the High Commissioner was invited only sporadically, and never participated in the semi-annual debates on the protection of civilians. This only changed in 2009 and was due to intense diplomatic efforts by certain members of the Council, most notably Austria. Austria chaired the Council in November 2009 when a periodic debate on protection was scheduled. The High Commissioner was invited to speak at that debate. When the next regular debate was about to be held in June 2010, Austria conducted informal consultations with other members of the Council and obtained their consent for another invitation. Securing consent for the invitation of the High Commissioner to the subsequent debate in November 2010 proved considerably easier.

The Responsibility to Protect

Another area that involves diplomacy at the UN Security Council for the prevention of the most serious human rights violations is the debate about the responsibility to protect. In September 2005, when world leaders gathered in New York for the World Summit, they included the responsibility to protect in the Summit Outcome document.[14] The document stated that each individual state has the responsibility to protect its populations from genocide, war crimes, ethnic cleansing and crimes against humanity.[15] It further established that the international community had a responsibility to use appropriate diplomatic, humanitarian and other peaceful means to help protect populations from these serious international crimes, and that the international

[14] UNGA Res 60/1 (2005), World Summit Outcome, UN Doc A/RES/60/1 (24 October 2005).

[15] *Ibid.*, para.138.

community was prepared to take collective action through the Security Council on this matter.[16] The latter raised considerable expectations about the Council embracing the responsibility to protect and implementing it in its actions. However, some members of the Security Council resisted the formal acceptance of the responsibility to protect. It took several months of negotiations at the Council to merely restate some of the world leaders' commitments set out in the Summit Outcome document in a Security Council resolution in 2006.[17] Since then the Council's resolutions have explicitly referred to the responsibility to protect, reminding governments and parties to different armed conflicts of *their* obligation to prevent genocide, war crimes, ethnic cleansing and crimes against humanity. Up to the present day, the Council has, however, stopped short of invoking *its* responsibility to protect when taking specific action. In early 2011, when discussing the situation in Libya, several members of the Security Council raised the responsibility to protect in the face of massive human rights violations in their statements before the Council and their comments to the media. When adopting its resolutions 1970 on 26 February 2011 and 1973 on 17 March 2011, the Security Council opted primarily for reminding the Libyan authorities of their responsibility to protect its population. Yet, in resolution 1973 the Council authorised the use of 'all necessary measures [...] to protect civilians and civilian populated areas under threat of attack',[18] thus coming quite close to formally invoking the principle as applicable to itself.

Final Comments

In conclusion, it seems fair to say that the very fact that human rights issues have attracted the Council's attention is very important for the overall promotion of human rights, even though this attention remains fragmented. By bringing rights concerns into the highest arena of multilateral diplomacy, the Council is in a position to send important messages about internationally inacceptable human rights behaviour.

---

[16] *Ibid.*, para.139.

[17] UNSC Res 1674 (2006) on Civilians in Armed Conflict, UN Doc S/RES/1674 (28 April 2006).

[18] UNSC Res 1973 (2011) on the Situation in Libya, UN Doc S/RES/1973 (17 March 2011), para.4.

There is obviously considerable potential for achieving more on several levels. The history of the Security Council's engagement with human rights shows that getting states to accept human rights as relevant to the Security Council's work has not been easy, nor is there a guarantee that this acceptance will prove permanent. Rather, the acceptance needs to be carefully cultivated and tended to by ongoing and strategically savvy diplomacy.

While outside the scope of this essay, the whole area of the implementation of the Council's decisions on the ground is also a topic where diplomatic efforts by and within the Council can play a significant role. It is arguably through the implementation of these decisions that the Council can make the most important contribution to the promotion and protection of human rights, and regular follow-up activities could advance these efforts. Finally, there is considerable and often underestimated room for diplomatic efforts by all UN member states to ensure that human rights are taken into account in all discussions of and measures taken by the Security Council.

CHAPTER 12

CONFERENCE DIPLOMACY AND HUMAN RIGHTS

Zdzisław Kędzia

On Conference Diplomacy

The role of diplomatic conferences, in particular those held at the level of heads of states or governments, started to increase once the classical view of the Burgundian diplomat Philippe de Commynes had been balanced by the Congress of Vienna (1814–1815), which was followed by similar gatherings and processes. De Commynes wrote in the 15th century: 'Two great princes who wish to establish good personal relations should never meet each other face to face, but ought to communicate through good and wise emissaries.'[1]

Historically, 'conference diplomacy' was gaining importance as a response to conflicts covering entire regions or bearing a global dimension. Diplomatic conferences or summits were perceived as a suitable framework to put an end to hostilities and open doors to post-conflict settlements. As Nicholas Eberstadt writes, in the 'inter-war' Europe, dominated by a series of crisis, 'the very fact that antagonists agreed to gather at the same table was held out as proof positive that 'Conference Diplomacy' was working'.[2]

Although this sort of diplomacy is rooted in the 'old diplomacy', which focused on the classical Westphalian principles of sovereignty and territoriality, it has somewhat flourished under the roof of the United Nations (UN) in the framework of 'new diplomacy'. The latter addresses issues governed by principles and norms which often balance the Westphalian order, such as human rights, humanitarian

[1] Quoted by C. W. Freeman, Jr. and S. Marks (primary contributors), 'Diplomacy' in *Encyclopædia Britannica*, available online at: http://www.britannica.com/EBchecked/topic/164602/diplomacy/10854/Conference-diplomacy?anchor=ref796011 [last accessed 15 January 2011].

[2] N. Eberstadt, '"Conference Diplomacy", All Over Again', The Nautilus Institute for Security and Sustainable Development, 6 July 2004, available at: http://oldsite.nautilus.org/fora/security/0425B_Eberstadt.html#sect2 [last accessed 15 January 2011].

and social issues, development, environment, and other contemporary items on the very broad international agenda.[3] International conferences have appeared, at least in some cases, to be a functional tool to look for global arrangements in these areas. Moreover, they offer a workable venue for the contemporary three tracks of diplomacy: official governmental channels, unofficial diplomatic activities (often involving governmental and non-governmental experts), and networking diplomacy based on interaction between social actors (often for advocacy purposes).

It is warrant to repeat the assessment made by the former UN Secretary-General Kofi Annan who said that the world conferences held under the auspices of the United Nations play a harmonising role, serve as an indispensable forum where diverse points of view are aired, where proposals are debated and where, most importantly, political consensus is achieved. As a result, the international community—governments, non-governmental organisations (NGOs), and representatives of the wider civil society—has been able to set a new course for a new era in global affairs.[4] In a similar spirit, another former Secretary-General, Boutros-Ghali, had recognised the world summits of the 1990s 'as a wholly new factor for achieving change on the world stage'. He associated himself with an unnamed 'bitter critic' of the conferences who nevertheless stressed that these events were not just 'talkathons' but, on the contrary, provided opportunities 'to seed international law with new norms and rights, many of them hidden in apparently routine language'.[5] Boutros-Ghali also said '[the world conferences] were in fact democratic [...] and the beginning of a new form of peoples' control of their own destinies on issues too large or too suppressed by special interests to be handled by domestic national politics'.[6] It seems that these words were primarily related to the relations between states and the role played at the conferences by those less

[3] W. R. Moomaw, 'New Diplomacy', The Fletcher School, Tufts University, available at: http://fletcher.tufts.edu/ierp/pdfs/NewDiplomacy.2.pdf [last accessed 15 January 2011].

[4] K. Annan, 'Preface' to the *UN Briefing Papers/The World Conferences* (New York: United Nations 1997), quoted by R. Reitano, 'UN-Sponsored Summits and "Citizen Diplomacy" Summits, Multilateral Diplomacy, and the United Nations', in J. P. Muldoon *et al.* (eds.), *Multilateral Diplomacy and the United Nations Today* (Boulder: Westview Press, 1999), p.119.

[5] B. Boutros-Ghali, *Unvanquished. A U.S.—U.N. Saga* (New York: Random House, 1999), p.174.

[6] *Ibid.*, p.175.

influential than the big powers. However, Boutros-Ghali's observation can also apply to the phenomenon of the 'third track' networking diplomacy present during the world conferences in the form of non-governmental forums and to their interaction with the intergovernmental level.

Divided Opinions

The UN reinvigorated the idea of conference diplomacy by setting up regular meetings of its bodies that partially recall the format of national parliaments, but often also bear the features of international conferences with their informal and formal preparatory processes and some sort of follow-up. More importantly from the discussed perspective, the world organisation and its agencies and programmes, and similarly, regional organisations, provide frameworks for global or regional conferences with open-ended participation that offer unique opportunities, almost impossible in another setting, such as a special dynamism of direct relations between different national delegations and delegates, synergy of efforts undertaken by governmental, non-governmental, and other actors, and finally, the genius of the Greek unity of time, venue and action based on the preparatory process leading up to the meeting itself. All this provides the chance for intensive negotiations leading to the reconciliation of interests based on the always helpful 'win-win' approach.

Yet, conference diplomacy also bears a considerable risk that the failure of a meeting, which sometimes is related to developments beyond the control of those directly involved, may constitute a major drawback in a specific area of international relations or even more generally. Remarkable and certainly worrying are comments by Calestous Juma that 'Africa is losing faith in conference diplomacy as a source of solutions to its persistent problems' which lead him to the conclusion that 'time has come for Africa to rethink its investment in multilateral diplomacy and redirect its efforts to new activities such as technology cooperation through bilateral partnerships'.[7] Juma does not question

[7] 'Africa Losing Faith in Conference Diplomacy', C. Juma for *Business Daily* (Nairobi), 20 September 2007, published on the website of the J. F. Kennedy School of Government, Harvard University, available at: http://belfercenter.ksg.harvard.edu/publication/17513/africa_losing_faith_in_conference_diplomacy.html [last accessed 15 January 2011].

the usefulness of conference diplomacy as such, only in his view this sort of diplomacy in the field of development draws too much on the limited resources of African countries, bringing very little in return.

Commentators heavily disagree in their assessments of both the very concept and impact of large international conferences. Some see them as an important and, by and large, a successful tool of new diplomacy, helping to reach an international consensus around an international agenda, and setting up law-making processes and new implementation and monitoring mechanisms. Others are sceptical, at the very least. Sometimes even the hosts of the United Nations world conferences cannot hide their mixed feelings. It was remarkable, indeed, that Kofi Annan published his first impressions about the 2005 World Summit the day after its closure under the title "The Glass at Least Half Full".[8] It was slightly better than to say: 'the glass half empty', but nevertheless…

Before referring to the arguments in favour of one or another position, let us look closer at the 1993 World Conference on Human Rights in Vienna (the Conference), which, after the Teheran Conference in 1968, was the second and so far the last global meeting on this topic. Was it successful? M. G. Schechter says that it was 'one of the most frequently criticized of the conferences of the 1990s'.[9] Although one can guess to what extent this relatively frequent criticism was a result of the importance attached to the Vienna meeting by a wide spectrum of public opinion, a divided attitude to its performance is a fact.

A Case Study—The Second World Conference on Human Rights

As far as a general assessment of the Conference is concerned, it has evolved considerably. On another occasion, I pointed to the fact that while reading the morning newspapers the day after the Conference, one could have had the feeling that the black scenario of conference diplomacy won the battle. The average tone was highly critical and the

[8] 'The Glass at Least Half Full', K. Annan for the *Wall Street Journal*, 19 September 2005, accessible at: http://www.un.org/News/ossg/sg/stories/articleFull.asp?TID=49&Type=Article [last accessed 15 January 2011].

[9] M. G. Schechter (ed.), *United Nations-sponsored World Conferences: Focus on Impact and Follow-up* (Tokyo/New York: United Nations University Press, 2001), p.219.

Conference was held almost meaningless.[10] It did not take too much time however, until the assessment became more positive, allowing the Conference to pass on to historical records as in many aspects a successful, even a landmark event. For several years afterwards, the 'spirit of Vienna' was being recalled with substantial nostalgia, in particular in times witnessing the deterioration of the international atmosphere. But, talking about the legacy of Vienna one has to go beyond the mystical level and stop evoking its 'spirit' only. Several substantive achievements decided about the impact of this Conference. Two years before its 20th anniversary, the Vienna Declaration and Programme of Action (VDPA)[11] remains one of the most frequently quoted basic programmatic documents in the area of human rights which would most probably not be the case if its substance were as weak as some critics say. The Vienna accord went far beyond just recording what everybody was aware of. Let us mention a few of the groundbreaking statements adopted after highly controversial negotiations.

The universality of human rights and the related responsibility of governments have been reiterated by all countries in unequivocal words: 'Human rights and fundamental freedoms are the birthright of all human beings; their protection and promotion is the first responsibility of Governments.'[12] Some more sceptical commentators were disappointed that the Conference was not able to close the chapter of the debate on the relationship between universality of human rights and diverse cultural traditions. First, one can have serious doubts whether it would be desirable to close this debate—aside from its feasibility. If not misused, it can only help to enrich the concept of universality, integrating diversified cultural roots into the common notion of universal rights and freedoms. Second, the Conference took place under the impact of somewhat contradicting objective factors, influencing not only the policies of states at the time, but also the minds of the participants. The end of the Cold War and the collapse of the Warsaw Pact, as well as the end of apartheid in South Africa evidently belonged to

[10] Z. Kedzia, 'The Road to Vienna: Negotiating the Vienna Declaration and Programme of Action' in Benedek *et al.* (eds.), *Global Standards—Local Action. 15 Years Vienna World Conference on Human Rights*, Conference Proceedings of the International Expert Conference held in Vienna on 28 and 29 August 2008, 16 Studienreihe des Ludwig Boltzmann Instituts für Menschenrechte (Viennna/Graz: NWV/Intersentia, 2009).

[11] Vienna Declaration and Programme of Action (VDPA), adopted by the World Conference on Human Rights, UN Doc A/CONF.157/23 (12 July 1993).

[12] Part.I, para.1 VDPA.

positive factors. But there were several other changes, perplexing rather than clarifying international relations. Indeed, the ideological division between communist East and liberal West had largely lost its ground. But, of course, life, including the international one, does not tolerate a longer standing vacuum. Projections of the future were ranging from the reinforced modernist visions to post-modernist scepticism, from cooperation and the solidarity paradigm to the 'clash of civilizations', from the optimistic perspective of the consolidation of democracy and sound economy to fears about the future facing, as it was named shortly before the Conference, the 'end of history'. Which of these visions is closer to today's reality and why may be an interesting topic for a Vienna+20 conference. However, in 1993, the compromise reached by the participants was not bad at all, even if the language of the relevant paragraph is not particularly striking by its beauty:

> All human rights are universal, indivisible and interdependent and interrelated. [...] While the significance of national and regional particularities and various historical, cultural and religious backgrounds must be borne in mind, it is the duty of States, regardless of their political, economic and cultural systems, to promote and protect all human rights and fundamental freedoms.'

This provision has been used on various occasions to clarify the responsibility of states for the promotion and protection of human rights which cannot be limited, suspended or waived because of the cultural or political specificity of the country.

Another example of groundbreaking statements—taking into account that this position has been endorsed by all states at a world summit—was the acceptance of the principle that 'in the framework of these purposes and principles [of the UN], the promotion and protection of all human rights is a legitimate concern of the international community.' This was a significant blow to the doctrine of the exclusive domestic jurisdiction used as a protective shield to prevent international criticism for serious human rights violations. And, even if this doctrine is from time to time recalled again in international fora, the principle is in place and helps to counter such attempts. Moreover, one can say that this principle paved the way for the subsequent developments in the crucial area of the international response to the gravest violations of human rights and humanitarian law. Already five years after the Vienna Conference, in an address to the then UN Commission on Human Rights, Secretary-General Kofi Annan made his memorable statement:

> I am here today to tell you that the next century must be the age of prevention. I am here to say that we can no longer claim that a lack of available resources prevents us from acting in time. Today's human rights violations are the causes of tomorrow's conflicts. This vicious circle of violations and conflict, leading to new violations, can and must be stopped.[13]

In 2005, the World Summit endorsed the fundamental principle of the responsibility to protect,[14] under elaboration since 2000[15] and drawn from the inspiration of the same Secretary-General.[16] The adoption of this principle had been facilitated by the Ezulwini Consensus endorsing it, reached by member states of African Union within the preparations for the 2005 World Summit.[17] The proclamation of the responsibility to protect at the Summit, as a result of a process leading up to this meeting, seems to be another example of the potential of conference diplomacy.

The proclamation of the interdependency of human rights, democracy and development was also a significant achievement of the Vienna Conference.[18] Some voices stressed that while linking human rights to democracy is fully justified, the same linking to development might be counterproductive. A lot has been said to demonstrate the linkage

[13] UN Press Release, UN Doc SG/SM/6487 HR/4355 (16 March 1998).

[14] UNGA Res 60/1 (2005), World Summit Outcome, UN Doc A/RES/60/1 (24 October 2005), paras.138-39.

[15] Report of the International Commission on Intervention and State Sovereignty on The Responsibility to Protect, published by the International Development Research Centre, Ottawa, December 2001, available at: http://www.iciss.ca/pdf/Commission-Report.pdf [last accessed 15 January 2011]; see also, Report of the High-level Panel on Threats, Challenges and Change, A More Secure World: Our Shared Responsibility, UN Doc A/59/565 (2 December 2004), para.55.

[16] Kofi A. Annan, '"We the Peoples" - The Role of the United Nations in the 21st Century', Millennium Report of the UN Secretary General, United Nations, 2000, p.43, available at: http://www.un.org/millennium/sg/report/full.htm [last accessed 15 January 2011]; Report of the Secretary-General, In Larger Freedom: Towards Development, Security and Human Rights for All, UN Doc A/59/2005 (21 March 2005), para.135.

[17] African Union Executive Council, The Common African Position on the Proposed Reform of the United Nations: "The Ezulwini Consensus", adopted at the 7th Extraordinary Session, 7–8 March 2005, Addis Ababa, Ethiopia, Ext/EX.CL/2 (VII), in particular point B.i, p.6.

[18] Part I, para.8 VDPA.

between development and human rights, to refer here only to Amartya Sen's "Development as Freedom".[19] However, let us stress that, by means of this statement, the Vienna Declaration and Programme of Action also announced that human rights were to be placed within the core activities of the United Nations. The process of mainstreaming human rights, rooted in this statement, led eventually to the crucial acknowledgement by the 2005 World Summit that

> peace and security, development and human rights are the pillars of the United Nations system and the foundations for collective security and well-being. We recognize that development, peace and security and human rights are interlinked and mutually reinforcing.[20]

A comparison of this statement with the language of the UN Charter shows the difference and progress made.

In the light of the Vienna Declaration and Programme of Action, the body of human rights standards is cohesive and coherent. Various categories of rights are interconnected and equally significant. The approach adopted throughout the Conference's document was based on this principle. When the participating states agreed that 'the international community must treat human rights globally in a fair and equal manner, on the same footing, and with the same emphasis',[21] the message was clear. This statement was about to put an end to the continuing attempts to establish a certain hierarchy between rights and freedoms, whereby priority happened to be attached to civil and political rights while economic, social and cultural rights were seen by some as imperfect. In the context of the long-standing division between the categories of rights, going back to the elaboration and adoption of two separate international Covenants in 1966,[22] the position taken by the Conference constituted an important breakthrough. It set the stage for the international debate in the coming years, even though also on this point agreements reached in Vienna did not put an end to allcontroversies. This is demonstrated for example by the tedious

---

[19] A. Sen, *Development as Freedom* (Oxford: Oxford University Press, 1999).

[20] UNGA Res 60/1 (2005), World Summit Outcome, UN Doc A/RES/60/1 (24 October 2005), para.9.

[21] Part I, para.5 VDPA.

[22] 1966 International Covenant on Civil and Political Rights (ICCPR), UNGA Res 2200A (XXI) (1966), UN Doc A/RES/2200 XXI (A) (16 December 1966), 999 UNTS 171; entered into force 23 March 1976; and 1966 International Covenant on Economic, Social and Cultural Rights (ICESCR), UNGA Res 2200A (XXI) (1966), UN Doc A/RES/2200 XXI (A) (16 December 1966), 933 UNTS 3; entered into force 3 January 1976.

negotiation process of the Optional Protocol to the International Covenant on Economic, Social, and Cultural Rights that needed another 15 years to be adopted by the General Assembly in December 2008.[23]

Several important legislative steps taken by the international community after 1993 benefited from a strong encouragement articulated in the Vienna Declaration and Programme of Action. Among them are the Optional Protocol to the Convention on the Elimination of All Forms of Discrimination against Women,[24] the Optional Protocol to the Convention against Torture and Other Cruel, Inhuman and Degrading Treatment or Punishment,[25] and the Optional Protocol to the International Covenant on Economic, Social and Cultural Rights, explicitly recommended by the Conference.[26] The roots of some other instruments may also be linked, although indirectly, to the discussions during the Vienna Conference, as e.g. of the International Convention for the Protection of All Persons from Enforced Disappearance,[27] the Convention on the Rights of Persons with Disabilities,[28] the Optional protocol to the Convention on the Rights of the Child on the Involvement of Children in Armed Conflict, and the Optional Protocol to the Convention on the Rights of the Child on the Sale of Children, Child Prostitution and Child Pornography.[29]

---

[23] 2008 Optional Protocol to the International Covenant on Economic, Social and Cultural Rights, UNGA Res 63/117 (2008), UN Doc A/RES/63/117 (10 December 2008); not yet in force.

[24] 1999 Optional Protocol to the Convention on the Elimination of All Forms of Discrimination against Women (OP-CEDAW), UNGA Res 54/4 (1999), UN Doc A/RES/54/4 (6 October 1999), 2131 UNTS 83; entered into force 22 December 2000.

[25] 2002 Optional Protocol to the Convention against Torture and Other Cruel, Inhuman or Degrading Treatment or Punishment (OP-CAT), UNGA Res 57/199 (2003), UN Doc A/RES/57/199 (9 January 2003), 2375 UNTS 237; entered into force 22 June 2006.

[26] See respectively, part II, paras.40, 60 and 75 VDPA.

[27] Part II, para.62 VDPA; 2006 International Convention for the Protection of All Persons from Enforced Disappearance (CPED), UNGA Res 61/177 (2006), UN Doc A/RES/61/177 (20 December 2006); entered into force 23 December 2010.

[28] Part II, paras.63-65 VDPA; 2006 Convention on the Rights of Persons with Disabilities (CRPD), UNGA Res 61/106 (2006), UN Doc A/RES/61/106 (13 December 2006); entered into force 3 May 2008.

[29] Respectively part II, paras.48 and 50 VDPA; 2000 Optional Protocol to the Convention on the Rights of the Child on the Involvement of Children in Armed Conflict (OP-CRC-AC), UNGA Res 54/263 (2000), UN Doc A/RES/54/263 (25 May 2000), 2173 UNTS 222; entered into force 12 February 2002; and 2000 Optional Protocol to the Convention on the Rights of the Child on the Sale of Children, Child Prostitution and Child Pornography (OP-CRC-SC), UNGA Res 54/263 (2000), UN Doc A/RES/54/263 (25 May 2000), 2171 UNTS 227; entered into force 18 January 2002.

Last but not least, the Vienna Conference led to the strengthening of the United Nations human rights mechanisms, including in particular the establishment of the position of the UN High Commissioner for Human Rights. One can wonder whether without the special dynamics of the World Conference and its preparatory process, and in particular without the negotiations during the Conference the push towards the creation of this fundamental UN function[30] would have had the sufficient power to successfully move through the General Assembly's debate in the autumn of 1993. Or in other words, whether the saga initiated by Rene Cassin's postulate raised in 1948, to create a world human rights attorney general would not have continued for the years to come. It is true that the compromise language of the Vienna Declaration and Programme of Action concerning the High Commissioner hammered out after a round of negotiations, involving ambassadors of some seventeen countries from all regions, sounds rather weak today. However, it was exactly the language of paragraph 18 of part II of the VDPA that set the tone for the debate in the General Assembly.[31] When the Working Group of the Third Committee on the follow-up to the World Conference started its work, two observations were clashing on the minds of participants in this exciting exercise. The scepticism regarding the chances for the establishment of the institution of the High Commissioner during the ongoing session of the General Assembly was probably dominating. However, another observation eventually better reflected the reality. Indeed, important recommendations of the world conferences most frequently had found their way, sooner or later, into the decision-making processes of United Nations bodies. So there was a silver line in the midst of scepticism which turned out to be more than just hope. And, against the doubters, the General Assembly decided already in December 1993 to establish the position of the High Commissioner for Human Rights. Twelve years later, the 2005 World Summit continued the work of the Vienna Conference by recommending the expansion of the capacities of the

[30] This time generated by Amnesty's International paper, 'A High Commissioner for Human Rights: Time for Action', AI Index IOR 41/35/93, October 1993.

[31] Para.18 VDPA reads: 'The World Conference on Human Rights recommends to the General Assembly that when examining the report of the Conference at its forty-eighth session, it begin, as a matter of priority, consideration of the question of the establishment of a High Commissioner for Human Rights for the promotion and protection of all human rights.'

Office of the High Commissioner, including doubling its budget, and the establishment of the Human Rights Council.

These are only some examples drawn from the Vienna Declaration and Programme of Action that may illustrate the importance of 1993 Conference. One should also acknowledge other aspects of its impact, in addition to its formal outcome. In particular, the Conference gave a strong impetus to governments and civil society to engage in human rights issues at various levels: international, regional, and national/local. The work of the Preparatory Committee, regional governmental and non-governmental preparatory meetings played an important role as the catalysts of such involvement. The Conference process instigated and was spearheaded by a multi-centred leadership in the human rights debate: governments were using this opportunity to position themselves in view of the fading Cold War divisions; NGOs used the Conference process as a platform for dialogue, programmes development, and consolidation of alliances for some human rights concepts or the protection of the human rights of specific groups. The most striking was the success of the women's caucus in effectively putting the rights of women on the agenda of the World Conference. In general, one can say that the Conference provided an effective leverage to postulates of organised groups and thus helped them to integrate their efforts as driving forces of the Conference process itself.

One can raise the question whether all these decisions and recommendations, initiated processes, and steps towards the strengthening of the protection of human rights would not have been possible without convening the Vienna Conference. In most cases, the answer should hypothetically be—yes, they would, although one can reasonably assume that the time needed to arrive at the results comparable with the Conference's outcome would be significantly longer. However, it would probably have been impossible to agree upon a broad set of principles and develop a comprehensive programmatic global platform for the promotion and protection of human rights without such a framework. Moreover, serious doubts may be raised whether at least some of the aforementioned principles and recommendations could have been worked out in the framework of the routine work of the General Assembly. Taking an example from another conference—2005 World Summit—would it have been possible to elaborate and adopt the responsibility to protect principle during regular sessions of the General Assembly or the Human Rights Council, under the political pressures dominating the scene during the last ten years or so?

All the positive findings about the Vienna Conference should not, of course, lead to a conclusion that its process and outcome do not deserve any criticism. For example, the Vienna Declaration and Programme of Action avoided any specific references to ongoing or recent human rights violations on a large scale. Those seeking to have a more precise language throughout the outcome document could be disappointed by a solid portion of probably unnecessary human rights rhetoric. In a couple of provisions, the language may imply that the international standards should be measured by national solutions and not the other way round. Also, the preparatory process, despite some clear achievements, had its remarkable flaws, such as ineffectively used time of the sessions of the Preparatory Committee. Other critical comments might also be made.

However, there is always a price for a common language capturing highly diversified views and equally varying interests. In the case of world conferences, therefore, what seems to actually count is their contribution to the progress in respective areas and not so much the difference between what could have been achieved in an ideal world and the final outcome. Some commentators might criticise this approach as minimalist. But one can argue that it could, indeed, be close to a minimalist position at the stage of planning a conference because the goals should always be ambitious and compelling. Nevertheless, while assessing the results of a conference the proposed approach seems to be more adequate.

Taking this into account, one can see the 1993 Vienna Conference as an effort which has contributed to the promotion and protection of human rights, by:

- reiterating and developing principles of the international system of human rights promotion and protection;
- identifying several structural challenges to human rights and ways to address them;
- adopting a comprehensive programme of action for the international community, including legislative and operational measures;
- strengthening international mechanisms in the area of human rights, including the establishment of the High Commissioner for Human Rights;
- raising human rights awareness and vigilance among political elites and the wider civil society, both at national and international levels, and thus, mobilising governments and public opinion for the cause of human rights;

- mounting the pressure of the international community on abusers of international law and moral; and
- providing authorisation and support for the mainstreaming of human rights into the United Nations programmes and activities.[32]

It seems that this assessment may apply *mutatis mutandis* to future human rights conferences, as well as to conference diplomacy in other fields than human rights. In view of the political conflicts accompanying some other conferences, one can wonder whether such a generalisation is justified. However, even the highly tensed 2001 World Conference against Racism, Xenophobia and related Intolerance in Durban was eventually able to adopt a comprehensive Declaration and Programme of Action. It is also interesting and encouraging to note that the 2009 Durban Review Conference produced results which have been widely welcomed. Having analysed *inter alia* the process of this last conference, the UN High Commissioner for Human Rights, Navanethem Pillay, stated: 'Let me conclude by saying that I have found diplomacy to be an effective and for ma new component to what is I believe a more holistic approach to human rights protection.'[33]

The Perspectives of Conference Diplomacy in the Human Rights Area—Is It Needed?

For several years, a lot of commentators have spoken about 'conference fatigue'.[34] Most frequently, criticisms pointed to:

---

[32] On the United Nations website on international conferences, the achievements of 1993 World Conference on Human Rights have been summarised rather modestly as follows: a) reaffirming international commitment to all human rights, and to strengthening the mechanisms for monitoring and promoting human rights worldwide; b) leading to the appointment of the first High Commissioner for Human Rights, to improve the ability of the UN to act quickly and efficiently to prevent rights violations and promote fundamental freedoms; c) instigating the inclusion of human rights as an integral element in UN peacekeeping missions, and declared the link between democracy, development and human rights; accessible at: http://www.un.org/News/facts/confercs.htm [last accessed 15 January 2011].

[33] Statement by Navanethem Pillay, United Nations High Commissioner for Human Rights, 'Human Rights Diplomacy: An Oxymoron?', Cambridge, Massachusetts (28 October 2009), available at: http://www.ohchr.org/EN/NewsEvents/Pages/DisplayNews.aspx?NewsID=9569&LangID=e [last accessed 6 August 2011]. On the review process, see also I. Salama, 'Human Rights Diplomacy from a UN Persepctive: A Complement to Advocay', Chapter 8 in the present volume, pp.139–40.

[34] M. G. Schechter, *United Nations-sponsored World Conferences,* 2001, summarises the views of both advocates and critics of conference diplomacy, pp.5–6.

- the duplicative nature of multilateral conferences organised in the framework of the United Nations if one takes into account the well developed structure of UN bodies mandated to address global issues;
- the discriminatory character of such meetings, with small and poor countries whose potential does not allow them to participate in the expensive and time-consuming process on an equal footing with more powerful states;
- the strong political bias of all intergovernmental meetings, including multilateral conferences, which leads to refocusing the attention from substantive issues to political interests;[35]
- the tendency to redefine problems at a low-key level when delegations seek compromises based on the lowest possible common denominator, which puts real changes into question and sometimes already achieved solutions at risk;
- the propensity on the part of a number of countries to reduce the impact of civil society, in particular NGOs; and
- the high financial costs of world conferences.

These critical comments are in many instances well-founded. Their careful analysis may help to avoid pitfalls accompanying conference diplomacy. They should be, however, considered in the context of the already discussed positive arguments about this kind of diplomacy—the more so as the United Nations are expected to host world conferences also in the future. The nature of the world organisation on the one hand, and on the other, the expectation that what is often not feasible in the top UN organs might be possible at world summits or other type of global conferences speak in favour of this observation.

In the case of human rights, the time which has elapsed since the Vienna meeting may prompt reflection on the need for a renewal of priorities, targets and benchmarks. Furthermore, one should not forget that for the youngest generation of human rights advocates, the Vienna Declaration and Programme of Action is already a historical document from a time preceding their births and also for that reason,

---

[35] It is interesting and encouraging to note that it was possible during the 2009 Durban Review Conference to overcome deep political tensions largely dominating the three UN conferences against racism, including the 2001 World Conference against Racism, Xenophobia and Related Intolerance in Durban. On this success see also I. Salama, 'Human Rights Diplomacy from a UN Perspective', Chapter 8 in the present volume, pp.139–41.

the time factor is not without significance. Nevertheless, more important is that new developments and challenges require visionary and programmatic adjustments. To address this need, conference diplomacy may again be appreciated as a handy tool. To recognise and accept this possibility is maybe a more rational approach than to go on the defensive and try to prevent holding new conferences, being guided by the aforementioned critical comments? In such a case, it would be a matter for preliminary discussions whether the international community should move from a type of a meeting with an all-inclusive agenda to specialised meetings addressing specific substantive areas (such as developing thematic programmes of action; addressing situations characterised by serious human rights violations; defining standard-setting needs and goals; addressing structural challenges to human rights; filling implementation gaps; raising human rights awareness and advancement of human rights on the international agenda).

Whatever type of conference should be on the horizon, there are some crucial factors to be taken into account in this respect:

- *A clear vision of the aims to be achieved*, with regard to substance, participatory framework, and international impact.
- *A well structured and participatory preparatory process*, enabling communication and cooperation among different stakeholders.
- *A target-oriented agenda* for a conference, involving input from all relevant actors.
- *A determined leadership*. This is a pre-condition for the success of diplomatic conferences as for any other collective effort. A multi-centred leadership, involving leading actors from various constituencies can ensure not only effective but also democratic decision-making process. The contribution by the conference host in this respect cannot be overestimated.
- *The role of the Office of the High Commissioner for Human Rights*. The Office should not only act in its secretariat role but, in particular, contribute to the conference process as the global centre of highly advanced professional knowledge and expertise in human rights.
- *An effective follow-up mechanism*. Such mechanisms may provide a pragmatic truth test for conference diplomacy. How self-evident this statement may be, the establishment of such mechanisms would mean the departure from presently existing modalities which unfortunately are largely ritual and formal.

- *Costs efficiency.* It is difficult to measure the tangibility of a conference against its financial implications. Nevertheless, the question of costs control is not only related to budgetary issues but also to a democratic and effective participation in the conference process by all relevant stakeholders.
- And lastly—*Zeitgeist.* The spirit of the time is influenced by a number of coefficients that are independent of the organisers of a conference and other leading actors. In any case, however, and as usual in diplomacy, confidence-building efforts undertaken before and throughout the process of such a conference by key players at different levels, both governmental and non-governmental, are particularly important to create a climate conducive to the conference outcome.

Having said that—it is difficult to forecast what the 'net generation'—as it was called by Don Tapscott in his "Growing up Digital"—would say about conference diplomacy. And, what would be the role and impact of 'digital diplomacy'?[36]

[36] D. Tapscott, *Growing up Digital: The Rise of the Net Generation* (New York: McGraw-Hill, 1998); and W. Dizard Jr., *Digital Diplomacy: U.S. Foreign Policy in the Information Age* (Westport, CT: Praeger, 2001).

CHAPTER 13

HUMAN RIGHTS DIPLOMACY: THE NGO ROLE

Peggy Hicks

Most of my colleagues would chaff at being called diplomats. There is a strong current among human rights activists that revels in being seen as outsiders, battling against corrupt and abusive governments. And, of course, we are also known for being decidedly un-diplomatic when the occasion warrants it. If human rights diplomacy is defined, however, as advocacy directed at governments and inter-governmental organisations to affect policy changes relating to human rights, it is a core function of non-governmental advocacy organisations like mine (Human Rights Watch). Human rights organisations have long since learned that it is not enough to document human rights abuses: we need to understand who is responsible for such abuses, why they occur, and what it will take to stop them.

Within the theatre of human rights diplomacy, non-governmental organisations (NGOs) take on many different roles. At times, the activities undertaken by NGOs are similar to those undertaken by governmental actors, but we also perform a number of functions that distinguish our work from governments. The discussion below highlights six different types of engagement by NGOs in human rights diplomacy, including our roles as: (1) catalysts; (2) advocates; (3) shapers of the debate; (4) partners in policy-making; (5) monitors; and (6) legitimisers and beneficiaries.

Catalysts

NGOs play a crucial role in instigating human rights diplomacy. By exposing abuses and pushing for accountability of those responsible for human rights violations, we act as catalysts for action by governments and other actors. When we put an issue into the public domain, governments are pushed to respond, and they recognise that failure to do so may provoke scrutiny and criticism by NGOs. Sometimes, the key role an NGO plays is simply to set a process of human rights change in motion.

Advocates

The mainstay of engagement by NGOs in human rights diplomacy is our traditional role as advocates for change. As advocates, NGOs monitor governmental efforts at 'human rights diplomacy' and push for stronger, more effective human rights engagement by governments. NGOs frequently engage, for example, with foreign ministries and diplomats to push for human rights concerns to play a more central role in bilateral relations with states with poor human rights records. We engage on issues ranging from individual cases of human rights abuse to broad policy discussions on human rights violations related to counter-terrorism efforts.

When governments engage in human rights diplomacy, progress can often hinge on agreeing to reciprocal treatment, promising benefits or threatening sanctions. Of course, NGOs are unable to employ those tools in our efforts to weigh in on how governments conduct their human rights diplomacy. Instead, there are four key ingredients to getting our voices heard: (1) information; (2) expertise; (3) media; and (4) public support. Different NGOs rely on each of these elements to different degrees.

For an organisation like Human Rights Watch, the information that we have about human rights abuses on the ground is often our biggest capital. Despite the relative wealth of resources that governments possess, we frequently find that our researchers have direct or more detailed information about situations under consideration, and that knowledge gives us entrée into policy discussions. Similarly, NGOs can bring helpful expertise into such discussions. Our input on how human rights problems should be pursued is informed by our engagement on a broad range of similar issues in a variety of situations, a perspective that can often be useful to governments considering a range of policy options.

In addition, NGOs are able to use the media to amplify our own voices. By making public statements, writing opinion pieces, and speaking with journalists, we turn a spotlight on how governments are engaging on human rights issues and make them more responsive to human rights concerns. Finally, by building public understanding and engagement on human rights issues, we can push governments to adopt more human rights friendly policies and hold them accountable when they do not.

Shapers of the Debate

A critical part played by NGOs in human rights diplomacy involves our ability to help frame the debate on a human rights issue. By taking consistent positions that are strongly supportive of human rights, we provide a helpful frame for discussions. NGOs are able to put forward an undiluted case for human rights, without having other interests moderate their views. Having a strong human rights case articulated expands the spectrum of policy options under discussion and makes it more likely that the policy point ultimately agreed upon will be closer to the human rights friendly end of the spectrum. Similarly, in many instances, our government interlocutors tell us that when we put our positions forward, it gives them a justification for pushing an issue that they had already wanted to take on, but on which they faced either internal or external resistance. At times, NGOs are knowingly providing support to one side in an ongoing policy debate within a government; for example where a foreign ministry may be supporting a more human rights friendly policy, but is encountering resistance from its own defence ministry.

NGOs also make a valuable contribution to human rights diplomacy by interjecting a human rights dimension into diplomacy on broader topics. NGOs often make a valuable contribution by pointing out the human rights implications, for example, of commerce, trade or energy policies. By drawing attention to the human rights dimensions within such a policy discussion, NGOs make it more likely that those responsible for human rights within the government will be brought into the discussion and that the human rights implications of the policy under discussion will be addressed.

Partners in Policy-Making

At times, NGOs are able to work in partnership with like-minded governments, and have a direct role in human rights diplomacy. The level of NGO engagement in such policy-making exercises varies greatly. In some cases, NGOs are officially consulted and their views become part of the record; in other instances, NGO experts are voting members of policy-setting commissions.

A good example of an environment in which NGOs have become partners with governments in policy-making is found in negotiations over treaties, such as recent campaigns to adopt the Convention on Cluster Munitions (CCM),[1] the Mine Ban Treaty[2] and the Convention on the Rights of Persons with Disabilities (CRPD).[3] NGOs were engaged in all facets of the development of and negotiations over these treaties, as the slogan adopted by persons with disabilities—'nothing about us without us'—demanded. Of course, even where NGOs have had a seat at the table, they do not participate on an equal footing with governments, and usually play more of a 'junior partner' role in such negotiations.

In such settings, NGOs are required to work simultaneously on two tracks. They participate at the negotiations table, while at the same time playing their usual role of monitoring engagement by governments and trying to influence the positions that governments are putting forward as well.

Through our consistent engagement on human rights issues, NGOs develop strong relationships with policy-makers that come into play at every level of decision-making. Policy-makers consult with NGO experts to get advice concerning policy options and views as to how particular approaches would be seen. This advice sometimes extends to offering language for resolutions, statements or agreements, which is accepted and used on the understanding that the NGO involved will not take credit for the contribution. These consultations can be particularly important in settings where NGOs do not have a full seat at the table, as has sometimes been the case when peace treaties are being negotiated, for example.

Monitors

NGOs also play a crucial role in holding human rights diplomats accountable. In the world of human rights diplomacy, there is a

[1] 2008 Convention on Cluster Munitions (CCM); entered into force 1 August 2010.

[2] 1997 Convention on the Prohibition of the Use, Stockpiling, Production and Transfer of Anti-Personnel Mines and on Their Destruction, 2056 UNTS 211; entered into force 1 March 1999.

[3] 2006 Convention on the Rights of Persons with Disabilities (CRPD), UNGA Res 61/106 (2007), UN Doc A/RES/61/106 (24 January 2007), Annex I; entered into force 3 May 2008.

remarkable ability for governments to behave inconsistently, to put it mildly. Governments that are strongly committed to equal protection on the basis of sexual orientation at home, for example, may take retrograde positions that question the need for such protections in their foreign policy. Governments that squelch freedom of expression at home may champion resolutions affirming free speech rights in intergovernmental bodies. NGOs monitor governments that engage in human rights diplomacy and are able to expose such hypocrisy. Moreover, we bring crucial information to the table about the credibility and motivations of governments engaging in human rights diplomacy. NGOs can expose that opposition to action on human rights crises in places like Burma or Georgia may reflect concern that the next stops for consideration would be Tibet or Chechnya.

Legitimisers and Beneficiaries

One of the underlying tensions that governments face in their human rights diplomacy involves their legitimacy in raising human rights issues with other governments. In this regard, civil society can also play a valuable role. When domestic NGOs are pushing for action on human rights, it gives greater legitimacy to international efforts to address those issues. International actors are able to avoid having their efforts framed as 'foreign intervention', and instead emphasise that they are simply backing domestic civil society in raising home-grown concerns.

NGOs are also on the receiving end of human rights diplomacy. Human rights diplomacy works, for example, to protect human rights defenders and to address laws that restrict the formation and operation of NGOs.

In playing these six roles relating to human rights diplomacy, NGOs work to strengthen human rights protections worldwide. At the same time, the NGO contribution to human rights diplomacy involves pushing governments to be more consistent and effective in their own diplomatic efforts on behalf of human rights. One frequent source of criticism of governments' human rights diplomacy involves over-reliance on 'quiet diplomacy' or human rights 'dialogues'. To be clear, NGO activists generally recognise that private engagement on human rights issues is a useful approach within the toolbox of methods that human rights diplomats need to employ. Where our differences with states surface, however, is when engagement in quiet diplomacy or human rights dialogue is really a pretext for doing little or nothing to address a serious human rights concern. For such strategies to be meaningful, the human rights diplomats that employ them must keep other possible approaches in the toolbox on the table. Quiet diplomacy is most effective when the target understands that the diplomacy will remain quiet only so long as there is real engagement and measurable progress. NGOs will continue to hold governments accountable not only for their actions on human rights, but also for their silence.

CHAPTER 14

NATIONAL HUMAN RIGHTS INSTITUTIONS AS DIPLOMACY ACTORS

KIRSTEN ROBERTS[1]

Introduction

Since the decision of the United Nations (UN) to formally call for the creation of national human rights institutions (NHRIs) in 1993,[2] and the subsequent work of the UN to actively promote their role as independent actors in the international human rights framework, the position of NHRIs has been developing. The mandate which national institutions derive from the Principles Relating to the Status of National Institutions (Paris Principles) to engage at the international level, coupled with support from international human rights mechanisms, particularly the Office of the High Commissioner for Human Rights (OHCHR), has meant that NHRIs are directly engaged in the international human rights framework in a manner and to an extent which may not have been envisaged at their inception. The importance given to NHRIs by the UN, and the activist nature of many individual national institutions and their regional and international coordinating

[1] The views expressed herein are solely those of the author. The author wishes to sincerely thank Jean-Paul Lehners, Professor of history at the University of Luxembourg, coordinator of the *Observatoire des Droits de l'Homme* and president of the Luxembourg Consultative Commission for Human Rights, for his support and very helpful comments on this draft. The author would also like to thank Katharina Rose, ICC Geneva Representative, for her comments on an early version of this draft.

[2] Principles relating to the Status of National Institutions (hereinafter: Paris Principles), annex to UNGA Res 48/134 (1993), UN Doc A/RES/48/134 (20 December 1993). It should be noted that several institutions which came to be recognised as NHRIs were already in existence in 1993. For instance, the Danish Centre for Human Rights, the forerunner to the Danish Institute for Human Rights, was established in 1987, the Canadian Human Rights Act founding the Canadian Human Rights Commission was adopted in 1977 and the French Consultative Commission on Human Rights (*Commission nationale consultative des droits de l'homme*) in its current composition was established in 1989. In addition, many ombudsmen, subsequently recognised as NHRIs, were established prior to 1993. For example, the Ombudsperson (*Procuraduría de los Derechos Humanos)* of Guatemala was founded in 1986.

bodies, has seen the boundaries of the roles and functions of NHRIs tested and expanded continuously over the past twenty years. This article discusses the emergence of NHRIs as institutions with a unique mandate and role, which are increasingly active in human rights diplomacy. In particular, it considers their creation and emerging position within the international human rights framework, their unique set of characteristics that are of particular benefit in the context of human rights diplomacy, and examples of their roles in this area.

The Emergence and Development of National Human Rights Institutions within the International Human Rights Framework

The idea of creating institutions for the promotion and protection of human rights at the national level has been in existence since the emergence of the modern international human rights system following the Second World War.[3] The lengthy period over which consideration was given to the creation of NHRIs culminated in the adoption of the Paris Principles on 20 December 1993 by the UN General Assembly. From the first proposal for the creation of such institutions at the national level in the middle of the twentieth century until the formalisation of guidelines for their establishment in 1993, they were envisaged as state institutions that would assist in the implementation of international human rights standards at the national level.[4] A set of guidelines endorsed by the then UN Commission on Human Rights and the UN General Assembly were elaborated during a Seminar on National and Local Institutions for the Promotion and Protection of Human Rights held in Geneva in 1978. These guidelines proposed that the functions of national institutions would be to 'act as a source of human rights

---

[3] In 1946, the Economic and Social Council (ECOSOC) invited UN member states to 'consider the desirability of establishing information groups or local human rights committees within their respective countries to collaborate with them in furthering the work of the Commission on Human Rights', see: ECOSOC Res 9 (II) (21 June 1946). ECOSOC Res 772 B (XXX) (25 July 1960) also called on states to establish national institutions.

[4] For further details, see: OHCHR, *A Handbook on the Establishment and Strengthening of National Human Rights Institutions for the Promotion and Protection of Human Rights* (New York/Geneva: United Nations, 1995). The handbook sets out developments relating to NHRIs between 1946 and 1993, and is available at: http://www.ohchr.org/Documents/Publications/training4en.pdf [last accessed 22 November 2010].

information for the Government and people of the country' as well as assisting in education and awareness raising, making recommendations and advising government.[5] The 1993 Paris Principles, which are the foundation for contemporary NHRIs, broadly reflect the same purpose and functions for national institutions. However, the Paris Principles include specification of an important additional role for NHRIs, which is of particular relevance for this article: their engagement at the international level, including encouraging ratification and implementation of international human rights treaties, contributing to the reporting procedure under international instruments, and cooperating with the UN human rights mechanisms and regional human rights bodies.[6]

The Application of the Paris Principles in the National Context

The Paris Principles encouraged the creation of national institutions founded in law and with a broad mandate to promote and protect human rights.[7] While the Principles set out the functions and composition of NHRIs, they were adopted as guidelines for their establishment. This means that in implementing the Principles, UN member states have considerable discretion when deciding on the form of institution to be created at the national level. States have the flexibility to develop the framework of the national institution to best suit their needs and institutional, cultural, legal and societal framework.[8] There

[5] Guidelines on the Structure and Functioning of National and Local Institutions for the Promotion and Protection of Human Rights, endorsed by UNGA Res 33/46 (1978), UN Doc A/RES/33/46 (18 December 1978). These guidelines are directly referenced in the Paris Principles. There were annual resolutions at the General Assembly relating to national institutions for the promotion and protection of human rights from 1978 onwards. It may also be noted that the annex to Res 32/123, celebrating the 30th Anniversary of the Universal Declaration of Human Rights suggested the 'establishment of national or local institutions for the promotion and protection of human rights', see: UN Doc A/RES/32/123 (16 December 1977), para.e). Other resolutions on national institutions include UNGA Res 34/49 (1979), UN Doc A/RES/34/49 (23 November 1979); UNGA Res 36/134 (1981), UN Doc A/RES/36/134 (14 December 1981); UNGA Res 38/123 (1983), UN Doc A/RES/38/123 (16 December 1983); UNGA Res 39/144 (1984), UN Doc A/RES/39/144 (14 December 1984); UNGA Res 40/123 (1985), UN Doc A/RES/40/123 (13 December 1985); UNGA Res 41/129 (1986), UN Doc A/RES/41/129 (4 December 1986).

[6] Paris Principles, para.3.

[7] *Ibid.*, paras.1 and 2.

[8] UNGA Res 48/134 (1993), UN Doc A/RES/48/134 (20 December 1993), to which the Paris Principles are annexed, 'encourages the establishment and strengthening of national institutions having regard to those principles and recognizing that it is the

are however, several key elements set out in the Paris Principles which are considered essential to all NHRIs: a foundation in national law (by way of legislation or the national constitution), independence from government, a mandate to promote and protect a broad range of international human rights standards, pluralism in membership, an independent appointment procedure of the institution's board, and responsibility to work with all actors in the field, including government and civil society.[9] These central elements give NHRIs a unique position within the international human rights framework and demonstrate the potentially important and distinctive role they can play in human rights diplomacy.

As a result of the broad discretion given in the Paris Principles, a diverse range of institutions have been created across the globe under the heading of NHRIs. These institutions can be broadly classified into four models:[10] human rights commissions,[11] ombuds institutions,[12] human rights institutes[13] and advisory committees.[14] However, even

right of each State to choose the framework that is best suited to its particular needs at the national level' (section 12).

[9] On this see also the General Observations of the International Coordinating Committee of National Human Rights Institutions, Sub-Committee on Accreditation, Geneva, June 2009, available at: www.nhri.net [last accessed 22 November 2010].

[10] For examples of varying mandates of NHRIs see: OHCHR, Survey on National Human Rights Institutions, Geneva (July 2009), available at: http://www.nhri.net/2009/Questionnaire%20-%20Complete%20Report%20FINAL-edited.pdf [last accessed 22 November 2010]; Comparative Study on Mandates of National Human Rights Institutions in the Commonwealth, Commonwealth Secretariat 2007; and, A. E. Pohjolainen, The Evolution of National Human Rights Institutions—The Role of the United Nations (Copenhagen: Danish Institute for Human Rights, 2006), available at: http://www.NHRI.net/pdf/Evolution_of_NHRIs.pdf [last accessed 22 November 2010].

[11] Commissions typically have a broad mandate which includes protection, promotion and monitoring. Examples of 'A'-status human rights commissions of this type of NHRIs include those in Australia, Canada, India, Ireland, New Zealand, Northern Ireland, Scotland, South Africa and Uganda.

[12] Ombuds-institutions traditionally focus on handling individual complaints. Examples of 'A'-status ombuds-institution NHRIs include those in Poland, Portugal and Spain. In the Americas, the term people's defender (*defensor/defensoría del pueblo*) is often used, for example for institutions in Bolivia, Ecuador, Paraguay and Venezuela.

[13] Institutes focus primarily on human rights education and research, and may have limited protection mandates. Examples of 'A'-status human rights institutes include those in Denmark, Germany and Norway.

[14] Consultative bodies (*commissions consultatifs*) mainly have an advisory mandate. Examples of 'A'-status institutions of this type include those in France, Greece, Luxembourg and Morocco. Generally on different NHRI models see also: OHCHR, Survey on National Human Rights Institutions, July 2009.

within these four categories, there are considerable differences in the size, structure and functions of institutions.[15] Depending on their structure and mandate, NHRIs' functions can include giving advice or recommendations on draft legislation; handling individual complaints; undertaking human rights enquiries; conducting inspection visits to prisons or other places of detention; engaging in human rights education and awareness raising, including promoting the ratification of and adherence to international treaties; and taking part in parallel reporting to UN human rights treaty bodies.

Despite the diversity of models, the Paris Principles remain the benchmark for the mandate and structure of NHRIs. The global coordinating body of NHRIs, the International Coordinating Committee of NHRIs (ICC), early on in its establishment, set up a committee to review the compliance of national institutions with the Paris Principles.[16] NHRIs that are fully compliant with the Paris Principles are given an 'A'-status accreditation by the ICC. This brings with it the recognition of the respective NHRI within the UN system, and includes the right to make statements before the Human Rights Council.[17] As of January 2010, there were sixty five NHRIs accredited as fully compliant with the Paris Principles and some twenty six others that were accredited as partly compliant or non-compliant.[18]

[15] For an overview of NHRIs in the European Union see: European Union Fundamental Rights Agency, National Human Rights Institutions in the EU Member States, 2010, available at: http://fra.europa.eu/fraWebsite/attachments/NHRI_en.pdf [last accessed 22 November 2010]; and K. Roberts, 'Regional Co-operation between National Human Rights Institutions from the European Perspective: Challenges and Opportunities', paper presented at the University of Melbourne Law School Workshop 'Creating Change? NHRIs (in) Action in the Asia-Pacific Region', 22 July 2009.

[16] The first accreditations took place in 1999, see: International Coordinating Committee of National Human Rights Institutions, Chart on the Status of National Human Rights Institutions, January 2010, accessible through: http://www.nhri.net/ [last accessed 22 November 2010].

[17] UNGA Res 60/251 (2006), establishing the Human Rights Council, provides that the Council is to 'work in close cooperation in the field of human rights with Governments, regional organizations, national human rights institutions and civil society', UN Doc A/RES/60/251 (3 April 2006). Res 5/1 of the Human Rights Council, on Rules of Procedure on Participation of and Consultation with Observers of the Council, UN Doc A/HRC/5/1 (16 May 2007), rule 7, provides for the participation of NHRIs.

[18] International Coordinating Committee of National Human Rights Institutions, Chart on the Status of National Human Rights Institutions, January 2010. The competence to decide on a national institution's compliance with the Paris Principles lies with the International Coordinating Committee of NHRIs and its Sub-Committee on Accreditation (SCA). The SCA assesses the compliance of NHRIs with the Paris

The Space for National Human Rights Institutions in the International Framework

Within the international human rights system NHRIs are *sui generis*. As neither state representatives, nor non-governmental organisations (NGOs), nor inter-governmental organisations, they occupy a unique space. The Paris Principles aimed at the creation of institutions that would act as an independent, direct link between the national and international systems for the protection of human rights. NHRIs can be said to occupy a '4th space'.[19] This space is one which has been created through the activities of NHRIs in a broad range of contexts, and which primarily exists through the engagement of NHRIs in what were previously the exclusive roles of the existing key actors within the international human rights framework—states, NGOs and international human rights mechanisms. It is this '4th space' which provides an interesting position from which NHRIs can apply human rights diplomacy.

The role of NHRIs in the promotion and protection of human rights thus overlaps to some extent with the roles of each of the above-mentioned key actors. First, the role that NHRIs frequently play in monitoring the application and implementation of international human rights agreements, and their advisory function in relation to the implementation of international standards at national level, was once primarily within the remit of international human rights mechanisms. Second, some of the space that NHRIs occupy today has traditionally been that of NGOs. NGOs have been regarded as the primary

Principles in law and practice. It has developed a series of guidelines known as General Observations and Templates, which serve as interpretative tools of the Paris Principles. The General Observations and Templates are available at: http://www.nhri.net/ [last accessed 22 November 2010]. See also: Report of the Secretary-General on Process Currently Utilized by the International Coordinating Committee of National Institutions for the Promotion and Protection of Human Rights to Accredit National Institutions in Compliance with the Paris Principles, UN Doc A/HRC/13/45 (18 January 2010).

[19] A number of commentators have referred to NGOs/civil society as the '3rd space', for example, R. P. Fairbanks II, 'The Political Economic Gradient' in R. A. Cnaan and C. M. Milofsky (eds.), *Handbook of Community Movements and Local Organisations* (Berlin: Springer, 2007); T. Kaplan 'Women's Rights as Human Rights: Women as Agents of Social Change' in M. Agosín (ed.), *Women, Gender & Human Rights: A Global Perspective* (New Brunswick: Rutgers University Press, 2001). G. Fellous referred to NHRIs as institutions of the 'third type', G. Fellous, *Les Institutions Nationales des Droits de l'Homme: Acteurs de Troisième Type* (Commission nationale consultative des droits de l'homme, 2006).

custodians of the concerns of civil society. However, because of their active engagement with civil society as well as their awareness of the broad range of domestic human rights concerns, national institutions also assume active roles in this area. Third, in providing authoritative, national-level voice on domestic human rights issues at the international level, NHRIs may be said to provide an alternative to the traditional role of the state in international fora.

Support for National Human Rights Institutions at the Regional and International Level

NHRIs are increasingly recognised as independent actors within the international human rights framework. This has been significantly supported by the UN, primarily through the OHCHR. The OHCHR has provided a forum for discussions on the structure and tasks of national institutions, promoted the establishment and development of NHRIs and provided direct support to both states and national institutions themselves. It has offered expert advice on the adoption of laws relating to NHRIs, and given direct technical and material assistance to NHRIs.[20] The active role of the UN in relation to NHRIs began with the establishment of a specialised support structure at the OHCHR, at first through the appointment of a Special Adviser on National Institutions.[21] This was followed by the establishment of the National Institutions Unit within the OHCHR, and subsequently the National Institutions and Regional Mechanisms Unit, which acts as a secretariat to the ICC.[22]

NHRIs themselves have also been active in developing their international role. An important factor in this context has been the establishment of regional and global networks coordinating the

[20] Report of the Secretary-General on National Institutions for the Promotion and Protection of Human Rights, UN Doc A/HRC/13/44 (15 January 2010), p.3, states that the OHCHR 'accords priority to the establishment and strengthening of [NHRIs] … [and] is also engaged in improving United Nations system-wide coordination on NHRIs, and supports their increased participation in the United Nations and regional human rights mechanisms'. See also, Commission on Human Rights Res 2005/74 on National Institutions for the Promotion and Protection of Human Rights, UN Doc E/CN.4/RES/2005/74 (20 April 2005); and ECOSOC, Report of the Secretary-General on Enhancing the Participation of National Human Rights Institutions in the Work of the Commission on Human Rights and its Subsidiary Bodies, UN Doc E/CN.4/2005/107 (19 January 2005).

[21] The post of the Special Adviser was established in 1995.

[22] See e.g. Report of the Secretary-General on National Institutions, 2010.

regional and international activities of NHRIs. There are four regional networks of national institutions, each with a regional coordinating structure, covering Africa, the Americas, Asia-Pacific and Europe respectively.[23] There is also a coordinating body at the international level, the ICC. The ICC was first established in 1993 and became a legal entity under Swiss law in 2008.[24] The ICC acts as a forum through which NHRIs can coordinate their international engagement.[25] It is headed by a Chair from one of its 'A'-status' NHRIs, who, among other tasks, acts as a high-level representative of the ICC in international meetings and events. The four regional networks, each led by a Chair elected from among the NHRIs of the respective region, act autonomously at the regional level. In addition, institutions engage individually with regional and international mechanisms for the promotion and protection of human rights. While the international and regional structures have a coordinating and networking function, they cannot be said to 'set policy' for the global community of NHRIs. However, they do act as an important forum for NHRIs to have a collective voice at the regional and international level.[26]

[23] These regional coordinating networks vary in strength, with the Asia-Pacific Forum of National Human Rights Institutions representing the most advanced model for regional cooperation. Established in 1996, it describes its activities as providing 'a framework for national human rights institutions to work together and cooperate on a regional basis through a wide range of services, including training, capacity building, networks and staff exchanges'. In October 2010 the Asia Pacific Forum was comprised of seventeen NHRIs from Afghanistan, Australia, India, Indonesia, Jordan, Malaysia, Maldives, Mongolia, Nepal, New Zealand, Palestine, Philippines, Qatar, Republic of Korea, Sri Lanka, Thailand and Timor-Leste. For more details see: http://www.asiapacificforum.net/ [last accessed 22 November 2010].

[24] See OHCHR website at: http://www.ohchr.org/en/countries/NHRI/pages/NHRImain.aspx [last accessed 22 November 2010]. UNGA Res 50/176 (1996) on National Institutions for the Promotion and Protection of Human Rights, takes note of the establishment of the ICC in 1993, UN Doc A/RES/50/176 (27 February 1996), para.7.

[25] The ICC Statute provides that the functions of the ICC include 'to coordinate at an international level the activities of NHRIs established in conformity with the Paris Principles, including such activities as: Interaction and cooperation with the United Nations, including the OHCHR, the Human Rights Council, its mechanisms, United Nations human rights treaty bodies, as well as with other international organisations; To promote the establishment and strengthening of NHRIs in conformity with the Paris Principles'. Statute of the International Coordinating Committee of National Human Rights Institutions as amended 24 March 2009 (Statute of the ICC), Article 7, is available at: http://www.nhri.net/ [last accessed 22 November 2010].

[26] Examples of some of the activities of the international and regional networks are outlined below.

Support at the UN level, as well as the activism of NHRIs, has resulted in other actors at the regional and international level increasingly formalising their engagement with NHRIs. This formal interaction takes place between individual NHRIs and regional or international organisations, through the four regional networks, and at the ICC level. For example, within the broader UN system, the United Nations Development Programme (UNDP) has begun to actively cooperate with OHCHR on the establishment and strengthening of NHRIs, and works with NHRIs at country level.[27] In the European region, regional human rights mechanisms such as the European Union Fundamental Rights Agency,[28] the Organisation for Security and Co-operation in Europe's (OSCE) Office for Democratic Institutions and Human Rights (ODIHR),[29] and the Council of Europe support and engage with NHRIs. In the Americas, the Organisation of American States (OAS) has issued resolutions to support the work of

[27] Report of the Secretary-General on National Institutions, 2010, para.86. See also, Address of UNDP Administrator Helen Clark to National Human Rights Institutions, 23 March 2010; and 'Human Rights: The Key to Keeping the Promise of 2015', UNDP Administrator Helen Clark Statement to OHCHR, 2 July 2010, both available at: http://www.undp.org/ [last accessed 22 November 2010]. UNDP and OHCHR have also jointly developed a toolkit for UN country teams on NHRIs.

[28] The Regulation founding the Fundamental Rights Agency, Council Regulation (EC) No 168/2007 (15 February 2007), Article 8(2)(a) provides '[T]o help it carry out its tasks, the Agency shall cooperate with… governmental organisations and public bodies competent in the field of fundamental rights in the Member States, including national human rights institutions'. Separately, the European Parliament has issued a resolution in support of NHRIs. European Parliament Resolution of 14 January 2009 on the Situation of Fundamental Rights in the European Union 2004-2008 called on member states to 'take measures to endow the national human rights institutions set up under the United Nations' 'Paris Principles' with independent status vis-à-vis the executive and sufficient financial resources, taking account, in particular, of the fact that one of these bodies' tasks is to review human rights policies with the aim of preventing failings and suggesting improvements, on the understanding that effectiveness is measured primarily by the way in which problems are prevented rather than simply resolved; [and] urges those member states which have not yet done so to set up the above-mentioned national human rights institutions'.

[29] The Document of the Copenhagen Meeting of the Conference on the Human Dimension of the CSCE of 1990 states in para.27: 'The participating States will also facilitate the establishment and strengthening of independent national institutions in the area of human rights and the rule of law, which may also serve as focal points for co-ordination and collaboration between such institutions in the participating States.' The Copenhagen Document is available at: http://www.osce.org/documents/odihr/1990/06/13992_en.pdf [last accessed 22 November 2010]. In 2007, ODIHR established a Focal Point for Human Rights Defenders and National Human Rights Institutions.

NHRIs[30] and the African Union has also formally recognised the role of NHRIs.[31]

The increasing engagement of the UN and regional human rights mechanisms with NHRIs demonstrates the acknowledgement of the valuable contribution that national institutions can make in furthering regional and international organisations' own institutional priorities, including supporting democratisation, the promotion of the rule of law and building stable and accountable public institutions. At the UN level, the increasing formalisation of the role of NHRIs has seen them gain direct access to the international human rights framework, including to treaty bodies and to the Human Rights Council.[32]

---

[30] OAS, Res AG/RES 2448 (XXXI X-O/09) on Strengthening the Role of National Institutions for the Promotion and Protection of Human Rights in the Organization of American States (4 June 2009) resolved to grant participation and speaking rights to NHRIs 'which are members of the Network of National Institutions for the Promotion and Protection of Human Rights of the Americas (Network of the Americas) accredited by the [ICC] with "A" status in accordance with the Paris Principles'. See also OAS, Res AG/RES 2421 (XXXVIII-O/08) on Strengthening the Role of National Institutions for the Promotion and Protection of Human Rights in the Organization of American States (3 June 2008); OAS, Permanent Council Report on Strengthening the Role of National Institutions for the Promotion and Protection of Human Rights in the Organization of American States, OEA/Ser.G CP/CG-1770/09 rev. 2 (29 April 2009); OAS, Res AG/RES. 2411 (XXXVIII-O/08) on Strengthening of the National Human Rights Systems of the Member States and Support for the Work of Defenders of the People, Defenders of the Population, and Human Rights Attorneys or Commissioners (Ombudsmen) (3 June 2008); and OAS, Res AG/RES. 2221 (XXXVI-O/06) on Strengthening of the National Human Rights Systems of the Member States and Support for the Work of Defenders of the People, Defenders of the Population, and Human Rights Attorneys or Commissioners (Ombudsmen) (6 June 2006).

[31] E.g. Article 30 of the 2008 Protocol on the Statute of the African Court of Justice and Human Rights provides that NHRIs are entitled to submit cases to the Court. While outside the direct scope of this chapter, ombudsmen—some of whom are also 'A'-status NHRIs—globally engage through the International Ombudsman Institute. There is also a network of the Ibero-American Ombudsmen. In Europe, equality bodies established under EU regulations are coordinated by *Equinet*. One or two of these equality bodies with a broader mandate are also recognised as NHRIs.

[32] See UNGA Res 60/251 (2006), establishing the Human Rights Council, UN Doc A/RES/60/251 (3 April 2006); and Res 5/1 of the Human Rights Council, on Rules of Procedure on Participation of and Consultation with Observers of the Council, UN Doc A/HRC/5/1 (16 May 2007), Rule 7. See also, OHCHR, Report on the International Workshop on Enhancing Cooperation between International and Regional Mechanisms for the Promotion and Protection of Human Rights, UN Doc A/HRC/15/56 (9 August 2010).

National Human Rights Institutions in Human Rights Diplomacy

Key Attributes of National Human Rights Institutions in the Context of Human Rights Diplomacy

Both the functions of NHRIs and their position within the international human rights framework mean that there is considerable potential for national institutions to utilise human rights diplomacy to further the promotion and protection of human rights.[33] There are certain attributes of NHRIs that are of particular importance to the role they play, and can play in the future, in the context of human rights diplomacy. These include: their expertise, perceived independence and impartiality, first-hand knowledge of the human rights situation on the ground, their role as a link between the international and national level and the cross-regional nature of NHRI networks. In the multi-level and multi-faceted context of human rights diplomacy, these attributes mean that national institutions can be active across a range of levels and in a large number of fora.

NHRIs' expertise in human rights in general and in relation to the human rights situation at the national level adds weight to their interventions. The composition of NHRIs, which usually includes specialist staff and ombudspersons or commissioners means that national institutions usually have considerable human rights expertise at their disposal. It can be the case that civil servants or career diplomats do not possess this same level of expertise, unless they have had the opportunity to work or study in the field of human rights. Moreover, outside field offices, an in-depth level of knowledge of the situation on the ground in a particular country will often not exist within regional or international human rights mechanisms. This means that NHRIs can provide authoritative voices on human rights issues and add

[33] For the purposes of this article, human rights diplomacy is defined as 'the utilisation of diplomatic negotiations/persuasion for the specific purpose of promoting and protecting human rights', as set out in the Report on the High-Level Workshop on Human Rights Diplomacy, Venice, 30-31 January 2009, Annex to the present volume, p.265. On a reflection of the characteristics of human rights diplomacy also see G. Ulrich, 'Framework for the Analysis of Human Rights Diplomacy', Chapter 2 in the present volume, pp.19–42; and R. Archer, 'A Short Reflection on Human Rights Diplomacy', Chapter 3 in the present volume, pp.43–58.

valuable insights and information in the elaboration of standards at the international level based on domestic experience.

The independence and impartiality of NHRIs is also crucial to their role in human rights diplomacy. NHRIs should maintain independence and impartiality from particular agendas or political positions—a factor that distinguishes them from national diplomats representing governmental positions. NHRIs' sole purpose is the promotion and protection of human rights—this can be identified as the core of their independence. They are almost exclusively 'loyal' to human rights principles. The value of this position in the context of human rights diplomacy should not be underestimated. NHRIs are also in a unique position of not being tied to any one actor. This freedom to engage with all actors strengthens the role which NHRIs can assume in human rights diplomacy.[34]

The universality of human rights is also underlined by the work of NHRIs and at the same time adds weight to their role in human rights diplomacy. NHRIs' work at the national level is centred on common international human rights standards, and this supports their role as a collective voice at the international level. The cross-regional nature of NHRIs' collective engagement means that their statements at the international level cannot be dismissed as merely reflecting the interests or views of one region, political persuasion or faith. Statements by the ICC represent national institutions from every region of the world.[35]

Finally, the linking function that NHRIs have between the national and international levels gives them a potentially unique role as human rights diplomacy actors. UN Secretary-General Ban Ki-moon's 2010 Report on NHRIs states:

> [NHRIs] play a crucial role in promoting and monitoring the effective implementation of international human rights standards at the national level, a role which is increasingly recognized by the international community.[36]

---

[34] In this context, see also the observations by R. Archer, 'A Short Reflection on Human Rights Diplomacy', Chapter 3 in the present volume. He identifies the need to manage asymmetry of networks as one of the key 'criteria for success' of human rights diplomacy (p.54). NHRIs can contribute to this task.

[35] As noted above, as of January 2010 the ICC of NHRIs represents sixty five 'A'-status institutions from Africa, the Americas, Asia-Pacific and Europe. There are also twenty six institutions with 'B'- or 'C'-status, many of whom also actively participate in the work of the ICC but who are not formally joined to ICC statements to for example the Human Rights Council.

[36] Report of the Secretary-General on National Institutions, 2010, p.3.

International initiatives are brought from and to the international level by national institutions, and are at the same time reinforced by them on the ground in their respective countries. Thus, an idea which begins at the international level can be discussed directly at the national level between the NHRI and their respective state structures; simultaneously, it can be discussed and reinforced by NHRIs individually and collectively at the international level. This cycle of mutually reinforcing activities at the national and international levels has considerable potential in the context of human rights diplomacy. In addition, the public sector positioning of NHRIs means that they often have access to state structures in ways and to an extent which is not possible for NGOs or civil society organisations.

Roles for National Human Rights Institutions in Human Rights Diplomacy

The functions of NHRIs at the national level, their position at the international level, and their unique characteristics mean that national institutions are already actively engaged in a wide range of activities which may be described as human rights diplomacy. A review of NHRIs' reports on their activities at the national, regional and international level, demonstrates the wide range of initiatives undertaken by NHRIs which come within the 'definition' of human rights diplomacy.[37] The following sections consider some of these initiatives of NHRIs at the multilateral, 'bilateral' and national level. The question of how human rights diplomacy is applied in order to strengthen NHRIs will also be examined. However, before considering some of these initiatives, it should be noted that given the different structures and mandates of NHRIs around the world, as well as their different stages of development, it might be the case that only a few NHRIs are active in all of these areas. Yet, many of the examples elaborated below may reflect areas of potential future activity for NHRIs.[38]

---

[37] E.g. Report of the Chair of the European Group of National Human Rights Institutions to ICC (23 March 2010); Asia-Pacific Forum Annual Report 2008; and Report to the Secretary-General on National Institutions, 2010.

[38] The OHCHR Survey on National Human Rights Institutions (July 2009), p.5, notes that 'the level of NHRI engagement with international and regional human rights mechanisms—particularly in following up on recommendations—remains significantly underdeveloped overall and reflects a limited familiarly with these systems'.

Multilateral Level

Within the multilateral framework, NHRIs have a recognised role in strengthening the examination of their state's human rights record by international and regional organisations. NHRIs can actively engage with the international treaty body system as well as the universal periodic review (UPR) process in order to enhance the promotion and protection of human rights at the national level.[39] The UN Secretary-General reported that in 2009, of sixty nine countries examined by treaty bodies that had a NHRI, thirty seven of the NHRIs participated in the process.[40] This engagement includes providing 'shadow' or alternative reports, supporting the involvement of NGOs and civil society organisations in the treaty body process, raising awareness of the treaty and the examination process at the national level, and engaging directly with the treaty body to pass on concerns and recommendations.[41]

Within the UPR process, NHRIs have a particularly active role to play in advocating for the adoption of strong and pertinent recommendations in the report on their state.[42] NHRIs provide stakeholder reports to the stakeholder summary, encourage and assist NGOs and civil society organisations to provide information, raise awareness of the UPR at the national level and comment on the state report. Prior to the hearings, NHRIs may engage directly with the diplomats of other member states during side events, and by directly lobbying on issues of concern for their country's UPR report. After the adoption of the report, NHRIs can make statements at the Human Rights Council concerning the implementation of the recommendations made to their state.[43] In addition to taking on this direct role at the international level, NHRIs also monitor their state's activities at the international and national level, and comment and report on these activities nationally and internationally.

---

[39] See *ibid.* for examples of areas of NHRI engagement with international mechanisms.

[40] Report of the Secretary-General on National Institutions, 2010, para.78.

[41] See e.g. Conclusions of the International Roundtable on the Role of National Human Rights Institutions and Treaty Bodies, Berlin, 23 and 24 November 2006, presented at Nineteenth meeting of chairpersons of the human rights treaty bodies Geneva, 21-22 June 2007, available at: http://www.nhri.net/pdf2006/Conclusions_Int_RT_rev8dec.pdf [last accessed 22 November 2010]; and A. Müller and F. Seidensticker, *The Role of National Human Rights Institutions in the UN Human Rights Treaty Body Process* (Berlin: German Institute for Human Rights, 2007).

[42] See Human Rights Council Res 5/1, UN Doc A/HRC/5/1 (16 May 2007).

[43] E.g. Universal Periodic Review, Information presented by the Asia Pacific Forum of National Human Rights Institutions, UN Doc A/HRC/14/NI/10 (31 May 2010).

NHRIs have also played a role in highlighting general human rights concerns and commenting on human rights situations within international fora. The UN Secretary-General reported that in 2009, an average of twenty NHRIs participated in each of the sessions of the Human Rights Council.[44] NHRIs' individual and collective statements covered a wide range of topics including thematic issues such as human rights education,[45] transitional justice,[46] the Convention on the Rights of Persons with Disabilities,[47] human rights and countering terrorism,[48] the Optional Protocol to the Convention on the Rights of the Child,[49] issues relating to the relationship between NHRIs and the UN human rights mechanisms including the role and functions of NHRIs,[50] and the need to strengthen international mechanisms such as the

---

[44] Report of the Secretary-General on National Institutions, 2010, para.77.

[45] See e.g. ICC Additional Statement on the Submission of the Draft Statement on Human Rights Education and Training to the Human Rights Council (16 March 2009); and Advisory Committee of the HRC, Draft "United Nations Declaration on Human Rights Education and Training", Concerted Contribution of National Human Rights Institutions Presented at the session of the Advisory Committee of the Human Rights Council, to be held in Geneva from 3 to 7 August 2009, information submitted by the International Coordinating Committee of National Institutions for the Promotion and Protection of Human Rights (ICC), UN Doc A/HRC/AC/3/NI/1 (4 August 2009), annex.

[46] E.g. Statement by the Network of African National Human Rights Institutions on Behalf of 'A'-status National Human Rights Institutions in Africa on the Report by the Office of the High Commissioner for Human Rights on Transitional Justice, UN Doc A/HRC/12/NI/1 (4 September 2009), annex.

[47] See e.g. ICC Chairperson statement on Article 33 and the Role of National Human Rights Institutions during a Panel Discussion on the Rights of Persons with Disabilities (5 March 2010), available at: http://www2.ohchr.org/english/issues/disability/2nd_debate.htm [last accessed 22 November 2010]; and European Group of National Human Rights Institutions, Statement on the Effective Implementation of National Frameworks on the Implementation and Monitoring of the Convention on the Rights of Persons with Disabilities (5 March 2010), accessible at: http://www.nhri.nic.in/2010/EUROPEAN_GROUP_OF_NHRIs_on_the_interactive_panel_debate_on_the _rights_of_persons_with_disabilities.pdf [last accessed 22 November 2010].

[48] E.g. Joint NHRI Statement of Afghanistan, Denmark, France, Greece, Germany, Great Britain, Ireland, Luxembourg, Norway and South Africa, under Agenda item 3: Report of the Special Rapporteur on the Promotion and Protection of Human Rights while Countering Terrorism (8 March 2010).

[49] E.g. Joint NHRI Statement of Germany, Great Britain, Ireland, Morocco, Namibia, the Philippines, Togo and Ukraine on the Rights of the Child, delivered at the 13th Regular Session under Agenda item 3: Report of the Working Group on the Optional Protocol to the Convention on the Rights of the Child, available at: http://www.nhri.nic.in/2010/JOINT_NHRIs_STATEMENT_ON_THE_RIGHTS_OF_THE_CHILD.pdf [last accessed 22 November 2010].

[50] E.g. ICC Statement of 3 March 2010 during the general segment of the 13th Session of the Human Rights Council, reiterating the importance of independent national institutions, the need for adequate funding, and urging member states to establish Paris Principle compliant NHRIs, and to strengthen those already in

treaty bodies and the special procedures of the Human Rights Council.[51] Regional networks have been particularly active in engaging with international mechanisms. For example, the Asia-Pacific Forum of NHRIs' Annual Report for 2007 notes that the Forum sent representatives to advocate policy on different human rights issues in Geneva on behalf of the ICC.[52]

NHRIs also act to mobilise support for regional or international conventions at the international level. For example, the 2009 Rabat Declaration of the African Network of NHRIs recognised the role of national institutions in awareness raising, promotion and dissemination of international and regional human rights instruments on transitional justice.[53] Individually and collectively, NHRIs also advocate for the reform and development of the international human rights framework—for example in relation to the reform of the Human Rights Council and the European Court of Human Rights.[54] The Association of Southeast Asian Nations (ASEAN) NHRI Forum submitted a position paper concerning the political declaration on the establishment of the ASEAN Intergovernmental Commission on Human Rights.[55]

existence. ICC Statement on the Secretary General's Reports on NHRIs and the Accreditation Process (4 March 2010), available at: http://www.nhri.nic.in/2009/ICC%20Statement%20on%20Secretary%20General%20Report%20on%20NHRIs%20and%20the%20ICC%20Accreditation%20process%20%20%20English.pdf [last accessed 22 November 2010].

[51] E.g., ICC Statement under Agenda Item 2: Annual Report of the High Commissioner for Human Rights (4 March 2010), noting the linking role of NHRIs, and encouraging the OHCHR to continue to facilitate and support NHRI engagement with the international mechanisms including the special procedures and treaty bodies, available at: http://www.nhri.nic.in/2009/ICC%20Statement%20Annual%20Report%20of%20the%20High%20Commissioner%20%20%20%20English.pdf [last accessed 22 November 2010].

[52] Asia-Pacific Forum of National Human Rights Institutions, Annual Report 2007, paras.6.1 and 9.3.

[53] Rabat Declaration, Seventh Conference of African NHRIs, Rabat, 3-5 November 2009, available at: www.nhri.net/2009/Rabat%20Declaration.final.doc [last accessed 22 November 2010].

[54] E.g. Response of the European Group of National Human Rights Institutions on the second Draft Declaration of the Interlaken Ministerial Conference (25 January 2010), available at: http://www.londonmet.ac.uk/research-units/hrsj/affiliated-centres/ehrac/activities-general/interlaken—ecthr-reforms.cfm [last accessed 22 November 2010].

[55] ASEAN NHRI Forum Position Paper Concerning the Political Declaration on the ASEAN Intergovernmental Commission on Human Rights, submitted at the 3rd Consultation Meeting with the High Level Panel, Jakarta (28 August 2009), available at: http://www.aseannhriforum.org/home/joint-statements.html [last accessed 22 November 2010].

NHRIs have an important role in contributing to the harmonisation of standards, and in promoting interaction between regional and international human rights mechanisms. They can take an active role in promoting engagement between regional human rights mechanisms and in sharing information on initiatives.[56] NHRIs are often the recipients of information on initiatives that are underway within regional and international mechanisms, and by sharing this information they can help to reduce overlaps and promote the harmonisation of standards. NHRIs also work directly with special procedures mandate-holders of the UN Human Rights Council on thematic issues.[57]

'Bilateral' Level

While NHRIs are primarily engaged at the multilateral level, they have also played a role, albeit less direct, in 'bilateral' diplomacy. Many NHRIs, particularly in recent years, have begun to work directly with NHRIs in other countries in information sharing and capacity building.[58] Through a peer-centred approach, NHRIs have the ability to find areas where they can engage even with states that have a particularly poor human rights record. Due to their unique status, as discussed

---

[56] OHCHR, Report on the International Workshop on Enhancing Cooperation between International and Regional Mechanisms for the Promotion and Protection of Human Rights, UN Doc A/HRC/15/56 (9 August 2010).

[57] For example, the ICC has engaged directly with the Special Representative of the Secretary General for Business and Human Rights, including at its 10th Biennial Conference hosted by the Scottish Human Rights Commission in Edinburgh, 8–10 October 2010. A Regional Workshop on the Role of African National Human Rights Institutions in Protecting the Human Rights of Internally Displaced Persons held in Nairobi, Kenya, 25-26 October 2008, heard from the Representative of the UN Secretary-General on the Human Rights of Internally Displaced Persons (IDPs) and discussed possible strategies for NHRIs in continuing or expanding their work on IDPs. See also generally on NHRIs and special procedures mandate-holders: Discussion Paper on Interaction between National Human Rights Institutions and Special Procedures, Annex X to the Report of the Secretary-General on National Institutions for the Promotion and Protection of Human Rights, UN Doc A/HRC/7/69 (14 January 2008), p. 56.

[58] Among the numerous examples are the Irish Human Rights Commission's experience sharing- and capacity building engagement with the Ethiopian Human Rights Commission, see: the 2009 Annual Report of the Irish Commission for details, at: www.ihrc.ie [last accessed 22 November 2010]). Many NHRIs also receive visits from other national institutions, see e.g.: Annual Report of the Australian Human Rights Commission 2007-2008, Chapter 11.4, at: http://www.hreoc.gov.au/about/publications/annual_reports/2007_2008/index.html [last accessed 22 November 2010]; and Asia-Pacific Forum of National Human Rights Institutions, Annual Report 2007, section 7.7 detailing staff placements and exchanges, and section 9.6, reporting on capacity building projects led by the Asia-Pacific Forum.

above, NHRIs may be able to engage and work in ways which states or NGOs cannot. For example, they can directly promote human rights standards in other countries, and engage in direct capacity development for other national level institutions. At times, this non-confrontational dialogue can almost be described as a 'parallel process' to the engagement of governments. In some cases it can facilitate dialogue between countries which may otherwise have no governmental 'bilateral' dialogue in place. It can also provide opportunities for greater understanding between cultures and regions.[59]

Another area in which some work has been done and which is also likely to increase in the future, is between NHRIs at the national level and their own country's development aid programmes. Support for national institutions forms part of many national development aid programmes and is included in the work of organisations such as UNDP and OSCE as part of their aims to promote democratisation and the rule of law. NHRIs can facilitate direct interaction between NHRIs in other countries and their own country's development aid programmes as well as supporting the institution building aspects of national development aid programmes and/or receiving support from development aid programmes for carrying out independent capacity building initiatives in other countries.[60]

An interesting example of a NHRI playing a direct role in this regard is the involvement of the Australian Human Rights Commission in two intergovernmental technical cooperation programmes. The 'China-Australia Human Rights Technical Cooperation Program' is described in the Australian Commission's Annual Report 2007-2008 as 'an integral part of Australia's annual inter-governmental Dialogue on Human Rights with China'.[61] The program 'aims to provide an

[59] The Arab-European NHRI Dialogue is an interesting example in this regard. The dialogue brings together NHRIs from among others, Denmark, France, Greece, Germany, Ireland, Sweden, Algeria, Egypt, Jordan, Mauritania, Morocco, Palestine and Qatar to discuss issues such as migration and women's rights. For more details see: http://aehrd.info/j02/ [last accessed 22 November 2010].

[60] For example, the New Zealand Human Rights Commission reported that in 2008 it had received financial support from the New Zealand Aid Programme (NZAID) for its work to strengthen respect for human rights globally and in the Asia-Pacific region in particular; see: New Zealand Human Rights Commission Annual Report 2008, p.26, available at: http://www.hrc.co.nz/hrc_new/hrc/cms/files/documents/03-Jun-2009_15-58-52_HRC_Annual_Report _2008.html [last accessed 22 November 2010].

[61] Australian Human Rights Commission, Annual Report 2007-2008, Chapter 11, available at: http://www.hreoc.gov.au/about/publications/annual_reports/2007_2008/index.html [last accessed 22 November 2010].

important information base of human rights principles, ideas and strategies which can be drawn upon in the development of Chinese policies and practices', and encompasses the themes women's and children's rights, the rights of ethnic minorities and the reform of legal systems.[62] Likewise, the 'Vietnam-Australia Dialogue on International Organisations and Legal Issues' focuses on access to justice, dissemination of information on legal rights and obligations, the rights of women, and awareness-raising of treaty obligations.[63]

Strengthening National Human Rights Institutions' Own Role

Because NHRIs have the explicit mandate to promote and protect human rights, action taken towards their establishment in countries where they do not yet exist or towards their strengthening where they already exist can be seen as an objective for which human rights diplomacy can be applied. NHRIs encourage states, as well as regional and international mechanisms to put the establishment and strengthening of NHRIs on their agendas.[64] One of the core activities undertaken by the ICC, the OHCHR and a range of regional human rights mechanisms is working to establish and strengthen NHRIs around the world,[65] and to enhance their role at the international level.[66] NHRIs own regional coordinating structures also provide support for NHRIs within their respective region, particularly in those regions which have regional secretariats, namely Africa and Asia-Pacific. For example, the OHCHR and the Asia-Pacific Forum, with the support of the Government of Samoa and the Pacific Islands Forum, held a workshop on the establishment of NHRIs in the Pacific in April 2009, resulting in the Samoa Declaration.[67] Similarly, the 2009-2010 Strategic Plan of the European Group of NHRIs lists building capacity of NHRIs in Europe as one of the priorities of the Group.[68] The Work Program of the

[62] *Ibid.* The report also lists a series of activities undertaken in 2007-2008 including workshops on domestic violence, women's labour rights and study visits from the judiciary and prison services.

[63] *Ibid.*, Chapter 11.2.

[64] See e.g. ICC Statement to the Human Rights Council 13th Session, 1 to 26 March 2010 under the General Segment (3 March 2010), available at: http://www.nhri.nic.in/2009/ICC%20Statement%20General%20Segment%203%20March%202010%20English.pdf [last accessed 22 November 2010].

[65] Article 5 Statute of the ICC.

[66] For examples of OHCHR activities in this area see: Report of the Secretary-General on National Institutions, 2010.

[67] *Ibid.*, para.55.

[68] European Group of National Human Rights Institutions Strategic Plan 2009–2010, available at: http://www.nhri.net [last accessed 22 November 2010].

Network of NHRIs of the Americas Region 2008-2010 states its vision as 'an organisation to build capacities of [NHRIs] of the Americas, individually as well as a Group'.[69] The African Network of NHRIs also has the strengthening and development of NHRIs as one of its missions.[70]

Sub-regionally, NHRIs also cooperate on joint initiatives and for capacity building. For example, the ASEAN NHRIs (Indonesia, Malaysia, the Philippines and Thailand) have adopted a cooperation agreement to carry out joint activities and develop regional strategies. Steps have also been taken to establish a West African Network of NHRIs,[71] and NHRIs from the Arab Region hold annual meetings.[72]

An interesting aspect of the work of NHRIs in strengthening their role is the accreditation function of the ICC. Assessments on the extent to which a NHRI complies with the Paris Principles are made by the Sub-Committee on Accreditation and adopted by the ICC. The recommendations made to individual NHRIs often have a direct impact at the national level and strengthen NHRIs positions. They can, for instance, result in the adoption or amendment of laws relating to NHRIs to improve their compliance with the Paris Principles.[73]

NHRIs are also active in advocating for a formalisation of their role within international and regional mechanisms. One interesting example in this regard concerns the Commission on the Status of Women (CSW). The Asia-Pacific Forum, with the support of the ICC,

---

[69] Work Program of the Network of National Human Rights Institutions for the Promotion and Protection of Human Rights of the Americas Region 2008-2010, p.3, available at: http://www.rindhca.org.ve/ [last accessed 22 November 2010].

[70] For the mission statement see: http://www.nanhri.org/ [last accessed 22 November 2010].

[71] Report of the Secretary-General on National Institutions, 2010, para.53.

[72] There is also a Commonwealth Forum of National Human Rights Institutions, at: http://www.commonwealthnhri.org/ [last accessed 22 November 2010].

[73] See e.g. Report and Recommendations of the Session of the Sub-Committee on Accreditation, Geneva, 26-30 March 2009. In relation to Qatar, the Committee expressed 'appreciation for the legislative changes that have increased the number of civil society representatives on the [National Human Rights Committee] NHRC, their majority status on the NHRC and the removal of voting rights for Government representatives'. In relation to Algeria, the Committee took note of 'a letter dated 25 March 2009 from the [National Consultative Commission for the Promotion and Protection of Human Rights] CNCPPDH President to the ICC Chair informing that the Prime Minister has instructed the Minister of Justice to elaborate a legislative text on the status of the CNCPPDH. This text is to be submitted to Parliament at its spring session 2009'. The report is available at: http://www.nhri.net/ [last accessed 22 November 2010].

has lobbied the CSW to give a formal position to NHRIs. To date, these efforts have resulted in formal government statements promoting the role of NHRIs in the CSW, a statement by the Chair of the Committee on the Elimination of All Forms of Discrimination Against Women (CEDAW) strongly encouraging CSW to consider how NHRIs could be fully integrated into its work, and the first specific reference to NHRIs in the 'Agreed Conclusions' of the CSW.[74]

National Level

NHRIs also advocate for international positions on human rights directly at the national level. National institutions have an advantage through their position and prominence at the domestic level in bringing concerns to the heart of their national systems. NHRIs are also able to bring international standards and concerns directly into the national system in ways and with a level of detail that may not be possible for actors based in New York or Geneva. Ministries of foreign affairs may sometimes have to 'negotiate' with other national departments or ministries on a governmental position to be taken at the international level, including in relation to the interpretation of international human rights law and the scope of obligations flowing from it. Such 'negotiations' may also be necessary for example in relation to the implementation of the outcomes of the UN treaty body processes at the national level. NHRIs have the possibility to support international level positions on different human rights issues and their implementation by directly advocating them to national ministries and departments.

NHRIs engage directly at the national level in discourse with different state actors, including parliaments.[75] Their reports are commonly

[74] See Report on NHRI Engagement with CSW, Deputy Director of the Asia-Pacific Forum, Pip Dargan (October 2009), available at: http://NHRI.net/2009/CSW_Update_Pip_Dargan_ICCB_Oct_09.Final_(2).pdf; for further information see also: http://www.asiapacificforum.net/services/international-regional/un/commission-on-the-status-of-women. Another interesting example in this regard in the initiative by the European Group of NHRIs to submit an *amicus curiae* intervention before the European Court of Human Rights, see: Report of the European Group—Regional Activities since ICC 21, presented at the 22nd meeting of the ICC, Geneva (March 2009), available at: http://www.nhri.net/2009/ITEM%207-Regional%20Report%20NHRI%20Int'l %20&%20Regl%20 EngagementEUROPEenglish.pdf [all last accessed 22 November 2010].

[75] For example, the Irish Human Rights Commission's Annual Report 2008 notes that its members met with parliamentary *(Oireachtas)* Committees on a number of occasions to follow up on observations the Commission had made or issues it had raised. The Report is accessible at: http://www.ihrc.ie/download/pdf/

laid before parliaments, and are frequently published and publicised in the media. In this way, they have the potential to hold the state to account for its action or inaction in addressing national human rights concerns, and in relation to the implementation of its international obligations.[76] NHRIs can also arrange briefings for opposition parties on their concerns in relation to the government's compliance with international treaties, for example through parliamentary committees. NHRIs can in addition act to increase the weight that is given to human rights at the top political levels of their country, both by encouraging national debate and engaging public pressure.

Future Challenges and Opportunities

NHRIs are increasingly engaged at every level of the human rights system: national, regional and international. They are providing additional and sometimes entirely new information on the human rights records of individual countries. They are also increasingly prominent as actors in multilateral forums. While the above sets out some of the areas in which NHRIs already engage in human rights diplomacy, there remains considerable untapped potential for NHRIs to further develop their '4th space' within the international human rights framework—separate from but working constructively with international organisations, governments and NGOs. This future expansion may, however, also bring about challenges that national institutions will have to contend with.

Challenges to National Human Rights Institutions' Role in Human Rights Diplomacy

A consequence of NHRIs' international engagement is the possibility that conflicts may arise between their national and international role.

---

annual_report_2008.pdf [last accessed 22 November 2020]. The National Commission for Human Rights of Jordan reported that it had signed Memoranda of Understanding with several governmental institutions including the Ministry of Education, the Ministry of Political Development and the Public Security Directorate, see: The National Centre for Human Rights Amman, Jordan, Report of Achievements, Opportunities, and Challenges, submitted to the APF 15th Annual Meeting, Bali, Indonesia, 3-5 August 2010, available at: http://www.asiapacificforum.net/ [last accessed 22 November 2010].

[76] E.g. OHCHR Survey on National Human Rights Institutions (July 2009), pp.26 and 31.

While at the domestic level NHRIs are for the most part viewed solely as *national* institutions, they are in fact also actors at the international level, both individually, and collectively through the activities of their coordinating bodies. The perception of NHRIs as primarily national-level actors means that they often lack a specific international mandate in their founding legislation. Even where an institution has an explicit international mandate, in practice this mandate can be limited to engagement on national issues such as producing alternative or 'shadow' reports to treaty bodies.[77] Both these elements can mean that institutions may not have financial or human resources to fulfil the international role promoted by international and regional organisations.

Furthermore, as national *sui generis* institutions, the role of NHRIs is not yet fully understood at the national level. NHRIs often have to justify their role nationally as independent institutions, and it is clear that many are not even given sufficient resources to act at the national level. A 2009 OHCHR survey of sixty one NHRIs reported that only twenty one of those surveyed considered their budget as sufficient to carry out their functions as effectively as possible. Ten per cent reported that their budget had significantly decreased in recent years, and economic pressures may see this number increase in the future.[78] Thus, while at the international level there are an increasing number of initiatives that target NHRIs for their implementation, at the national level national institutions may not be able to actuate these new roles.[79] While the ICC and particularly the regional coordinating bodies can provide information on the realities of NHRI capacity at the international level and can support NHRIs in fulfilling their international role, this conflict could lead to difficulties in future. Situations may arise where NHRIs pull back from international engagement,

---

[77] *Ibid.*, p.43.

[78] *Ibid.*, p.17.

[79] It may be noted that some NHRIs have also been designated as the relevant national mechanisms under Article 3 of the 2002 Optional Protocol to the Convention against Torture and other Cruel, Inhuman or Degrading Treatment or Punishment (OP-CAT), UNGA Res 57/99 (2003), UN Doc A/RES/57/199 (9 January 2003), 2375 UNTS 237; entered into force 22 June 2006, and under Article 33 of the 2006 Convention on the Rights of Persons with Disabilities, UNGA Res 61/611 (2006), UN Doc A/RES/61/106 (13 December 2006); entered into force 3 May 2008. Both mechanisms require sufficient—usually additional—resources in order to be properly implemented.

considering that their key mandate as actors at the national level does not allow for such engagement.

One of the biggest challenges for the future collective position of NHRIs at the international level is their independence. Currently, the ICC monitors the independence of NHRIs and sets their accreditation status. However, the Statute of the ICC dictates that there is no 'emergency' measure to suspend the 'A' status of an institution. Thus, where an institution acts in a manner that might be considered as undermining its independence, or where a country has experienced a coup or other crisis which may impact the independence of government and of the NHRI, the institution will nonetheless retain an 'A'-status, which includes for example the possibility to make statements before the Human Rights Council and to interact with international mechanisms in other ways for a period of at least one year.[80]

There is also a particular challenge in assessing whether NHRIs are truly independent actors at the national level. The ICC has invited NGOs to make submissions to the Sub-Committee on Accreditation about the national institution in their country, which may assist in ensuring that the ICC has the most information available to it in relation to the actual work and independence of an institution. However, if questions arise as to the value and reliability of the 'A'-status, and the international community considers that it cannot rely on NHRIs as independent actors, the role of NHRIs within the international human rights framework may be jeopardised. The future effectiveness of NHRIs at the international level will largely depend on maintaining NHRIs' independence and ensuring the credibility of the 'A'-status designation. Ensuring NHRIs' ability to fulfil their mandates by maintaining their work at the national level as their primary focus, while acting collectively to promote human rights standards internationally is equally important.

Opportunities for an Enhanced Role in Human Rights Diplomacy

NHRIs are still in the process of strengthening their position in relation to regional and international human rights mechanisms. The work being undertaken in fora such as the Commission on the Status of Women is evidence of the way there is to go in having the role of national institutions formalised within the international human rights

[80] Article 18 Statute of the ICC.

framework. However, the scope of the work of NHRIs across different levels and in different fora indicates the potential which exists for national institutions to promote and protect human rights through human rights diplomacy. There is still a relatively low international engagement of NHRIs. As noted above, in 2009 on average twenty NHRIs out of a possible sixty five participated in each Human Rights Council session,[81] and only about fifty per cent of NHRIs which had the possibility to do so provided a stakeholder report for their state's UPR.[82]

Structurally, there are a number of steps which could be taken by NHRIs to strengthen their role at the international level. The ICC has a permanent presence in Geneva. However, expanding into a permanent ICC office in Geneva to ensure active engagement by NHRIs at a high level with the members of the Human Rights Council and senior civil servants at the UN, has great potential to enhance the role of NHRIs and to ensure that their voices are heard on key human rights issues. At the regional level, the establishment or strengthening of secretariats in all four geographical regions modelled along the lines of the successful Asia-Pacific Forum will allow for enhanced interaction between NHRIs and regional human rights mechanisms, as well as ensuring strong regional voices within the ICC.

In addition, at present there is a lack of systematic documentation or centralised recording of the work of NHRIs that would give a comprehensive overview of the scope of their national, regional and international activities. Such documentation could assist NHRIs in identifying their strengths as well as areas in which they could undertake additional work. At the same time, it would allow the wider human rights community to understand NHRIs' role and functions more fully. A more strategic approach could also be adopted by NHRIs at the national level, such as holding periodic meetings with ministries of foreign affairs and other departments, and regularly sending them position papers and statements of regional NHRI coordination bodies and the ICC. Clearly, there is also substantial scope for greater collaboration between NHRIs and major NGOs at the international level, as demonstrated by the publication "Preventing Torture: An Operational

81 Report of the Secretary-General on National Institutions, 2010, para.77.
82 *Ibid.*, para.76.

Guide for National Human Rights Institutions",[83] produced jointly by the Asia-Pacific Forum, the Association for the Prevention of Torture and OHCHR in 2010.

The clearest opportunities for strengthening and expanding the future role of NHRIs in human rights diplomacy will come from the support provided by international and regional human rights mechanisms, including through a further formalisation of NHRIs' roles within these fora. NHRIs' activities at the international and regional level, often directly critical of governments, can mean that they come under pressure at the national level from the recriminations of disgruntled governments. It is vital therefore, that NHRIs receive the constant support of the international community. However, the international community must be cognisant of the fact that NHRIs' work at the international level can place them in a precarious position nationally.

Conclusion

Over the past twenty years NHRIs have emerged as a new actor in the international human rights framework. Although the extent of their functions and roles are not yet fully understood and although NHRIs are still in the process of developing into mature, stable institutions, they have already played an active role in helping to create a culture of human rights and in the promotion and protection of human rights at the international and domestic levels. While the effectiveness of NHRIs as actors in human rights diplomacy is difficult to assess, it is clear that they are active across a wide range of areas within the international human rights framework and are strengthening the link between the national and international levels. There is considerable strength and potential in the individual and collective work of NHRIs at the international level, and in the scope of their peer-to-peer capacity building and information sharing activities. The national, 'bi-lateral', sub-regional, regional and international nature of NHRIs' work is almost unique in breadth and character. If it is accepted that the promotion

[83] Asia-Pacific Forum, Association for the Prevention of Torture (APT) and the Office of the High Commissioner for Human, *Preventing Torture: An Operational Guide for National Human Rights Institutions*, (May 2010), available at: http://www.apt.ch/index.php?option=com_docman&task=cat_view&gid=237&Itemid =250& lang =en [last accessed 22 November 2010].

and protection of human rights in one country benefits all countries and individuals, then a strong role for NHRIs is likely to emerge and develop further over the next decade, and will likely see them using their unique position to advance the promotion and protection of human rights through means of human rights diplomacy.

CHAPTER 15

THE RELEVANCE OF THE MULTI-STAKEHOLDER APPROACH AND MULTI-TRACK DIPLOMACY FOR HUMAN RIGHTS DIPLOMACY

Wolfgang Benedek

Multi-stakeholder approaches, whether in the form of public private partnerships or multi-stakeholder partnerships in the multilateral and regional context, are becoming increasingly relevant in international affairs. At the same time, the theory of multi-track diplomacy appears to offer useful insights for human rights diplomacy although it has been largely developed as a new approach to ensure peace and security. In this contribution, I will mainly focus on the relevance of these two approaches to public diplomacy for various forms of human rights diplomacy.

Theory of Multi-track Diplomacy and the Multi-stakeholder Approach

While the leading actors of traditional diplomacy are the diplomatic officials of states,[1] multi-track diplomacy is characterised by a broader approach to the role of diplomacy, based on the involvement of actors beyond the state, including civil society.[2] The trend towards multi-track diplomacy is the result of the growing number of internationally active, well-connected and increasingly influential non-state actors.[3] It is based on the experience that non-state actors can play an important role in the resolution of conflicts in different fields, in particular in the area of human rights.

[1] For a traditional approach to diplomacy see H. Kissinger, *Diplomacy* (New York: Simon & Schuster, 1994).

[2] See D. Wehrenfennig, 'Multi-Track Diplomacy and Human Security', *Human Security Journal* 7 (2008), 80.

[3] See W. Benedek, 'The Emerging Global Civil Society: Achievements and Prospects' in V. Rittberger and M. Nettesheim (eds.), *Authority in the Global Political Economy* (Houndsmills/New York: Palgrave Macmillan, 2008), pp.170–85.

Where traditional diplomacy is conceived by diplomatic officials and conducted top-down, multi-track diplomacy argues for a bottom-up approach that first searches to identify the human needs of the population to be targeted by a diplomatic measure. This focus on people and the bottom-up approach to diplomacy, which often includes mainstreaming human rights and gender issues into traditionally politico-diplomatic spheres,[4] has also contributed to the fact that multi-track diplomacy is often called 'human diplomacy'.[5] There are also large conceptual overlaps with the approach of 'public diplomacy' that focuses on the involvement of non-official actors.[6] While space does not permit to enter into a conceptual discussion, all these approaches share a new and broader conception of democracy and promote a more inclusive approach towards stakeholders. This allows multi-track diplomacy to answer more directly to the diplomatic challenges faced by a world of changing power differentials and emerging actors.[7] Among these emerging actors that multi-track diplomacy seeks to involve are academics, civil society organisations, the media and parliamentarians.

With regard to the participation of academics in diplomacy, certain advantages exist, but some risks are also involved. Diplomats have to take the interest of their states into account and, in a similar way, officials of international organisations are also limited by the mandate, powers and purposes of their institutions. In meetings, this is often reflected in the typical opening sentence of participants: 'I am speaking in my personal capacity'. Academics are usually more committed to better understanding a matter, if not the famous 'search for the truth', but they might be quite 'undiplomatic' when it comes to a situation

---

[4] On the challenges and the potential of mainstreaming a 'soft' approach, such as human security and multi-track, into 'hard' approaches, such as peace operations (or traditional diplomacy), see W. Benedek, M. C. Kettemann and M. Möstl (eds.), *Mainstreaming Human Security in Peace Operations and Crisis Management. Policies, Problems, Potential* (London: Routledge, 2010).

[5] Compare C. M. Constantinou, *Human Diplomacy and Spirituality*, Discussion Papers in Diplomacy, 2006, available at: http://www.clingendael.nl/publications/2006/20060400_cli_paper_dip_issue103.pdf [last accessed 3 December 2010].

[6] On public diplomacy see J. M. Wallner (eds.), *The Public Diplomacy Reader* (Washington: Institute of World Politics Press, 2007), available online at: http://goo.gl/iHZa2 [last accessed 3 December 2010]; or N. Snow and P. M. Taylor, *The Routledge Handbook of Public Diplomacy* (London: Routledge, 2009).

[7] See L. Diamond and J. McDonald, *Multi-Track Diplomacy: A Systems Approach to Peace* (Sterling, VA: Kumarian Press, 1996); see also Institute for Multi-Track Diplomacy, 'What is Multi-Track Diplomacy?', available at: http://www.imtd.org/at-a-glance/mission/working-methods/what-is-multi-track-diplomacy/ [last accessed 3 December 2010].

which requires a more careful approach. Non-governmental organisations (NGOs), on the other hand, usually have an element of advocacy in their work, which strengthens and limits their role at the same time. There is strong evidence that including more actors in diplomatic endeavours leads to more sustainable results;[8] their inclusion does not, however, *per se* guarantee a self-interest-free diplomacy.

Exclusively relying on non-state actor approaches to diplomacy is problematic: The results reached in purely academic environments, for instance, are unofficial and non-binding. States are still needed to implement them. Thus, academic multi-track diplomats have to develop solutions with an eye to the realities on the ground.

The media can also play a useful role in informing about and sometimes amplifying concerns, but there is the problem of generalisation and exaggeration.[9] There have been cases where the media has contributed to the causes of conflict and undermined holistic diplomatic solutions.

What is often missing in traditional approaches to diplomacy is the involvement of parliamentarians, who, like in the case of the European Parliament, can play an important role to enhance the democratic legitimacy of diplomatic solutions to conflicts. There are parliamentary assemblies of the Council of Europe and even of the North Atlantic Treaty Organisation (NATO) or the Cotonou Agreement, but there is no parliamentary body on the level of the United Nations (UN). This has to be considered as an important gap. The Inter-Parliamentary Union in Geneva cannot compensate for this fact.[10]

A multi-track approach has the advantage of involving more public actors, which can give additional support to human rights diplomacy and increase public interest. The approach can also ensure a more objective and realistic debate. This recognition is reflected in the fact that the European Union (EU) has supported the invitation of NGOs to a number of international conferences in order to take views from the ground into account, and push the diplomatic process towards becoming more inclusive. The Vienna World Conference on Human

---

[8] H. Saunders, *A Public Peace Process: Sustained Dialogue to Transform Racial and Ethnical Conflicts* (New York: St. Martin's Press, 1999).

[9] E. Gilboa, 'Media Diplomacy' in W. Donsbach (ed.), *The International Encyclopaedia of Communication* (London: Blackwell, 2008).

[10] On the Inter-Parliamentary Union see: www.ipu.org [last accessed 3 December 2010].

Rights in 1993 exemplified this inclusive approach, which has since become a general practice.

Similar to the concept of multi-track diplomacy, the multi-stakeholder approach aims to involve all relevant stakeholders on a largely equal footing. Conceptually, the multi-stakeholder approach has successfully been used with regard to the governance of the information society, in the context of post-conflict situations, for the solution of environmental problems and in particular regarding the promotion and protection of human rights. The inclusivity of multi-stakeholder approaches generates legitimacy and increases the effectiveness of the measures taken.

Examples from Practice

Practice shows that a number of states and international and supranational organisations have used both, the concept of multi-track diplomacy and the notion of multi-stakeholder partnerships (and their combination) in their efforts to conduct a more comprehensive, holistic and sustainable human rights diplomacy. The following examples from practice show both the advantages and the potential pitfalls of these approaches.

One example for the potential of the multi-stakeholder approach in the context of the governance of the information society is the Internet Governance Forum (IGF) that was established after the World Summit on the Information Society in Geneva and Tunis in 2003 and 2005. The IGF's mandate is to bring together all stakeholders—i.e. governments, international organisations, business, NGOs and academics—to discuss all issues concerning the information society on a yearly basis.[11] The IGF cannot take decisions, nor even draft recommendations or common conclusions.[12] But the discussion process involving multiple stakeholders generates results through creative, lively and open debate, and through persuasive policy suggestions in reaction to common problems. The disadvantage of the process is that results are less visible and/or less clear-cut. They are, nonetheless, quite real. IGF participants

[11] See W. Benedek, V. Bauer and M. C. Kettemann (eds.), *Internet Governance and the Information Society. Global Perspectives and European Dimensions* (Utrecht: Eleven International Publishing, 2008).

[12] J. Malcolm, *Multi-Stakeholder Governance and the Internet Governance Forum* (Perth: Terminus Press, 2008).

include key people of the information society who take the results back to their institutions. This decentralised distribution of results by different members of the information society has contributed to the success of the IGF. Apart from that, the successful formula of multi-stakeholderism as exemplified by the IGF has been copied by regional and even national internet governance forums.[13]

Strangely enough, representatives from the UN human rights system were present in the person of the Special Rapporteur on Freedom of Expression only since the IGF in Sharm el Sheikh in 2009, even though stakeholders discuss a large number of human rights issues, for example child protection or freedom of expression. The Council of Europe by contrast actively uses the IGF as an opportunity to advance its human rights agenda, and has participated with a large delegation since the Forum was founded. The UN Educational, Scientific and Cultural Organisation (UNESCO), the Organisation for Security and Co-operation in Europe (OSCE), human rights NGOs and academics specialised in human rights are also among the participants.

This experience raises the question of whether the multi-stakeholder approach—and even multi-stakeholder partnerships which have a stronger continuity—could also be used to increase the effectiveness of UN human rights bodies, and to give a fresh momentum to the discussion about strategies to be pursued in their reform process. This discussion also resembles the debate on UN partnerships: a partnership-based approach is relied on by the UN to strengthen their activities in the fields of development and human rights in order to implement goals more effectively.[14]

In the past, multi-track diplomacy has developed mainly in the context of ensuring or restoring peace and security. The observation underlying the multi-track approach is that diplomacy is not only a

---

[13] These include *inter alia* the yearly European Dialogue on Internet Governance (EuroDIG) (http://www.eurodig.org), the national Internet Governance Forum in the US in July 2010 (http://igfusa.wordpress.com/2010/05/11/2010-igf-usa-at-georgetown-law-center-in-dc-july-21), sub-regional forums, such as the one held in Uganda in September 2010 (http://www.eaigf.or.ke), and regional forums like the Asian Forum in June 2010 (http://rigf.asia) [all last accessed 3 December 2010].

[14] See C. Malena, 'Strategic Partnership: Challenges and Best Practices in the Management and Governance of Multi-Stakeholder Partnerships Involving UN and Civil Society Actors' (2004) Background paper for the Multi-Stakeholder Workshop on Partnerships and UN-Civil Society Relations, New York, available at: http://www.un.org/reform/civilsociety/pdfs/pocantino_booklet.pdf [last accessed 22 August 2010].

matter for diplomats, but also for a variety of other, often non-state actors including civil society, individual citizens, NGOs, or church groups like San Egidio in Rome, but also academic institutions or business—with the role of the media deserving special attention.[15] Think tanks can play a major role in multi-track diplomacy and other institutions can make essential contributions through funding other actors. In the context of human rights diplomacy, the EU practice of funding a substantial research agenda in the field of human rights is worth mentioning. Fourteen different consortia conducting EU-funded research in the field of human rights and democracy in the wider sense met for the first time in December 2008 in Brussels.

An example of good practice—and of the potential of combining a commitment to multi-stakeholderism and to multi-track diplomacy—is the dialogue conducted in the framework of the Asia-Europe Meeting (ASEM), in which EU countries meet with ten ASEAN countries, including China. There is a 'magic formula' according to which all country delegations should consist of a representative of the government, an NGO representative who can also come from a trade union, and an academic representative. It has helped to avoid superficial discussions and governments cannot give an embellished account of the situation in their country without being corrected by other members of their delegation. Sometimes the results of the dialogue are published and show a quite substantive debate. In this way a multi-stakeholder approach is combined with multi-track diplomacy.[16]

Another example is the EU-China-Dialogue: The political dialogue of governmental representatives is preceded by a seminar in which NGOs and academics play a major role. The main purpose is to openly discuss the issues selected so far by diplomats, and to reach joint conclusions and recommendations—i.e. the debates are outcome-oriented. There have been some shortcomings in the past with regard to the preparation of the seminars. Due to diplomatic problems, they were sometimes organised at too short notice, or had to be cancelled because the admissions of certain NGOs proved to be unacceptable to the Chinese side. There is also a problem with regard to the follow-up,

---

[15] Compare the nine different tracks of diplomacy identified for multi-track diplomacy: Institute for Multi-Track Diplomacy, 'What is Multi-Track Diplomacy?', available at: http://www.imtd.org/at-a-glance/mission/working-methods/what-is-multi-track-diplomacy/ [last accessed 3 December 2010].

[16] See Asia-Europe Foundation, The Third Informal ASEM Seminar on Human Rights, Singapore 2000.

which is largely non-existent. Of late, a new formula has been adopted by the EU that gives the responsibility for following up on the results of the debate to a consortium of academic institutions in the EU, and also allows for additional activities that will benefit the process.[17] It remains to be seen, however, to what extent such seminars should remain result-oriented. The need to come up with results is often a heavy burden on the discussion and, as can be seen from multi-stakeholder approaches in other contexts, the absence of pressure to produce a concrete outcome can lead to a more open discussion—and to results which can be achieved indirectly. However, the effectiveness of different strategies will always depend on the particular context.

Another example to be mentioned is the Human Security Network that was formed in 1999 and consists of 13 member states from different regions of the world, plus South Africa as an observer. Annual ministerial meetings are open to the participation of NGOs, international organisations and academics. Depending on the issues selected, multi-stakeholder discussions take place which can lead to conclusions and recommendations on specific projects, like the campaign against anti-personnel landmines (which was even awarded the 1997 Nobel Peace Prize), or the coalition against cluster munitions. Both coalitions were constituted to promote the abolition of these weapons as multi-stakeholder partnerships in the best sense. Importantly, these coalitions have led to extremely successful treaty negotiations—the 1997 Mine Ban Treaty[18] and the 2010 Convention on Cluster Munitions[19]—and thus serve as prime evidence of the concrete impact multi-stakeholder partnerships and multi-track diplomacy can have on the development of human rights law and international humanitarian law.[20]

Several conferences recently organised by Austria also show the advantage of multi-stakeholder and multi-track approaches. For

[17] See W. Benedek, 'EU Action on Human and Fundamental Rights in 2009' in W. Benedek *et al.* (eds.), *European Yearbook on Human Rights 2010* (Vienna/Antwerp, 2010), 94; and generally K. Kinzelbach, 'The EU Human Rights Dialogue with China and the 2008 Olympic Games' in Benedek *et al.* (eds.), *European Yearbook on Human Rights 2009* (Vienna/Antwerp, 2009), 37–60.

[18] 1997 Convention on the Prohibition of the Use, Stockpiling, Production and Transfer of Anti-Personnel Mines and on Their Destruction, 2056 UNTS 211; entered into force 1 March 1999.

[19] 2008 Convention on Cluster Munitions; entered into force 1 August 2010.

[20] For the International Campaign to Ban Landmines (ICBL) see: http://www.icbl.org/intro.php; and the Cluster Munition Coalition: http://www.stopclustermunitions.org [both last accessed 3 December 2010].

example, the international expert conference organised 15 years after the World Conference on Human Rights in Vienna, dedicated to the topic 'Global Standards—Local Action' (30 August to 1 September 2008), brought together experts and governmental and inter-governmental representatives for the purpose of evaluating the outcome of the Vienna World Conference after 15 years and to identify new challenges. Again, there was a focus on producing an outcome document in the form of conclusions for which rapporteurs together with moderators of the three working groups held during the conference were responsible.[21]

Another conference worth mentioning is the Euro-Arab-Dialogue organised in Vienna in December 2008 on the topic of the situation of women, civil society and youth in the Arab world. The participants came partly from the governments of the Arab League and EU countries, including the European Commission. NGOs, academic participants as well as representatives from religious denominations were also active in the working groups, the results of which were reported to the plenary. Again, it was quite difficult within the limited time to come to significant conclusions. This would require a more structured form of debate which is difficult to achieve with a large number of participants with different backgrounds and priorities.[22]

Examples for multi-stakeholder partnerships and their relevance for the improvement of human rights situations can also be found in post-conflict contexts, where multi-stakeholder partnerships can enhance empowerment, freedom from fear and freedom from want, and thus promote human security and peace-building. In the so-called MultiPart Project (Multi-Stakeholder Partnerships in Post-conflict Situations) financed by the EU under the 7th Framework Programme, the concept of multi-stakeholder partnerships in post-conflict and conflict

---

[21] See W. Benedek *et al.* (eds.), *Global Standards—Local Action. 15 Years Vienna World Conference on Human Rights*, Conference Proceedings of the International Expert Conference held in Vienna on 28 and 29 August 2008, 16 Studienreihe des Ludwig Boltzmann Instituts für Menschenrechte (Vienna/Graz: NWV/Intersentia, 2009).

[22] For all background papers, talks and summaries, see Austrian Federal Ministry for European and International Affairs, 'International Conference "Europe and the Arab World - Connecting Partners in Dialogue"', available at: http://www.bmeia.gv.at/en/foreign-ministry/foreign-ministry/international-conference-europe-and-the-arab-world-connecting-partners-in-dialogue.html [last accessed 3 December 2010].

situations has been researched on, focusing on 12 case studies from Afghanistan, the Democratic Republic of the Congo and Kosovo. The results show that if the concept of multi-stakeholder partnership is taken seriously and meets certain criteria like transparency, participation, ownership, empowerment of local actors, accountability and sustainability, it can indeed make a contribution to good governance and confidence-building as well as to addressing security and development concerns. What turned out to be crucial was the involvement of government and civil society, i.e. local actors and the provision of adequate space to meet local concerns. This contributed to enhance human security and peace-building efforts.[23]

The work of UN human rights bodies, in particular of the Human Rights Council, is characterised by a strong involvement of experts, for example as members of the Human Rights Council Advisory Committee or serving as special procedures mandate-holders. These experts, and also NGOs, have important influence on issues ranging from agenda-setting to concrete negotiations of new standards. NGOs rely on different means of human rights diplomacy, such as negotiating directly with governments, addressing multilateral human rights bodies, and mobilising public support. Accordingly, the approach of multi-track diplomacy is daily practice within the UN. In a similar way, the human rights diplomacy of the EU often uses academic expertise and NGOs in pursuing EU human rights policies.

Conclusions

In conclusion it can be said that the multi-stakeholder approach combined with a multi-track approach can improve the quality of diplomatic engagements and processes, and increase the legitimacy of their outcomes. Certainly, the question what to do with the results will need to be answered mainly at the governmental level, but the non-governmental level should also be involved in all phases of follow-up and implementation as much as possible. In this way, results of multi-stakeholder and multi-track processes will be better disseminated, and conclusions communicated more effectively. The possibility to build

[23] See: www.multi-part.eu [last accessed 3 December 2010].

on the networks developed during the multi-stakeholder discussions for the implementation of conclusions also holds considerable potential.

Generally, multi-stakeholder events could benefit from better preparation, a more clearly structured agenda and carefully selected participants who should have demonstrated competence in the field. There needs to be an opportunity for participants to provide feedback as well as to engage in follow-up activities, in order to ensure continuity—perhaps through establishing a permanent secretariat. Isolated events are often criticised for not leading to sustainable results. Academics sometimes even feel somewhat misused if they are invited to debates defined by others, who also pull the strings and insist upon phrasing conclusions in a certain way. Sometimes this is aggravated by late invitations not allowing for adequate preparation, by the lack of feedback on the outcome of the event, as well as by the absence of follow-up work. In this way, there is also the risk that such events become counterproductive. On the other hand, there are a number of examples of good practice, in particular when the results are published and the event is prepared with the assistance of NGOs or academic institutions. These actors can usually invest more efforts and time than ministries that often lack the capacity to do so.

These findings are also relevant for human rights dialogues and human rights partnerships, which could benefit from more emphasis on preparation and follow-up processes to make full use of the existing potential. A multi-stakeholder approach, if not a true multi-stakeholder partnership, should characterise the whole undertaking. Also, the question whom to invite can usefully be resolved through preparatory consultations among different stakeholders.

Accordingly, a more strategic approach to human rights diplomacy needs to be developed in order to achieve substantive results, which are also sustainable. There is always the danger of superficiality, of exaggerated expectations and, consequently, disappointment. In this context, it might be useful to draw up guidelines of how to plan and administer multi-stakeholder and multi-track events, making use of the numerous past experiences reflecting good and bad practices for future projects of a similar nature, in particular in the field of human rights diplomacy.

That being said, the specificities of human rights diplomacy should always be given close attention. In some cases, bilateral diplomacy or silent diplomacy—such as quick *demarches* sent by the EU—can be more effective than organising a broad multi-stakeholder event. Without going into more details at this point, it can however be plausibly argued, that in the vast majority of situations a multi-stakeholder-based multi-track approach to human rights diplomacy will lead to better, more legitimate and more sustainable results. The examples and reasons given in this contribution are proof of this.

ANNEX

European Inter - University Centre for Human Rights and Democratisation

The University of Nottingham Human Rights Law Centre

Adam Mickiewicz University, Poznan

HIGH-LEVEL WORKSHOP ON HUMAN RIGHTS DIPLOMACY

Venice, 30–31 January 2009

Report

1. Introduction

A High-Level Workshop on Human Rights Diplomacy was convened by the European Inter-University Centre for Human Rights and Democratisation (EIUC), the University of Nottingham Human Rights Law Centre and the Adam Mickiewicz University Poznan on 30-31 January 2009 in the Monastery of San Nicolò Venice—Lido.

The main purpose of the high-level workshop was to explore the notion, dimensions and means of human rights diplomacy with a view to better understanding the sector and promoting good practice. To this end, it brought together diplomats, academics, civil society actors, special procedure mandate-holders, United Nations (UN) treaty body members, senior personnel of intergovernmental organisations and current and former high diplomatic office holders. The list of participants is in section 5.

The discussion was organised in eight sessions covering different aspects of human rights diplomacy. Each session started with two-four short presentations delivered by the participants, followed by lively and rich debates. Chatham House Rules applied. The programme is in section 4.

This report seeks to present the key issues identified and the range of views expressed at the high-level workshop. It does not draw conclusions or make recommendations. However, it is planned to further explore the key issues and results outlined in this report in an edited volume on human rights diplomacy. Though completed following consultation with workshop panellists, the report remains an output of the organisers.

The report has been drafted by Amrei Müller of the Human Rights Law Center, University of Nottingham, with input from Agnieszka Bienczyk-Missala of the Institute of International Relations, University of Warsaw. Our warm thanks to both for their expert assistance both during the workshop and in the preparation of the present report. Thanks also to EIUC staff members Anna Schulz, Michelle Farrell, Christian Volk and Alessandra Silanos for their assistance in the organisation of the workshop.

Zdzisław Kędzia
Michael O'Flaherty
George Ulrich

2. Background and Key Questions

The examination of the potentials and challenges of human rights diplomacy has been identified as a very timely undertaking by the convenors of the high-level workshop. On the one hand, there has been a proliferation of diplomatic initiatives with the aim to promote the implementation of human rights, in particular after the 1993 Second World Conference on Human Rights in Vienna. On the other hand, there is no systematic analysis of the work of these diplomatic initiatives and of actors involved in human rights diplomacy, of the means they employ, of their success and failure, of their interaction with each other and of many more questions related to the opportunities and challenges for human rights diplomacy. This gap was recognised as one of the reasons why the potential of human rights diplomacy has not been exploited to its full extent. It was also noted that the risks and pitfalls of advancing human rights by diplomatic means are not well understood.

Participants of the workshop were invited to reflect on and discuss the following key questions/issues:

- A working definition of 'diplomacy' as 'the art of persuasion in international affairs' (Marshall Green) was put forward. Participants were invited to examine the usefulness of this definition for human rights diplomacy as well as their understanding of what activities fall under human rights diplomacy.
- Who are the actors in human rights diplomacy and what is their role?
- What is the relationship between human rights diplomacy and general diplomacy with human rights objectives? Shall they be integrated or shall they be used in parallel?
- How can coherence be achieved among the different actors involved in human rights diplomacy? Is coherence necessary?
- What are the core tools/instruments of human rights diplomacy?
- What is the role of international human rights law in human rights diplomacy?
- Finally, participants were urged to indentify good, bad and promising practice in human rights diplomacy.

3. Human Rights Diplomacy

3.1 Characterisation of Human Rights Diplomacy

The engagement in some form of negotiation with counterparts whose goals and interests are different, with the aim to persuade them as far as possible or to even dissuade them from certain actions, was identified as a distinguishing feature of diplomacy. The related element of reciprocity was recognised as equally important. Human rights diplomacy is the utilisation of diplomatic negotiations/persuasion for the specific purpose of promoting and protecting human rights.

Departing from this broad understanding of human rights diplomacy, almost all human rights promotion and protection work by states, international governmental organisations, non-governmental organisations (NGOs), independent experts, national human rights institutions (NHRIs), ombudspersons, academics and other actors can be identified as human rights diplomacy. Examples were given of how different actors, even those established with the specific mandate to further the promotion and protection of human rights, were engaged in some form of negotiation to pursue their goals. To name but a few of these examples: the Office of the High Commissioner for Human Rights (OHCHR) engages in lengthy negotiations with states when opening country offices; UN special rapporteurs to the UN Human Rights

Council (HRC) may have to make concessions when they negotiate the terms of reference for visits to specific countries, for the sake of gaining access to these countries; even judicial bodies, such as the European Court of Human Rights (ECtHR) have mechanisms that are dominated by negotiation-based elements, for instance procedures to achieve a friendly settlement between the parties; and even in situations where persuasion seems to be no option and for example some sort of sanctions are employed against a certain actor, this is always done with the aim to start new negotiations.

However, the work of judicial bodies adjudicating human rights should fall outside the definition of human rights diplomacy, with the exception of certain limited aspects of their work. Judicial bodies' function is to apply and interpret the law, and not to negotiate it. In this connection it has to be highlighted that not all human rights work includes an element of reciprocity and negotiation. For example, a large part of the human rights advocacy work done by the UN High Commissioner, the special rapporteurs, NGOs and academics is based on revealing (non-negotiable) facts, outcome of scientific research or statistics. Such work can be supported by human rights diplomacy, and the interaction between different actors involved in (diplomatic or non-diplomatic) human rights work has to be given further thought.

Thus, it was suggested to search for a definition of human rights diplomacy that would recognise the involvement of a wide range of actors in human rights diplomacy, but at the same time take a narrower view on the functions, activities or types of human rights work that actually fall under human rights diplomacy.

There are also risks and pitfalls in employing diplomatic means to seek the promotion and protection of human rights. Among them is the risk that human rights standards may be watered down if compromises found through diplomatic negotiations are going too far, that some actors may engage in diplomatic action with exactly this intention to deteriorate established human rights standards, and that some states may use diplomatic means to minimise and refuse criticism of their human rights record ('bad' human rights diplomacy). Moreover, some actors instrumentalise human rights in their diplomatic efforts to achieve other foreign policy goals not related to the promotion and protection of human rights. This reveals that using diplomacy as a tool to promote human rights (human rights diplomacy) has to be distinguished from using human rights as a tool for diplomacy. The discussion in the following sections relates to the former ('good') human rights diplomacy.

Human rights diplomacy should use diplomatic means (negotiations) to further the promotion and implementation of human rights, but should avoid making compromises on norms or results of fact-finding. In particular, the non-derogable core of international human rights law shall not be negotiable in any diplomatic effort. This does not exclude that certain actors, in particular states, are and can be selective in the human rights norms they advocate through diplomatic means.

A difficulty is that human rights professionals are often reluctant to link their work to diplomacy, even though this has changed to some extent recently. Traditionally, diplomacy was thought of as a cool-headed pursuit of national interest by states, devoid of moral content and value judgement. Diplomacy was understood as *realpolitik* at international level. Meanwhile, the work of human rights always related to the promotion of universal ideals, principles and values transcending the national. This made it difficult to find common ground between human rights work and diplomacy. However, it has changed in recent years due to developments in two areas: first, human rights professionals recognised that the implementation of all human rights is a continuous process that requires direct engagement with governments to assist them in finding solutions for their human rights problems; and second, the rights-consciousness and sense of injustice of the global public as well as of governments has increased considerably in recent years, a consequence being that human rights are gradually more incorporated into the work of foreign ministries.

3.2 The Practice of Bilateral Human Rights Diplomacy by States

The driving factors and motives of bilateral human rights diplomacy by states are diverse: First, the acknowledgement that the protection of human rights is critical for stability and security as well as for sustainable social and economic development in third countries has advanced the understanding within governments that the promotion and protection of human rights in third countries serves national interests. Second, the promotion of the observance of universal human rights standards agreed upon by states has become a legitimate concern of the international community, and can therefore no longer be ignored in foreign policy. Third and related to this, a moral commitment towards the victims of violations of human rights is increasingly felt to influence diplomatic action. Bilateral human rights diplomacy is also driven by domestic factors such as demands and lobbying activities by NGOs, parliamentarians, the media, exile groups, etc.

States engaging in human rights diplomacy have different tools and strategies at their disposal: Sending confidential or public *demarches*, the calling in of ambassadors, issuing public statements of concern, raising human rights issues in meetings at the political level, engaging in regular human rights dialogues and consultations with specific countries (including on individual cases), monitoring the human rights situations in third countries through embassies, supporting human rights defenders and engaging in capacity development of governments and NGOs to deal with human rights issues. In addition, there are more 'punitive'/confrontational measures that can be taken to effect change in the conduct of another state in the field of human rights, such as suspending or threatening the suspension of cooperation in other fields or even the entire diplomatic relations.

The decision of what tool should be used and when depends very much on the overall situation, including on the attitude and political will of the state concerned. In case the state concerned is open to address its human rights challenges in a cooperative manner, pursuing constructive and confidential dialogues on human rights questions, supplemented by concrete technical cooperation can be the most promising strategy. Meanwhile, the strategy employed to address a deteriorating human rights situation or individual cases in rather uncooperative countries is one of escalation, i.e. starting with the milder, usually confidential tools, moving to stronger, public and even confrontational measures, if necessary.

Engaging in human rights diplomacy at the bilateral level successfully requires sensitivity and adequate knowledge of the specific situation, its background, its dynamics and possible cultural issues involved. Action must always be based on reliable information. In this context, it is also important to identify the right entity, body or actor within the state concerned, and not to confine interaction to ministries of foreign affairs. In case it is planned to take measures on behalf of individuals, it is important to clarify whether these measures are in the best interest of the individuals by consulting them directly or those close to them.

Human rights diplomacy at the bilateral level cannot be separated from human rights diplomacy at the regional and multilateral (UN) level. First, bilateral human rights diplomacy can support multilateral processes and mandates. Bilateral action can urge other states to cooperate with multilateral mechanisms, e.g. the universal periodic review (UPR) process of the UN HRC, the special procedures mandate-holders of the HRC and the UN treaty bodies (TMBs). Bilateral human rights diplomacy can also encourage other states to request OHCHR technical cooperation or establish OHCHR field presence. Second, the output from multilateral processes can be used in bilateral human rights diplomacy, such as concluding observations of TMBs, resolutions of the HRC, outcome documents of the UPR, etc. In particular the impact of the HRC's activities could be improved considerably through greater diplomatic support at the bilateral level. Third, the interaction with the multilateral and regional level is an important tool for bilateral human rights diplomacy. For example, if bilateral efforts do not produce the desired results, the issue can be raised at the regional or multilateral level; in return, it can also be offered to discontinue an initiative at multilateral or regional level, in case progress is achieved or certain benchmarks are met.

One of the main challenges for bilateral human rights diplomacy is to ensure its coherence and consistency. A tendency is observed that the instruments of bilateral diplomacy are used in an uneven and uncoordinated way. For example, there are no criteria or guidelines for when states take diplomatic action for human rights. Often, diplomats and politicians do not possess sufficient knowledge on human rights issues, and too little efforts are being made to invest in building their sustained human rights capacity. Bilateral human rights diplomacy is too reactive, inconsistent and not sustainable, concentrating on action related to specific cases or (topical) issues that are pushed forward by actors at national level. Bilateral diplomatic initiatives are also not always coordinated with initiatives of other bilateral, regional or multilateral actors or mechanisms. Thus, the need to develop a systematic and long-term approach in bilateral human rights diplomacy that helps to set priorities, to make strategic choices and to ensure the transparency of this process, is beyond question.

Another main challenge for bilateral human rights diplomacy remains the question of how to ensure its credibility and to avoid the reproach of applying double-standards. It largely depends on how states deal with their own human rights issues—in particular to what extent they are open to external scrutiny of their own human rights record and are prepared to respond to criticism and recommendations by regional and multilateral bodies/mechanisms. To name but a few examples: many high-income states are late with reporting to UN TMBs and take at best half-hearted measures to implement the concluding observations of these bodies and so far very few high-income countries ratified the Convention on the Protection of the Rights of Migrant Workers. This prevents high-income states to 'lead by example.' Credibility is also undermined when there is little or no willingness to allow for reciprocity in human rights diplomacy or when too little effort is made to seriously engage with the agenda of the other party. In this connection it is desirable to put the notion of partnership and mutual review to the centre of bilateral human rights diplomacy.

Foreign policy in other areas not directly related to human rights, for instance trade, energy and security policies as well as the Common Agricultural Policy (for EU member states) can weaken the credibility of human rights diplomacy. Diplomatic initiatives to promote and protect human rights must therefore be supported at high political level, and must be an integral part of overall foreign policy. It has to be made sure that human rights diplomacy is not 'outsourced' to a few human rights experts, but that it is mainstreamed into all aspects of foreign policy. One step towards the resolving of credibility issues is to achieve a better coordination and cooperation between diplomatic initiatives of bilateral, regional and multilateral human rights mechanism so that initiatives at one level can step in when the credibility of initiatives at another level has been questioned.

The question of how to measure the impact of states' bilateral human rights diplomacy remains a further challenge. Effectiveness of diplomatic initiatives for human rights is difficult to determine, and depends very much on the responsiveness of the state concerned. No quantitative and qualitative data is available for assessing the effectiveness of human rights diplomacy, and no systematic review of good and bad practices in bilateral human rights diplomacy has been conducted so far.

3.3 The Practice of Multilateral (UN) Human Rights Diplomacy by States

There is a fundamental difference between bilateral and multilateral human rights diplomacy of states: bilateral human rights diplomacy has been used almost exclusively by high-income countries to advance the protection of human rights in other states. By contrast, multilateral human rights diplomacy brings together all states to discuss and build a common standard for the protection of individuals (and groups). Assisting each other in the implementation of these common standards through various activities including but not limited to monitoring and building governmental capacity in the field of human rights is also part of multilateral human rights diplomacy. Multilateral human rights diplomacy reflects states' collective responsibility for the promotion and protection of human rights.

The UPR process of the UN HRC which treats all states in the same way will contribute to the building of a truly collectively owned human rights system, including a common sense of responsibility for the promotion and protection of human rights. The fact that many countries of the 'Global South' have developed some sense of common ownership of the HRC—even if not always in a way as desired by human rights professionals—can be seen as a first step into this direction. In this context, it is also positively noticed that the participation of ambassadors in the work of the HRC, in particular in the UPR, has become more intense recently, notably if compared to the rather low level of ambassadors' participation in the procedures of the former UN Commission on Human Rights. Nevertheless, the HRC could go further and organise more special sessions and *ad hoc* briefings, and not just adopt resolutions.

The possible role of the OHCHR in multilateral human rights diplomacy by states was examined further. Even though OHCHR has already been compiling reports that serve as the basis for UPR process and has contributed greatly to 'set it going', it was noted that the OHCHR could play a more proactive role to help increase the positive output of the process. Suggestions to achieve this ranged from OHCHR giving legal expert advice to all actors involved in the UPR process; to give states who review the human rights performance of other states the opportunity to obtain information about the states concerned from OHCHR, for example by letting OHCHR give briefing sessions on the human rights records of states that are due to be reviewed in the UPR process; to allow OHCHR to bring up its own issues into the UPR process; to make sure that the output of the UPR does not undermine established human rights norms or contradict the findings of TMBs; and to support the implementation of the output of the UPR. The latter has to involve other UN agencies, in particular UN country teams.

The trend of states acting in blocks rather than in their individual capacity as states within the HRC has upsides and downsides. On the one hand, it can speed up the finding of a consensus; and blocks that are formed around thematic issues can contribute to bringing and/or to keeping an issue on the agenda. On the other hand, acting in regional blocks can prevent true debates on human rights issues, in particular when it is doubtful whether the finding of the consensus within a block is the outcome of a thorough consultation process. Another danger is that the formation of thematic blocks on controversial human rights issues can generate the formation of strong 'anti-blocks' which hardens fronts rather than bringing the issue forward and promoting the finding of a consensus. Moreover, blocks seem to strengthen the 'giving-taking' format of diplomacy that should, at the end of the day, be oriented on human rights protection.

Diplomacy in the multilateral (UN) space should also become more inclusive with regard to the actors involved. NGOs, NHRIs, trade unions, parliamentarians and possibly private actors from all regions shall be included in the work of the HRC. Some participants noted, in addition, that the UN in general and its human rights system in particular should become more accessible to ordinary people, for example through the establishment of a 'UN people's assembly'. Making use of the multi-stakeholder approach (see below, pp.275–76) seems to be a promising undertaking to address this challenge.

Multilateral human rights diplomacy by states is often not sufficiently effective in dealing with urgent issues, such as new human rights challenges or gross violations of human rights. Based on states' common responsibility to protect human rights it was suggested that in such situations there has to be a strong 'reign of ambassadors', pushing for action together with the UN High Commissioner for Human Rights, her Office and the UN Secretary-General. A current issue with regard to which such a 'reign of ambassadors' would be desirable is an initiative to make the Durban Review Conference in April 2009 a success.

Non-implementation and non-compliance with resolutions and other documents of the HRC are also among the great challenges for multilateral human rights diplomacy. Systematising follow-up activities at all levels by all actors, including through enhanced cooperation with and support from other UN bodies and agencies working on the ground could contribute to reducing the 'implementation gap'.

A further big challenge multilateral human rights diplomacy by states has to engage with, are attempts of some states to work towards the erosion of well-established human rights norms and principles, downright undermining the effectiveness of the UN human rights system. There is no clear strategy to meet this challenge. However, on the positive side, there are also states that became strong human rights advocates recently, making positive contributions to the work of the multilateral human rights mechanisms.

The meetings of states parties to different universal human rights treaties could be used in a better way as a forum for multilateral human rights diplomacy. Opportunities for discussion are missed in these meetings where representatives of many states come together, when their action is limited to electing members for the TMB of the treaty in question.

Conference diplomacy

Another forum for multilateral human rights diplomacy by states is the holding of world conferences on human rights. World conferences offer a forum for exchange among states and other actors involved in human rights work which are usually not interacting on the same level, can contribute to confidence building and the forming of important alliances (see also below, pp.275–76 on the multi-stakeholder approach). World conferences can be a trigger for worldwide public mobilisation on specific human rights issues and they can contribute to the development of international human rights law through the adoption of a concluding document. Actors at national level can use these documents as a reference point for their daily work. Conference diplomacy can be in particular useful for pushing issues forward that cannot be discussed in the normal UN framework.

Risks of conference diplomacy were also identified: there is always a risk that world conferences fail to produce an outcome, or that the outcome only reflects the lowest common denominator which does at best prevent receiving setbacks on a certain question. The work of permanent bodies and mechanisms with a specific mandate to promote and protect human rights can be duplicated by human rights conferences, and the enormous efforts and resources required for organising and following-up on world conferences may outweigh the benefits they may bring. Procedures at world conferences can also turn out to be discriminatory against small or poor states.

3.4 The Practice of Multilateral Human Rights Diplomacy at the Regional Level

'Internal' human rights diplomacy of regional organisations

Human rights diplomacy involving organs of regional organisations (like the Council of Europe (CoE), the Organisation for Security and Co-operation in Europe (OSCE), the European Union, the Organisation of American States (OAS), the African Union (AU), the Association of Southeast Asian Nations (ASEAN) and the Arab League), their member states and other actors from the region has certain advantages over bilateral and multilateral (UN) human rights diplomacy, and can complement human rights diplomacy at these two other levels.

Regional mechanisms for the promotion and protection of human rights are usually perceived as more effective than international mechanisms. This is based on various facts, including the following: regional mechanism relate more closely to regionally shared values and priorities; they are more responsive to region-specific human rights problems; they can relate human rights more easily to other issues, such as questions of regional security; and they are easier accessible for a whole range of actors than the multilateral (UN) system. Their work is usually broader and goes deeper than that of multilateral mechanisms: regional mechanisms 'interfere' to a greater extent at the national level of their member states, for instance through election observation (in Europe/Central Asia, the OSCE observes election, an activity that is no longer pursued by the UN) or through the establishment of regional human rights courts. Regional mechanisms also have a greater network with actors on the ground and are often directly present in every member state. These and other factors contribute to the stronger political will of states to conform to decisions of regional bodies.

Regional organisations can also prevent their member states from engaging in bilateral diplomatic action that is detrimental to the promotion and protection of human rights in third states. For example, when one member state of the EU has a particularly strong interest with regard to a third state that would normally cause diplomatic action overriding human rights diplomacy, internal pressure from the organs of the EU and other member states can prevent this. This is particularly promising in areas where the EU has adopted clear human rights policy guidelines on which all member states have agreed. Sometimes, however, the EU can also prevent (good) bilateral human rights diplomacy initiatives when member states wait for the EU to act, but such action is never taken, whatever the reasons.

In addition to the mentioned challenges faced at multilateral (UN) level (see above, pp.269–70), 'internal' regional human rights diplomacy encounters the following problems: First, there is a danger that regional mechanisms unnecessarily duplicate the work of multilateral (UN) or national mechanisms and *vice versa*, and therefore place a needless burden on states' resources. However, not all duplication should be seen as negative, since some duplication may be necessary to effect change. An example is the prevention of torture: despite the existence of multiple multilateral (UN), regional and national monitoring mechanisms for its prevention, there is no country in the world that eradicated torture completely.

Second, the existence of regional and global mechanisms opens the possibility for states to pick and chose the 'easiest' mechanism(s), and to avoid cooperation with the 'harder' ones (forum shopping). Better coordination and interaction between multilateral (UN), regional and national mechanisms can help to prevent unnecessary duplication as well as forum shopping by states.

And third, states prevent regional human rights mechanisms to develop their full capacity, for example by appointing or electing less competent staff which is further encouraged by the trading of votes among governments. Budgets of regional mechanisms are kept low by intent.

'External' human rights diplomacy of regional organisations

Regional organisations, in particular the EU, also pursue human rights diplomacy towards third states. Many of the instruments and tools at the EU's disposal are similar to those of bilateral human rights diplomacy (see above, p.267). The same is true for the challenges faced by the EU human rights diplomacy (see above, pp.268–69). However, there are some tools and challenges that are specific to EU human rights diplomacy.

The EU conducts regular human rights dialogues with third states. Currently, around thirty human rights dialogues between the EU and third states are ongoing. Even though EU guidelines provide that dialogues should be established with countries which are willing and committed to improving their human rights performance, this is interpreted very broadly and dialogues are held with 'difficult' countries as well. Human rights dialogues can be a very successful tool when the partner is open and willing to engage into true dialogue. On the other hand, dialogues with more 'difficult' countries can consist largely of stonewalling, longwinded presentations devoid of substance or attacks on the EU. Some states also use the fact that dialogues exist to avoid discussing human rights in other meetings, or claim that the existence of a dialogue with the EU makes it no longer necessary for them to cooperate with other regional or UN procedures. In cases where human rights dialogues fail to produce any result the EU can suspend them, based on the findings of regular reviews of the dialogues. In practice, however, the EU is reluctant to suspend dialogues, since they are preferred to taking a more confrontational approach or to closing all channels to possibly influence the human rights situation in a particular third country.

Through the European Instrument for Democracy and Human Rights (EIDHR) the European Commission funds civil society organisations worldwide that promote human rights. This is an innovative and successful tool of human rights diplomacy with regard to some third countries since it recognises the role of non-state actors in the promotion and protection of human rights and aims to better integrate them into the process of implementing human rights at local levels. Some states, however, regard the EIDHR an interference with their domestic affairs, and create obstacles for EU funds to reach civil society organisations.

Financial cooperation directly with cooperative governments can also be a very effective tool for EU human rights diplomacy, as many human rights violations stem from lack of capacity. A challenge in this context is to prevent third states from stripping out all sensitive elements from projects, undermining all chances for true success.

The EU also tries to link its efforts to promote and protect human rights to other areas of its external policies, in particular to trade policies. This provides a higher degree of leverage for EU human rights diplomacy. Access to GSP (Generalised System of Preferences) is linked in negative (possible withdrawal of GSP benefits) or positive (granting additional GSP+) ways to a particular country's human rights performance. However, sanctions related to the GSP regulation have not been used very frequently so far, and the credibility of the mechanism is questioned by the fact that many countries with poor human rights records continue to benefit from it.

The European Parliament is involved in human rights diplomacy with third states. It adopts resolutions on human rights situations in third countries and organises missions to third countries. It also acts as a watchdog over the human rights diplomacy of the Council of the EU and the European Commission. At times, the activities of the European Parliament in the field of human rights diplomacy are highly unpredictable since not all MPs are 'human rights minded' and may have other legitimate interests, for example trade links between their constituency and a third country.

EU human rights diplomacy is most effective with regard to human rights issues on which there is a broad internal consensus among member states. This is usually the case in areas where human rights guidelines have been adopted that define a policy objective and identify means to pursue it. Examples are the guidelines on the death penalty and the prohibition of torture. In human rights questions where there is little or no internal consensus among EU member states initiating diplomatic action can be a difficult and very slow process, since 27 EU member states have to engage in a consultative process before action can be taken. The adoption of human rights guidelines for other areas may therefore be advantageous.

Due to this requirement of consensus before external action can be taken, it remains particularly difficult for the EU to react quickly to crisis situations or new challenges for the implementation of human rights. This is reinforced by the fact that the EU was not originally founded with the aim to promote and protect human rights through external policies, but to harmonise economic and trade policies among its member states. The EU therefore also faces difficulties to speak with one voice or to initiate action on human rights issues within global forums, including in the UN HRC. As for bilateral human rights diplomacy, one of the main challenges for EU human rights diplomacy is its credibility (see above, pp.268–69).

Different regional organisations also engage in dialogues on human rights (inter-regional human rights diplomacy). For instance, regular Asia-Europe Meetings (ASEM) are held between the EU and ten ASEAN countries, among them China. Every other year ASEM includes a dialogue on specific human rights issues. ASEM-dialogues are not limited to dialogues among diplomats or politicians, but every country delegation should include an NGO or trade union representative and an academic representative, in addition to a representative of the government. This particular format of the ASEM-dialogues has contributed to more thorough discussions as governments cannot give an embellished account of the human rights situation in their countries without being corrected by other members of their delegations. Similarly, regular Euro-Arab-Dialogues bring together government representatives of member states of the EU and the Arab League, NGOs, academics and religious representatives from both regions to discuss different human rights issues.

Generally, such inter-regional multi-stakeholder dialogues could benefit from better preparation, a clearly structured agenda and carefully selected participants who have sufficient competence in relevant fields. There is also a need to follow-up on the results of these dialogues in order to ensure continuity and impact.

Inter-regional human rights diplomacy between other regional organisations such as the AU, ASEAN, OAS, the Arab League, OSCE or CoE could be encouraged.

Multi-stakeholder approach and multi-track diplomacy

While the ASEM- and Euro-Arab-Dialogues already include actors beyond governmental representatives, human rights diplomacy at all levels could benefit from better inclusion of other actors, such as NGOs, academic institutions, parliamentarians, church groups and business in addition to representatives of governments and intergovernmental organisations. In this respect, the multi-stakeholder approach and the theory of multi-track diplomacy which have been successfully applied in other fields, such as the governance of information society, the solution of environmental problems and peace and security, can offer useful insights for human rights diplomacy. The inclusivity of the multi-stakeholder approach could enhance the legitimacy, efficacy and quality of human rights diplomacy.

The multi-stakeholder approach and the concept of multi-track diplomacy aim to involve all relevant stakeholders on a largely equal level, to discuss commonly identified problems in an open and pervasive debate and to generate responses. An example is the multi-stakeholder approach to the governance of the information society, as it can be observed in the Internet Governance Forum (IGF) established after the World Summit on the Information Society in Geneva 2003 and Tunis 2005.

Even though results from these multi-stakeholder discussions may be less visible than those of other multilateral meetings, they deploy their effect through the participants who take them back to their respective context or institution. The wider network of actors involved in multi-stakeholder negotiations can also ease the implementation of the outcome of such negotiations, since ideally the inclusive discussions should have increased the knowledge about and degree of identification with them.

Reviewing the rich experience from different multi-stakeholder/multi-track diplomacy events and identifying good and bad practices could benefit future projects of a similar nature including in the field of multilateral and regional human rights diplomacy.

3.5 The Practice of Human Rights Diplomacy by Inter-governmentally Appointed Office Holders

The role of the UN High Commissioner and her Office

The UN High Commissioner and her Office (OHCHR) have a moral, a political and an administrative task which are sometimes not easy to reconcile. With minimal funds, OHCHR has to hold together an office that has to facilitate and coordinate the work the different bodies of the UN human rights system, to engage with states at the country level and to react to the human rights dimension of crises and new threats.

The High Commissioner should develop her own strong identity and exercise leadership in human rights diplomacy with the support of her Office. She should spearhead and coordinate human rights diplomacy at all levels, in partnership with regional and national actors. The High Commissioner should initiate diplomatic action in particular in times of crisis, to prevent gross violations of human rights and to expose and address the human rights dimensions of new challenges, such as the food emergency, the global financial crisis, climate change or cloning. She should have the means to call on the responsibility and accountability of actors at different levels, and in particular activate adequate responses by the HRC and other UN bodies and agencies. However, to exercise this leadership function, the High Commissioner and her Office need the ongoing political support of states, regional organisations, the UN Secretary-General and other UN bodies and agencies. The High Commissioner needs routine access to the UN Security Council and a considerable presence on the ground through her Office. OHCHR also needs to be present with regional organisations to activate or support leadership at regional level in situations where this seems more appropriate than exercising leadership herself.

OHCHR should focus on the prevention of human rights violations by supporting the building of national protection systems if it wants to truly affect the difference in the lives of people that human rights promise to make. This requires, *inter alia*, entering into dialogues about the best ways to implement universal human rights in specific local contexts. To this end, OHCHR should strongly partner with states, advise them on their possibilities to implement human rights, ideally through increased presence in the field. Field presence expansion, however, is limited by resource constraints as well as by a 'push-back' in inter-governmental fora against the operationalisation of human rights mainstreaming on the ground. OHCHR therefore has to develop good contacts and modes of cooperation with UN country teams which can further the implementation of human rights with OHCHR's advice. Related to this is OHCHR's immense 'internal' human rights diplomacy task with regard to other UN bodies and agencies: to mainstream human rights into the work of all UN bodies and agencies so that they can all become involved in human rights diplomacy.

Focussing on the prevention of human rights violations would also require OHCHR to establish early-warning mechanisms that assist in identifying hot spots and factors that could lead to gross violations of human rights. Greater attention to systematic discrimination and violations of economic, social and cultural rights could be useful in this regard. OHCHR should also support the entities of the international criminal justice system and regional conflict prevention mechanisms by working toward putting human rights into the centre of their work.

OHCHR should develop into a 'centre of expertise' on human rights issues. This could be facilitated by a review of good practice of the implementation of human rights at all levels and by bringing the output of such review to the attention of states and other actors. For this, the OHCHR does not only need a larger, reliable budget, it should also develop a more complete doctrine of human rights diplomacy that can guide its actions. This would contribute to enhancing the authority of the OHCHR, and states may become more inclined to approach the OHCHR to obtain its independent advice on the implementation of human rights (OHCHR as a 'trusted guardian').

Reviewing the experience and success of the OSCE High Commissioner on National Minorities (HCNM) could give some inspiration of how OHCHR's performance could be improved. However, it must be kept in mind that one aspect of the successful work of the HCNM in the late 1990s was the rather unusual openness and willingness of Eastern European governments to engage with regional mechanisms. Human rights are rarely a priority at the highest political level—a fact that regularly challenges the chances for successful human rights diplomacy by OHCHR.

Experience of the OSCE High Commissioner on National Minorities

While the OSCE HCNM is not a High Commissioner for the promotion and protection of human rights but a security mechanism, it makes wide use of human rights treaties in its work. This is based on the insight that conflict prevention, security and the protection of human rights are inextricably linked. Human rights are normative and therefore describe ends which guide the HCNM's work, linking them up with mechanisms for conflict and dispute resolution.

Much of the success of the HCNM is based on the fact that it manages to 'be inside the state' and to directly assist states in finding practicable and creative solutions to the problems and conflicts they experience. The HCNM is involved in drafting national laws, treaties and even political accords, in developing national policies, in the building of strong national institutions and engages with political parties. A very good understanding of the process of governance at all levels, including the roles and functions of different institutions and the way of thinking and interests of politicians is an important precondition for allowing such direct involvement in the making of substantive policies. HCNM interacts with all state institutions. At the same time, sufficient subject-specific knowledge about the problem to be solved is required for HCNM to influence solutions.

Human rights law plays an important role in the HCNM's work. It sets limits to negotiable points, and is used as an overall framework to generate solutions. Since governments have agreed on human rights in international negotiations in their peoples' interests, human rights are a legitimate framework for the shaping of national policies and solving of problems. Efforts are made to recall to government officials that the implementation of human rights is actually in their interest. In other words, HCNM recognises the interest-based approach of politics and tries to utilise it for the implementation of human rights.

Often it is unclear how human rights norms work in a specific case, and therefore ways to implement them need to be clarified. Developing guidelines on different possibilities for the implementation of human rights can be useful in this regard, and can be achieved by reviewing practice, jurisprudence, resolutions and documents of relevant bodies, etc. Sometimes such process of specification can result in the creation of further norms. The more precise and practical the guidance for the implementation of a particular norm can be made for a specific situation, the more likely governments are to follow the suggestion. Knowledge of 'what works' is very important in this context. At the same time, this specification of human rights norms for implementation at the national level is crucial to fulfil the promise of human rights to give every individual the chance to live a life in freedom and dignity (closing of the implementation gap).

Effective coordination and cooperation with other actors is also an important component of success in the work of the HCNM. Knowledge and understanding of the functioning, activities and assets of other multilateral, regional and national actors and regular exchange and dialogue with them is central in this regard. Through maintaining contacts with other actors, a fourth or fifth party can be brought in easily by HCNM if the situation so requires ('joining hands—linking arms').

From the work of the NCHM it is clear that sufficient and stable funding of inter-governmentally appointed office holders is important for their work. The effective use of these funds is equally important. Frequently, there may also be various possibilities to mobilise funds from outside sources.

Role of the UN Secretary-General

Human rights diplomacy by the UN Secretary-General may have a decisive impact on the integration of human rights into inter-state dialogue and the placement of human rights high on the agenda of international fora. Making human rights an integral part of Secretary-General's good offices and conflict-resolution proposals would be a convincing strategy to link human rights with the UN's peace efforts. As far as in-house diplomacy is concerned, the determination of the Secretary-General to link human rights with peace and development is a prerequisite for a successful mainstreaming of human rights within the UN system. In coordination and cooperation with the UN High Commissioner and her Office, the UN Secretary-General could also initiate diplomatic action on the promotion and protection of human rights. The Secretary-General should fully support all diplomatic action of OHCHR. Depending on the situation at hand, it has to be decided whether the UN Secretary-General or the High Commissioner should act first.

3.6 Human Right Diplomacy by Other Actors

Academic institutions

Academic institutions are involved in human rights diplomacy through different activities that can greatly contribute to the prevention of human rights violations and the building of a 'human rights culture'. For example, the Raul Wallenberg Institute has established an educational human rights programme in Beijing. It has negotiated with the Chinese government since the mid-1990, and was able to open an office in 2001. It supports the 'Research Direction in Human Rights' at Beijing University Law School, trains university lecturers in various aspects of human rights as well as teachers in the National Prosecutors College, has developed a Chinese-language textbook on human rights with the collection of international and Chinese human rights jurisprudence and it promotes the creation of a Chinese NHRI.

Another role of academics in human rights diplomacy is their inclusion into human rights dialogues, conferences or other interactive processes on human rights issues at the governmental level. Their involvement can, for example, prevent 'diplomatic superficiality' of dialogues, since academics are more likely to speak open about problems, and may have thought through problems and solutions more carefully than diplomats. On the other hand, there is a risk that dialogues are blocked by sensitive states when the suggestion is made to include academics.

Non-governmental organisations

Many activities of NGOs can be described as human rights diplomacy, since they involve elements of negotiations and discussions with policy makers to effect change. However, there rarely is an element of reciprocity in the interaction between NGOs and governmental officials or representatives of intergovernmental organisations.

Rooted in their focus on fact-finding and monitoring, and the related lack of expertise of how to engage in diplomatic action, NGOs were particularly affected by the mentioned hesitation of many human rights professionals to engage in diplomacy that might compromise human rights standards (see above, pp.266–67). However, NGOs largely recognised that bringing about change requires action beyond naming and shaming, including the provision of assistance in finding solutions entailing discussion and negotiation.

Different roles of NGOs in human rights diplomacy complementing the actions of others were discussed:

First, NGOs can instigate human rights diplomacy by exposing certain facts, and call upon those responsible to take necessary action.

Second, NGOs can shape debates by taking strong positions. This can provide support within internal policy debates for those seeking to push for strong human rights positions, and allows them to demand vigorous action from the government.

Third, NGOs can become involved in human rights diplomacy behind the scenes in situations where there is no direct space for NGO engagement. This can include assisting governments to prepare for negotiations on human rights related issues, providing information and language for resolutions, agreements, etc. or pushing key issues into the public domain with the help of the media.

Fourth, in situations where NGO involvement is permitted at some level, NGOs can participate directly in negotiations or convince governments of their position and encourage them to put it on the table.

Fifth, NGOs act as lobbyists or advocates pushing those involved in human rights diplomacy to take a particular position. The lack of reciprocity is sometimes a problem in this type of action, but it can be compensated by offering information or expertise, or by applying public pressure. Public advocacy is one of the most essential tools for human rights diplomacy by NGOs, since it helps to keep the discussion focused and honest, promoting outcomes that address the underlying problems or threats.

Sixth, NGOs' monitoring functions are vital for their own successful engagement in human rights diplomacy and that of other actors. Through monitoring, human rights dimensions of certain policies can be exposed, the true motivation of certain actors involved in human rights diplomacy can be disclosed, shortcomings in the implementation of human rights can be revealed and those accountable for such failures can be identified.

Last, NGOs can be beneficiaries of human rights diplomacy, for instance when diplomatic action is taken by other actors on behalf of NGOs or human rights defenders.

UN agencies (UNICEF)

Human rights diplomacy of the UN Children's Fund (UNICEF) is centred on the support of the implementation of the Convention on the Rights of the Child (CRC). The CRC contains a reference to UNICEF which legitimises UNICEF's activities in this field and establishes the organisation's accountability. With the focus on children's rights, often perceived as less political than human rights in general, diplomatic action by UNICEF has a considerable potential for success. Children's rights diplomacy can generally serve as a good entry point for human rights diplomacy, in particular with regard to countries that are less open to human rights.

While in the early 1990s UNICEF focused on the promotion of universal ratification of the CRC, this focus shifted towards the support for its implementation. This includes the following activities: UNICEF supports governments in the preparation of their periodic reports to the CRC-Committee. To make the process of the preparation of these reports as inclusive as possible,

UNICEF encourages the participation of all relevant governmental institutions, NGOs, academic institutions, other UN agencies, etc. UNICEF facilitates country visits of members of the CRC-Committee for the purpose of the promotion of the Committee's concluding observations and a discussion on their implementation. Through its projects, UNICEF also provides technical assistance for the implementation of concluding observations. By compiling and disseminating the concluding observations and general comments of the CRC-Committee at national levels, UNICEF enhances the visibility of the Committee. Furthermore, UNICEF provides direct support to the Committee by briefing its new members and by giving independent information on specific countries. UNICEF has also participated in further standard setting on children's rights.

The adoption of the CRC and UNICEF's involvement in diplomatic action for its implementation also had important internal implications for UNICEF's work. Through the process of mainstreaming, human rights were brought into every aspect of UNICEF's work. UNICEF adopted a statement of commitment on human rights, issued guiding principles for staff and provided for staff training in human rights issues.

The challenge was to transform the normative into operational tools that could be used to effect the implementation of children's rights through UNICEF's activities. Human rights principles began to reshape UNICEF's country programme guidance, bridging commitments and legal obligations undertaken by states with action to promote their concrete implementation. Supporting the drafting of national legislation on child protection, collection of clearly disaggregated data allowing the detection of any form of discrimination, focusing on particularly marginalised groups of children and promoting national ownership of programmes through consultative processes are only a few examples of the results of this process. One of the greatest challenges in the process remains not to replace a country's leadership and ownership in the implementation of children's rights (involving governmental institutions, local NGOs and other actors).

Another difficulty faced by UNICEF is the question of how, when and in which forum 'sensitive issues' should be raised. Questions related to the security of the persons concerned, including UNICEF' staff and the organisation's credibility are connected to this difficulty. There is no guidance on when to express concern privately and to engage in dialogue to solve the issue, when to issue a public statement or even a condemnation with a threat to suspend the programme. It is also unclear whether the matter can be referred to another UN agency of body.

UN treaty bodies

UN human rights treaty bodies, in addition to their quasi-judicial function, engage in 'constructive dialogues' with states based on states' periodic reports on their efforts to implement human rights treaties. TMBs adopt their concluding observations delineating suggestions to states of how to improve the implementation of human rights. This diplomatic work of TMBs, focussing on the outlining of policy options for the implementation of human rights has had some success. Surveys from different countries suggest that the overall compliance with concluding observations is quite significant. Given the strong tradition of consensus in the work of TMBs as well as their limited meeting-time and budget, adopting a judicial model with which to asses this aspect of TMB work seems to be unrealistic and inappropriate.

Diplomatic tools can be integrated further in the work of the UN TMBs, for example through the inclusion of additional actors in the 'constructive dialogue'. To enhance the specificity and practicality of concluding observations, it would also be desirable to increase the number of TMB members who have a sound understanding of how governments work. Furthermore, TMB members should change their perception of the role of OHCHR: they should not merely see it as their secretariat, but as a diplomatic partner for the promotion of human rights at the country level.

3.7 Future Challenges and Opportunities for Human Rights Diplomacy

As long as criticism or recommendations from outside actors relating to violations or (non-)implementation of human rights within states are seen as something negative, more often than not provoking defensive moves, skilful diplomatic action is required to press ahead with the implementation of human rights. Equally, the recognition that the implementation of human rights is an ongoing process that requires incremental approaches highlights the need for continuous dialogues and negotiations among different actors to identify the best ways to move forward at a time. Both insights point to the importance of diplomatic action for the promotion and protection of human rights.

With this in mind, the following challenges and opportunities for human rights diplomacy and for pursuing this discussion on human rights diplomacy were identified at the end of the workshop:

Achieving true inclusiveness: applying the multi-stakeholder approach to human rights diplomacy seems to be a promising strategy to improve its outreach, effectiveness and legitimacy. In addition to actors discussed, the role of NHRIs, business, local governments, cities, health institutions, educational institutions, the legal profession, etc. in human rights diplomacy could be further explored. The regional, inter-regional and global linking between NGOs, the value of unexpected alliances and peer processes (e.g. peer cities) and their relevance for human rights diplomacy could be examined. The analysis of human rights diplomacy by other national and regional actors beyond the European ones would be desirable. For example, the potential of the 'Global South' to become a 'generator' (participant) of human rights diplomacy and to leave behind its primary role as a 'recipient' should be explored further. The gender dimension of human rights diplomacy should also be discussed. With regard to this project, an inclusive approach would require a wider representation from other geographical regions and regional organisations beyond Europe and North America.

Conditions of effectiveness: while these have to be explored further in a review of practices of human rights diplomacy, the following conditions contribute to its effectiveness: a credible status of the actors which includes that they have a clear understanding of themselves, a clear purpose, an achievable mission or outcome and the presence of open-mindedness and trust. The latter requires the willingness to engage with the position of the other party, i.e. a strong attitude of respect towards one another. Without trust, human rights diplomacy can quickly create a defensive siege mentality between the parties, and undermine the main aim of human rights diplomacy to build the counterpart's ownership of human rights. For actors working on the ground, it is essential to deploy human rights literate and sensitive staff that is able to bring norms together with wisdom of programming for the effective implementation of human rights in specific local contexts.

What shall human rights diplomacy take on? There are many areas where human rights do not command the thinking, but where human rights are relevant. Including these areas in human rights diplomacy needs engagement with other large professional constituencies that have another culture and values and that are not familiar with human rights. Thus, it requires a human rights diplomacy which recognises that human rights are advanced alongside with other aims. In such cases, a 'listening diplomacy' to create conditions for engagement seems to be an appropriate first step.

Identify criteria for success and failure: a review of good and bad practice in human rights diplomacy could help to identify models of good practice.

Coherence and consistency: the complexity of multi-layered human rights diplomacy is huge, and it is questionable whether coherence and consistency in human rights diplomacy is achievable, in particular because actions taken by different actors will always be based on political assessments. However, there is a need for a collective endeavour of different actors towards reinforcing each other's actions ('orchestration'), and strategies for effective sequencing of diplomatic action should be explored. One could also think in systems of cross-referral. In any case, human rights diplomacy may sometimes look less consistent from the outside than it in fact is, due to issues of confidentiality.

4. Workshop Programme

Friday, 30 January 2009

9.30 Opening Session

Welcome on behalf of institutional organisers

Preliminary overview: what human rights diplomacy is about

Introduction of workshop participants

Presenters:

George Ulrich, *Senior Research Fellow, EIUC*

Michael O'Flaherty, *Professor of Applied Human Rights, University of Nottingham; Member of UN Human Rights Committee*

Dzidek Kędzia, *Professor of Constitutional Law, Adam Mickiewicz University of Poznan; Member of UN Committee on Economic, Social and Cultural Rights*

10.30 Coffee break

11.00 ***Session 2:***
Main contemporary forms of human rights diplomacy

Presenters:

KYUNG-WHA KANG, *Deputy UN High Commissioner for Human Rights*

MANFRED NOWAK, *Professor for International Human Rights, University of Vienna; UN Special Rapporteur on Torture*

DZIDEK KĘDZIA, *Professor of Constitutional Law, Adam Mickiewicz University of Poznan; Member of UN Committee on Economic, Social and Cultural Rights*

12.45 Lunch

14.30 ***Session 3:***
The practice of bilateral human rights diplomacy by States

Presenters:

ENGELBERT THEUERMANN, *Director for Human Rights, Federal Ministry for European and International Affairs, Austria*

FRANÇOIS ZIMERAY, *Ambassador for Human Rights, France*

16.00 Coffee break

16.30 ***Session 4:***
The practice of multilateral human rights diplomacy by States

Presenters:

VITIT MUNTARBHORN, *Professor of Law at Chulalongkorn University, Bangkok;*

UN Special Rapporteur on the situation of human rights in the Democratic People's Republic of Korea

LUIS ALFONSO DE ALBA, *Ambassador, Permanent Mission of Mexico to the United Nations and other International Organisations in Geneva*

18.00 End of Session

20.00 Dinner in Venice

Saturday, 31 January 2009

9.00 ***Session 5:***
The practice of multilateral human rights diplomacy at the regional level

Presenters:

SILVIA ESCOBAR, *Special Mission Ambassador for Human Rights, Spanish Ministry for Foreign Affairs*

CHRISTIAN STROHAL, *Ambassador, Permanent Mission of Austria to the United Nations and other International Organisations in Geneva*

WOLFGANG BENEDEK, *Professor, Institute of International Law and International Relations, University of Graz*

JEAN-PAUL JACQUÉ, *Honorary Director General and Special Counsellor, Council of the EU*

10.15 ***Session 6:***
The practice of human rights diplomacy by inter-governmentally appointed office holders

Presenters:

BERTRAND RAMCHARAN, *Former Acting UN High Commissioner for Human Rights*

JOHN PACKER, *Director, Human Rights Centre, University of Essex*

11.30 Coffee break

12.00 ***Session 7:***
Human rights diplomacy by other actors

Presenters:

HURST HANNUM, *Professor of International Law, The Fletcher School of Law and Diplomacy, Tufts University*

MARTA SANTOS PAIS, *Director, UNICEF-Innocenti Research Centre*

PEGGY HICKS, *Advocacy Director, Human Rights Watch*

MICHAEL O'FLAHERTY, *Member of the UN Human Rights Committee*

13.15 Lunch

15.00 ***Session 8:***
Future challenges and opportunities for human rights diplomacy

Presenters:

ROBERT ARCHER, *Executive Director, International Council of Human Rights Policy*

TIYANJANA MALUWA, *Associate Dean and Director of Penn State School of International Affairs*

IBRAHIM SALAMA, *Chief of Human Rights Treaty Branch, UN OHCHR*

16.30 Coffee break

17.00 ***Concluding session:***
Summary of conference findings and plenary discussion

18.00 End of Session

20.30 Dinner on Lido

5. List of Participants

Kalliope Agapiou-Josephides, *University of Cyprus*

Luis Alfonso de Alba, *Ambassador, Permanent Mission of Mexico to the United Nations and other International Organisations in Geneva*

Robert Archer, *Executive Director, International Council of Human Rights Policy*

Wolfgang Benedek, *Professor of International Law, Institute for International Law and International Relations, Karl-Franzens-Universität Graz*

Agnieszka Bienczyk-Missala, *Institute of International Relations, University of Warsaw*

Silvia Escobar, *Special Mission Ambassador for Human Rights, Spanish Ministry for Foreign Affairs*

Michelle Farrell, *E.MA Teaching Fellow*

Peggy Hicks, *Advocacy Director, Human Rights Watch*

Hurst Hannum, *Professor of International Law, The Fletcher School of Law and Diplomacy, Tufts University*

Jean-Paul Jacqué, *Honorary Director General and Special Counsellor, Council of the EU*

Kyung-wha Kang, *Deputy UN High Commissioner for Human Rights*

Dzidek Kedzia, *Professor of Constitutional Law, Adam Mickiewicz University of Poznan; Member of UN Committee on Economic, Social and Cultural Rights*

Tobias King, *DG Relex, European Commission*

Jean-Paul Lehners, *Professor of History, University of Luxembourg*

Tiyanjana Maluwa, *Associate Dean and Director of Penn State School of International Affairs*

Fabrizio Marrella, *E.MA Programme Director, EIUC*

Amrei Müller, *Human Rights Law Centre, University of Nottingham*

Vitit Muntarbhorn, *UN Special Rapporteur on the Situation of Human Rights in the Democratic People's Republic of Korea; Chulalongkorn University, Bangkok*

Manfred Nowak, *UN Special Rapporteur on Torture; Professor for International Human Rights, University of Vienna*

Michael O'Flaherty, *Professor of Applied Human Rights, University of Nottingham; Member of UN Human Rights Committee*

John Packer, *Director, Human Rights Centre, University of Essex*

Bertrand Ramcharan, *Former Acting UN High Commissioner for Human Rights*

Marta Santos Pais, *Director, UNICEF-Innocenti Research Centre*

Ibrahim Salama, *Chief of Human Rights Treaty Branch, UN OHCHR*

Anna Natalia Schulz, *E.MA Teaching Fellow*

Christian Strohal, *Ambassador, Permanent Mission of Austria to the United Nations and other International Organisations in Geneva*

Engelbert Theuermann, *Director for Human Rights, Federal Ministry for European and International Affairs, Austria*

George Ulrich, *Senior Research Fellow, EIUC*

SELECT BIBLIOGRAPHY

Baehr, P. R. and Castermans-Holleman, M., *The Role of Human Rights in Foreign Policy*, 3rd edn (The Hague: Palgrave Macmillan, 2004).

Bartels, L., *Human Rights Conditionality in the EU's International Agreements* (Oxford: Oxford University Press, 2005).

Bell, C., *Peace Agreements and Human Rights* (Oxford: Oxford University Press, 2000).

Benedek, W., 'EU Action on Human and Fundamental Rights in 2009', in W. Benedek *et al.* (eds.), *European Yearbook on Human Rights 2010* (Vienna/Antwerp, 2010).

Benedek, W., *et al.* (eds.), *Global Standards—Local Action. 15 Years Vienna World Conference on Human Rights*, Conference Proceedings of the International Expert Conference held in Vienna on 28 and 29 August 2008, 16 Studienreihe des Ludwig Boltzmann Instituts für Menschenrechte (Wien/Graz: NWV/Intersentia, 2009).

Berridge, G. R., *Diplomacy: Theory and Practice*, 4th edn, (Basingstoke: Palgrave Macmillan, 2010).

Boutros-Ghali, B., *Unvanquished. A U.S.—U.N. Saga* (New York: Random House, 1999).

Brett, R., 'The Role of NGOs—An Overview' in G. Alfredsson *et al* (eds.), *International Human Rights Monitoring Mechanisms: Essays in Honour of Jakob Th. Möller* (The Hague: Martinus Nijhoff, 2001), pp.845–58.

Chigas, D., 'Preventive Diplomacy and the Organisation for Security and Co-operation in Europe: Creating Incentives for Dialogue and Co-operation' in A. Chayes and H. Chayes (eds.), *Preventing Conflict in the Post-Communist Wold. Mobilizing International and Regional Organizations* (Washington: Brookings Institute, 1996).

Claude, R. P. and Weston, B. (eds.), *Human Rights in the World Community* (Philadelphia: University of Pennsylvania Press, 1992).

Constantinou, C. M., *Human Diplomacy and Spirituality*, Discussion Papers in Diplomacy, 2006, available at: http://www.clingendael.nl/publications/2006/20060400_cli_paper_dip_issue103.pdf.

De Feyter, K., Parmentier, S., Timmerman, C. and Ulrich, G. (eds.), *The Local Relevance of Human Rights* (Cambridge: Cambridge University Press (forthcoming 2011)).

Diamond L. and McDonald, J., *Multi-Track Diplomacy: A Systems Approach to Peace* (Sterling, VA: Kumarian Press, 1996).

Dickson, B., 'Law, Diplomacy and Conflict: State Crises and the Role of the European Convention on Human Rights' (unpublished paper delivered at a conference on The Diplomacy of Human Rights, 7 December 2007, co-organised by the Irish Centre for Human Rights and University of Paris II).

Dizard Jr., W., *Digital Diplomacy: U.S. Foreign Policy in the Information Age* (Westport, CT: Praeger, 2001).

Doyle, J., 'Irish Diplomacy on the UN Security Council 2001–2002: Foreign Policy Making in the Light of Day', *Irish Studies in International Affairs* 15 (2004), 73–102.

Eberstadt, N., '"Conference Diplomacy"—All Over Again', The Nautilus Institute for Security and Sustainable Development, 2004, available at: http://oldsite.nautilus.org/fora/security/0425B_Eberstadt.html#sect2.

Fischer, H., Lorion, S. and Ulrich, G., *Beyond Activism: The Impact of the Resolutions and other Activities of the European Parliament in the Field of Human Rights outside the European Union* (Venice: Marsilio Editori, 2007).

Forsythe, D. P., 'The UN Secretary-General and Human Rights: The Question of Leadership in a Changing Context' in B. Rivilin and L. Gordenker (eds.), *The Challenging Role of the UN Secretary-General* (Westport, Connecticut: Praeger, 1993), pp.211–32.

Forsythe, D. P., *Human Rights in International Relations*, 2nd edn, (Cambridge: Cambridge University Press, 2006).

Gaer, F. D., 'A Voice Not an Echo: Universal Periodic Review and the UN Treaty Body System', *Human Rights Law Review* 7 (2007), 121–35.

Habermas, J., 'Remarks on Legitimation through Human Rights' *Philosophy and Social Criticism* 24 (1998), 157–171.

Hannum, H., 'Human Rights in Conflict Resolution: The Role of the Office of the High Commissioner for Human Rights in UN Peacemaking and Peacebuilding', *Human Rights Quarterly* 28 (2006), 1–85.

Hansen, C., 'Non-Governmental Organisations and the European Union's Promotion of Human Rights in China: NGO Influence or No Influence?', *EU Diplomacy Papers* 4 (2010), College of Europe, Bruges.

Heyns, C. and Viljoen, F., 'The Impact of the United Nations Human Rights Treaties on the Domestic Level', *Human Rights Quarterly* 23 (2001), 483–535.

Humphrey, J., *Human Rights and the United Nations: A Great Adventure* (New York: Transnational Publishers, 1984).

International Council on Human Rights Policy, *Human Rights Standards: Learning from Experience*, 2006.

Kędzia, Z., 'The Road to Vienna: Negotiating the Vienna Declaration and Programme of Action' in Benedek *et al.* (eds.), *Global Standards—Local Action. 15 Years Vienna World Conference on Human Rights*, Conference Proceedings of the International Expert Conference held in Vienna on 28 and 29 August 2008, 16 Studienreihe des Ludwig Boltzmann Instituts für Menschenrechte (Viennna/Graz: NWV/Intersentia, 2009).

Kemp, W. A. (ed.), *Quiet Diplomacy in Action: The OSCE High Commissioner on National Minorities* (Boston: Kluwer Law International, 2001).

Khaliq, U., *Ethical Dimensions of the Foreign Policy of the European Union* (Cambridge: Cambridge University Press, 2008).

King, T. 'Human Rights in European Foreign Policy: Success or Failure of Post-modern Diplomacy?', *European Journal of International Law* 10 (1999), 313–37.

King, T., 'Human Rights in the Development Policy of the European Community', *Netherlands Yearbook of International Law* 28 (1997), 51–99.

Kinzelbach, K., 'The EU Human Rights Dialogue with China and the 2008 Olympic Games' in Benedek *et al.* (eds.), *European Yearbook on Human Rights 2009* (Vienna/Antwerp, 2009) 37–60.

Leino, P., 'European Universalism? The EU and Human Rights Conditionality', *Yearbook of European Law* 24 (2005), 329–383.

Livermore J. D. and Ramcharan, B. G., 'Purposes and Principles. The Secretary-General's Role in Human Rights', in B. Rivilin and L. Gordenker (eds.), *The Challenging Role of the UN Secretary-General* (Westport, Connecticut: Praeger, 1993), pp. 213–48.

MacDonald, D. B., Patman, R. G. and Mason-Parker, B. (eds.), *The Ethics of Foreign Policy* (Hampshire: Ashgate, 2007).

MacLean, G., *The Changing Perception of Human Security: Coordinating National and Multilateral Responses—The United Nations and the New Security Agenda* (Ottawa: UNAC, 1998).

Malcolm, J., *Multi-Stakeholder Governance and the Internet Governance Forum* (Perth: Terminus Press, 2008).

Manners, I., 'Normative Power Europe: A Contradiction in Terms?', *Journal of Common Market Studies* 40(2) (2002), 235–58.

Mertus, J., *Bait and Switch: Human Rights and US Foreign Policy* (New York/London: Routledge, 2008).
Minear, L. and Smith, H. (eds.), *Humanitarian Diplomacy: Practitioners and Their Craft* (New York: United Nations University Press, 2007).
Moomaw, W. R., 'New Diplomacy', The Fletcher School, Tufts University, available at: http://fletcher.tufts.edu/ierp/pdfs/NewDiplomacy.2.pdf.
Muldoon, J. P. *et al* (eds.), *Multilateral Diplomacy and the United Nations*, 2nd edn, (Boulder: Westview Press, 2005).
Müller, L. (ed.), *The First 365 Days of the United Nations Human Rights Council*, Swiss Federal Department of Foreign Affairs, Political Affairs Division IV, 2007.
Müllerson, R., *Human Rights Diplomacy* (London: Routledge, 1997).
O'Flaherty, M., 'Reform of the UN Human Rights Treaty Body System: Locating the Dublin Statement', *Human Rights Law Review* 10 (2010), 319–35.
O'Flaherty, M., 'Sierra Leone's Peace Process: The Role of the Human Rights Community', *Human Rights Quarterly* 26 (2004), 29–62.
O'Flaherty, M., 'The Concluding Observations of United Nations Human Rights Treaty Bodies', *Human Rights Law Review* 6 (2006), 27–52.
O'Flaherty, M. (ed.), *The Human Rights Field Operation: Law, Theory and Practice* (Aldershot: Ashgate, 2007).
O'Flaherty, M. and Ulrich, G. (eds.), *The Professional Identity of the Human Rights Field Officer* (Farnham: Ashgate, 2010).
Packer, J., 'The OSCE High Commissioner on National Minorities' in G. Alfredsson *et al.* (eds.), *International Human Rights Monitoring Mechanisms: Essays in Honour of Jakob Th. Möller* (The Hague: Martinus Nijhoff, 2001), pp.641–56.
Pohjolainen, E., *The Evolution of National Human Rights Institutions—The Role of the United Nations* (Copenhagen: Danish Institute for Human Rights, 2006), available at: http://www.NHRI.net/pdf/Evolution_of_NHRIs.pdf.
Ramcharan, B. G., *A UN High Commissioner in Defence of Human Rights* (The Hague: Martinus Nijhoff, 2005).
Ramcharan, B. G., *Preventive Diplomacy at the UN* (Indiana, Indiana University Press, 2008).
Ramcharan, B. G., *The International Law and Practice of Early Warning and Preventive Diplomacy: The Emerging Global Watch* (Dordrecht: Martinus Nijhoff, 1991).
Ramcharan, B. G., *The UN High Commissioner for Human Rights and the Challenges of International Protection* (The Hague: Martinus Nijhoff, 2002).
Ramcharan, B. G., *Humanitarian Good Offices in International Law. The Good Offices of the UN Secretary-General in the Field of Human Rights* (The Hague: Martinus Nijhoff, 1983).
Robinson, M., *A Voice for Human Rights* (Philadelphia: University of Pennsylvania Press, 2006).
Roth, K., 'A Façade of Action: The Misuse of Dialogue and Cooperation with Rights Abusers', Human Rights Watch, World Report 2011.
Rothchild, D., *et al.*, *Sovereignty as Responsibility: Conflict Management in Africa* (Washington D.C: Brookings Institution Press, 1996).
Saunders, H., *A Public Peace Process: Sustained Dialogue to Transform Racial and Ethnical Conflicts* (New York: St. Martin's Press, 1999).
Schechter, M. G. (ed.), *United Nations-sponsored World Conferences: Focus on Impact and Follow-up* (Tokyo/New York: United Nations University Press, 2001).
Smith, K., *European Union Foreign Policy in a Changing World* (Cambridge: Polity Press, 2008).
Snow, N. and Taylor, P. M., *The Routledge Handbook of Public Diplomacy* (London: Routledge, 2009).
U Thant, S., *View from the UN* (Newton Abbot: David and Charles, 1978).

Ulrich, G., 'Universal Human Rights: An Unfinished Project' in K. Hastrup (ed.), *Human Rights on Common Grounds? The Quest for Universality* (The Hague/ London/New York: Kluwer Law International, 2001).

Vincent, R. J., (eds.), *Foreign Policy and Human Rights: Issues and Responses* (Cambridge: Cambridge University Press, 1986).

Wallner, J. M. (eds.), *The Public Diplomacy Reader* (Washington: Institute of World Politics Press, 2007).

Wehrenfennig, D., 'Multi-Track Diplomacy and Human Security', *Human Security Journal* 7 (2008), 80–88.

INDEX

academic institutions, 1, 6, 7, 18, 256, 257, 260, 275, 279, 281
accountability, 21, 118, 169, 217, 259, 276, 280
advocacy
  human rights, 8, 20, 23, 25, 28n16, 29, 30, 34, 41, 49, 81, 83, 129, 134, 137, 153, 266, 271
  non-governmental, 1, 217
  public, 5, 18, 53, 129, 132–134, 280
Afghanistan, 230n23, 237n48, 259
African Union (AU), 6, 180, 207n17, 232, 272
Agenda for Peace, 176n8
alternative reports, 236
Amnesty International, 47, 48, 84, 108, 168n57
Annan, K., 34, 176, 188, 197, 202n4, 204n8, 207n16
Arab League, 258, 272, 275
Arbour, L., 64n11, 147
armed conflict, 2, 15, 60, 86n24, 103n5, 113, 114, 140, 182, 188n30, 192–199
Armenia, 12, 67, 107, 118–119
'Arria Formula,' 195–196
Article 19 ICCPR. *See* freedom of expression
Asia-Europe Meetings (ASEM), 63n6, 256n16, 275
Asian Human Rights Commission (AHRC), 35
Association for the Prevention of Torture, 248n83
Association of Southeast Asian Nations, 6, 238, 272
  Intergovernmental Commission on Human Rights, 238n55
asymmetry of status, 9, 52
Australia, 90, 226n11, 230n23, 240, 241
  Australian Human Rights Commission, 239n58, 240n61
Austria, 59, 71, 198, 257
Azerbaijan, 107

bad practice, 260, 269, 276, 283
best practices. *See* good practices
blasphemy, 31
Bosnia and Herzegovina, 105
bottom-up approach, 17, 149, 252
Boutros-Ghali, B., 175, 176, 202n5, 203
Brahimi, L., 165n43
Brazil, 40

campaigning, 8, 25, 26, 30, 50
capacity building, 35, 133, 162, 170, 230n23, 239n58, 240, 242, 248
Chechnya, 12, 113–115, 221
children's rights. *See* rights of the child
child soldiers, 67, 137, 196
China, 32n23, 32n24, 37, 38, 44, 46, 47, 57, 75, 79, 84n19, 88n26, 95n49, 164n40, 240, 256, 257n17, 275
China-Australia Human Rights Technical Cooperation Program, 240
civil and political rights, 78, 93n41, 130n2, 159n20, 208n22
civil society, 1, 10–12, 19, 27, 28n19, 46, 50, 51, 60n2, 61–63n6, 65, 66, 68, 72, 83, 84, 87, 88, 94n48, 95n49, 96, 100, 104, 108, 114, 131, 134, 137, 140, 141, 145, 147–149, 158, 159, 161–165, 167, 185, 202, 211, 212, 214, 221, 226, 227n17, 228n19, 229, 235, 236, 242n73, 251n3, 252, 255n14, 256, 258, 259, 264, 273, 274
'clash of civilizations,' 206
climate change, 36, 50, 57, 66, 70, 177, 178, 276
cloning, 179, 276
coherence, 61, 148
  in human rights diplomacy, 9, 14, 49, 58, 98, 142, 265, 268, 283
Cold War, 3, 4, 14, 33, 78, 137, 158, 175, 191, 193, 205, 211
colonisation, 14, 40, 192
Committee on the Elimination of All Forms of Discrimination Against Women, 243
Committee on the Elimination of Racial Discrimination, 147
complementarity, 110, 131, 170
compromise, 7, 11, 19, 33, 42, 49, 52, 81, 206, 210, 214, 266, 279
conditionality, 44, 78n5

conference, 66, 73n9, 106, 136n10, 139, 140n21, 167, 196, 253, 257, 258n22, 279, 285
  diplomacy, 15n34, 16, 36, 201–216, 271–272
confidence-building measures, 5, 133, 134
confidentiality, 49, 51, 53, 58, 66n13, 133, 169, 283
confrontational measures, 10, 267, 268
Confucius Peace Prize, 38
Congress of Vienna, 201
Convention against Torture and Other Cruel, Inhuman or Degrading Treatment or Punishment, 93n42
  Optional Protocol to the, 15, 97n55, 189n31, 209n25, 245n79
Convention on Cluster Munitions, 220n1, 257n19
Convention on the Elimination of All Forms of Discrimination against Women, 136n10, 156, 161n26
  Optional Protocol to the, 209n24
Convention on the Protection of the Rights of All Migrant Workers and Members of Their Families, 97n57, 136n10, 156n8, 269
Convention on the Rights of Persons with Disabilities, 156n9, 209n28, 220n3, 237n47, 245n79
Convention on the Rights of the Child, 93n43, 117n27, 156n5, 161n29, 162n30, 280
  Optional protocol to the Convention on the Rights of the Child on the Involvement of Children in Armed Conflict, 209n29
  Optional Protocol to the Convention on the Rights of the Child on the Sale of Children, Child Prostitution and Child Pornography, 209n29
cooperation
  suspension of, 10, 267
coordination, 59, 61–63, 67, 120, 133, 143, 229n20, 247, 269, 273, 278, 279
Coordination Committee of Special Procedures, 143
corporal punishment, 116n25, 117n28
Cotonou Agreement, 91n35, 253
Council of Europe
  Commissioner for Human Rights
    assessment report of, 105
    assessment visits of, 104, 105
    country visits of (*see* assessment visits of)
    impartiality of, 12, 102, 104, 121
    independence of, 12, 102, 104, 109, 121
    as intermediary, 12, 136
    mandate of, 2, 101–103
    presence in the field, 12
    'Viewpoints' of the, 109n12
  Committee of Ministers, 101n1, 102n4, 103n6, 105, 106n8, 109, 121, 125–128, 169–170
  Congress of Local and Regional Authorities, 109, 110
  Parliamentary Assembly, 105, 108–110, 121, 122, 126–127
    Monitoring Committee of, 119
counter-terrorism measures, 79, 110, 112, 116, 118
credibility, 7, 11, 12, 71, 79, 98, 121, 134, 221, 246, 268, 269, 274, 281
crimes against humanity, 183, 185, 198, 199
cultural relativism, 31n21, 80, 136

death penalty
  abolition of, 64n10, 65, 66, 81, 85
  International Commission against the, 64n10
de Cuéllar, P., 174, 181
demarches
  confidential, 10, 86, 267
  public, 10, 70, 77, 86, 267
Democratic Republic of Congo (DRC), 65, 195n9, 198
democratisation, 99n61, 232, 240
Denmark, 59, 75, 226n13, 237n48, 240n59
deprivation of liberty, 119
development
  assistance, 70, 186
  cooperation, 32, 35, 77n2
  global partnerships for, 152
  governmental agencies, 17
  policies, 68, 78, 90n32
dialogue
  Council Guidelines on Human Rights Dialogues (EU), 87
  human rights, 10, 11, 28, 35n29, 44, 66, 67, 77, 84, 86n24, 87, 88n25, 89n29, 90, 94n48, 95n49, 106, 222, 257n17, 260, 267, 273, 279

diplomacy
  bilateral, 17, 239, 260, 268
  'classical,' 3, 6, 7, 9, 10, 17, 19, 25, 39, 44–45, 48, 51–53, 56, 57, 201
  humanitarian, 2n1, 133n5, 143n24, 165n43, 181
  human rights
    'bad,' 1, 5n10, 29, 30, 34, 39, 41, 266, 269, 276, 283
    credibility of, 7, 11, 71, 134, 221, 268, 269, 274
    definition, concept of, 8, 9, 20, 23n10, 25, 70, 100, 132, 153, 235, 252, 265, 266
    effectiveness of, 6, 54, 58, 248, 269, 282
    expertise-based, 41, 142, 145, 146, 153
    good faith, 1, 5, 29
    hybrid form of, 9, 16, 54, 57, 58
    instruments of, 5, 6, 11, 151, 265, 266, 268, 273
    key challenges of, 130
    legitimacy of, 6, 143, 221, 275, 282
    principled, 8, 11, 13, 81
    risks and pitfalls of, 6, 7, 265, 266
    'success' of, 7, 9, 10, 15, 20, 39, 45, 51, 54–56, 76, 133, 139, 141, 143n25, 151, 165, 181, 215, 204, 234n34, 255, 268, 277
    tools of, 4, 5, 6, 10, 61, 65, 69, 70, 81, 87, 130, 133, 134, 153, 165, 218, 265, 267, 268, 273, 280
    voices in, 9, 28n16, 47–49, 145, 218
  inter-state, 1, 3, 17, 278
  listening, 57, 74, 283
  multilateral, 5n11, 70, 123, 191, 199, 203, 259, 268, 269–275
  multi-layered, 7, 9, 14, 283
  multi-track, 6, 17n41, 63n6, 251–261, 275–276
  preventive, 174n1, 176n8, 177
  'public,' 70, 71, 251, 252n6
  quiet (*see* silent)
  silent, 123, 260
  traditional (*see* 'classical')
Dominican Republic, 65, 192n2
double-standards, 4, 31n21, 79, 134, 269
Dublin Statement on the Process of Strengthening of the United Nations Human Rights Treaty Body System, 149n34
  Response by Non-governmental Organizations to the, 167n53
Durban Review Conference, 12, 130, 139–141, 143, 146, 153, 213, 214n35, 271
  Outcome Document, 139n19

East Timor, 195n11
economic, social and cultural rights, 31, 86, 187n26, 208n22, 209n23, 277
  Committee on, 156, 157, 161n23, 166n45, 167n48, 283, 284, 286
El Salvador, 92, 93n40
Equality commissions/body, 107, 116, 124
Euro-Arab-Dialogue, 258, 275
European Agency for Fundamental Rights, 62, 112, 231
European Commission, 2, 66, 84n18, 90n30, 93n40, 98n58, 99n61, 258, 273, 274
European Commission for Democracy through Law. *See* Venice Commission
European Convention of Human Rights, 78, 111, 125
European Court of Human Rights, 62, 91, 97, 109, 117, 122, 169, 238, 243n74, 266
European External Action Service, 67
European Instrument for Democracy and Human Rights (EIDHR), 95n50–52, 96, 273, 274
European Parliament
  Committee on Civil Liberties, Justice and Home Affairs, 112
  human rights diplomacy of, 11, 84, 94, 274
  Members of the, 85
  Sub-Committee on Human Rights, 85, 112
European Security Strategy, 79, 80n12
European Union (EU)
  annual NGO forum, 94n47
  Annual Report on Human Rights, 77, 85n21
  Common Agricultural Policy, 269
  Council Working Group on Human Rights (COHOM), 66, 67, 82
  Council Working Group on OSCE and Council of Europe, 111
  Counter-Terrorism Coordinator, 111
  foreign policy, 11, 66n13, 71, 78n5, 79n11, 80, 83, 88n27, 89, 94
  framework agreements, 11, 90
  Generalised System of Preferences (GSP), 274

Guidelines on Human Rights, 11, 28n19, 35n29, 66n14, 71n5, 72, 86n24, 87, 88n25, 89n29, 94n48, 97, 111
High Representative for Foreign Affairs and Security Policy, 40
human rights dialogues, 11, 35n29, 66, 67, 77, 86n24, 87, 88n25, 89n29, 90, 94n48, 95n49, 257n17, 273
policies in the area of Justice, Freedom and Security
Stockholm Programme, 98n59
Political and Security Committee, 111
Presidency of the
Irish, 72
Spanish, 67, 68
Swedish, 67
trade agreements, 80, 94
trade policy, 91, 94
Extra-judicial killings, 97
Ezulwini Consensus, 207n17

Fact-finding, 7, 28, 103, 104, 182, 183, 266, 279
Fair trial guarantees, 34
Finland, 59, 71, 164n40
France, 59, 64n11, 65, 226n14, 237n48, 240n59
freedom of assembly, 81, 86
freedom of expression, 31, 33, 41, 81, 86, 221, 225
Expert seminar on Freedom of Expression and Advocacy of Religious Hatred that Constitutes Incitement to Discrimination, Hostility or Violence, 12, 31n22, 130, 136n12, 142–147, 153
Special Rapporteur on, 255
freedom of thought, consciousness and religion, 87, 144
'defamation of religions,' 41, 136, 143, 145, 150

gender equality, 67
genocide, 182n15, 183, 185, 198, 199
Special Adviser on the Prevention of, 182, 183
Georgia, 12, 67, 119, 120n34, 221
Germany, 49, 59, 226n13, 237n48, 240n59
Gil-Robles, Á., 113, 114n18, 115n19
good governance, 80, 92n39, 93n44, 259
good offices, 14, 120, 173n1, 174, 176, 179–181, 278
good practices, 45, 57, 58, 104, 146, 159, 169, 170, 256, 260, 264, 277, 283
Green, M., 165, 265
Gulf Cooperation Council, 135

Hammarskjold, D., 174
hate speech, 136, 146
health institutions, 6, 282
High-Level Workshop on Human Rights Diplomacy, 5, 264
Participants of the, 265
Report on, 6n12, 23n10, 25n12, 28n17, 165n41, 233n33
humanitarian
access, 2, 120
good offices, 14, 173n1, 174, 176, 179–181
intervention, 5n10, 176
relief, 181
human rights
adjudication, 23n10, 266
ambassador(s), 2, 10, 59, 60, 65
Spanish, 9, 59, 61, 63, 64, 67, 68
approach, 36n31, 48, 104
and business, 1, 6, 46, 51n4, 72, 239n57, 256, 275, 282
Committee, 19, 31n22, 157n13, 158n17, 159n20, 160n22, 168n56, 224n3
defenders, 10, 37, 46, 66, 67, 71, 72, 74n18, 75, 86n24, 98, 103n6, 108, 111n15, 112, 221, 231n29, 267, 280
dialogue (*see* dialogue)
diplomacy (*see* diplomacy)
education, 178, 180, 184, 189, 190, 226n13, 227, 237n45
expertise, 149, 233
indicators, 113
national action plan on, 62, 104, 113, 188
national protection systems, 14, 179, 180, 187, 188, 190, 276
negotiations, 15, 18, 32, 50, 131, 139, 142, 149, 259, 265, 266, 278, 280
principles, 43, 46, 121, 234, 241, 281
standard-setting, 29, 42, 45
treaties, 15, 16, 35, 92, 122, 142, 148, 157n11, 162n34, 181, 187, 189, 190, 225, 271, 277, 281
treaty bodies
concluding observations of, 62, 104, 142, 157n12, 281
as diplomatic actors, 13n30, 160, 163, 155–171, 269

general comments of, 104, 142, 171, 281
Meeting of Chairpersons of, 143, 236n41
reform process, 13, 167, 255
state reports to, 149, 161n24–26, 164
strengthening of, 13, 51, 53, 74, 130, 147–149, 167n50, 171, 230n25
universal culture of, 178, 180, 189, 190
universality of, 31, 34n27, 46, 60, 77, 97, 178, 205, 234
violations
gross, 5, 114, 175, 179, 188, 271, 276, 277
large scale, 212
Human Rights Watch, 19n1, 84, 108, 164n39, 217, 218
Human Security Network, 74, 257
Hungary, 59, 192n3
hypocrisy, 16, 221

India, 40, 46, 47, 226n11, 230n23
indigenous peoples, 46
individual communications, 171
information sharing, 239, 248
inspection visits, 227
Inter-governmental organisation, 1, 2, 4, 6, 10, 11, 16, 165, 217, 228
Inter-governmental Working Group on the Right to Development, 130, 149, 151
interim measures, 171, 181
International Committee of the Red Cross, 50, 183
International Conference on Population and Development, 36
International Convention for the Protection of All Persons from Enforced Disappearance, 156n10, 209n27
International Convention on the Elimination of All Forms of Racial Discrimination, 156n3
International Covenant on Civil and Political Rights, 31n22, 93n41, 130n2, 143, 144n27, 145n29, 155n1, 158n16, 160, 187n25, 208n22
International Covenant on Economic, Social and Cultural Rights (ICESCR), 155n2, 187n26, 208n22
Optional Protocol to the, 15, 209n23
International Criminal Court (ICC), 14, 25, 37n32, 47, 48n3, 50, 74, 95n51, 137n15, 178, 186, 188, 190, 223n1, 227, 229, 230n24, 231
International Federation for Human Rights, 108
international humanitarian law, 15, 66, 86n24, 111n15, 257
international human rights law, 6–8, 12, 13, 15, 21n4, 24, 116, 130, 135, 136, 143, 144n26, 145n29, 146, 243, 265, 266, 271
International Labour Organisation (ILO), 92, 157
Convention No 87, 92
International relations
constructivist theory, 63
'idealist turn,' 22, 38
realist paradigm, 22
Internet Governance Forum (IGF), 254n12, 255n13, 275
Inter-Parliamentary Union, 253n10
Iran, 89
Ireland, 49, 69–75, 164n38, 167n48, 226n11, 237n48, 240n59
Department of Foreign Affairs, 72

judicial proceedings, 165
jurisdiction, 60, 157, 162, 165, 187, 206
justice, 14, 42, 78n6, 82, 88, 112, 113, 115, 116n26, 118, 178–180, 184, 188, 190, 232n31, 237n46, 238, 241, 277

Kant, I., 38n34
Ki-moon, B., 40, 173, 177, 178, 180, 185, 234
Kosovo, 259

landmines, 50, 137, 257n20
leadership, 53, 75, 132n4, 139–141, 146, 173n1, 177–181, 211, 215, 276, 281
legal proceedings, 24, 27, 42
legal profession, 6, 282
legal remedies, 18
Lie, T., 174
light weapons. *See* small arms
Lord's Resistance Army, 197

mainstreaming, 47, 61, 99n60, 100n62, 111, 131, 132, 137, 208, 213, 252n4, 276, 279, 281
Mandela, N., 192
Marrakech Statement on Strengthening the Relationship between NHRIs and the Human Rights Treaty Bodies System, 149n35, 167n51

media, 28, 87, 105, 109, 112, 118, 123, 131, 140, 199, 218, 244, 252, 253n9, 256, 267, 280
Millennium Declaration, 150n39
Millennium development goals, 152
monitoring
  human rights, 24n11, 43, 97, 109, 110, 142, 157n14, 161n28, 223, 234, 267
  by non-governmental organisations, 6, 46, 220, 267, 279, 280
multi-stakeholder approach, 6, 17n41, 29, 63n6, 251–261, 271, 275–276, 282

national human rights institutions (NHRIs)
  accreditation of, 226n9, 227n16, 227n18, 238n50, 242n73, 246
  African Network of, 238, 242
  Asia-Pacific Forum of, 230n23, 238, 241, 243, 247, 248
  European Group of, 235n37, 237n47, 238n54, 241n68, 243n74
  independence and impartiality of, 16, 233, 234
  International Coordinating Committee of, 129, 130, 134, 226, 227, 230n25, 241, 242, 245–247
    Sub-Committee on Accreditation, 227n18
  Pacific Islands Forum of, 241
  Rabat Declaration of the African Network of, 238n53
  West African Network of, 242
national protection systems, 14, 179, 180, 187, 188, 190, 276
negotiation, 1, 5–8, 11, 15, 16, 18, 25, 27, 28, 32, 35, 36, 41, 45, 50, 51n4, 52, 53, 56–58, 61, 80, 90, 131, 133n5, 139, 142, 143, 149, 150, 165, 166, 191, 199, 203, 205, 209, 210, 220, 233n33, 243, 257, 259, 265–266, 275, 278–280, 282
Netherlands, The, 35, 59, 164n38
networking, 202, 203, 230
Nobel Peace Prize, 37, 38, 257
non-governmental organisations (NGOs)
  as advocates, 16, 52, 218, 280
  as beneficiaries of human rights diplomacy, 16, 221, 280
  as catalysts, 16, 211, 217
  exposing abuses, 16, 217
  involvement in negotiations, 280
  as monitors, 16, 217, 220–221
  as partners in policy-making, 16, 217, 219–220
non-state actors, 137, 196, 251, 256, 274
non-state armed groups, 196
North Atlantic Treaty Organisation (NATO), 253
Northern Ireland Human Rights Commission, 115, 116
Norway, 59, 70, 73, 74n18, 226n13, 237n48

Office for the Coordination of Humanitarian Affairs (OCHA), 112, 174
Office of the United Nations High Commissioner for Human Rights (OHCHR), 6, 12, 13, 35, 48, 56, 112, 131, 135, 141, 148, 153, 163, 176, 177, 181, 184, 189
  National Institutions and Regional Mechanisms Unit, 229
ombudsman, 61, 107, 110, 114, 118
Organisation for Security and Co-operation in Europe (OSCE)
  High Commissioner on National, 2, 61, 62, 64, 86, 112, 231, 240, 255, 272, 275
  Minorities (HCNM), 6, 7n18, 112, 135, 136, 277
  Human Dimension Implementation Meeting, 96, 112
  Office for Human Rights and Democratic Institutions (ODHIR), 112, 231
  Permanent Council, 112
  Representative on Freedom of the Media, 112
Organisation of American States (OAS), 6, 231, 272, 275

Paris Principles. *See* Principles relating to the Status of National Institutions
parliamentarians, 1, 110, 253, 267, 270, 275
parliaments, 6, 12, 61, 84, 102, 122, 127, 203, 243, 244
participation, 57, 63n6, 79, 95n49, 106, 159n20, 162, 164, 198, 203, 216, 227, 229, 232n30, 232n32, 252, 257, 259, 270, 281
peace agreements, 70, 183n16, 184, 185
peacebuilding, 14, 184–185, 190

peacekeeping, 14, 112, 180, 184–185, 190, 193, 213
peacemaking, 14, 176n8, 180, 183–184, 190
peer processes, 51, 239, 278, 282
persuasion, 1, 5, 25, 26, 30, 48n3, 56, 75, 81, 87, 129, 133, 165, 191, 233n33, 234, 265, 266
political freedom, 33, 79
political pressure, 1, 18, 211
poverty reduction, 35
Poznan Statement on the Reforms of the UN Human Rights Treaty Body System, 149, 167n52
pressure, 1, 16, 18, 28n16, 40, 41, 48, 50, 83, 84, 88, 94, 113, 133, 134, 136, 139n18, 196, 211, 213, 244, 245, 248, 257, 272, 280
Principles relating to the Status of National Institutions, 16, 224–227, 230, 242
prisoner of war, 120
privacy, 34
prohibition of torture, 34, 115, 274
protection of civilians, 197, 198
public private partnerships, 251

Raul Wallenberg Institute, 279
reciprocity, 1, 7, 11, 21, 38, 81, 265, 266, 269, 279, 280
relief, 4, 135n8, 180, 181, 190
religious groups, 1, 6, 265, 275
reservations, 37, 42, 117, 136n10, 167
responsibility to protect, 14, 21n5, 176, 178, 180, 183, 185–188, 190, 194, 198, 199, 207, 211, 271
  Special Adviser on the, 182
rights-based approach, 32, 35, 100
rights of lesbians, gays, bisexuals and transsexuals (LGBTs), 67
rights of the child, 66, 86n24, 93n43, 113, 117, 156n5, 161n25, 161n39, 162n30, 209n29, 237n49, 280
  Committee on the, 161n25, 162n32, 167n46, 280
right to development
  declaration of the, 151
  High-level Task Force on the, 149, 151, 152n43
  Working Group on the, 13, 130, 149, 151, 152n43
Rome Statue of the International Criminal Court, 137
rule of law, 42, 46, 77–80, 90, 122, 186, 231, 232, 240
Russia, Russian Federation, 57, 67, 83n16, 107, 113, 114n18, 120

Sakharov Prize for Freedom of Thought, 85
Samoa Declaration, 241
sanctions, 26, 87, 91, 92, 121, 192, 194, 195, 218, 266, 274
Second World War, 42, 224
selectivity, 40, 138, 164n39
Sen, A., 208
'shadow' reports. *See* alternative reports
small arms, 137
small states
  advantages of, 10, 69, 71
  disadvantages of, 10, 69, 71
South Africa, 14, 40, 46, 65, 192, 194, 205, 226, 237n48, 257
  apartheid regime, 14, 40, 192, 205
South Ossetia, 12, 119, 120
sovereignty, 21, 157, 191, 201, 207n15
Spain, 10n21, 59–68, 226n12
  Spanish Ministry of Foreign Affairs and Cooperation, 59, 61, 64
special procedure mandate-holders, 2, 6, 7, 13, 24, 28, 47, 55, 61, 129, 142, 144, 181, 183, 259, 264, 268
Special Representative for Children and Armed Conflict, 182
Sri Lanka, 65, 70, 93n44, 117, 197, 230
Subcommittee on Prevention of Torture and other Cruel, Inhuman or Degrading Treatment or Punishment, 157
Sudan, 70, 188, 195n9
Sweden, 59, 240n59
Switzerland, 65, 72–75, 148, 149, 164n40

technical assistance, 1, 18, 35, 88, 89, 98, 170, 281
territorial integrity, 114
Thant, U., 174n3
Tibet, 221
torture
  prevention of, 66, 86, 94, 109n13, 157, 248n83, 273
  prohibition of, 34, 115, 274
trade unions, 6, 51, 61, 62, 270
transnational corporations, 18

transparency, 9, 49, 51, 57, 58, 84, 88, 108, 133, 139n18, 149n36, 169, 259, 268
travel bans, 195
trust, 9, 12, 49, 51, 53–55, 57, 58, 141, 283

Union of Socialist Soviet Republics (USSR), 4, 192
United Kingdom, 2, 115–118
  Anti-terrorism, Crime and Security Act 2001, 115
  anti-terrorism legislation, 115
  asylum system, 115
  Equalities and Human Rights Commission, 116
  Foreign and Commonwealth Office, 73
  House of Lords, 115
  Joint Committee on Human Rights of the Parliament of the United Kingdom of Great Britain and Northern Ireland, 115
  juvenile justice system, 115
  Parliamentary and Health Service Ombudsman, 118n32
United Nations Charter, 14, 77, 137, 165, 208
  Article 99 of the, 14, 177–178, 180–183, 190
United Nations Children's Fund (UNICEF), 6, 112, 113, 161n28, 162n30, 280–281
United Nations Climate Change Conference, 36
United Nations Commission on Human Rights, 39, 40n37, 151n41, 151n42, 176, 193, 196, 224, 270
United Nations Commission on the Status of Women (CSW), 242, 243n74
United Nations Conference on Environment and Development
  in Cancun 2010, 36
  in Copenhagen 2009, 36
United Nations country teams, 138, 231n27, 270, 276
United Nations Department of Political Affairs, 184
United Nations Development Programme (UNDP), 56, 231n27, 240
United Nations Economic and Social Council (ECOSOC), 156, 177, 224n3
United Nations Educational, Scientific and Cultural Organisation (UNESCO), 64n11, 255
United Nations General Assembly (UNGA), 64, 139, 174, 177, 181, 186, 192, 210, 211, 224
  Third Committee of, 67
United Nations Global Compact, 51
United Nations High Commissioner for Human Rights (UNHCHR), 2, 6, 12, 14, 15, 40, 48, 56, 64n11, 73, 112, 130, 132n4, 133, 134, 135n10, 136, 137–148, 153, 173, 176–179, 182, 188, 193, 194, 196–198, 210, 213, 266, 271, 276, 279
United Nations High Commissioner for Refugees (UNHCR), 112
United Nations Human Rights Council
  Advisory Committee, 109n13, 237, 259
  'bloc dynamics' in, 75
  participation of ambassadors in the work of, 270
  special sessions of, 182, 270
United Nations Peace-building Commission, 184
United Nations Secretariat, 130, 131, 141, 181, 247
United Nations Secretary-General, 2, 6, 14, 15, 34, 40, 51n4, 64n8, 65, 165, 173–190, 202, 207, 234, 236, 237, 271, 276, 278–279
United Nations Security Council, 6, 14, 15, 74, 138, 177, 181–184, 191–200
  public debates of the, 197n13
  resolution 1325 on Women, Peace and Security, 64
  Working Group on Children and Armed Conflict, 194, 196–197
United States, 4, 46, 73, 146, 194, 255n13
  State Department, 47, 82n15
Universal Declaration of Human Rights (UDHR), 47, 78, 174, 225
Universal Periodic Review (UPR), 11, 14, 39, 62, 73n11, 112, 131, 138, 155, 163, 164n40, 169–171, 188, 236, 247, 268, 270
  recommendations, 164n40, 170, 236
universal values, 19, 21, 39
universities. *See* academic institutions
use of force, 22n9, 26, 44
Uzbekistan, 57

value systems, 32
Venice Commission, 107
Vienna Declaration and Programme of Action, 15n35, 21, 22n6, 60n2, 175, 205n10, 208–212, 214
Vienna World Conference on Human Rights, 2, 15, 60, 137, 205n10, 253–254, 258

Waldheim, K., 174
war crimes, 183, 185, 198, 199
Warsaw Pact, 205
Westphalian principles, 201
women's rights, 67, 80, 228n19, 240n59
World Conference against Racism, Racial Discrimination, Xenophobia and Related Intolerance, 139, 213, 214n35
  Durban Declaration and Programme of Action, 139, 213, 214n35
World Summit on the Information Society, 254, 275
World Summit Outcome Document (2005), 185, 198n14, 207n14, 208n19

Xiaobo, L., 37, 38

www.ingramcontent.com/pod-product-compliance
Lightning Source LLC
La Vergne TN
LVHW081514300926
849161LV00006B/1177
* 9 7 8 9 0 0 4 1 9 5 1 6 5 *